The Norton Psychology Reader

The Norton Psychology Reader

EDITED BY

Gary Marcus

NEW YORK UNIVERSITY

W. W. NORTON & COMPANY
NEW YORK • LONDON

W. W. Norton & Company has been independent since its founding in 1923, when William Warder Norton and Mary D. Herter Norton first published lectures delivered at the People's Institute, the adult education division of New York City's Cooper Union. The Nortons soon expanded their program beyond the Institute, publishing books by celebrated academics from America and abroad. By mid-century, the two major pillars of Norton's publishing program—trade books and college texts—were firmly established. In the 1950s, the Norton family transferred control of the company to its employees, and today—with a staff of four hundred and a comparable number of trade, college, and professional titles published each year—W. W. Norton & Company stands as the largest and oldest publishing house owned wholly by its employees.

Editor: Jon Durbin
Editorial Assistant: Kelly Rolf
Director of Manufacturing—College: Roy Tedoff
Managing Editor—College: Marian Johnson

Library of Congress Cataloging-in-Publication Data

The Norton psychology reader / [compiled by] Gary Marcus.
    p. cm.

    ISBN 0-393-92712-1 (pbk.)

    1. Psychology.   I. Marcus, Gary F. (Gary Fred)

    BF121.N63 2005
    150—dc22   2005048247

W. W. Norton & Company, Inc. 500 Fifth Avenue, New York, NY 10110
www.wwnorton.com

W. W. Norton & Company Ltd., Castle House, 75/76 Wells Street, London WIT 3QT

6 7 8 9 0

To Athena

CONTENTS

ACKNOWLEDGMENTS

Many of these authors served as inspiration when I entered the field of psychology, and in editing this volume, my greatest debt is plainly to them. I also want to extend my heartfelt thanks to Jon Durbin for commissioning this project, to Kelly Rolf for securing permission to reprint these fine pieces, and especially to Athena Vouloumanos, for her love, encouragement, and superlative editorial advice.

PREFACE

In NYU's massive twelve-story library, you can find books on psychology on nearly every floor. Memory, cognitive psychology, and the interpretation of dreams on the fourth floor, culture on the fifth floor, human relationships, nonverbal communication, and self-actualization on the seventh, language on the eighth, psychiatry, psychotherapy, and neuroanatomy on the ninth. Ranging from the molecular concerns of physiological psychologists through the reaction-time studies of cognitive psychologists to the animal studies of comparative psychologists and the studies of community-level interactions that are the stuff of social psychology, psychology is one of the broadest disciplines known to science.

Scarcely 150 years old, the discipline of psychology is still relatively new, considerably less well-understood than physics or chemistry, and in many ways much more challenging. Described by the *American Heritage Dictionary* as "The science that deals with mental processes and behavior," the charge of psychology is to discover everything there is to know about the mind and how it relates to behavior.

In this short book, there is only room to scratch the surface. My aim is not to provide the last word, but the first, to introduce you to three dozen of psychology's finest thinkers— scientists and journalists with exceptional psychological insight. The selections in this sampler had to meet just two criteria: they had to be great psychology, and they had to be great writing. Although the pieces in this short book won't teach you everything there is to know about psychology, my hope is that they will leave you wanting more.

Nearly every selection was written to be accessible not just to specialists but to any bright, interested reader. They can be read in order, in tandem with a traditional introductory psychology textbook, but each one is self-contained, so it's okay to skip around. Whether you are a student in an introductory psychology class, a professional in a different field, or just an interested layperson, if you want to learn more about the passions and puzzles of academic psychology, by all means, dive right in.

The Norton Psychology Reader

CHAPTER ONE

PIONEERS

Psychology has come a long way in the last 150 years, but not so far that we can't recognize the questions and concerns of the field's earliest thinkers, and not so far that we can't still learn from them.

Perhaps no scholar better exemplifies the twin goals of this book than William James (1842–1910), who was both a cofounder of the field of psychology and an exceptional writer, a scholar who showed definitively that good science doesn't need to be hard to read. This first selection is drawn from James's monumental *The Principles of Psychology* (1890). Almost as soon as it was published, *Principles* became standard reading for virtually all psychologists. The book presaged the field of evolutionary psychology, pioneered the notion of stream-of-consciousness, and helped formulate a theory of emotion that is still a touchstone for much thinking in the field.

The selection here, taken from the introduction to James's magnum opus, serves as a reminder of how central to psychology is the problem of relating the mind to the brain. Even before he began *Principles*, James was what we might nowadays call a physiological psychologist, dissecting the brains and optic nerves of frogs in an effort to understand the neural basis of perception, and so it is no accident here that for James the question of relating the mind to the brain is pivotal.

If James was the founder of modern studies of consciousness, Sigismund Schlomo Freud (1856–1939) (better known as Sigmund) was father to the modern study of the *unconscious*. Like James, Freud spent much of his early days trying to relate brain and mind—his 1895 *Project for a Scientific Psychology* still bears rereading in that connection—but Freud soon switched from a direct interest in the physiological function of the brain to an abiding interest in the development of human personality, with a special emphasis on the relation between mental disorders and early-childhood experience.

To modern eyes, Freud seems far too focused on speculative notions like penis envy, the Oedipus complex (according to which every young boy wishes that he could marry his mother), and the interpretation of dreams; furthermore, the notion of heredity is almost entirely absent.

Other ideas, like the notion that we could repress unpleasant memories, remain controversial.

But even if some of Freud's specific suggestions no longer seem valid, his influence on contemporary psychology cannot be underestimated. While only a tiny minority of active researchers in psychology directly employ specific psychoanalytic ideas, virtually everyone now takes for granted one of the principles Freud cared about most: the importance of unconscious mental processes. Among therapists, even the most skeptical accept and build upon the notion that Freud laid out in "The Unconscious" (1915): that we are not always aware of why we do the things we do. Beck's well-known cognitive therapy (see Chapter 17), for example, all but dismisses the Freudian emphasis on early psychosexual development, yet still revolves around getting patients in better touch with their unconscious mental processes. As later chapters will make clear, the unconscious also plays a central role in the modern studies of cognitive psychology (for example, Wegner's selection on consciousness in Chapter 9) and social psychology (as in Cialdini's studies of persuasion in Chapter 13). Though written almost a century ago, the selection here still stands as a powerful argument in understanding what lies beneath the surface of the mind.

From *The Principles of Psychology*

William James

Psychology is the Science of Mental Life, both of its phenomena and of their conditions. The phenomena are such things as we call feelings, desires, cognitions, reasonings, decisions, and the like; and, superficially considered, their variety and complexity is such as to leave a chaotic impression on the observer. The most natural and consequently the earliest way of unifying the material was, first, to classify it as well as might be, and, secondly, to affiliate the diverse mental modes thus found, upon a simple entity, the personal Soul, of which they are taken to be so many facultative manifestations. Now, for instance, the Soul manifests its faculty of Memory, now of Reasoning, now of Volition, or again its Imagination or its Appetite. This is the orthodox 'spiritualistic' theory of scholasticism and of common-sense. Another and a less obvious way of unifying the chaos is to seek common elements *in* the divers mental facts rather than a common agent behind them, and to explain them constructively by the various forms of arrangement of these elements, as one explains houses by stones and bricks. The 'associationist' schools of Herbart in Germany, and of Hume, the Mills and Bain in Britain, have thus constructed a *psychology without a soul* by taking discrete 'ideas,' faint or vivid, and showing how, by their cohesions, repulsions, and forms of succession, such things as reminiscences, perceptions, emotions, volitions, passions, theories, and all the other furnishings of an individual's mind may be engendered. The very Self or *ego* of the individual comes in this way to be viewed no longer as the pre-existing source of the representations, but rather as their last and most complicated fruit.

Now, if we strive rigorously to simplify the phenomena in either of these ways, we soon become aware of inadequacies in our method. Any particular cognition, for example, or recollection, is accounted for on the soul-theory by being referred to the spiritual faculties of Cognition or of Memory. These faculties themselves are thought of as absolute properties of the soul;

that is, to take the case of memory, no reason is given why we should remember a fact as it happened, except that so to remember it constitutes the
essence of our Recollective Power. We may, as spiritualists, try to explain our
memory's failures and blunders by secondary causes. But its *successes* can invoke no factors save the existence of certain objective things to be remembered on the one hand, and of our faculty of memory on the other. When, for
instance, I recall my graduation-day, and drag all its incidents and emotions
up from death's dateless night, no mechanical cause can explain this process,
nor can any analysis reduce it to lower terms or make its nature seem other
than an ultimate *datum*, which, whether we rebel or not at its mysterious-
ness, must simply be taken for granted if we are to psychologize at all.
However the associationist may represent the present ideas as thronging
and arranging themselves, still, the spiritualist insists, he has in the end to
admit that *something*, be it brain, be it 'ideas,' be it 'association,' *knows* past
time *as* past, and fills it out with this or that event. And when the spiritualist calls memory an 'irreducible faculty,' he says no more than this admission
of the associationist already grants.

    And yet the admission is far from being a satisfactory simplification
of the concrete facts. For why should this absolute god-given Faculty retain
so much better the events of yesterday than those of last year, and, best of
all, those of an hour ago? Why, again, in old age should its grasp of childhood's events seem firmest? Why should illness and exhaustion enfeeble
it? Why should repeating an experience strengthen our recollection of it?
Why should drugs, fevers, asphyxia, and excitement resuscitate things long
since forgotten? If we content ourselves with merely affirming that the faculty of memory is so peculiarly constituted by nature as to exhibit just
these oddities, we seem little the better for having invoked it, for our explanation becomes as complicated as that of the crude facts with which we
started. Moreover there is something grotesque and irrational in the sup-
position that the soul is equipped with elementary powers of such an ingeniously intricate sort. Why *should* our memory cling more easily to the
near than the remote? Why should it lose its grasp of proper sooner than
of abstract names? Such peculiarities seem quite fantastic; and might, for
aught we can see *a priori*, be the precise opposites of what they are.
Evidently, then, *the faculty does not exist absolutely, but works under conditions*; and *the quest of the conditions* becomes the psychologist's most interesting task.

However firmly he may hold to the soul and her remembering faculty, he must acknowledge that she never exerts the latter without a *cue*, and that something must always precede and *remind* us of whatever we are to recollect. "An *idea!*" says the associationist, "an idea associated with the remembered thing; and this explains also why things repeatedly met with are more easily recollected, for their associates on the various occasions furnish so many distinct avenues of recall." But this does not explain the effects of fever, exhaustion, hypnotism, old age, and the like. And in general, the pure associationist's account of our mental life is almost as bewildering as that of the pure spiritualist. This multitude of ideas, existing absolutely, yet clinging together, and weaving an endless carpet of themselves, like dominoes in ceaseless change, or the bits of glass in a kaleidoscope, —whence do they get their fantastic laws of clinging, and why do they cling in just the shapes they do?

For this the associationist must introduce the order of experience in the outer world. The dance of the ideas is a copy, somewhat mutilated and altered, of the order of phenomena. But the slightest reflection shows that phenomena have absolutely no power to influence our ideas until they have first impressed our senses and our brain. The bare existence of a past fact is no ground for our remembering it. Unless we have seen it, or somehow *undergone* it, we shall never know of its having been. The experiences of the body are thus one of the conditions of the faculty of memory being what it is. And a very small amount of reflection on facts shows that one part of the body, namely, the brain, is the part whose experiences are directly concerned. If the nervous communication be cut off between the brain and other parts, the experiences of those other parts are non-existent for the mind. The eye is blind, the ear deaf, the hand insensible and motionless. And conversely, if the brain be injured, consciousness is abolished or altered, even although every other organ in the body be ready to play its normal part. A blow on the head, a sudden subtraction of blood, the pressure of an apoplectic hemorrhage, may have the first effect; whilst a very few ounces of alcohol or grains of opium or hasheesh, or a whiff of chloroform or nitrous oxide gas, are sure to have the second. The delirium of fever, the altered self of insanity, are all due to foreign matters circulating through the brain, or to pathological changes in that organ's substance. The fact that the brain is the one immediate bodily condition of the mental operations is indeed so universally admitted nowadays that I need spend no more time in illustrating it, but will simply postulate it and pass on. The whole remainder of the book will be more or less of a proof that the postulate was correct.

Bodily experiences, therefore, and more particularly brain-experiences, must take a place amongst those conditions of the mental life of which Psychology need take account. *The spiritualist and the associationist must both be 'cerebralists,'* to the extent at least of admitting that certain peculiarities in the way of working of their own favorite principles are explicable only by the fact that the brain laws are a codeterminant of the result.

Our first conclusion, then, is that a certain amount of brain-physiology must be presupposed or included in Psychology.

In still another way the psychologist is forced to be something of a nerve-physiologist. Mental phenomena are not only conditioned *a parte ante* by bodily processes; but they lead to them *a parte post*. That they lead to *acts* is of course the most familiar of truths, but I do not merely mean acts in the sense of voluntary and deliberate muscular performances. Mental states occasion also changes in the calibre of blood-vessels, or alteration in the heart-beats, or processes more subtle still, in glands and viscera. If these are taken into account, as well as acts which follow at some *remote period* because the mental state was once there, it will be safe to lay down the general law that *no mental modification ever occurs which is not accompanied or followed by a bodily change*. The ideas and feelings, e.g., which these present printed characters excite in the reader's mind not only occasion movements of his eyes and nascent movements of articulation in him, but will some day make him speak, or take sides in a discussion, or give advice, or choose a book to read, differently from what would have been the case had they never impressed his retina. Our psychology must therefore take account not only of the conditions antecedent to mental states, but of their resultant consequences as well.

But actions originally prompted by conscious intelligence may grow so automatic by dint of habit as to be apparently unconsciously performed. Standing, walking, buttoning and unbuttoning, piano-playing, talking, even saying one's prayers, may be done when the mind is absorbed in other things. The performances of animal *instinct* seem semi-automatic, and the *reflex acts* of self-preservation certainly are so. Yet they resemble intelligent acts in bringing about the *same ends* at which the animals' consciousness, on other occasions, deliberately aims. Shall the study of such machine-like yet purposive acts as these be included in Psychology?

The boundary-line of the mental is certainly vague. It is better not to be pedantic, but to let the science be as vague as its subject, and include such phenomena as these if by so doing we can throw any light on the main business in hand. It will ere long be seen, I trust, that we can; and that we gain much more by a broad than by a narrow conception of our subject. At a certain stage in the development of every science a degree of vagueness is what best consists with fertility. On the whole, few recent formulas have done more real service of a rough sort in psychology than the Spencerian one that the essence of mental life and of bodily life are one, namely, 'the adjustment of inner to outer relations.' Such a formula is vagueness incarnate; but because it takes into account the fact that minds inhabit environments which act on them and on which they in turn react; because, in short, it takes mind in the midst of all its concrete relations, it is immensely more fertile than the old-fashioned 'rational psychology,' which treated the soul as a detached existent, sufficient unto itself, and assumed to consider only its nature and properties. I shall therefore feel free to make any sallies into zoology or into pure nerve-physiology which may seem instructive for our purposes, but otherwise shall leave those sciences to the physiologists.

Can we state more distinctly still the manner in which the mental life seems to intervene between impressions made from without upon the body, and reactions of the body upon the outer world again? Let us look at a few facts.

If some iron filings be sprinkled on a table and a magnet brought near them, they will fly through the air for a certain distance and stick to its surface. A savage seeing the phenomenon explains it as the result of an attraction or love between the magnet and the filings. But let a card cover the poles of the magnet, and the filings will press forever against its surface without its ever occurring to them to pass around its sides and thus come into more direct contact with the object of their love. Blow bubbles through a tube into the bottom of a pail of water, they will rise to the surface and mingle with the air. Their action may again be poetically interpreted as due to a longing to recombine with the mother-atmosphere above the surface. But if you invert a jar full of water over the pail, they will rise and remain lodged beneath its bottom, shut in from the outer air, although a slight deflection from their course at the outset, or a re-descent towards the rim of the jar when they found their upward course impeded, would easily have set them free.

If now we pass from such actions as these to those of living things, we notice a striking difference. Romeo wants Juliet as the filings want the magnet; and if no obstacles intervene he moves towards her by as straight a line as they. But Romeo and Juliet, if a wall be built between them, do not remain idiotically pressing their faces against its opposite sides like the magnet and the filings with the card. Romeo soon finds a circuitous way, by scaling the wall or otherwise, of touching Juliet's lips directly. With the filings the path is fixed; whether it reaches the end depends on accidents. With the lover it is the end which is fixed, the path may be modified indefinitely.

Suppose a living frog in the position in which we placed our bubbles of air, namely, at the bottom of a jar of water. The want of breath will soon make him also long to rejoin the mother-atmosphere, and he will take the shortest path to his end by swimming straight upwards. But if a jar full of water be inverted over him, he will not, like the bubbles, perpetually press his nose against its unyielding roof, but will restlessly explore the neighborhood until by re-descending again he has discovered a path round its brim to the goal of his desires. Again the fixed end, the varying means!

Such contrasts between living and inanimate performances end by leading men to deny that in the physical world final purposes exist at all. Loves and desires are to-day no longer imputed to particles of iron or of air. No one supposes now that the end of any activity which they may display is an ideal purpose presiding over the activity from its outset and soliciting or drawing it into being by a sort of *vis a fronte*. The end, on the contrary, is deemed a mere passive result, pushed into being *a tergo*, having had, so to speak, no voice in its own production. Alter the pre-existing conditions, and with inorganic materials you bring forth each time a different apparent end. But with intelligent agents, altering the conditions changes the activity displayed, but not the end reached; for here the idea of the yet unrealized end co-operates with the conditions to determine what the activities shall be.

The pursuance of future ends and the choice of means for their attainment are thus the mark and criterion of the presence of mentality in a phenomenon. We all use this test to discriminate between an intelligent and a mechanical performance. We impute no mentality to sticks and stones, because they never seem to move for *the sake of* anything, but always when pushed, and then indifferently and with no sign of choice. So we unhesitatingly call them senseless.

Just so we form our decision upon the deepest of all philosophic problems: Is the Kosmos an expression of intelligence rational in its inward nature, or a brute external fact pure and simple? If we find ourselves, in contemplating it, unable to banish the impression that it is a realm of final purposes, that it exists for the sake of something, we place intelligence at the heart of it and have a religion. If, on the contrary, in surveying its irremediable flux, we can think of the present only as so much mere mechanical sprouting from the past, occurring with no reference to the future, we are atheists and materialists.

In the lengthy discussions which psychologists have carried on about the amount of intelligence displayed by lower mammals, or the amount of consciousness involved in the functions of the nerve-centres of reptiles, the same test has always been applied: Is the character of the actions such that we must believe them to be performed *for the sake* of their result? The result in question, as we shall hereafter abundantly see, is as a rule a useful one,— the animal is, on the whole, safer under the circumstances for bringing it forth. So far the action has a teleological character; but such mere outward teleology as this might still be the blind result of *vis a tergo*. The growth and movements of plants, the processes of development, digestion, secretion, etc., in animals, supply innumerable instances of performances useful to the individual which may nevertheless be, and by most of us are supposed to be, produced by automatic mechanism. The physiologist does not confidently assert conscious intelligence in the frog's spinal cord until he has shown that the useful result which the nervous machinery brings forth under a given irritation *remains the same when the machinery is altered*. If, to take the stock-instance, the right knee of a headless frog be irritated with acid, the right foot will wipe it off. When, however, this foot is amputated, the animal will often raise the *left* foot to the spot and wipe the offending material away.

Pflüger and Lewes reason from such facts in the following way: If the first reaction were the result of mere machinery, they say; if that irritated portion of the skin discharged the right leg as a trigger discharges its own barrel of a shotgun; then amputating the right foot would indeed frustrate the wiping, but would not make the *left* leg move. It would simply result in the right stump moving through the empty air (which is in fact the phenomenon sometimes observed). The right trigger makes no effort to discharge the left barrel if the right one be unloaded; nor does an electrical machine ever get restless because it can only emit sparks, and not hem pillow-cases like a sewing-machine.

If, on the contrary, the right leg originally moved for the *purpose* of wiping the acid, then nothing is more natural than that, when the easiest means of effecting that purpose prove fruitless, other means should be tried. Every failure must keep the animal in a state of disappointment which will lead to all sorts of new trials and devices; and tranquillity will not ensue till one of these, by a happy stroke, achieves the wished-for end.

In a similar way Goltz ascribes intelligence to the frog's optic lobes and cerebellum. We alluded above to the manner in which a sound frog imprisoned in water will discover an outlet to the atmosphere. Goltz found that frogs deprived of their cerebral hemispheres would often exhibit a like ingenuity. Such a frog, after rising from the bottom and finding his farther upward progress checked by the glass bell which has been inverted over him, will not persist in butting his nose against the obstacle until dead of suffocation, but will often re-descend and emerge from under its rim as if, not a definite mechanical propulsion upwards, but rather a conscious desire to reach the air by hook or crook were the mainspring of his activity. Goltz concluded from this that the hemispheres are not the seat of intellectual power in frogs. He made the same inference from observing that a brainless frog will turn over from his back to his belly when one of his legs is sewed up, although the movements required are then very different from those excited under normal circumstances by the same annoying position. They seem determined, consequently, not merely by the antecedent irritant, but by the final end,—though the irritant of course is what makes the end desired.

Another brilliant German author, Liebmann, argues against the brain's mechanism accounting for mental action, by very similar considerations. A machine as such, he says, will bring forth right results when it is in good order, and wrong results if out of repair. But both kinds of result flow with equally fatal necessity from their conditions. We cannot suppose the clockwork whose structure fatally determines it to a certain rate of speed, noticing that this speed is too slow or too fast and vainly trying to correct it. Its conscience, if it have any, should be as good as that of the best chronometer, for both alike obey equally well the same eternal mechanical laws—laws from behind. But if the *brain* be out of order and the man says "Twice four are two," instead of "Twice four are eight," or else "I must go to the coal to buy the wharf," instead of "I must go to the wharf to buy the coal," instantly there arises a consciousness of error. The wrong performance, though it obey the same mechanical law as the right, is nevertheless condemned,—condemned as contradicting the inner law—the law from in front, the purpose or ideal for which the brain *should* act, whether it do so or not.

We need not discuss here whether these writers in drawing their conclusion have done justice to all the premises involved in the cases they treat of. We quote their arguments only to show how they appeal to the principle that *no actions but such as are done for an end, and show a choice of means, can be called indubitable expressions of Mind.*

I shall then adopt this as the criterion by which to circumscribe the subject-matter of this work so far as action enters into it. Many nervous performances will therefore be unmentioned, as being purely physiological. Nor will the anatomy of the nervous system and organs of sense be described anew. The reader will find in H. N. Martin's *Human Body,* in G. T. Ladd's *Physiological Psychology,* and in all the other standard Anatomies and Physiologies, a mass of information which we must regard as preliminary and take for granted in the present work. Of the functions of the cerebral hemispheres, however, since they directly subserve consciousness, it will be well to give some little account.

From *The Unconscious*

Sigmund Freud

We have learnt from psycho-analysis that the essence of the process of re-pression lies, not in putting an end to, in annihilating, the idea which rep-resents an instinct, but in preventing it from becoming conscious. When this happens we say of the idea that it is in a state of being 'unconscious', and we can produce good evidence to show that even when it is unconscious it can produce effects, even including some which finally reach conscious-ness. Everything that is repressed must remain unconscious; but let us state at the very outset that the repressed does not cover everything that is un-conscious. The unconscious has the wider compass: the repressed is a part of the unconscious.

How are we to arrive at a knowledge of the unconscious? It is of course only as something conscious that we know it, after it has undergone trans-formation or translation into something conscious. Psycho-analytic work shows us every day that translation of this kind is possible. In order that this should come about, the person under analysis must overcome certain resis-tances—the same resistances as those which, earlier, made the material con-cerned into something repressed by rejecting it from the conscious.

I. Justification for the Concept of the Unconscious

Our right to assume the existence of something mental that is unconscious and to employ that assumption for the purposes of scientific work is dis-puted in many quarters. To this we can reply that our assumption of the un-conscious is *necessary* and *legitimate*, and that we possess numerous proofs of its existence.

It is *necessary* because the data of consciousness have a very large num-ber of gaps in them; both in healthy and in sick people psychical acts often occur which can be explained only by presupposing other acts, of which, nevertheless, consciousness affords no evidence. These not only include parapraxes and dreams in healthy people, and everything described as a psychical symptom or an obsession in the sick; our most personal daily experience acquaints us with ideas that come into our head we do not know from where, and with intellectual conclusions arrived at we do not know how. All these conscious acts remain disconnected and unintelligible if we insist upon claiming that every mental act that occurs in us must also necessarily be experienced by us through consciousness; on the other hand, they fall into a demonstrable connection if we interpolate between them the unconscious acts which we have inferred. A gain in meaning is a perfectly justifiable ground for going beyond the limits of direct experience. When, in addition, it turns out that the assumption of there being an unconscious enables us to construct a successful procedure by which we can exert an effective influence upon the course of conscious processes, this success will have given us an incontrovertible proof of the existence of what we have assumed. This being so, we must adopt the position that to require that whatever goes on in the mind must also be known to consciousness is to make an untenable claim.

We can go further and argue, in support of there being an unconscious psychical state, that at any given moment consciousness includes only a small content, so that the greater part of what we call conscious knowledge must in any case be for very considerable periods of time in a state of latency, that is to say, of being psychically unconscious. When all our latent memories are taken into consideration it becomes totally incomprehensible how the existence of the unconscious can be denied. But here we encounter the objection that these latent recollections can no longer be described as psychical, but that they correspond to residues of somatic processes from which what is psychical can once more arise. The obvious answer to this is that a latent memory is, on the contrary, an unquestionable residuum of a *psychical* process. But it is more important to realize clearly that this objection is based on the equation—not, it is true, explicitly stated but taken as axiomatic—of what is conscious with what is mental. This equation is either a *petitio principii* which begs the question whether everything that is psychical is also necessarily conscious; or else it is a matter of convention, of nomenclature. In this latter case it is, of course, like any other convention, not open to refutation. The question remains, however, whether the convention is so expedient that we are bound to adopt it. To this we may reply that the conventional equation of the psychical with the conscious is totally inexpedient. It disrupts psychical continuities, plunges us into the insoluble difficulties of psycho-physical parallelism, is open to the reproach that for no obvious reason it over-estimates the part played by consciousness, and that it forces us prematurely to abandon the field of psychological research without being able to offer us any compensation from other fields.

It is clear in any case that this question—whether the latent states of mental life, whose existence is undeniable, are to be conceived of as conscious mental states or as physical ones—threatens to resolve itself into a verbal dispute. We shall therefore be better advised to focus our attention on what we know with certainty of the nature of these debatable states. As far as their physical characteristics are concerned, they are totally inaccessible to us: no physiological concept or chemical process can give us any notion of their nature. On the other hand, we know for certain that they have abundant points of contact with conscious mental processes; with the help of a certain amount of work they can be transformed into, or replaced by, conscious mental processes, and all the categories which we employ to describe conscious mental acts, such as ideas, purposes, resolutions and so on, can be applied to them. Indeed, we are obliged to say of some of these latent states that the only respect in which they differ from conscious ones is precisely in the absence of consciousness. Thus we shall not hesitate to treat them as objects of psychological research, and to deal with them in the most intimate connection with conscious mental acts.

The stubborn denial of a psychical character to latent mental acts is accounted for by the circumstance that most of the phenomena concerned have not been the subject of study outside psycho-analysis. Anyone who is ignorant of pathological facts, who regards the parapraxes of normal people as accidental, and who is content with the old saw that dreams are froth [*'Träume sind Schäume'*] has only to ignore a few more problems of the psychology of consciousness in order to spare himself any need to assume an unconscious mental activity. Incidentally, even before the time of psycho-analysis, hypnotic experiments, and especially post-hypnotic suggestion, had tangibly demonstrated the existence and mode of operation of the mental unconscious.

The assumption of an unconscious is, moreover, a perfectly *legitimate* one, inasmuch as in postulating it we are not departing a single step from our customary and generally accepted mode of thinking. Consciousness makes each of us aware only of his own states of mind; that other people, too, possess a consciousness is an inference which we draw by analogy from their observable utterances and actions, in order to make this behaviour of theirs intelligible to us. (It would no doubt be psychologically more correct to put it in this way: that without any special reflection we attribute to everyone else our own constitution and therefore our consciousness as well, and that this identification is a *sine qua non* of our understanding.) This inference (or this identification) was formerly extended by the ego to other human beings, to animals, plants, inanimate objects and to the world at large, and proved serviceable so long as their similarity to the individual ego was overwhelmingly great; but it became more untrustworthy in proportion as the difference between the ego and these 'others' widened. To-day, our critical judgement is already in doubt on the question of consciousness in animals; we refuse to admit it in plants and we regard the assumption of its existence in inanimate matter as mysticism. But even where the original inclination to identification has withstood criticism—that is, when the 'others' are our fellow-men—the assumption of a consciousness in them rests upon an inference and cannot share the immediate certainty which we have of our own consciousness.

Psycho-analysis demands nothing more than that we should apply this process of inference to ourselves also—a proceeding to which, it is true, we are not constitutionally inclined. If we do this, we must say: all the acts and manifestations which I notice in myself and do not know how to link up with the rest of my mental life must be judged as if they belonged to someone else: they are to be explained by a mental life ascribed to this other person. Furthermore, experience shows that we understand very well how to interpret in other people (that is, how to fit into their chain of mental events) the same acts which we refuse to acknowledge as being mental in ourselves. Here some special hindrance evidently deflects our investigations from our own self and prevents our obtaining a true knowledge of it.

This process of inference, when applied to oneself in spite of internal opposition, does not, however, lead to the disclosure of an unconscious; it leads logically to the assumption of another, second consciousness which is united in one's self with the consciousness one knows. But at this point, certain criticisms may fairly be made. In the first place, a consciousness of which its own possessor knows nothing is something very different from a consciousness belonging to another person, and it is questionable whether such a consciousness, lacking, as it does, its most important characteristic, deserves any discussion at all. Those who have resisted the assumption of an unconscious *psychical* are not likely to be ready to exchange it for an unconscious *consciousness*. In the second place, analysis shows that the different latent mental processes inferred by us enjoy a high degree of mutual independence, as though they had no connection with one another, and knew nothing of one another. We must be prepared, if so, to assume the existence in us not only of a second consciousness, but of a third, fourth, perhaps of an unlimited number of states of consciousness, all unknown to us and to one another. In the third place—and this is the most weighty argument of all—we have to take into account the fact that analytic investigation reveals some of these latent processes as having characteristics and peculiarities which seem alien to us, or even incredible, and which run directly counter to the attributes of consciousness with which we are familiar. Thus we have grounds for modifying our inference about ourselves and saying that what is proved is not the existence of a second consciousness in us, but the existence of psychical acts which lack consciousness. We shall also be right in rejecting the term 'subconsciousness' as incorrect and misleading. The well-known cases of *'double conscience'* (splitting of consciousness) prove nothing against our view. We may most aptly describe them as cases of a splitting of the mental activities into two groups, and say that the same consciousness turns to one or the other of these groups alternately.

In psycho-analysis there is no choice for us but to assert that mental processes are in themselves unconscious, and to liken the perception of them by means of consciousness to the perception of the external world by means of the sense-organs. We can even hope to gain fresh knowledge from the comparison. The psycho-analytic assumption of unconscious mental activity appears to us, on the one hand, as a further expansion of the primitive animism which caused us to see copies of our own consciousness all around us, and, on the other hand, as an extension of the corrections undertaken by Kant of our views on external perception. Just as Kant warned us not to overlook the fact that our perceptions are subjectively conditioned and must not be regarded as identical with what is perceived though unknowable, so psycho-analysis warns us not to equate perceptions by means of consciousness with the unconscious mental processes which are their object. Like the physical, the psychical is not necessarily in reality what it appears to us to be. We shall be glad to learn, however, that the correction of internal perception will turn out not to offer such great difficulties as the correction of external perception—that internal objects are less unknowable than the external world.

QUESTIONS

1. Why did James argue that "a certain amount of brain-physiology must be presupposed or included in Psychology"? What did he mean by this? Does this view seem more or less correct early in the twenty-first century?

2. In a passage that presages the cognitive revolution in psychology (see the introduction to Chapter 7), James speaks of "fixed ends" with "varying means." What point is he trying to make?

3. Freud's central claim is that "all conscious acts remain disconnected and unintelligible if we insist upon claiming that every mental act that occurs in us must all necessarily be experienced by us through consciousness." Drawing on this, and the selection as a whole, explain Freud's view on the importance of the unconscious for understanding psychology.

CHAPTER TWO

METHODS

Psychology is only as good as its methods. To understand what goes on in the mind and to explain human behavior, we must be able to accurately measure mental processes that are not straightforwardly observable. As in any field, scientific advances are often driven by methodological innovation. The recent explosion in brain imaging, for example, can be traced in part to advances in techniques for measuring neural activity in a relatively safe fashion, without having to breach the skull or use radioactive tracers.

But whether psychologists use the latest high-tech devices for brain scanning or paper-and-pencil questionnaires, all good experimental work is based on a keen understanding of statistics and the logic of scientific inference—the central focus of the two readings in this chapter. The first, taken from Darrell Huff's ironically titled *How to Lie with Statistics*, is a classic from 1954; the second is taken from Keith Stanovich's more recent *How to Think Straight About Psychology* (2001).

Huff's guide isn't specifically about psychology, but no matter. His straightforward advice remains sound and applicable half a century later. In this particular selection, Huff focuses on the complex relationship between cause and effect, causation and correlation: the bane of all psychological research. Every good psychologist wants to know whether some A causes some B, but all too often we are left with something less definitive: an understanding of how A *correlates* with B—with no certainty about whether A *causes* B (rather than, say, B causing A or some third factor C causing both). For example, if we know that business acumen correlates with risktaking, it might be that taking risks leads to success in business, that success in business encourages people to take risks, or that some third factor, say, assertiveness, leads to both. Correlation is never the same as causation, and Huff explains why.

Like Huff, what Stanovich is really after is the distinction between data and explanation, between mere observation and genuine understanding. Working through a series of cases, including the infamous tale of Clever

Hans, the turn-of-the-twentieth-century horse who allegedly understood arithmetic, Stanovich illustrates the importance of what he calls comparison, control, and manipulation, quite possibly the three most essential tools in any psychologist's toolkit.

Both selections encourage a healthy skepticism, and in interpreting psychology, there could be no more valuable tool.

From *How to Lie with Statistics*

Darrell Huff

Somebody once went to a good deal of trouble to find out if cigarette smokers make lower college grades than nonsmokers. It turned out that they did. This pleased a good many people and they have been making much of it ever since. The road to good grades, it would appear, lies in giving up smoking; and, to carry the conclusion one reasonable step further, smoking makes dull minds.

This particular study was, I believe, properly done: sample big enough and honestly and carefully chosen, correlation having a high significance, and so on.

The fallacy is an ancient one which, however, has a powerful tendency to crop up in statistical material, where it is disguised by a welter of impressive figures. It is the one that says that if B follows A, then A has caused B. An unwarranted assumption is being made that since smoking and low grades go together, smoking causes low grades. Couldn't it just as well be the other way around? Perhaps low marks drive students not to drink but to tobacco. When it comes right down to it, this conclusion is about as likely as the other and just as well supported by the evidence. But it is not nearly so satisfactory to propagandists.

It seems a good deal more probable, however, that neither of these things has produced the other, but both are a product of some third factor. Can it be that the sociable sort of fellow who takes his books less than seriously is also likely to smoke more? Or is there a clue in the fact that somebody once established a correlation between extroversion and low grades—a closer relationship apparently than the one between grades and intelligence? Maybe extroverts smoke more than introverts. The point is that when there are many reasonable explanations you are hardly entitled to pick one that suits your taste and insist on it. But many people do.

To avoid falling for the *post hoc* fallacy and thus wind up believing many things that are not so, you need to put any statement of relationship through a sharp inspection. The correlation, that convincingly precise figure that seems to prove that something is because of something, can actually be any of several types.

One is the correlation produced by chance. You may be able to get together a set of figures to prove some unlikely thing in this way, but if you try again, your next set may not prove it at all. As with the manufacturer of the tooth paste that appeared to reduce decay, you simply throw away the results you don't want and publish widely those you do. Given a small sample, you are likely to find some substantial correlation between any pair of characteristics or events that you can think of.

A common kind of co-variation is one in which the relationship is real but it is not possible to be sure which of the variables is the cause and which the effect. In some of these instances cause and effect may change places from time to time or indeed both may be cause and effect at the same time. A correlation between income and ownership of stocks might be of that kind. The more money you make, the more stock you buy, and the more stock you buy, the more income you get; it is not accurate to say simply that one has produced the other.

Perhaps the trickiest of them all is the very common instance in which neither of the variables has any effect at all on the other, yet there is a real correlation: A good deal of dirty work has been done with this one. The poor grades among cigarette smokers is in this category, as are all too many medical statistics that are quoted without the qualification that although the relationship has been shown to be real, the cause-and-effect nature of it is only a matter of speculation. As an instance of the nonsense or spurious correlation that is a real statistical fact, someone has gleefully pointed to this: There is a close relationship between the salaries of Presbyterian ministers in Massachusetts and the price of rum in Havana.

Which is the cause and which the effect? In other words, are the ministers benefiting from the rum trade or supporting it? All right. That's so far-fetched that it is ridiculous at a glance. But watch out for other applications of *post hoc* logic that differ from this one only in being more subtle. In the case of the ministers and the rum it is easy to see that both figures are growing because of the influence of a third factor: the historic and world-wide rise in the price level of practically everything.

And take the figures that show the suicide rate to be at its maximum in June. Do suicides produce June brides—or do June weddings precipitate suicides of the jilted? A somewhat more convincing (though equally unproved) explanation is that the fellow who licks his depression all through the winter with the thought that things will look rosier in the spring gives up when June comes and he still feels terrible.

Another thing to watch out for is a conclusion in which a correlation has been inferred to continue beyond the data with which it has been demonstrated. It is easy to show that the more it rains in an area, the taller the corn grows or even the greater the crop. Rain, it seems, is a blessing. But a season of very heavy rainfall may damage or even ruin the crop. The positive correlation holds up to a point and then quickly becomes a negative one. Above so-many inches, the more it rains the less corn you get.

We're going to pay a little attention to the evidence on the money value of education in a minute. But for now let's assume it has been proved that high-school graduates make more money than those who drop out, that each year of undergraduate work in college adds some more income. Watch out for the general conclusion that the more you go to school the more money you'll make. Note that this has not been shown to be true for the years beyond an undergraduate degree, and it may very well not apply to them either. People with Ph.D.s quite often become college teachers and so do not become members of the highest income groups.

A correlation of course shows a tendency which is not often the ideal relationship described as one-to-one. Tall boys weigh more than short boys on the average, so this is a positive correlation. But you can easily find a six-footer who weighs less than some five-footers, so the correlation is less than 1. A negative correlation is simply a statement that as one variable increases the other tends to decrease. In physics this becomes an inverse ratio: The further you get from a light bulb the less light there is on your book; as distance increases light intensity decreases. These physical relationships often have the kindness to produce perfect correlations, but figures from business or sociology or medicine seldom work out so neatly. Even if education generally increases incomes it may easily turn out to be the financial ruination of Joe over there. Keep in mind that a correlation may be real and based on real cause and effect—and still be almost worthless in determining action in any single case.

Reams of pages of figures have been collected to show the value in dollars of a college education, and stacks of pamphlets have been published to bring these figures—and conclusions more or less based on them—to the attention of potential students. I am not quarreling with the intention. I am in favor of education myself, particularly if it includes a course in elementary statistics. Now these figures have pretty conclusively demonstrated that people who have gone to college make more money than people who have not. The exceptions are numerous, of course, but the tendency is strong and clear.

The only thing wrong is that along with the figures and facts goes a totally unwarranted conclusion. This is the *post hoc* fallacy at its best. It says that these figures show that if *you* (your son, your daughter) attend college you will probably earn more money than if you decide to spend the next four years in some other manner. This unwarranted conclusion has for its basis the equally unwarranted assumption that since college-trained folks make more money, they make it because they went to college. Actually we don't know but that these are the people who would have made more money even if they had not gone to college. There are a couple of things that indicate rather strongly that this is so. Colleges get a disproportionate number of two groups of kids: the bright and the rich. The bright might show good earning power without college knowledge. And as for the rich ones . . . well, money breeds money in several obvious ways. Few sons of rich men are found in low-income brackets whether they go to college or not.

The following passage is taken from an article in question-and-answer form that appeared in *This Week* magazine, a Sunday supplement of enormous circulation. Maybe you will find it amusing, as I do, that the same writer once produced a piece called "Popular Notions: True or False?"

Q: What effect does going to college have on your chances of remaining unmarried?

A: If you're a woman, it skyrockets your chances of becoming an old maid. But if you're a man, it has the opposite effect—it minimizes your chances of staying a bachelor.

Cornell University made a study of 1,500 typical middle-aged college graduates. Of the men, 93 per cent were married (compared to 83 per cent for the general population).

But of the middle-aged women graduates only 65 per cent were married. Spinsters were relatively three times as numerous among college graduates as among women of the general population.

When Susie Brown, age seventeen, reads this she learns that if she goes to college she will be less likely to get a man than if she doesn't. That is what the article says, and there are statistics from a reputable source to go with it. They go with it, but they don't back it up; and note also that while the statistics are Cornell's the conclusions are not, although a hasty reader may come away with the idea that they are.

Here again a real correlation has been used to bolster up an unproved cause-and-effect relationship. Perhaps it all works the other way around and those women would have remained unmarried even if they had not gone to college. Possibly even more would have failed to marry. If these possibilities are no better than the one the writer insists upon, they are perhaps just as valid conclusions: that is, guesses.

Indeed there is one piece of evidence suggesting that a propensity for old-maidhood may lead to going to college. Dr. Kinsey seems to have found some correlation between sexuality and education, with traits perhaps being fixed at pre-college age. That makes it all the more questionable to say that going to college gets in the way of marrying.

Note to Susie Brown: It ain't necessarily so.

A medical article once pointed with great alarm to an increase in cancer among milk drinkers. Cancer, it seems, was becoming increasingly frequent in New England, Minnesota, Wisconsin, and Switzerland, where a lot of milk is produced and consumed, while remaining rare in Ceylon, where milk is scarce. For further evidence it was pointed out that cancer was less frequent in some Southern states where less milk was consumed. Also, it was pointed out, milk-drinking English women get some kinds of cancer eighteen times as frequently as Japanese women who seldom drink milk.

A little digging might uncover quite a number of ways to account for these figures, but one factor is enough by itself to show them up. Cancer is predominantly a disease that strikes in middle life or after. Switzerland and the states mentioned first are alike in having populations with relatively long spans of life. English women at the time the study was made were living an average of twelve years longer than Japanese women.

Professor Helen M. Walker has worked out an amusing illustration of the folly in assuming there must be cause and effect whenever two things vary together. In investigating the relationship between age and some physical characteristics of women, begin by measuring the angle of the feet in walking. You will find that the angle tends to be greater among older women. You might first consider whether this indicates that women grow older because they toe out, and you can see immediately that this is ridiculous. So it appears that age increases the angle between the feet, and most women must come to toe out more as they grow older.

Any such conclusion is probably false and certainly unwarranted. You could only reach it legitimately by studying the same women—or possibly equivalent groups—over a period of time. That would eliminate the factor responsible here. Which is that the older women grew up at a time when a young lady was taught to toe out in walking, while the members of the younger group were learning posture in a day when that was discouraged.

When you find somebody—usually an interested party—making a fuss about a correlation, look first of all to see if it is not one of this type, produced by the stream of events, the trend of the times. In our time it is easy to show a positive correlation between any pair of things like these: number of students in college, number of inmates in mental institutions, consumption of cigarettes, incidence of heart disease, use of X-ray machines, production of false teeth, salaries of California school teachers, profits of Nevada gambling halls. To call some one of these the cause of some other is manifestly silly. But it is done every day.

Permitting statistical treatment and the hypnotic presence of numbers and decimal points to befog causal relationships is little better than superstition. And it is often more seriously misleading. It is rather like the conviction among the people of the New Hebrides that body lice produce good health. Observation over the centuries had taught them that people in good health usually had lice and sick people very often did not. The observation itself was accurate and sound, as observations made informally over the years surprisingly often are. Not so much can be said for the conclusion to which these primitive people came from their evidence: Lice make a man healthy. Everybody should have them.

As we have already noted, scantier evidence than this—treated in the statistical mill until common sense could no longer penetrate to it—has made many a medical fortune and many a medical article in magazines, including professional ones. More sophisticated observers finally got things straightened out in the New Hebrides. As it turned out, almost everybody in those circles had lice most of the time. It was, you might say, the normal condition of man. When, however, anyone took a fever (quite possibly carried to him by those same lice) and his body became too hot for comfortable habitation, the lice left. There you have cause and effect altogether confusingly distorted, reversed, and intermingled.

From *How to Think Straight about Psychology*

Keith Stanovich

This chapter starts with a quiz. Don't worry; it's not about what you read in the last chapter. In fact, it should be easy because it's about the observable motion of objects in the world, something with which we have all had much experience. There are just three questions in the quiz.

For the first, you will need a piece of paper. Imagine that a person is whirling a ball attached to a string around his or her head. Draw a circle that represents the path of the ball as viewed from above the person's head. Draw a dot somewhere on the circle and connect the dot to the center of the circle with a line. The line represents the string, and the dot represents the ball at a particular instant in time. Imagine that at exactly this instant, the string is cut. Your first task is to indicate with your pencil the subsequent flight of the ball.

For your next problem, imagine that you are a bomber pilot flying toward a target at 500 miles per hour at a height of 20,000 feet. To simplify the problem, assume that there is no air resistance. The question here is: At which location would you drop your bomb: before reaching the target, directly over the target, or when you have passed the target? Indicate either a specific distance in front of the target, directly over the target, or a specific distance past the target.

Finally, imagine that you are firing a rifle from shoulder height. Assume that there is no air resistance and that the rifle is fired exactly parallel to the ground. If a bullet that is dropped from the same height as the rifle takes one-half second to hit the ground, how long will it take the bullet that is fired from the rifle to hit the ground if its initial velocity is 2,000 feet per second?

And the answers—oh, yes, the answers. They appear later on in this chapter. But, first, in order to understand what the accuracy of our knowledge about moving objects has to do with psychology, we need to explore more fully the nature of the experimental logic that scientists use.

Comparison, Control, and Manipulation

Although many large volumes have been written on the subject of scientific methodology, it is simply not necessary for the layperson, who may never actually carry out an experiment, to become familiar with all the details and intricacies of experimental design. The most important characteristics of scientific thinking are actually quite easy to grasp. Scientific thinking is based on the ideas of comparison, control, and manipulation. To achieve a more fundamental understanding of a phenomenon, a scientist compares conditions in the world. Without this comparison, we are left with isolated instances of observations, and the interpretation of these isolated observations is highly ambiguous.

By comparing data patterns under different conditions, scientists rule out certain explanations and confirm others. They construct their comparisons so that the outcome will eliminate a number of alternative theories that may have been advanced as explanations. That is, they try to weed out the maximum number of incorrect explanations. They do this either by directly controlling the experimental situation or by observing the kinds of naturally occurring situations that allow them to test alternative explanations.

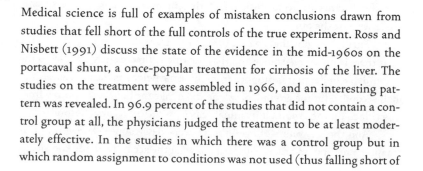

Medical science is full of examples of mistaken conclusions drawn from studies that fell short of the full controls of the true experiment. Ross and Nisbett (1991) discuss the state of the evidence in the mid-1960s on the portacaval shunt, a once-popular treatment for cirrhosis of the liver. The studies on the treatment were assembled in 1966, and an interesting pattern was revealed. In 96.9 percent of the studies that did not contain a control group at all, the physicians judged the treatment to be at least moderately effective. In the studies in which there was a control group but in which random assignment to conditions was not used (thus falling short of true experimental design), 86.7 percent of the studies were judged to have shown at least moderate effectiveness. However, in the studies in which there was a control group formed by true random assignment, only 25 percent of the studies were judged to have shown at least moderate effectiveness. Thus, the effectiveness of this particular treatment—now known to be ineffective—was vastly overestimated by studies that did not employ complete experimental controls. Ross and Nisbett (1991) note that "the positive results found using less formal procedures were the product either of 'placebo effects' or of biases resulting from nonrandom assignment." Ross and Nisbett discuss how selection effects may operate to cause spurious positive effects when random assignment is not used. For example, if the patients chosen for a treatment tend to be "good candidates" or those with vocal and supportive families, there may be differences between them and the control group irrespective of the effectiveness of the treatment.

The tendency to see the necessity of acquiring comparative information before coming to a conclusion is apparently not a natural one—which is why training in all the sciences includes methodology courses that stress the importance of constructing control groups. The "nonvividness" of the control group—the group treated just like the experimental group except for the absence of a critical factor—makes it difficult to see how essential such a group is. Psychologists have done extensive research on the tendency for people to ignore essential comparative (control group) information. For example, in a much researched paradigm (Shanks, 1995; Stanovich & West, 1998), subjects are shown a 2 × 2 matrix such as the one shown here that summarizes the data from an experiment.

	Improvement	No Improvement
Treatment	200	75
No treatment	50	15

The numbers in the table represent the number of people in each cell. Specifically, 200 people received the treatment and showed improvement in the condition being treated, 75 received the treatment and showed no improvement, 50 received no treatment and showed improvement, and 15 received no treatment and showed no improvement. The subjects are asked to indicate the degree of effectiveness of the treatment. Many subjects think that the treatment in question is effective, and a considerable number of subjects think that the treatment has substantial effectiveness. They focus on the large number of cases (200) in the cell indicating people who received treatment and showed improvement. Secondarily, they focus on the fact that more people who received treatment showed improvement (200) than showed no improvement (75). In fact, the particular treatment tested in this experiment is completely ineffective.

In order to understand why the treatment is ineffective, it is necessary to concentrate on the two cells that represent the outcome for the control group (the no-treatment group). There we see that 50 of 65 subjects in the control group, or 76.9 percent, improved when they got *no* treatment. This contrasts with 200 of 275, or 72.7 percent, who improved when they received the treatment. Thus, the percentage of improvement is actually larger in the no-treatment group, an indication that this treatment is totally ineffective. The tendency to ignore the outcomes in the no-treatment cells and focus on the large number in the treatment/improvement cell seduces many people into viewing the treatment as effective. In short, it is relatively easy to draw people's attention away from the fact that the outcomes in the control condition are a critical piece of contextual information in interpreting the outcome in the treatment condition (see Doherty, Chadwick, Garavan, Barr, & Mynatt, 1996).

The Case of Clever Hans, the Wonder Horse

The necessity of eliminating alternative explanations of a phenomenon by the use of experimental control is well illustrated by a story that is famous in the annals of behavioral science: that of Clever Hans, the mathematical horse. More than 80 years ago, a German schoolteacher presented to the public a horse, Clever Hans, that supposedly knew how to solve mathematical problems. When Hans was given addition, subtraction, and multiplication problems by his trainer, he would tap out the answer to the problems with his hoof. The horse's responses were astoundingly accurate.

Many people were amazed and puzzled by Clever Hans's performance. Was the horse really demonstrating an ability thus far unknown in his species? Imagine what the public must have thought. Compelling testimonials to Hans's unique ability appeared in the German press. One Berlin newspaper reporter wrote that "this thinking horse is going to give men of science a great deal to think about for a long time to come" (Fernald, 1984, p. 30), a prediction that turned out to be correct, though not quite in the way the reporter expected. A group of "experts" observed Hans and attested to his abilities. Everyone was baffled. And bafflement was bound to remain as long as the phenomenon was observed merely in isolation and as long as no controlled observations were carried out. The mystery was soon dispelled, however, when a psychologist, Oskar Pfungst, undertook systematic studies of the horse's ability (Spitz, 1997).

In the best traditions of experimental design, Pfungst systematically manipulated the conditions under which the animal performed, thus creating "artificial" situations (see Chapter 7) that would allow tests of alternative explanations of the horse's performance. After much careful testing, Pfungst found that the horse did have a special ability, but it was not a mathematical one. In fact, the horse was closer to being a behavioral scientist than a mathematician. You see, Hans was a very careful observer of human behavior. As it was tapping out its answer, it would watch the head of the trainer or other questioner. As Hans approached the answer, the trainer would involuntarily tilt his head slightly, and Hans would stop. Pfungst found that the horse was extremely sensitive to visual cues. It could detect extremely small head movements. Pfungst tested the horse by having the problems presented in such a way that the presenter did not know the answer to the problem or by having the trainer present the problem away from the horse's view. The animal lost its "mathematical abilities" when the questioner did not know the answer or when the trainer was out of view.

The case of Clever Hans is a good context in which to illustrate the importance of carefully distinguishing between the *description* of a phenomenon and the *explanation* of a phenomenon. That the horse tapped out the correct answers to mathematical problems presented by the trainer is not in dispute. The trainer was not lying. Many observers attested to the fact that the horse actually did tap out the correct answers to mathematical problems presented by the trainer. It is in the next step that the problem arises: making the inference that the horse was tapping out the correct answers because the horse had mathematical abilities. Inferring that the horse had mathematical abilities was a *hypothesized explanation* of the phenomenon. It did not follow logically, from the fact that the horse tapped out the correct answers to mathematical problems that the horse had mathematical abilities. Positing that the horse had mathematical abilities was only one of many possible explanations of the horse's performance. It was an explanation that could be put to empirical test. When put to such a test, the explanation was falsified.

Before the intervention of Pfungst, the experts who looked at the horse had made this fundamental error: They had not seen that there might be alternative explanations of the horse's performance. They thought that, once they had observed that the trainer was not lying and that the horse actually did tap out the correct answers to mathematical problems, it necessarily followed that the horse had mathematical abilities. Pfungst was thinking more scientifically and realized that that was only one of many possible explanations of the horse's performance, and that it was necessary to set up controlled conditions in order to differentiate alternative explanations. By having the horse answer questions posed by the trainer from behind a screen, Pfungst set up conditions in which he would be able to differentiate two possible explanations: that the horse had mathematical abilities or that the horse was responding to visual cues. If the horse actually had such abilities, putting the trainer behind a screen should make no difference in its performance. On the other hand, if the horse was responding to visual cues, then putting the trainer behind a screen should disrupt its performance. When the latter happened, Pfungst was able to rule out the hypothesis that the horse had mathematical abilities (Spitz, 1997).

Many classic experiments in psychology involve this logic of prying apart the natural relationships that exist in the world so that it can be determined which variable is the dominant cause. Psychologist Harry Harlow's famous experiments (Anderson & Anderson, 1996; Harlow, 1958) provide a case in point. Harlow wanted to test a prevailing hypothesis about infant-mother attachment: that the attachment resulted from the mother providing the infant's source of food. However, the problem was that, of course, mothers provide much more than nourishment (comfort, warmth, caressing, stimulation, etc.). Harlow (1958) examined the behavior of infant macaque monkeys in situations in which he isolated only one of the variables associated with attachment by giving the animals choices among "artificial" mothers. For example, he found that the contact comfort provided by a "mother" made of terrycloth was preferred to that provided by a "mother" made of wire mesh. After two weeks of age, the infant preferred a cold terrycloth mother to a warm wire one, a finding indicating that the contact comfort was more attractive than warmth (Harlow & Suomi, 1970). Finally, Harlow found that the infants preferred the terrycloth mother even when their nourishment came exclusively from a wire mother. Thus, the hypothesis that attachment was due solely to the nourishment provided by mothers was falsified. This was possible only because Harlow was able to pry apart variables that naturally covary in the real world.

In short, it is often necessary for scientists to create special conditions that will test a particular theory about a phenomenon. Merely observing the event in its natural state is rarely sufficient. People observed falling and moving objects for centuries without arriving at accurate principles and laws about motion and gravity. Truly explanatory laws of motion were not derived until Galileo and other scientists set up some rather artificial conditions for the observation of the behavior of moving objects. In Galileo's time, smooth bronze balls were rarely seen rolling down smooth inclined planes. Lots of motion occurred in the world, but it was rarely of this type. However, it was just such an unnatural situation, and others like it, that led to our first truly explanatory laws of motion and gravity. Speaking of laws of motion, didn't you take a little quiz earlier in this chapter?

Intuitive Physics

Actually, the three questions posed at the beginning of this chapter were derived from the work of Michael McCloskey, a psychologist at Johns Hopkins University. McCloskey (1983) has studied what he calls "intuitive physics," that is, people's beliefs about the motion of objects. Interestingly, these beliefs are often at striking variance from how moving objects actually behave (Catrambone, Jones, Jonides, & Seifert, 1995; diSessa, 1996).

For example, in the first problem, once the string on the circling ball is cut, the ball will fly in a straight line at a 90-degree angle to the string (tangent to the circle). McCloskey found that one-third of the college students who were given this problem thought, incorrectly, that the ball would fly in a curved trajectory (see also, Catrambone et al., 1995). About half of McCloskey's subjects, when given problems similar to the bomber pilot example, thought that the bomb should be dropped directly over the target, thus displaying a lack of understanding of the role of an object's initial motion in determining its trajectory. The bomb should actually be dropped five miles before the plane reaches the target. The subjects' errors were not caused by the imaginary nature of the problem. When subjects were asked to walk across a room and, while moving, drop a golf ball on a target on the floor, the performance of more than half of them indicated they did not know that the ball would move forward as it fell. Finally, many people are not aware that the bullet fired from the rifle will hit the ground at the same time as a bullet dropped from the same height.

You can assess your own performance on this little quiz. Chances are that you missed at least one if you have not had a physics course recently. "Physics course!" you might protest. "Of course, I haven't had a physics class recently. This quiz is unfair!" But hold on a second. Why should you *need* a physics course? You have seen literally hundreds of falling objects in your lifetime. You have seen them fall under *naturally occurring* conditions. Moving objects surround you every day, and you are seeing them in their "real-life" state. You certainly cannot claim that you have not experienced moving and falling objects. Granted, you have never seen anything quite like the bullet example. But most of us have seen children let go of whirling objects, and many of us have seen objects fall out of planes. And besides, it seems a little lame to protest that you have not seen these exact situations. Given your years of experience with moving and falling objects, why can't you accurately predict what will happen in a situation only slightly out of the ordinary?

McCloskey's work demonstrates something of fundamental importance in understanding why scientists behave as they do. Despite extensive experience with moving and falling objects, people's intuitive theories of motion are remarkably inaccurate. It is critical to understand that the layperson's beliefs are inaccurate precisely because his or her observations are "natural," rather than controlled in the manner of the scientist's. Thus, if you missed a question on the little quiz at the beginning of the chapter, don't feel ignorant or inadequate. Simply remember that some of the world's greatest minds observed falling objects for centuries without formulating a physics of motion any more accurate than that of the average high-school sophomore. In an article in *Scientific American*, McCloskey (1983) observed that many of his subjects had held an incorrect theory about motion that was very similar to one held to be true some three centuries before Newton. McCloskey's modern subjects and medieval philosophers had something in common: Both groups had had much exposure to the motion of objects in the ordinary world, but none under the artificially created conditions of scientific manipulation, control, and comparison.

Even large amounts of personal experience are insufficient to prevent misconceptions about the nature of physical motion. Writing about the history of the development of knowledge about banked turns in aircraft, pilot

William Langewiesche (1993) noted that pilots in the early part of the twentieth century resisted the use of instrumentation such as gyroscopes because they believed in "instinctive balance." However, these "instincts" failed to uncover the existence of unfelt banks in clouds. Enough crashes and near crashes finally taught pilots a sobering lesson: No amount of instinct would substitute for knowledge of the actual physics of flight (Langewiesche, 1993).

Intuitive Psychology

Philosopher Paul Churchland (1988) argued that, if our intuitive (or "folk") theories about objects in motion are inaccurate, it is hard to believe that our folk theories in the more complex domain of human behavior could be correct:

> Our early folk theories of motion were profoundly confused, and were eventually displaced entirely by more sophisticated theories. Our early folk theories of the structure and activity of the heavens were wildly off the mark, and survive only as historical lessons in how wrong we can be. Our folk theories of the nature of fire, and the nature of life, were similarly cockeyed. And one could go on, since the vast majority of our past folk conceptions have been similarly exploded.... But the phenomenon of conscious intelligence is surely a more complex and difficult phenomenon than any of those just listed. So far as accurate understanding is concerned, it would be a miracle if we had got that one right the very first time, when we fell down so badly on all the others.

Biologist E. O. Wilson (1998) suggested the reason why Churchland's speculation is probably correct when he pointed out that "the brain is a machine assembled not to understand itself, but to survive. Because these two ends are basically different, the mind unaided by factual knowledge from science sees the world only in little pieces. It throws a spotlight on those portions of the world it must know in order to live to the next day.... That is why even today people know more about their automobiles than they do about their own minds—and why the fundamental explanation of mind is an empirical rather than a philosophical or religious quest."

When we look at the actual literature on people's theories of behavior, we find that Churchland's speculation turns out to be right. In Chapter 1, we illustrated that a number of commonsense (or folk) beliefs about human behavior are wrong. Many more examples are contained in Alfie Kohn's book *You Know What They Say . . . : The Truth about Popular Beliefs* (1990) and in

Sergio Della Sala's book *Mind Myths: Exploring Popular Assumptions about the Mind and Brain* (1999). Although written for the general public, both books rely on evidence in the peer-reviewed scientific literature for their conclusions. Many of the popular beliefs discussed in them concern human behavior. For example, it turns out that there is no evidence that highly religious people are more altruistic than less religious people (Paloutzian, 1983; Smith, Wheeler, & Diener, 1975). Many studies have indicated that there is no simple relationship between degree of religiosity and the tendency to engage in charitable acts, to aid other people in distress, or to abstain from cheating other people (Paloutzian, 1983). Indeed, within a large research literature, there is no indication at all that people high in religiosity are any more likely to be charitable or to help their fellows than are people who identify themselves as atheists.

The list of popular beliefs that are incorrect is long. For example, many people believe that a full moon affects human behavior. It doesn't (see Byrnes & Kelly, 1992; Coates, Jehle, & Cottington, 1989; Culver, Rotton, & Kelly, 1988; Rotton & Kelly, 1985). Some people believe that "opposites attract." They don't (see Buss, 1985; Buss & Barnes, 1986; Murstein, 1980). Some people believe that "familiarity breeds contempt." It doesn't (see Bornstein, 1989). Some people believe that blind people are blessed with supersensitive hearing. They're not (see Niemeyer & Starlinger, 1981; Stankov & Spilsbury, 1978). And the list goes on and on and on. Consult Kohn's (1990) book for a readable account of a couple of dozen popular beliefs about behavior that are not supported by empirical evidence (all of the trends listed here are probabilistic, of course).

The many inadequacies in people's intuitive theories of behavior illustrate why we need the controlled experimentation of psychology: so that we can progress beyond our flat-earth conceptions of human behavior to a more accurate scientific conceptualization.

QUESTIONS

1. Find a report of a psychological or medical study in your daily newspaper. See whether that study reports any correlational data, and assess whether the results are described as demonstrating a causal relationship. Does the story make any of the mistakes that Huff points out? Are there any reasonable alternative explanations? How would you rewrite the report to make it more logically sound?

2. The title of the chapter in Huff's book from which the selection here is taken is "Post Hoc Rides Again," which alludes to the Latin expression *post hoc, propter hoc*, "after the fact, therefore because of the fact." What does the Latin mean, and how does the saying, the name of a common logical fallacy, relate to psychology?

3. Comparison, control, and manipulation might be of little use if common sense could tell us all we needed to know about the mind and behavior. But, according to Stanovich, popular beliefs are often wrong and "we need the controlled experimentation of psychology ... so that we can progress beyond our flat-earth conceptions of human behavior to a more accurate scientific conceptualization." Would Freud have been sympathetic to this view? Why or why not?

CHAPTER THREE

EVOLUTION AND GENES

Whatever shape the human mind has, it must have been, like the rest of the body, shaped by evolution. In the first selection in this chapter, Steven Pinker, one of the world's leading advocates of the field known as evolutionary psychology, argues that we will never truly understand the mind until we understand the tasks for which it evolved. In his book *How the Mind Works* (1997), Pinker argues that natural selection has shaped just about every aspect of psychology you might imagine: how we choose our mates, how we treat our families, how we reason about falling objects, even what kinds of landscapes we prefer.

If evolution truly did shape the mind, it must have done so by shaping our genes. But what is the relationship between genes and psychology? Cartoons joke of genes for specific traits—music genes, sports genes, even genes for propensity to talk about the weather—but real genes build proteins, not specific traits or behaviors. In my own book, *The Birth of the Mind* (2004), I wrestle with these questions, asking what the growing literature in developmental neurobiology can tell us about the origins of the human mind. In the selection included here, I take the first step toward connecting these previously disparate fields by clarifying the power and limits of individual genes.

From *How the Mind Works*

Steven Pinker

Reverse-Engineering the Psyche

The complex structure of the mind is the subject of this book. Its key idea can be captured in a sentence: The mind is a system of organs of computation, designed by natural selection to solve the kinds of problems our ancestors faced in their foraging way of life, in particular, understanding and outmaneuvering objects, animals, plants, and other people. The summary can be unpacked into several claims. The mind is what the brain does; specifically, the brain processes information, and thinking is a kind of computation. The mind is organized into modules or mental organs, each with a specialized design that makes it an expert in one arena of interaction with the world. The modules' basic logic is specified by our genetic program. Their operation was shaped by natural selection to solve the problems of the hunting and gathering life led by our ancestors in most of our evolutionary history. The various problems for our ancestors were subtasks of one big problem for their genes, maximizing the number of copies that made it into the next generation.

On this view, psychology is engineering in reverse. In forward-engineering, one designs a machine to do something; in reverse-engineering, one figures out what a machine was designed to do. Reverse-engineering is what the boffins at Sony do when a new product is announced by Panasonic, or vice versa. They buy one, bring it back to the lab, take a screwdriver to it, and try to figure out what all the parts are for and how they combine to make the device work. We all engage in reverse-engineering when we face an interesting new gadget. In rummaging through an antique store, we may find a contraption that is inscrutable until we figure out what it was designed to do. When we realize that it is an olive-pitter, we suddenly understand that the metal ring is designed to hold the olive, and the lever lowers an X-shaped blade through one end, pushing the pit out through the other end. The shapes and arrangements of the springs, hinges, blades, levers, and rings all make sense in a satisfying rush of insight. We even understand why canned olives have an X-shaped incision at one end.

In the seventeenth century William Harvey discovered that veins had valves and deduced that the valves must be there to make the blood circulate. Since then we have understood the body as a wonderfully complex machine, an assembly of struts, ties, springs, pulleys, levers, joints, hinges, sockets, tanks, pipes, valves, sheaths, pumps, exchangers, and filters. Even today we can be delighted to learn what mysterious parts are for. Why do we have our wrinkled, asymmetrical ears? Because they filter sound waves coming from different directions in different ways. The nuances of the sound shadow tell the brain whether the source of the sound is above or below, in front of or behind us. The strategy of reverse-engineering the body has continued in the last half of this century as we have explored the nanotechnology of the cell and of the molecules of life. The stuff of life turned out to be not a quivering, glowing, wondrous gel but a contraption of tiny jigs, springs, hinges, rods, sheets, magnets, zippers, and trapdoors, assembled by a data tape whose information is copied, downloaded, and scanned.

The rationale for reverse-engineering living things comes, of course, from Charles Darwin. He showed how "organs of extreme perfection and complication, which justly excite our admiration" arise not from God's foresight but from the evolution of replicators over immense spans of time. As replicators replicate, random copying errors sometimes crop up, and those that happen to enhance the survival and reproduction rate of the replicator tend to accumulate over the generations. Plants and animals are replicators, and their complicated machinery thus appears to have been engineered to allow them to survive and reproduce.

Darwin insisted that his theory explained not just the complexity of an animal's body but the complexity of its mind. "Psychology will be based on a new foundation," he famously predicted at the end of *The Origin of Species*. But Darwin's prophecy has not yet been fulfilled. More than a century after he wrote those words, the study of the mind is still mostly Darwin-free, often defiantly so. Evolution is said to be irrelevant, sinful, or fit only for speculation over a beer at the end of the day. The allergy to evolution in the social and cognitive sciences has been, I think, a barrier to understanding. The mind is an exquisitely organized system that accomplishes remarkable feats no engineer can duplicate. How could the forces that shaped that system, and the purposes for which it was designed, be irrelevant to understanding it? Evolutionary thinking is indispensable, not in the form that many people think of—dreaming up missing links or narrating stories about the stages of Man—but in the form of careful reverse-engineering. Without reverse-engineering we are like the singer in Tom Paxton's "The Marvelous Toy," reminiscing about a childhood present: "It went ZIP! when it moved, and POP! when it stopped, and WHIRRR! when it stood still; I never knew just what it was, and I guess I never will."

Only in the past few years has Darwin's challenge been taken up, by a new approach christened "evolutionary psychology" by the anthropologist John Tooby and the psychologist Leda Cosmides. Evolutionary psychology brings together two scientific revolutions. One is the cognitive revolution of the 1950s and 1960s, which explains the mechanics of thought and emotion in terms of information and computation. The other is the revolution in evolutionary biology of the 1960s and 1970s, which explains the complex adaptive design of living things in terms of selection among replicators. The two ideas make a powerful combination. Cognitive science helps us to understand how a mind is possible and what kind of mind we have. Evolutionary biology helps us to understand *why* we have the kind of mind we have.

The evolutionary psychology of this book is, in one sense, a straightforward extension of biology, focusing on one organ, the mind, of one species, *Homo sapiens*. But in another sense it is a radical thesis that discards the way issues about the mind have been framed for almost a century. The premises of this book are probably not what you think they are. Thinking is computation, I claim, but that does not mean that the computer is a good metaphor for the mind. The mind is a set of modules, but the modules are not encapsulated boxes or circumscribed swatches on the surface of the brain. The organization of our mental modules comes from our genetic program, but that does not mean that there is a gene for every trait or that learning is less important than we used to think. The mind is an adaptation designed by natural selection, but that does not mean that everything we think, feel, and do is biologically adaptive. We evolved from apes, but that does not mean we have the same minds as apes. And the ultimate goal of natural selection is to propagate genes, but that does not mean that the ultimate goal of people is to propagate genes. Let me show you why not.

The human mind is a product of evolution, so our mental organs are either present in the minds of apes (and perhaps other mammals and vertebrates) or arose from overhauling the minds of apes, specifically, the common ancestors of humans and chimpanzees that lived about six million years ago in Africa. Many titles of books on human evolution remind us of this fact: *The Naked Ape, The Electric Ape, The Scented Ape, The Lopsided Ape, The Aquatic Ape, The Thinking Ape, The Human Ape, The Ape That Spoke, The Third Chimpanzee, The Chosen Primate.* Some authors are militant that humans are barely different from chimpanzees and that any focus on specifically human talents is arrogant chauvinism or tantamount to creationism. For some readers that is a reductio ad absurdum of the evolutionary framework. If the theory says that man "at best is only a monkey shaved," as Gilbert and Sullivan put it in *Princess Ida,* then it fails to explain the obvious fact that men and monkeys have different minds.

We *are* naked, lopsided apes that speak, but we also have minds that differ considerably from those of apes. The outsize brain of *Homo sapiens sapiens* is, by any standard, an extraordinary adaptation. It has allowed us to inhabit every ecosystem on earth, reshape the planet, walk on the moon, and discover the secrets of the physical universe. Chimpanzees, for all their vaunted intelligence, are a threatened species clinging to a few patches of forest and living as they did millions of years ago. Our curiosity about this difference demands more than repeating that we share most of our DNA with chimpanzees and that small changes can have big effects. Three hundred thousand generations and up to ten megabytes of potential genetic information are enough to revamp a mind considerably. Indeed, minds are probably easier to revamp than bodies because software is easier to modify than hardware. We should not be surprised to discover impressive new cognitive abilities in humans, language being just the most obvious one.

None of this is incompatible with the theory of evolution. Evolution is a conservative process, to be sure, but it can't be all *that* conservative or we would all be pond scum. Natural selection introduces differences into descendants by fitting them with specializations that adapt them to different niches. Any museum of natural history has examples of complex organs unique to a species or to a group of related species: the elephant's trunk, the narwhal's tusk, the whale's baleen, the platypus' duckbill, the armadillo's armor. Often they evolve rapidly on the geological timescale. The first whale evolved in something like ten million years from its common ancestor with its closest living relatives, ungulates such as cows and pigs. A book about whales could, in the spirit of the human-evolution books, be called *The Naked Cow*, but it would be disappointing if the book spent every page marveling at the similarities between whales and cows and never got around to discussing the adaptations that make them so different.

To say that the mind is an evolutionary adaptation is not to say that all behavior is adaptive in Darwin's sense. Natural selection is not a guardian angel that hovers over us making sure that our behavior always maximizes biological fitness. Until recently, scientists with an evolutionary bent felt a responsibility to account for acts that seem like Darwinian suicide such as celibacy, adoption, and contraception. Perhaps, they ventured, celibate people have more time to raise large broods of nieces and nephews and thereby propagate more copies of their genes than they would if they had their own children. This kind of stretch is unnecessary, however. The reasons, first articulated by the anthropologist Donald Symons, distinguish evolutionary psychology from the school of thought in the 1970s and 1980s called sociobiology (though there is much overlap between the approaches as well).

First, selection operates over thousands of generations. For ninety-nine percent of human existence, people lived as foragers in small nomadic bands. Our brains are adapted to that long-vanished way of life, not to brand-new agricultural and industrial civilizations. They are not wired to cope with anonymous crowds, schooling, written language, government, police, courts, armies, modern medicine, formal social institutions, high technology, and other newcomers to the human experience. Since the modern mind is adapted to the Stone Age, not the computer age, there is no need to strain for adaptive explanations for everything we do. Our ancestral environment lacked the institutions that now entice us to nonadaptive choices, such as religious orders, adoption agencies, and pharmaceutical companies, so until very recently there was never a selection pressure to resist the enticements. Had the Pleistocene savanna contained trees bearing birth-control pills, we might have evolved to find them as terrifying as a venomous spider.

Second, natural selection is not a puppetmaster that pulls the strings of behavior directly. It acts by designing the generator of behavior: the package of information-processing and goal-pursuing mechanisms called the mind. Our minds are designed to generate behavior that would have been adaptive, on average, in our ancestral environment, but any particular deed done today is the effect of dozens of causes. Behavior is the outcome of an internal struggle among many mental modules, and it is played out on the chessboard of opportunities and constraints defined by *other* people's behavior. A recent cover story in *Time* asked, "Adultery: Is It in Our Genes?" The question makes no sense because neither adultery nor any other behavior can be in our genes. Conceivably a *desire* for adultery can be an indirect product of our genes, but the desire may be over-ridden by *other* desires that are also indirect products of our genes, such as the desire to have a trusting spouse. And the desire, even if it prevails in the rough-and-tumble of the mind, cannot be consummated as overt behavior unless there is a partner around in whom that desire has also prevailed. Behavior itself did not evolve; what evolved was the mind.

From *The Birth of the Mind: How a Tiny Number of Genes Create the Complexities of Human Thought*

Gary Marcus

Proteins are long chains of twenty or so basic molecules known as amino acids that are twisted and folded into complex three-dimensional structures such as fibers, tubes, globules, and sheets. Amino acids, in turn, are particular arrangements of carbon, hydrogen, oxygen, and nitrogen atoms. (Your body makes many of these amino acids, but nine are "essential" because they can only come from your diet. Animal meats typically contain all the missing amino acids, but many plant products do not—lysine, for example, is absent in many grains—which is why vegetarians must carefully balance, or "complement," their sources of protein.)

There are literally hundreds of thousands of different proteins in a human body. An average cell has thousands of different proteins, and, all told, they make up more than half the body's dry weight. In addition to enzymes, there is a huge range of other proteins. For example, keratin (the principal protein in hair) and collagen (the principal protein in skin) help to build the structures of the body. Others, such as prolactin and insulin, are hormones used for communication between (and within) organs. Still others serve as everything from motors to couriers (such as hemoglobin, which exists to transport oxygen). And then there are *channels*, complex cellular gates that open and close to control the flow of molecules into and out of a cell, and *receptors*, receivers of biochemical signals that can be thought of as sentinels that capture messages and convey their content to the inside of a cell without letting the messengers themselves through the membrane walls. Proteins are involved in just about every aspect of life.

The first step toward the Protein Template conception of genes, which held that genes were involved in all proteins, not just enzymes, came in the

1940s. Up until then, many scientists thought that genes were just one more special kind of protein, but in 1944 a largely unsung American biologist named Oswald Avery discovered otherwise. His great advance came in a study of the uncomfortably familiar bacterium we know as *pneumococcus*. Pneumococcus comes in two varieties, a lethal, "smooth-coated" S strain and a normally harmless, "rough" R strain, so named for their appearance under a microscope. In the late 1920s, British biologist Frederick Griffiths discovered that heat-killed S strain (which on its own was not lethal) could "transform" normally safe R-strain bacteria into deadly killers. But Griffiths was not able to explain why. Avery cracked the case by a process of elimination, ruling out, one by one, all the substances contained within the S strain until the only substance left was a mysterious sticky acid that had first been identified in 1869 by a Swiss biochemist named Friederich Miescher. That mysterious sticky stuff—DNA—was enough *all by itself* to transform the ordinary R into deadly R. In modern language, what made transformed R deadly was genetic material incorporated from S-strain DNA.

The bottom line? Scientists could now point to the material basis of heredity, to Mendel's factors, to genes. But rather than being made of some special kind of protein, genes were made of DNA (deoxyribonucleic acid). To find out more about genes, then, scientists would clearly need to figure out how this molecule, DNA, worked. At that point, researchers knew relatively little about DNA. From Miescher's original discovery of the substance in 1869 (just four years after Mendel published his paper on the pea), scientists knew what DNA was made of: carbon, hydrogen, oxygen, nitrogen, and phosphorus. A decade and a half later, in 1885, German biologist Albrecht Kossel discovered that DNA included four types of alkaline (opposite of acidic) molecules known as "bases," which he named cytosine, thymine, guanine, and adenine, and which we now refer to as nucleotides. But the exact composition of DNA, and how those bases related to one another, seemed to differ from one species to the next. For example, the proportion of guanine was higher in the thymus of an ox than it was in the thymus of a person. Unexplained were biochemist Erwin Chargaff's 1950 "laws": The amount of cytosine always seemed to match the amount of guanine, and the amount of thymine always seemed to match the amount of adenine.

With Avery's discovery, and independent confirmation from Alfred Hershey and Martha Chase that followed in 1952, there was soon a race to figure out DNA's exact shape and the way that its molecules fit together. The smart money was on Linus Pauling, the world's leading authority on chemical bonds. True to biology's *Daily Racing Form*, Pauling, who later won two Nobel Prizes, was first to publish—but his hypothesis turned out to be flawed; his triple helix idea nowadays can only be found in science fiction. Before Pauling could spot his own error, he was overtaken by two ambitious newcomers, a twenty-five-year-old American who had only recently finished his Ph.D. dissertation, and a thirty-something British graduate student who had yet to finish his.

I am speaking, of course, about James Watson and Francis Crick. What the famous team discovered, in February 1953 (with the help of critical X rays that were taken by Rosalind Franklin and Maurice Wilkins), was that the DNA molecule was a double helix: two twisted sugar-phosphate ladders connected by rungs made up of pairs of nucleotide bases. The idea of a helix wasn't new. What was new was the understanding of the way in which the bases fit together: Each individual rung was made up of a pair of "unlike" bases, either an adenine (A) and a thymine (T), or a guanine (G) and a cytosine (C). The reason that the amount of adenine correlated so well with the amount of thymine was that they always came in pairs—Chargaff's laws had been explained and the structure of DNA deciphered.

"It has not escaped our notice," Watson and Crick famously wrote, "that the specific pairing we have postulated immediately suggests a possible copying mechanism for the genetic material." The immediate significance of their theory was in the way it connected to Mendel's questions about heredity. An organism could resemble its parent only if Mendel's factors could be transferred from parent to child, and that, in turn, required that there be some way to make copies of the factors. DNA provided for that possibility: Information was contained in the sequence of nucleotides, and the two strands of the substance could separate and serve as templates for more strands—voilà, biological Xerox.

The conception of genes as templates for proteins grew out of efforts to figure out what all those A, C, G, and T nucleotides were for. Almost immediately, a physicist named George Gamow took a first stab, guessing that the amino acids that make up a protein might somehow stick into crevices between the rungs of the DNA ladder. Which protein emerged from a given DNA sequence would, in Gamow's theory, be a matter of which amino acids fit into the crevice between its nucleotides. Gamow's crevice theory was wrong in its details—proteins are not formed through direct interaction

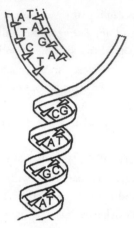

FIGURE 1——DNA, AND THE PROCESS OF ITS REPLICATION
Source: Tim Fedak

with the DNA (and the crevices between nucleotides are irrelevant for this process)—but the spirit of his idea was correct: One of the main ways that genes exert their influence is by providing templates for proteins.

As became clear in the early 1960s, sequences of three nucleotides, known as triplets, or *codons*, get translated into amino acids, with each triplet standing for a different amino acid. For example, triplets of T-C-G get translated into serine, triplets of G-T-T into glutamine, and so forth, each codon serving as a template for a different amino acid. Series of triplets were translated into the chains of amino acids, which in turn fold up into the complex three-dimensional molecules we know as proteins. (Aficionados will realize that I'm oversimplifying in several ways. DNA must first be copied, or "transcribed," onto RNA (ribonucleic acid), an intermediate complement of DNA, before it gets translated into amino acids. Furthermore, there are sixty-four codons but only twenty amino acids, so sometimes two, three, or even six different codons serve as templates for a single amino acid; for our purposes, these details will not matter.)

The conception of genes as protein templates is partly correct, and it's what many people think of when they think of genes. Genes genuinely do provide

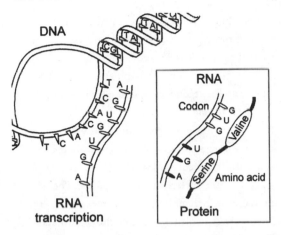

Figure 2——From DNA to RNA to Protein
Source: Tim Fedak

templates for protein building, and many disorders—mental and physical—
are the result of small "errors" in protein templates. Sickle-cell anemia, for
example, is caused by a single spelling error in the 861-nucleotide-long gene
for building hemoglobin, the four-part protein that allows red blood cells to
carry oxygen. Blood cells with ordinary hemoglobin look like dimpled discs;
sickled blood cells are so named because when they are not bearing oxygen
they form a crescent, or sickle, shape, the direct consequence of change in a
single nucleotide from an A to a T. Sickled cells have a front and a back, and
when they lack oxygen they tend to fit together like the top and bottom of a
Lego brick, forming chains that can clog arteries and block the flow of blood.
Most of the time, such cells commit suicide, but occasionally the clots persist
and one of the body's organs may be damaged, sometimes leading to death.
(Like many disorders, sickle-cell anemia is most severe in people who inherit
two copies of the errant gene, one from each parent. When only a single copy
is inherited, the normal copy can do some of the work and the illness is far
less severe. The disorder may persist in the population because even a single
copy of the "mutant" gene conveys a resistance to malaria.)

   Not all genetically influenced disorders, however, can be traced to errors in protein templates. Even the Protein Template Theory was incomplete
in a significant way. Proteins are marvelous molecular machines, but what

makes one animal different from the next is not just its set of proteins, but the *arrangement* of those proteins, and, remarkably, the arrangements, too, are a product of the genes. The Protein Template Theory captured only half the real story. Each gene actually has two parts: the protein template, which is widely known, and a second part that provides *regulatory* information about *when that template should be used.*

This final, crucial insight—that genes provide not just templates but also instructions for regulating when a gene should be translated into protein—came in 1961 in Jacques Monod and François Jacob's investigations of the eating habits of the bacterium *Escherichia coli.* These insights led scientists to refine the Protein Template Theory into the theory of genes that is now considered correct, which I will call the Autonomous Agent Theory. Monod and Jacob's study began with the observation that *E. coli* could quickly switch from a diet of glucose (its preferred sugar) to one of lactose (the sugar found in milk). In ordinary glucose-rich environments, *E. coli* doesn't bother to make enzymes for metabolizing lactose. But when glucose becomes scarce, the bacteria switch their diet in the space of a few minutes. To do that, they must produce thousands of copies of enzymes, such as galactosidase, a molecule that facilitates the breakdown of lactose to galactose and glucose.

What Monod and Jacob discovered is that the genes for these lactose enzymes switched on or off *as needed* according to a simple logical system. The templates for lactose-metabolizing enzymes are translated into proteins if and only if exactly two things are true. First, the bacterium *must* have lactose around, and second, the bacterium must *not* have access to glucose. The logical juxtaposition of these two requirements (IF lactose AND NOT glucose) should instantly ring a bell with any reader who has computer programming experience—for the requirement "IF X AND NOT Y" is of a piece with the billions of IF-THEN rules that guide the world's software. What Jacob and Monod had discovered, in essence, was that each gene acts like a single line in a computer program.

The net result is a kind of mass empowerment: Every gene is a free agent authorized to act on its own, hence the Autonomous Agent Theory. As soon as the IF part of a gene's IF-THEN rule is satisfied, the process of translating the template part of a gene into its corresponding protein commences. There is no form to fill out in triplicate, no waiting for approval. Patrick Bateson and Richard Dawkins have described the genome as a whole (the collection of all the genes in a given organism) as a recipe, but it is also possible to think of each individual gene as a recipe for a particular protein; on the latter analogy, what IF-THEN gene regulation means is that *each recipe can act on its own.*

IF-THEN

Understanding how genomes contribute to the construction of body and brain is thus a matter of understanding how the two parts of every gene— the regulatory IF and the protein template THEN—work together to guide the fates of individual cells. Nearly every cell contains a complete copy of the genome (which is why one can grow a carrot from a clipping or clone a sheep from a single cell). But most cells specialize for particular tasks, some signing up for service in the circulatory system, others in the digestive tract or the nervous system, relocating and even committing suicide when their job requires it. And it is from that process of specialization, in the individual decisions of the trillions of cells that make up a body, in how cells spend their lives, in how they grow, slip, slide, divide, and differentiate, that the structure of the body and brain emerge. (Or fail to emerge, for most birth defects stem in one way or another from errors in these basic processes.)

What makes one cell different from the next is not which genes it has copies of, but rather *which of those genes are switched on.* The recipe for hemoglobin is only followed in red blood precursors, the recipe for human growth hormone only in the pituitary gland. Some genes are expressed only in the brain, others only in the kidneys or the liver, or in a particular kind of cell, or in a particular place within a cell, and many genes are just as choosy about *when* they are expressed as they are about *where* they are expressed. Some genes (such as those that build proteins that help convert sugar to energy) are on almost all the time in almost every cell, but most are on (or most active) only at select times, during particular situations (for example, during cell division or gastrointestinal inflammation), or at particular moments in embryological development (such as during the leg-growing, tail-shedding process of tadpole-to-frog metamorphosis). In this way, by switching on only at specific times and places, genes modulate the growth of proteins in different ways in different cells. With IFS that are tied to particular times and types of cells, each cell can develop in its own unique way.

What drives the embryo forward in development—and what drives a monkey embryo to become a monkey rather than a grapefruit—is each species' unique set of IF-THENS and the different ways in which they drive cells to develop and specialize. If genes are like lines in a computer program—an IF that controls when a gene will be expressed, a THEN that says what protein it will build if it is expressed—they are a special kind of computer program, one that is followed not by a central processor but autonomously, by individual genes in individual cells.

With one more trick—*regulatory proteins* that control the expression of other genes—nature is able to tie the whole genetic system together, allowing gangs of otherwise unruly free-agent genes to come together in exquisite harmony. Rather than acting in absolute isolation, most genes act as parts of elaborate networks in which the expression of one gene is a precondition for the expression of the next. The THEN of one gene can satisfy the IF of another and thus induce it to turn on. In this way, a single gene that is at the top of a complex network can indirectly launch a cascade of hundreds or thousands of others, leading to, for example, the development of an eye or a limb.

In the words of Swiss biologist Walter Gehring, such genes can serve as "master control genes" that exert enormous power in a growing system. *Pax6*, for example, is a regulatory protein that plays a role in eye development, and Gehring has shown that artificially activating that one gene in the right spot on a fruit fly's antenna can lead to an extra eye, right there on the fly's antenna—a simple regulatory protein IF that leads, directly and indirectly, to the expression of approximately 2,500 other genes.

The IFS and THENS can even lead a single organism to develop in different ways in different circumstances. The African butterfly *Bicyclus anyana*, for instance, comes in two different forms depending on the season, a colorful wet-season form, and a duller brown dry-season form. Which one develops is determined only late in the larval stage of the butterfly's development, probably on the basis of a temperature-sensitive gene that triggers different cascades depending on the climate. Genetically identical butterflies raised in a warm laboratory tend to take on the wet-season form, whereas those raised in cooler temperatures tend to take on the dry-season form. It would be impossible for the genome to "know" in advance whether a particular larva will develop in the wet season or the dry season, so instead nature has endowed the *B. anyana* genome with IF-THEN instructions for handling both and machinery for letting the environment determine the most appropriate phenotype.

History and Geography

In simple organisms, many of the IF-THEN cascades of development are driven primarily by a cell's history. The growth of the *Caenorhabditis elegans* roundworm is so regular that biologists have taken to drawing "fate maps," or "lineages," diagrams that would make a genealogist feel at home. Each newly fertilized egg divides four times, each time budding off from a different founder cell, each of which, under normal circumstances, has a specific destiny. For example, the founder cell known as "D" generally gives rise to muscle cells, and founder cell "AB" generally gives rise to neural cells, muscle cells, and a set of "hypodermal cells" that lie in a layer beneath the skin's surface. The first few generations are shown in the first figure here. By the time all the great-great-great-grandchildren are born, the chart is a lot more complicated, but it still looks like a family tree, as in the second figure.

In the nematode, most cells appear almost as if they were on autopilot, going about their business independently, according to a strict schedule, even if, say, the head is missing. In mammals, cells do use a bit of history, but they also rely heavily on molecular signposts that tell growing cells where they are. In complex, three-dimensional biological structures like the human heart or arm, the body makes use of at least three different systems, or *axes* (plural of "axis"), for indicating position, each depending on a different set of genes and proteins. In the arm, the *proximal-distal* axis starts from the shoulder and runs down to the fingertips. The *anterior-posterior* axis runs from the thumb to the pinkie, and the *dorsal-ventral* system runs from the

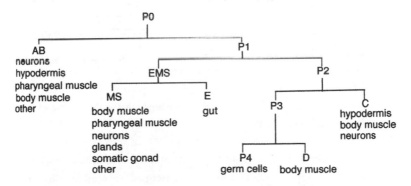

FIGURE 3——CELL FATE IN AN EARLY C. *ELEGANS* EMBRYO
Source: Reprinted with the permission of William B. Wood

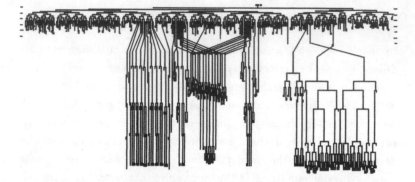

FIGURE 4——FURTHER DEVELOPMENT IN C. *ELEGANS*
Source : Reprinted with the permission of Cynthia Kenyon and Sir John Sulston

back of the hand to the palm. Every cell in the arm can be defined in terms of where it is on those three axes: how far it is from the shoulder, whether it is closer to the palm or the back of the hand, and how far along the axis it is from the thumb to the little finger.

The contrast between mammals and worms was once thought to be so great that Nobel laureate Sydney Brenner once joked that there were two basic plans of development, the "European Plan" and the "American Plan":

> The European way is for the cells to do their own thing and not to talk to their neighbors very much. Ancestry is what counts, and once a cell is born in a certain place it will stay there and develop according to rigid rules; it does not care about the neighborhood, and even its death is programmed. If it dies in an accident, it cannot be replaced. The American way is quite the opposite. Ancestry does not count, and in many cases a cell may not even know its ancestors or where it came from. What counts are the interactions with its neighbors. It frequently exchanges information with its fellow cells and often has to move to accomplish its goals and find its proper place. It is quite flexible and competes with other cells for a given function. If it dies in an accident, it can readily be replaced.

In truth, all animals make use of both kinds of information, albeit in somewhat different proportions. Despite its apparent reliance on ancestry, the hermaphroditic worm still uses positional information to, for example, configure its egg-laying opening (otherwise known as the worm's vulva).

The worm's vulva generally consists of exactly twenty-two cells, which originate, under normal circumstances, at a cell known as $P6_p$, regular as clockwork. But the worm will still grow a vulva if inquisitive experimenters use a laser to destroy $P6_p$. As developmental biologist Judith Kimble discovered, there are actually six skin cells that have the potential to give rise to the vulva. Which one actually does so is determined not by a blueprint but by a protein signal that is secreted from a cell known as the "anchor cell." The skin cell closest to the anchor cell then gives rise to the primary vulva cells, while the two adjacent skin cells become secondary vulva cells. If the anchor cell is destroyed (by the zap of the laser beam), no vulva grows. If the anchor cell is shifted toward the head, the vulva shifts in the same direction, centering around the anchor cell's new position rather than around its ordinary position. What triggers the vulva program is thus not an absolute cue to location but a functional one, a triggering of a receptor for a cue given off by the anchor cell.

In mammals, many of a cell's IF-THEN decisions depend on a mix of ancestry and signals. One of the first studies to pit the two against each other came in the 1950s. Embryologist John Saunders Jr. took presumptive thigh tissue (tissue that would ordinarily turn into a thigh) from a chicken embryo and implanted it onto the edge of the wing bud of another chick embryo. The transplanted tissue didn't simply fill in the missing part of the wing tip, but it didn't turn into a thigh, either. Neither ancestry nor neighborhood won out. Instead, claws sprouted from the ends of the chicken's wings. The transplanted tissue retained a memory (in the form of molecular markers) of its lineage (from the leg) and combined that with the positional cues from its new environment (in the edge of the wing bud), rendering dramatic the complex calculus of combining position and ancestry. And it is that same calculus that allows presumptive eye cells to become stomach cells and presumptive somatosensory cells to become visual cells: By including position in the equations that determine cell fate, the growing mammal automatically achieves a large degree of flexibility.

What propels an embryo from one stage to the next—and makes one species different from another—is not a blueprint but rather an enormous autonomous library of the instructions contained within its genome. Each gene does double duty, specifying both a recipe for a protein and a set of regulatory conditions for when and where it should be built. Taken together, suites of these IF-THEN genes give cells the power to act as parts of complicated improvisational orchestras. Like real musicians, what they play depends on both their own artistic impulses and what the other members of the orchestra are playing. As we will see in the next chapter, every bit of this process—from the Cellular Big 4 to the combination of regulatory cues—holds as much for development of the brain as it does for the body.

How much can you do with a system like that? Consider the power of groups of simpleminded ants that work together to build a colony. Outside of DreamWorks Studios, individual ants can do little more than follow one chemical trail or another, pretty much insensitive to the rest of the world around them, yet their collective action yields great complexity.

In a similar way, individual genes are not particularly clever—this one only cares about that molecule, that one only about some other molecule. The regulatory region that controls insulin production, for example, looks for signs that it is in the pancreas, but it can easily be fooled. It's not smart enough to look around and realize that it might be the victim of a party prank played in a Petri dish. But that simplicity is no barrier to building enormous complexity. If you can build an ant colony with just a few different kinds of simpleminded ants (workers, drones, and the like), think what you can do with 30,000 cascading genes, deployed at will.

QUESTIONS

1. What kind(s) of evidence could scientists use to test hypotheses about the evolution of the mind?

2. People often think of genomes as deterministic blueprints that dictate the details of our lives. Why does the notion of genes as IF-THENS challenge that view?

3. Find a recent news story that discusses a gene that has something to do with psychology. What metaphors does the story use in describing genes? To what extent does the story discuss an environmental role for the trait in question?

THE BRAIN

The human brain is the seat of our mental life and, as such, the material basis of all psychology. Change someone's brain, through drugs or trauma, and you change their psychology. Scientists didn't always know this—Aristotle thought the function of the brain was to cool the blood—but nowadays, in the era of brain scans and prescription drugs like Prozac, lithium, and Xanax, the importance of the brain to mind and behavior can no longer be denied.

One of the first clues to the connection between brain and mind came over 150 years ago, when an accidental explosion drove an iron rod straight through the head of a railway construction worker named Phineas Gage. Miraculously, Gage survived. But, as Antonio Damasio explains in *Descartes' Error* (1994), the damage to Gage's brain permanently altered his personality and cognitive capacities.

Gage's story is part of what we now know as neuropsychology, a field that seeks to understand the mind by studying people with brain injuries. Oliver Sacks is perhaps the best-known contemporary practitioner, a neurologist with a keen eye and a gift for writing. His book *The Man Who Mistook His Wife for a Hat* (1985) was the first work of neuropsychology I ever read, and it remains one of my favorites. The title essay refers to a patient, Dr. P., who has visual agnosia, a neurological condition that leaves him unable to recognize even familiar faces and objects. A rose may be a rose to Gertrude Stein, but Dr. P sees a rose as nothing more than "a convoluted red form with a linear green attachment." That he could perceive color and even to some extent shape without recognizing objects tells us something important about how the brain analyzes the visual world.

In a less well-known but no less moving case study, "The Tale of the Disembodied Lady," Sacks describes Christina, a patient who has a deficit in a sense—proprioception, or the awareness of one's body in space—which many people may not realize they have. As is so often the case, Sacks's keen observations give insight not just into mind and brain, but also into the human condition.

From *Descartes' Error: Emotion, Reason, and the Human Brain*

Antonio R. Damasio

Phineas P. Gage

It is the summer of 1848. We are in New England. Phineas P. Gage, twenty-five years old, construction foreman, is about to go from riches to rags. A century and a half later his downfall will still be quite meaningful.

Gage works for the Rutland & Burlington Railroad and is in charge of a large group of men, a "gang" as it is called, whose job it is to lay down the new tracks for the railroad's expansion across Vermont. Over the past two weeks the men have worked their way slowly toward the town of Cavendish; they are now at a bank of the Black River. The assignment is anything but easy. The terrain is uneven in every direction and is filled with hard, stratified rock. Rather than twist and turn the tracks around every escarpment, the strategy is to blast the stone now and then to make way for a straighter and more level path. Gage oversees all these tasks and is equal to them in every way. He is five-foot-six and athletic, and his movements are swift and precise. He looks like a young Jimmy Cagney, a Yankee Doodle dandy dancing his tap shoes over ties and tracks, moving with vigor and grace.

In the eyes of his bosses, however, Gage is more than just another able body. They say he is "the most efficient and capable" man in their employ. This is a good thing, because the job takes as much physical prowess as keen concentration, especially when it comes to preparing the detonations. Several steps have to be followed, in orderly fashion. First, a hole must be drilled in the rock. After it is filled about halfway with explosive powder, a fuse must be inserted, and the powder covered with sand. Then the sand must be "tamped in," or pounded with a careful sequence of strokes from an iron rod. Finally, the fuse must be lit. If all goes well, the powder will explode into the rock; the sand is essential, for without its protection the explosion would be directed away from the rock. The shape of the iron and the way it is played are also important. Gage, who has had an iron manufactured to his specifications, is a virtuoso of this thing.

Now for what is going to happen. It is four-thirty on this hot afternoon. Gage has just put powder and fuse in a hole and told the man who is helping him to cover it with sand. Someone calls from behind, and Gage looks away, over his right shoulder, for only an instant. Distracted, and before his man has poured the sand in, Gage begins tamping the powder directly with the iron bar. In no time he strikes fire in the rock, and the charge blows upward in his face.

The explosion is so brutal that the entire gang freezes on their feet. It takes a few seconds to piece together what is going on. The bang is unusual, and the rock is intact. Also unusual is the whistling sound, as of a rocket hurled at the sky. But this is more than fireworks. It is assault and battery. The iron enters Gage's left cheek, pierces the base of the skull, traverses the front of his brain, and exits at high speed through the top of the head. The rod has landed more than a hundred feet away, covered in blood and brains. Phineas Gage has been thrown to the ground. He is stunned, in the afternoon glow, silent but awake. So are we all, helpless spectators.

"Horrible Accident" will be the predictable headline in the Boston *Daily Courier* and *Daily Journal* of September 20, a week later. "Wonderful Accident" will be the strange headline in the *Vermont Mercury* of September 22. "Passage of an Iron Rod Through the Head" will be the accurate headline in the *Boston Medical and Surgical Journal*. From the matter-of-factness with which they tell the story, one would think the writers were familiar with Edgar Allan Poe's accounts of the bizarre and the horrific. And perhaps they were, although this is not likely; Poe's gothic tales are not yet popular, and Poe himself will die the next year, unknown and impecunious. Perhaps the horrible is just in the air.

Noting how surprised people were that Gage was not killed instantly, the Boston medical article documents that "immediately after the explosion the patient was thrown upon his back"; that shortly thereafter he exhibited "a few convulsive motions of the extremities," and "spoke in a few minutes"; that "his men (with whom he was a great favourite) took him in their arms and carried him to the road, only a few rods distant (a rod is equivalent to $5\frac{1}{2}$ yards, or $16\frac{1}{2}$ feet), and sat him into an ox cart, in which he rode, sitting erect, a full three quarters of a mile, to the hotel of Mr. Joseph Adams"; and that Gage "got out of the cart himself, with a little assistance from his men."

Let me introduce Mr. Adams. He is the justice of the peace for Cavendish and the owner of the town's hotel and tavern. He is taller than Gage, twice as round, and as solicitous as his Falstaff shape suggests. He approaches Gage, and immediately has someone call for Dr. John Harlow, one of the town physicians. While they wait, I imagine, he says, "Come, come, Mr. Gage, what have we got here?" and, why not, "My, my, what troubles we've seen." He shakes his head in disbelief and leads Gage to the shady part of the hotel porch, which has been described as a "piazza." That makes it sound grand and spacious and open, and perhaps it is grand and spacious, but it is not open; it is just a porch. And there perhaps Mr. Adams is now giving Phineas Gage lemonade, or maybe cold cider.

An hour has passed since the explosion. The sun is declining and the heat is more bearable. A younger colleague of Dr. Harlow's, Dr. Edward Williams, is arriving. Years later Dr. Williams will describe the scene: "He at that time was sitting in a chair upon the piazza of Mr. Adams' hotel, in Cavendish. When I drove up, he said, 'Doctor, here is business enough for you.' I first noticed the wound upon the head before I alighted from my carriage, the pulsations of the brain being very distinct; there was also an appearance which, before I examined the head, I could not account for: the top of the head appeared somewhat like an inverted funnel; this was owing, I discovered, to the bone being fractured about the opening for a distance of about two inches in every direction. I ought to have mentioned above that the opening through the skull and integuments was not far from one and a half inch in diameter; the edges of this opening were everted, and the whole wound appeared as if some wedge-shaped body had passed from below upward. Mr. Gage, during the time I was examining this wound, was relating the manner in which he was injured to the bystanders; he talked so rationally and was so willing to answer questions, that I directed my inquiries to him in preference to the men who were with him at the time of the accident, and who were standing about at this time. Mr. G. then related to me some of the circumstances, as he has since done; and I can safely say that neither at that time nor on any subsequent occasion, save once, did I consider him to be other than perfectly rational. The one time to which I allude was about a fortnight after the accident, and then he persisted in calling me John Kirwin; yet he answered all my questions correctly."

The survival is made all the more amazing when one considers the shape and weight of the iron bar. Henry Bigelow, a surgery professor at Harvard, describes the iron so: "The iron which thus traversed the skull weighs thirteen and a quarter pounds. It is three feet seven inches in length, and one and a quarter inches in diameter. The end which entered first is pointed; the taper being seven inches long, and the diameter of the point one quarter of an inch; circumstances to which the patient perhaps owes his life. The iron is unlike any other, and was made by a neighbouring blacksmith to please the fancy of the owner." Gage is serious about his trade and its proper tools.

Surviving the explosion with so large a wound to the head, being able to talk and walk and remain coherent immediately afterward—this is all surprising. But just as surprising will be Gage's surviving the inevitable infection that is about to take over his wound. Gage's physician, John Harlow, is well aware of the role of disinfection. He does not have the help of antibiotics, but using what chemicals are available he will clean the wound vigorously and regularly, and place the patient in a semi-recumbent position so that drainage will be natural and easy. Gage will develop high fevers and at least one abscess, which Harlow will promptly remove with his scalpel. In the end, Gage's youth and strong constitution will overcome the odds against him, assisted, as Harlow will put it, by divine intervention: "I dressed him, God healed him."

Phineas Gage will be pronounced cured in less than two months. Yet this astonishing outcome pales in comparison with the extraordinary turn that Gage's personality is about to undergo. Gage's disposition, his likes and dislikes, his dreams and aspirations are all to change. Gage's body may be alive and well, but there is a new spirit animating it.

Gage Was No Longer Gage

Just what exactly happened we can glean today from the account Dr. Harlow prepared twenty years after the accident. It is a trustworthy text, with an abundance of facts and a minimum of interpretation. It makes sense humanly and neurologically, and from it we can piece together not just Gage but his doctor as well. John Harlow had been a schoolteacher before he entered Jefferson Medical College in Philadelphia, and was only a few years into his medical career when he took care of Gage. The case became his life-consuming interest, and I suspect that it made Harlow want to be a scholar, something that may not have been in his plans when he set up his medical practice in Vermont. Treating Gage successfully and reporting the results to his Boston colleagues may have been the shining hours of his career, and he must have been disturbed by the fact that a real cloud hung over Gage's cure.

Harlow's narrative describes how Gage regained his strength and how his physical recovery was complete. Gage could touch, hear, and see, and was not paralyzed of limb or tongue. He had lost vision in his left eye, but his vision was perfect in the right. He walked firmly, used his hands with dexterity, and had no noticeable difficulty with speech or language. And yet, as Harlow recounts, the "equilibrium or balance, so to speak, between his intellectual faculty and animal propensities" had been destroyed. The changes became apparent as soon as the acute phase of brain injury subsided. He was now "fitful, irreverent, indulging at times in the grossest profanity which was not previously his custom, manifesting but little deference for his fellows, impatient of restraint or advice when it conflicts with his desires, at times pertinaciously obstinate, yet capricious and vacillating, devising many plans of future operation, which are no sooner arranged than they are abandoned.... A child in his intellectual capacity and manifestations, he has the animal passions of a strong man." The foul language was so debased that women were advised not to stay long in his presence, lest their sensibilities be offended. The strongest admonitions from Harlow himself failed to return our survivor to good behavior.

These new personality traits contrasted sharply with the "temperate habits" and "considerable energy of character" Phineas Gage was known to have possessed before the accident. He had had "a well balanced mind and was looked upon by those who knew him as a shrewd, smart businessman, very energetic and persistent in executing all his plans of action." There is no doubt that in the context of his job and time, he was successful. So radical was the change in him that friends and acquaintances could hardly recognize the man. They noted sadly that "Gage was no longer Gage." So different a man was he that his employers had to let him go shortly after he returned to work, for they "considered the change in his mind so marked that they could not give him his place again." The problem was not lack of physical ability or skill; it was his new character.

The unraveling continued unabated. No longer able to work as a foreman, Gage took jobs on horse farms. He would work at one place or another briefly, only to quit in a capricious fit or be let go because of poor discipline.

As Harlow notes, he was good at "always finding something which did not suit him." Then came his career as a circus attraction. Gage was featured at Barnum's Museum in New York City, vaingloriously showing his wounds and the tamping iron. (Harlow states that the iron was a constant companion, and points out Gage's strong attachment to objects and animals, which was new and somewhat out of the ordinary. This trait, what we might call "collector's behavior," is something I have seen in patients who have suffered injuries like Gage's, as well as in autistic individuals.)

Then far more than now, the circus capitalized on nature's cruelty. The endocrine variety included dwarfs, the fattest woman on earth, the tallest man, the fellow with the largest jaw; the neurological variety included youths with elephant skin, victims of neurofibromatosis—and now Gage. We can imagine him in such Fellinian company, peddling misery for gold.

Four years after the accident, there was another theatrical coup. Gage left for South America. He worked on horse farms, and eventually was a stagecoach driver in Santiago and Valparaiso. Little else is known about his expatriate life except that in 1859 his health was deteriorating.

In 1860, Gage returned to the United States to live with his mother and sister, who had since moved to San Francisco. At first he was employed on a farm in Santa Clara, but he did not stay long. In fact, he moved around often, occasionally finding work as a laborer in the Bay Area. It is clear that he was not an independent person and that he could not secure the type of steady, remunerative job that he had once held. The end of the fall was nearing.

In my mind is a picture of 1860s San Francisco as a bustling place, full of adventurous entrepreneurs engaged in mining, farming, and shipping. That is where we can find Gage's mother and sister, the latter married to a prosperous San Francisco merchant (D. D. Shattuck, Esquire), and that is where the old Phineas Gage might have belonged. But that is not where we would find him if we could travel back in time. We would find him drinking and brawling in a questionable district, not conversing with the captains of commerce, as astonished as anybody when the fault would slip and the earth would shake threateningly. He had joined the tableau of dispirited people who, as Nathanael West would put it decades later, and a few hundred miles to the south, "had come to California to die."

The meager documents available suggest that Gage developed epileptic fits (seizures). The end came on May 21, 1861, after an illness that lasted little more than a day. Gage had a major convulsion which made him lose consciousness. A series of subsequent convulsions, one coming soon on the heels of another, followed. He never regained consciousness. I believe he was the victim of *status epilepticus*, a condition in which convulsions become nearly continuous and usher in death. He was thirty-eight years old. There was no death notice in the San Francisco newspapers.

Why Phineas Gage?

Why is this sad story worth telling? What is the possible significance of such a bizarre tale? The answer is simple. While other cases of neurological damage that occurred at about the same time revealed that the brain was the foundation for language, perception, and motor function, and generally provided more conclusive details, Gage's story hinted at an amazing fact: Somehow, there were systems in the human brain dedicated more to reasoning than to anything else, and in particular to the personal and social dimensions of reasoning. The observance of previously acquired social convention and ethical rules could be lost as a result of brain damage, even when neither basic intellect nor language seemed compromised. Unwittingly, Gage's example indicated that something in the brain was concerned specifically with unique human properties, among them the ability to anticipate the future and plan accordingly within a complex social environment; the sense of responsibility toward the self and others; and the ability to orchestrate one's survival deliberately, at the command of one's free will.

The most striking aspect of this unpleasant story is the discrepancy between the normal personality structure that preceded the accident and the nefarious personality traits that surfaced thereafter—and remained for the rest of Gage's life. Gage had once known all he needed to know about making choices conducive to his betterment. He had a sense of personal and social responsibility, reflected in the way he had secured advancement in his job, cared for the quality of his work, and attracted the admiration of employers and colleagues. He was well adapted in terms of social convention and appears to have been ethical in his dealings. After the accident, he no longer showed respect for social convention; ethics were violated; the decisions he made did not take into account his best interest, and he was given to invent tales "without any foundation except in his fancy," in Harlow's words. There was no evidence of concern about his future, no sign of forethought.

The alterations in Gage's personality were not subtle. He could not make good choices, and the choices he made were not simply neutral. They were not the reserved or slight decisions of someone whose mind is diminished and who is afraid to act, but were instead actively disadvantageous. Gage worked hard at his downfall. One might venture that either his value system was now different, or, if it was still the same, there was no way in which the old values could influence his decisions. No evidence exists to tell us which is true, yet my investigation of patients with brain damage similar to Phineas Gage's convinces me that neither explanation captures what really happens in those circumstances. Some part of the value system remains and can be utilized in abstract terms, but it is unconnected to real-life situations. When the Phineas Gages of this world need to operate in reality, the decision-making process is minimally influenced by old knowledge.

Another important aspect of Gage's story is the discrepancy between the degenerated character and the intactness of the several instruments of mind—attention, perception, memory, language, intelligence. In this type of discrepancy, known in neuropsychology as *dissociation*, one or more performances within a general profile of operations are at odds with the rest. In Gage's case the impaired character was dissociated from the otherwise intact cognition and behavior. In other patients, with lesions elsewhere in the brain, language may be the impaired aspect, while character and all other cognitive aspects remain intact; language is then the "dissociated" ability. Subsequent study of patients similar to Gage has confirmed that his specific dissociation profile occurs consistently.

It must have been hard to believe that the character change would not resolve itself, and at first even Dr. Harlow resisted admitting that the change was permanent. This is understandable, since the most dramatic elements in Gage's story were his very survival, and then his survival without a defect that would more easily meet the eye: paralysis, for example, or a speech defect, or memory loss. Somehow, emphasizing Gage's newly developed social shortcomings smacked of ingratitude to both providence and medicine. By 1868, however, Dr. Harlow was ready to acknowledge the full extent of his patient's personality change.

Gage's survival was duly noted, but with the caution reserved for freakish phenomena. The significance of his behavioral changes was largely lost. There were good reasons for this neglect. Even in the small world of brain science at the time, two camps were beginning to form. One held that psychological functions such as language or memory could never be traced to a particular region of the brain. If one had to accept, reluctantly, that the brain did produce the mind, it did so as a whole and not as a collection of parts with special functions. The other camp held that, on the contrary, the brain did have specialized parts and those parts generated separate mind functions. The rift between the two camps was not merely indicative of the infancy of brain research; the argument endured for another century and, to a certain extent, is still with us today.

Whatever scientific debate Phineas Gage's story elicited, it focused on the issue of localizing language and movement in the brain. The debate never turned to the connection between impaired social conduct and frontal lobe damage. I am reminded here of a saying of Warren McCulloch's: "When I point, look where I point, not at my finger." (McCulloch, a legendary neurophysiologist and a pioneer in the field that would become computational neuroscience, was also a poet and a prophet. This saying was usually part of a prophecy.) Few looked to where Gage was unwittingly pointing. It is of course difficult to imagine anybody in Gage's day with the knowledge *and* the courage to look in the proper direction. It was acceptable that the brain sectors whose damage would have caused Gage's heart to stop pumping and his lungs to stop breathing had not been touched by the iron rod. It was also acceptable that the brain sectors which control wakefulness were far from the iron's course and were thus spared. It was even acceptable that the injury did not render Gage unconscious for a long period. (The event anticipated what is current knowledge from studies of head injuries: The style of the injury is a critical variable. A severe blow to the head, even if no bone is broken and no weapon penetrates the brain, can cause a major disruption of wakefulness for a long time; the forces unleashed by the blow disorganize brain function profoundly. A penetrating injury in which the forces are concentrated on a narrow and steady path, rather than dissipate and accelerate the brain against the skull, may cause dysfunction only where brain tissue is actually destroyed, and thus spare brain function elsewhere.) But to understand Gage's behavioral change would have meant believing that normal social conduct required a particular corresponding brain region, and this concept was far more unthinkable than its equivalent for movement, the senses, or even language.

A Landmark by Hindsight

There is no question that Gage's personality change was caused by a circumscribed brain lesion in a specific site. But that explanation would not be apparent until two decades after the accident, and it became vaguely acceptable only in this century. For a long time, most everybody, John Harlow included, believed that "the portion of the brain traversed, was, for several reasons, the best fitted of any part of the cerebral substance to sustain the injury": in other words, a part of the brain that did nothing much and was thus expendable. But nothing could be further from the truth, as Harlow himself realized. He wrote in 1868 that Gage's mental recovery "was only partial, his intellectual faculties being decidedly impaired, but not totally lost; nothing like dementia, but they were enfeebled in their manifestations, his mental operations being perfect in kind, but not in degree or quantity." The unintentional message in Gage's case was that observing social convention, behaving ethically, and making decisions advantageous to one's survival and progress require knowledge of rules and strategies *and* the integrity of specific brain systems. The problem with this message was that it lacked the evidence required to make it understandable and definitive. Instead the message became a mystery and came down to us as the "enigma" of frontal lobe function. Gage posed more questions than he gave answers.

To begin with, all we knew about Gage's brain lesion was that it was probably in the frontal lobe. That is a bit like saying that Chicago is probably in the United States—accurate but not very specific or helpful. Granted that the damage was likely to involve the frontal lobe, where exactly was it within that region? The left lobe? The right? Both? Somewhere else too? As you will see in the next chapter, new imaging technologies have helped us come up with the answer to this puzzle.

Then there was the nature of Gage's character defect. How did the abnormality develop? The primary cause, sure enough, was a hole in the head, but that just tells why the defect arose, not how. Might a hole anywhere in the frontal lobe have the same result? Whatever the answer, by what plausible means can destruction of a brain region change personality? If there are specific regions in the frontal lobe, what are they made of, and how do they operate in an intact brain? Are they some kind of "center" for social behavior? Are they modules selected in evolution, filled with problem-solving algorithms ready to tell us how to reason and make decisions? How do these modules, if that is what they are, interact with the environment during development to permit normal reasoning and decision making? Or are there in fact no such modules?

What were the mechanisms behind Gage's failure at decision making? It might be that the knowledge required to reason through a problem was destroyed or rendered inaccessible, so that he no longer could decide appropriately. It is possible also that the requisite knowledge remained intact and accessible but the strategies for reasoning were compromised. If this was the case, which reasoning steps were missing? More to the point, which steps are there for those who are allegedly normal? And if we are fortunate enough to glean the nature of some of these steps, what are their neural underpinnings?

Intriguing as all these questions are, they may not be as important as those which surround Gage's status as a human being. May he be described as having free will? Did he have a sense of right and wrong, or was he the victim of his new brain design, such that his decisions were imposed upon him and inevitable? Was he responsible for his acts? If we rule that he was not, does this tell us something about responsibility in more general terms? There are many Gages around us, people whose fall from social grace is disturbingly similar. Some have brain damage consequent to brain tumors, or head injury, or other neurological disease. Yet some have had no overt neurological disease and they still behave like Gage, for reasons having to do with their brains or with the society into which they were born. We need to understand the nature of these human beings whose actions can be destructive to themselves and to others, if we are to solve humanely the problems they pose. Neither incarceration nor the death penalty—among the responses that society currently offers for those individuals—contribute to our understanding or solve the problem. In fact, we should take the question further and inquire about our own responsibility when we "normal" individuals slip into the irrationality that marked Phineas Gage's great fall.

Gage lost something uniquely human, the ability to plan his future as a social being. How aware was he of this loss? Might he be described as self-conscious in the same sense that you and I are? Is it fair to say that his soul was diminished, or that he had lost his soul? And if so, what would Descartes have thought had he known about Gage and had he had the knowledge of neurobiology we now have? Would he have inquired about Gage's pineal gland?

From *The Man Who Mistook His Wife for a Hat and Other Clinical Tales*

Oliver Sacks

The aspects of things that are most important for us are hidden because of their simplicity and familiarity. (One is unable to notice something because it is always before one's eyes.) The real foundations of his enquiry do not strike a man at all.

—Wittgenstein

What Wittgenstein writes here, of epistemology, might apply to aspects of one's physiology and psychology—especially in regard to what Sherrington once called 'our secret sense, our sixth sense'—that continuous but unconscious sensory flow from the movable parts of our body (muscles, tendons, joints), by which their position and tone and motion is continually monitored and adjusted, but in a way which is hidden from us because it is automatic and unconscious.

Our other senses—the five senses—are open and obvious; but this—our hidden sense—had to be discovered, as it was, by Sherrington, in the 1890s. He named it 'proprioception', to distinguish it from 'exteroception' and 'interoception', and, additionally, because of its indispensability for our sense of *ourselves*; for it is only by courtesy of proprioception, so to speak, that we feel our bodies as proper to us, as our 'property', as our own. (Sherrington 1906, 1940.)

What is more important for us, at an elemental level, than the control, the owning and operation, of our own physical selves? And yet it is so automatic, so familiar, we never give it a thought.

Jonathan Miller produced a beautiful television series, *The Body in Question*, but the body, normally, is never in question; our bodies are beyond question; or perhaps beneath question—they are simply, unquestionably, there. This unquestionability of the body, its certainty, is, for Wittgenstein, the start and basis of all knowledge and certainty. Thus, in his last book (*On Certainty*), he opens by saying: 'If you do know that *here is one hand*, we'll grant you all the rest.' But then, in the same breath, on the same opening page: 'What we can ask is whether it can make sense to doubt it . . .'; and, a little later, 'Can I doubt it? Grounds for *doubt* are lacking!'

Indeed, his book might be titled *On Doubt*, for it is marked by doubting, no less than affirming. Specifically, he wonders—and one in turn may wonder whether these thoughts were perhaps incited by his working with patients, in a hospital, in the war—he wonders whether there might be situations or conditions which take away the certainty of the body, which do give one grounds to doubt one's body, perhaps indeed to lose one's entire body in total doubt. This thought seems to haunt his last book like a nightmare.

Christina was a strapping young woman of twenty-seven, given to hockey and riding, self-assured, robust, in body and mind. She had two young children, and worked as a computer programmer at home. She was intelligent and cultivated, fond of the ballet, and of the Lakeland poets (but not, I would think, of Wittgenstein). She had an active, full life—had scarcely known a day's illness. Somewhat to her surprise, after an attack of abdominal pain, she was found to have gallstones, and removal of the gallbladder was advised.

She was admitted to a hospital three days before the operation date, and placed on an antibiotic for microbial prophylaxis. This was purely routine, a precaution, no complications of any sort being expected at all. Christina understood this, and being a sensible soul had no great anxieties.

The day before surgery Christina, not usually given to fancies or dreams, had a disturbing dream of peculiar intensity. She was swaying wildly, in her dream, very unsteady on her feet, could hardly feel the ground beneath her, could hardly feel anything in her hands, found them flailing to and fro, kept dropping whatever she picked up.

She was distressed by this dream ('I never had one like it,' she said, 'I can't get it out of my mind'), so distressed that we requested an opinion from the psychiatrist. 'Pre-operative anxiety,' he said. 'Quite natural, we see it all the time.'

But later that day *the dream came true*. Christina did find herself very unsteady on her feet, with awkward flailing movements, and dropping things from her hands.

The psychiatrist was again called—he seemed vexed at the call, but also, momentarily, uncertain and bewildered. 'Anxiety hysteria,' he now snapped, in a dismissive tone. 'Typical conversion symptoms—you see them all the while.'

But the day of surgery Christina was still worse. Standing was impossible—unless she looked down at her feet. She could hold nothing in her hands, and they 'wandered'—unless she kept an eye on them. When she reached out for something, or tried to feed herself, her hands would miss, or overshoot wildly, as if some essential control or coordination was gone.

She could scarcely even sit up—her body 'gave way'. Her face was oddly expressionless and slack, her jaw fell open, even her vocal posture was gone.

'Something awful's happened,' she mouthed, in a ghostly flat voice. 'I can't feel my body. I feel weird—disembodied.'

This was an amazing thing to hear, confounded, confounding. 'Disembodied'—was she crazy? But what of her physical state then? The collapse of tone and muscle posture, from top to toe; the wandering of her hands, which she seemed unaware of; the flailing and overshooting, as if she were receiving no information from the periphery, as if the control loops for tone and movement had catastrophically broken down.

'It's a strange statement,' I said to the residents. 'It's almost impossible to imagine what might provoke such a statement.'

'But it's hysteria, Dr. Sacks—didn't the psychiatrist say so?'

'Yes, he did. But have you ever seen a hysteria like this? Think phenomenologically—take what you see as a genuine phenomenon, in which her state-of-body and state-of-mind are not fictions, but a psychophysical whole. Could anything give such a picture of undermined body and mind?'

'I'm not testing you,' I added. 'I'm as bewildered as you are. I've never seen or imagined anything quite like this before ...'

I thought, and they thought, we thought together.

'Could it be a biparietal syndrome?' one of them asked.

'It's an "as if",' I answered: '*as if* the parietal lobes were not getting their usual sensory information. Let's *do* some sensory testing—and test parietal lobe function, too.'

We did so, and a picture began to emerge. There seemed to be a very profound, almost total, proprioceptive deficit, going from the tips of her toes to her head—the parietal lobes were working, *but had nothing to work with*. Christina might have hysteria, but she had a great deal more, of a sort which none of us had ever seen or conceived before. We put in an emergency call now, not to the psychiatrist, but to the physical medicine specialist, the physiatrist.

He arrived promptly, responding to the urgency of the call. He opened his eyes very wide when he saw Christina, examined her swiftly and comprehensively, and then proceeded to electrical tests of nerve and muscle function. 'This is quite extraordinary,' he said. 'I have never seen or read about anything like this before. She has lost all proprioception—you're right—from top to toe. She has no muscle or tendon or joint sense whatever. There is slight loss of other sensory modalities—to light touch, temperature, and pain, and slight involvement of the motor fibres, too. But it is predominantly position-sense—proprioception—which has sustained such damage.'

'What's the cause?' we asked.

'You're the neurologists. You find out.'

By afternoon, Christina was still worse. She lay motionless and toneless; even her breathing was shallow. Her situation was grave—we thought of a respirator—as well as strange.

The picture revealed by spinal tap was one of an acute polyneuritis, but a polyneuritis of a most exceptional type: not like Guillain-Barré syndrome, with its overwhelming motor involvement, but a purely (or almost purely) sensory neuritis, affecting the sensory roots of spinal and cranial nerves throughout the neuraxis.

Operation was deferred; it would have been madness at this time. Much more pressing were the questions: 'Will she survive? What can we do?'

'What's the verdict?' Christina asked, with a faint voice and fainter smile, after we had checked her spinal fluid.

'You've got this inflammation, this neuritis . . .' we began, and told her all we knew. When we forgot something, or hedged, her clear questions brought us back.

'Will it get better?' she demanded. We looked at each other, and at her: 'We have no idea.'

The sense of the body, I told her, is given by three things: vision, balance organs (the vestibular system), and proprioception—which she'd lost. Normally all of these worked together. If one failed, the others could compensate, or substitute—to a degree. In particular, I told of my patient Mr. MacGregor, who, unable to employ his balance organs, used his eyes instead. And of patients with neurosyphilis, *tabes dorsalis*, who had similar symptoms, but confined to the legs—and how they too had to compensate by use of their eyes. And how, if one asked such a patient to move his legs, he was apt to say: 'Sure, Doc, as soon as I find them.'

Christina listened closely, with a sort of desperate attention.

'What I must do then,' she said slowly, 'is use vision, use my eyes, in every situation where I used—what do you call it?—proprioception before. I've already noticed,' she added, musingly, 'that I may "lose" my arms. I think they're one place, and I find they're another. This "proprioception" is like the eyes of the body, the way the body sees itself. And if it goes, as it's gone with me, *it's like the body's blind*. My body can't "see" itself if it's lost its eyes, right? So *I* have to watch it—be its eyes. Right?'

'Right,' I said, 'right. You could be a physiologist.'

'I'll *have* to be a sort of physiologist,' she rejoined, 'because my physiology has gone wrong, and may never *naturally* go right...'

It was as well that Christina showed such strength of mind, from the start, for, though the acute inflammation subsided, and her spinal fluid returned to normal, the damage it did to her proprioceptive fibres persisted—so that there was no neurological recovery a week, or a year, later. Indeed there has been none in the eight years that have now passed—though she has been able to lead a life, a sort of life, through accommodations and adjustments of every sort, emotional and moral no less than neurological.

That first week Christina did nothing, lay passively, scarcely ate. She was in a state of utter shock, horror and despair. What sort of a life would it be, if there were no natural recovery? What sort of a life, every move made by artifice? What sort of a life, above all, if she felt disembodied?

Then life reasserted itself, as it will, and Christina started to move. She could at first do nothing without using her eyes, and collapsed in a helpless heap the moment she closed them. She had, at first, to monitor herself by vision, looking carefully at each part of her body as it moved, using an almost painful conscientiousness and care. Her movements, consciously monitored and regulated, were at first clumsy, artificial, in the highest degree. But then—and here both of us found ourselves most happily surprised, by the power of an ever-increasing, daily increasing, automatism—then her movements started to appear more delicately modulated, more graceful, more natural (though still wholly dependent on use of the eyes).

Increasingly now, week by week, the normal, unconscious feedback of proprioception was being replaced by an equally unconscious feedback by vision, by visual automatism and reflexes increasingly integrated and fluent. Was it possible, too, that something more fundamental was happening? That the brain's visual model of the body, or body-image—normally rather feeble (it is, of course, absent in the blind), and normally subsidiary to the proprioceptive body-model—was it possible that *this*, now the proprioceptive body model was lost, was gaining, by way of compensation or substitution, an enhanced, exceptional, extraordinary force? And to this might be added a compensatory enhancement of the vestibular body-model or body-image, too . . . both to an extent which was more than we had expected or hoped for.

Whether or not there was increased use of vestibular feedback, there was certainly increased use of her ears—auditory feedback. Normally this is subsidiary, and rather unimportant in speaking—our speech remains normal if we are deaf from a head cold, and some of the congenitally deaf may be able to acquire virtually perfect speech. For the modulation of speech is normally proprioceptive, governed by inflowing impulses from all our vocal organs. Christina had lost this normal inflow, this afference, had lost her normal proprioceptive vocal tone and posture, and therefore had to use her ears, auditory feedback, instead.

Besides these new, compensatory forms of feedback, Christina also started to develop— it was deliberate and conscious in the first place, but gradually became unconscious and automatic— various forms of new and compensatory 'feed-forward' (in all this she was assisted by an immensely understanding and resourceful rehabilitative staff).

Thus at the time of her catastrophe, and for about a month afterwards, Christina remained as floppy as a ragdoll, unable even to sit up. But three months later, I was startled to see her sitting very finely—too finely, statuesquely, like a dancer in mid-pose. And soon I saw that her sitting was, indeed, a pose, consciously or automatically adopted and sustained, a sort of forced or wilful or histrionic posture, to make up for the continuing lack of any genuine, natural posture. Nature having failed, she took to 'artifice', but the artifice was suggested by nature, and soon became 'second nature'. Similarly with her voice—she had at first been almost mute.

This too was projected, as to an audience from a stage. It *was* a stagey, theatrical voice—not because of any histrionism, or perversion of motive, but because there was still no natural vocal posture. And with her face, too—this still tended to remain somewhat flat and expressionless (though her inner

emotions were of full and normal intensity), due to lack of proprioceptive facial tone and posture, unless she used an artificial enhancement of expression
(as patients with aphasia may adopt exaggerated emphases and inflections).

But all these measures were, at best, partial. They made life possible—
they did not make it normal. Christina learned to walk, to take public transport, to conduct the usual business of life—but only with the exercise of great
vigilance, and strange ways of doing things—ways which might break down
if her attention was diverted. Thus if she was eating while she was talking, or
if her attention was elsewhere, she would grip the knife and fork with painful
force—her nails and fingertips would go bloodless with pressure; but if there
were any lessening of the painful pressure, she might nervelessly drop them
straightaway—there was no in-between, no modulation, whatever.

Thus, although there was not a trace of neurological recovery (recovery
from the anatomical damage to nerve fibres), there was, with the help of intensive and varied therapy—she remained in hospital on the rehabilitation
ward, for almost a year—a very considerable functional recovery, i.e. the ability to function using various substitutions and other such tricks. It became
possible, finally for Christina to leave the hospital, go home, rejoin her children. She was able to return to her home-computer terminal, which she now
learned to operate with extraordinary skill and efficiency, considering that
everything had to be done by vision, not feel. She had learned to operate—
but how did she feel? Had the substitutions dispersed the disembodied
sense she first spoke of?

The answer is—not in the least. She continues to feel, with the continuing loss of proprioception, that her body is dead, not-real, not-hers—
she cannot appropriate it to herself. She can find no words for this state, and
can only use analogies derived from other senses: 'I feel my body is blind and
deaf to itself . . . it has no sense of itself'—these are her own words. She has
no words, no direct words, to describe this bereftness, this sensory darkness
(or silence) akin to blindness or deafness. She has no words, and we lack
words too. And society lacks words, and sympathy, for such states. The blind,
at least, are treated with solicitude—we can imagine their state, and we treat
them accordingly. But when Christina, painfully, clumsily, mounts a bus, she
receives nothing but uncomprehending and angry snarls: 'What's wrong
with you, lady? Are you blind—or blind-drunk?' What can she answer—
'I have no proprioception'? The lack of social support and sympathy is an additional trial—disabled, but with the nature of her disability not clear—she

is not, after all, manifestly blind or paralysed, manifestly anything—she tends to be treated as a phoney or a fool. This is what happens to those with disorders of the hidden senses (it happens also to patients who have vestibular impairment, or who have been labyrinthectomised).

Christina is condemned to live in an indescribable, unimaginable realm—though 'non-realm', 'nothingness', might be a better words for it. At times she breaks down—not in public, but with me: 'If only I could *feel!*' she cries. 'But I've forgotten what it's like . . . I *was* normal, wasn't I? I *did* move like everyone else?'

'Yes, of course.'

'There's no "of course". I can't believe it. I want proof.'

I show her a home movie of herself with her children, taken just a few weeks before her polyneuritis.

'Yes, of course, that's me!' Christina smiles, and then cries: 'But I can't identify with that graceful girl any more! She's gone, I can't remember her, *I can't even imagine her*. It's like something's been scooped right out of me, right at the centre . . . that's what they do with frogs, isn't it? They scoop out the centre, the spinal cord, they *pith* them . . . That's what I am, *pithed*, like a frog . . . Step up, come and see Chris, the first pithed human being. She's no proprioception, no sense of herself—disembodied Chris, the pithed girl!' She laughs wildly, with an edge of hysteria. I calm her—'Come now!' while thinking, 'Is she right?'

For, in some sense, she *is* 'pithed', disembodied, a sort of wraith. She has lost, with her sense of proprioception, the fundamental, organic mooring of identity—at least of that corporeal identity, or 'body-ego', which Freud sees as the basis of self: 'The ego is first and foremost a body-ego.' Some such depersonalisation or derealisation must always occur, when there are deep disturbances of body perception or body image—Weir Mitchell saw this, and incomparably described it, when he was working with amputees and nerve-damaged patients in the American Civil War—and in a famous, quasi-fictionalised account, but still the best, phenomenologically most accurate, account we have, said (through the mouth of his physician-patient, George Dedlow):

> 'I found to my horror that at times I was less conscious of myself, of my own existence, than used to be the case. This sensation was so novel that at first it quite bewildered me. I felt like asking someone constantly if I were really

George Dedlow or not; but, well aware of how absurd I should seem after such a question, I refrained from speaking of my case, and strove more keenly to analyse my feelings. At times the conviction of my want of being myself was overwhelming and most painful. It was, as well as I can describe it, a deficiency in the egoistic sentiment of individuality.'

For Christina there is this general feeling—this 'deficiency in the egoistic sentiment of individuality'—which has become less with accommodation, with the passage of time. And there is this specific, organically based, feeling of disembodiedness, which remains as severe, and uncanny, as the day she first felt it. This is also felt, for example, by those who have high transections of the spinal cord—but they of course, are paralysed; whereas Christina, though 'bodiless', is up and about.

There are brief, partial reprieves, when her skin is stimulated. She goes out when she can, she loves open cars, where she can feel the wind on her body and face (superficial sensation, light touch, is only slightly impaired). 'It's wonderful,' she says. 'I feel the wind on my arms and face, and then I know, faintly, I *have* arms and a face. It's not the real thing, but it's something—it lifts this horrible, dead veil for a while.'

But her situation is, and remains, a 'Wittgensteinian' one. She does not know 'Here is one hand'—her loss of proprioception, her de-afferentiation, has deprived her of her existential, her epistemic, basis—and nothing she can do, or think, will alter this fact. She cannot be certain of her body— what would Wittgenstein have said, in her position?

In an extraordinary way, she has both succeeded and failed. She has succeeded in operating, but not in being. She has succeeded to an almost incredible extent in all the accommodations that will, courage, tenacity, independence and the plasticity of the senses and the nervous system will permit. She has faced, she faces, an unprecedented situation, has battled against unimaginable difficulties and odds, and has survived as an indomitable, impressive human being. She is one of those unsung heroes, or heroines, of neurological affliction.

But still and forever she remains defective and defeated. Not all the spirit and ingenuity in the world, not all the substitutions or compensations the nervous system allows, can alter in the least her continuing and absolute loss of proprioception—that vital sixth sense without which a body must remain unreal, unpossessed.

Poor Christina is 'pithed' in 1985 as she was eight years ago and will remain so for the rest of her life. Her life is unprecedented. She is, so far as I know, the first of her kind, the first 'disembodied' human being.

Postscript

Now Christina has company of a sort. I understand from Dr. H. H. Schaumberg, who is the first to describe the syndrome, that large numbers of patients are turning up everywhere now with severe sensory neuronopathies. The worst affected have body-image disturbances like Christina. Most of them are health faddists, or are on a megavitamin craze, and have been taking enormous quantities of Vitamin B6 (Pyridoxine). Thus there are now some hundreds of 'disembodied' men and women—though most, unlike Christina, can hope to get better as soon as they stop poisoning themselves with Pyridoxine.

QUESTIONS

1. Skip ahead to Donald Hoffman's essay in Chapter 5. Does Dr. P.'s deficit (mentioned in the introduction to this chapter) fit with Hoffman's concept of vision by construction?

2. Would you expect athletes to have exceptional proprioceptive systems? Why or why not? How might you test your hypothesis?

3. Do you know anyone who has had a stroke (or other accident) that affected his or her brain? What aspects of the person's mental function were impaired? Which were spared?

CHAPTER FIVE

SENSATION AND PERCEPTION

Seeing the world around you involves more than just opening your eyes. Although perception often seems effortless, the process by which the brain converts patterns of light into an understanding of objects is truly astounding, and even today only incompletely understood.

From its title onward, Donald Hoffman's book *Visual Intelligence* (1998) captures one of the most important yet often underappreciated aspects of vision: that it is not just about perceiving brightness and color, it is about using your brain to make supremely educated guesses about what's out there in the world. Any digital camera can sharpen an image, but it takes a human being (or at least a very clever animal) to *understand* what it is seeing. By probing the nature of our visual intelligence—and describing what he calls "vision by construction"—Hoffman cuts to the core of one of our most powerful senses.

In a selection from his book *Sensory Exotica* (1999), Howard C. Hughes reminds us that our five familiar senses—hearing, seeing, smelling, tasting, and touching—are not the only senses found in the animal world. Describing a panoply of senses that we as humans don't have (or have in only limited ways), such as echolocation, navigation by internal compass, and even "electroreception," Hughes uses the perceptions of other creatures to bring our own world view into sharper relief.

From *Visual Intelligence:*
How We Create What We See

Donald D. Hoffman

You are a creative genius. Your creative genius is so accomplished that it appears, to you and to others, as effortless. Yet it far outstrips the most valiant efforts of today's fastest supercomputers. To invoke it, you need only open your eyes. This might sound like the mantra of a new therapy, or the babble of a fortune cookie. But it is, instead, the reasoned conclusion of researchers in the field of cognitive science. What happens when you see is not a mindless process of stimulus and response, as behaviorists thought for much of the twentieth century, but a sophisticated process of construction whose intricacies we are now beginning to understand. In a fraction of a second your visual intelligence can construct the strut and colors of a peacock, or the graceful run of a leopard, or the fireworks of an ocean sunset, or the nuances of light in a forest at dusk, or any of countless other scenes of such subtlety and complexity. In repertoire and speed you far surpass the greatest of painters.

You are a visual virtuoso. Perhaps, though, you are unaware of or flatly disbelieve in your innate talent. My goal is to persuade you otherwise, to present you with the evidence uncovered by researchers in the cognitive sciences, evidence that, quite frankly, has come as a surprise to the researchers themselves. Indeed, rumor has it, an early researcher at MIT so underestimated vision that he assigned it to a graduate student as a summer project, a mere warm-up for more substantial forays into human and artificial intelligence. Now, a few decades later, thousands of researchers in a variety of disciplines work full-time to explore the genius of vision. What they have found will, I suspect, prod even the most jaded of viewers to awe.

Your visual prowess is nowhere more impressive than when you view a natural scene. But to appreciate that prowess it is best to begin with something far simpler. This is, after all, the method of science: study first the simple, then the complex. Try arithmetic before calculus. In this spirit, let's look first at a simple figure, a mere trifle for the constructive powers of your visual intelligence. Here is the "ripple":

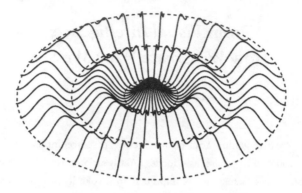

This figure is of course a drawing on a flat—or, more precisely, two-dimensional (2D)—surface. You can check this, should you wish to, by touching it. But the figure also appears to be, as the name "ripple" suggests, a surface that is far from flat, and that undulates in space like waves on a pond. You can check this by viewing the figure. Indeed, *try* to see the ripple as flat; I have never succeeded.

Logic dictates that the ripple cannot be at once flat and not flat, so either the hand or the eye (or both) must be in error. Everyone to whom I have shown the ripple has opted to believe the hand. So assume for now that the hand is right and the figure is flat. Then your visual system has made a serious error: it has constructed an elaborate ripple in space despite ample evidence that this construction is unwarranted. And it perseverates in this error, ignoring your better judgment that the figure must be flat. This might not seem the virtuoso performance I mentioned a moment ago.

There is, as we shall see, method to this visual madness. But for now, look again at the ripple and note that it has three parts: a bump in the center, a circular wave around the bump, and another circular wave on the outside. As an aid to discuss the figure, I drew dashed curves along the boundaries of these parts.

We have gone from bad to worse. Your visual system not only fabricates the ripple, it then endows it with parts. But could it be that the dashed curves—and not your visual system—are the real culprits here, and that without the dashed curves you would see no parts? You can check that this is not so. Simply turn the figure, or your head, upside down. You now see an inverted ripple with new parts: the dashed curves now lie on crests of waves and not, as before, in the troughs between waves. Turning the figure upright restores the original parts. And if you turn the figure slowly you can catch it in the act of flipping from one set of parts to the other. So the dashed curves aren't the culprits, since the parts you see in the inverted ripple don't always respect those curves.

Has your visual system gone off the deep end? It constructs from whole cloth a ripple in space and then proceeds to embellish it with mutable parts. Shall we henceforth distrust the witness of vision, knowing now its penchant to perjure?

This last conclusion is of course too hasty. Our evidence, so far, suggests only a single mistake, not inveterate fabrication. To establish the harsher verdict, we must consider more evidence. That we shall do through much of this book. In the process we shall find that your construction of the ripple and its parts follows a beautiful logic. But for now consider next the "magic square":

Magic square   Magic square   Almost gone!

The middle figure consists of sixteen lines at random orientations. You might see, in addition, four edges that form the boundary of a square. And the square itself might look a brighter white than the rest of the page. But a photometer, a device which measures light intensity by catching and counting light particles, would discern neither the edges nor the brighter interior of this square.

Logic again dictates that the figure cannot at once contain and not contain a bright square, so either the photometer or your visual system (or both) must be in error. Everyone to whom I have shown the magic square has opted to believe the photometer. So assume for now that the photometer is right and the figure has no bright square. Then your visual system has again made a serious error, and of the same type it did with the ripple: elaborate fabrication.

The magic square appears as well in the figure on the left. But when I superpose the left and middle figures to obtain the figure on the right, the magic square almost disappears. This seems to make no sense. If the left figure and the middle figure each prompt your visual system to construct a square, then we should expect, if anything, that superposing them would prompt your visual system to construct another, more salient, square. After all, there is now twice the "evidence" for a square, since there are now twice as many lines that terminate along its presumed boundary. Why build a square based on small evidence, and yet refuse to build one when there is more? This example, and the ripple, suggest that your visual system not only fabricates, it does so willy-nilly.

This charge is again too hasty. We will find that your visual system fabricates, and does so chronically—but not willy-nilly. There is a compelling logic to your construction, and deconstruction, of the magic square.

Now consider the "devil's triangle," a fiendish figure devised in 1934 by Oscar Reutersvärd:

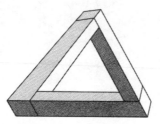

Once again we catch vision in the act of perjury. Its testimony to a solid triangle extended in depth is flatly contradicted by evidence from the hand. But this time we also catch vision in that joy of opposing counsel: self-contradiction. The triangle that is so confidently fabricated by vision, and which vision will not retract despite the witness of the hand, is not consistent. You could not build it with lumber and nails, which is why it's sometimes called the "impossible triangle."

This is striking. It suggests that vision not only fabricates, it does so, at times, unconstrained by reality. Constrained fabrication we might endure, but fabrication unconstrained goes well beyond the pale. Perhaps, though, the devil's triangle is exceptional. Perhaps the visual system fabricates an inconsistency simply because there is no way, given this figure, to fabricate anything else. If so, we might excuse the visual system on grounds that it must, by nature, fabricate and that no consistent fabrication could be had. This explanation is attractive because it would avoid accusing vision of gratuitous inconsistency, and would confine all inconsistencies to such rarities as psychology labs and exhibitions of Escher.

An admirable try, but it won't work. There are, as it happens, many (infinitely many!) different objects one can build with lumber and nails that, if photographed from the proper angle, give the same image as the devil's triangle. The psychologist Richard Gregory has taken the time to build one. His construction looks something like this:

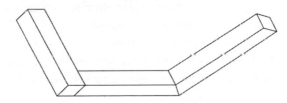

If you construct this with wood and view it from just the right angle, you can see the devil's triangle. Of course, what you construct with wood is not the devil's triangle itself, since that is impossible. Instead what you construct with wood is another object which, when viewed from the appropriate angle, leads you to see the devil's triangle.

So we can't excuse the visual system on grounds it had no consistent options; it had them, all right, and either ignored or discarded them. But, as we shall find, there is no need to excuse the visual system at all. Its fabrication of the devil's triangle is governed by elegant principles, and knowing these principles we can predict when its fabrications will be consistent or inconsistent.

And this, we shall find, is typical of your visual intelligence. Its nature is to construct, and to do so according to principles. Without exception, everything you see you construct: color, shading, texture, motion, shape, visual objects, and entire visual scenes. The three examples we just considered—the ripple, the magic square, and the devil's triangle—are simple demonstrations of your visual intelligence and its genius to construct.

But wait. If you construct all you see, then since you see this book, you construct it as well. And if that's so, then why should you buy it and why should I get royalties? What right have I to copyright your construction?

This question has more than passing interest to me as an author, and I shall have to raise a distinction to rescue my royalties. We use the phrase "what you see" in at least two ways. Sometimes we use it to mean "the way things look to you," "the way they visually appear to you," "the way you visually experience them."

Philosophers call this the *phenomenal* sense. Someone with delirium tremens may see, in the phenomenal sense, a pink elephant in the room, even though the rest of us do not. Someone normal may see, in the phenomenal sense, the devil's triangle, even though what is seen can't be built with wood. You see the depth and parts of the "ripple" in the phenomenal sense. You also see the edges and brightness of the magic square in the phenomenal sense. Photometers can't discern what you see in this sense of "see," and so they can't discern the magic square.

We also use the phrase "what you see" to mean roughly "what you interact with when you look." This is the *relational* sense. Someone with delirium tremens can, simultaneously, see a pink elephant in the phenomenal sense and fail to see a pink elephant in the relational sense—if there is in fact no pink elephant. A thing must exist to be seen in the relational sense. Suppose you are the only thing that exists (a strange idea called *solipsism*). Then you could never see anything else in the relational sense, since there would be nothing else to interact with. You might still, of course, continue to see in the phenomenal sense, since you might continue to have visual experiences.

So when I say that your visual intelligence constructs what you see, I mean "see" in the phenomenal sense: you construct your visual experience. When you look at this book, everything you see, i.e., everything you visually experience, is your construction: the thickness of the spine, the white color and rectangular shape of the pages, the black color and curved shapes of the letters—no less than the ripple, the magic square, and the devil's triangle.

But when you see this book there is also, I hope you will agree, something that you see relationally, something with which you interact. If so, that thing is something I helped to create (by typing at a computer terminal), and therefore I get to keep my royalty. Philosophical distinctions can indeed be of practical value!

This distinction, however, might cost you more than money, it might cost you worry. Just what are these things that we interact with when we see, and how do they relate to our visual experiences? Interesting issues lurk here, but we shall have to postpone them until later. But here, in brief, is a metaphor I find useful. The relation between what you see phenomenally and what you see relationally is like the relation between icons and software on a computer. When you use, say, that neat paint program or word processor on your PC, you interact with megabytes of software of such complexity that its creation took talented programmers many months of concerted effort. Fortunately for you, they made their software "user-friendly" so you don't need to know its grisly innards. They gave you colorful icons and clever graphical tools that make it easy to get your work done. As a result, you can be an expert user of that paint program without knowing how to write a program—indeed, without even knowing about or believing in programs. But every time you click an icon or drag a paintbrush you in fact interact with a complex unseen world of software (and hardware). The relation between icons and software is systematic but arbitrary; those icons could take many different forms and colors, as they often do from one paint program to the next, and still have the same function. Similarly, our visual experiences serve as our user-friendly icon interface with those things we relationally see (whatever they are). Experienced chairs, books, cars, trees, and stars are all icons of this interface.

We'll explore this "icon metaphor" in more detail later. For now, however, and for most of the book, we'll explore the genius of your visual intelligence to construct visual experiences—that is, to construct your icon interface.

"The only difference between genius and stupidity," said an unknown wag, "is that genius is limited." This is precisely the finding of cognitive science. You are a genius at a few things, like vision and language, whether or not you have a high IQ. One must be severely retarded (or have a special handicap) before failing to see or talk. Your genius at vision, like your genius at language, is innate, safely wired into your brain under the influence of your genes. (However, the brain itself, with its neurons, is part of the icon interface. It is the icon we see when we peek inside skulls.)

But vision, unlike language, is a genius we share with many other animals. Of course, vision varies widely from species to species, and in many respects it's a mistake to think that vision in other species resembles vision in humans. To underline this point, the biologist Adrian Horridge prefers to call the vision of insects *semivision*. But the vision, or semivision, of other species is impressive in its own right. Goldfish have color vision—in fact they have four color receptors, compared to our three—and "color constancy": they can continue to find, say, green objects despite changes in color of the ambient light in their tank. Honeybees have color constancy and can see the magic square. They can also navigate using the sun as a compass, even if it's hidden behind a cloud: they find it via the polarization of ultraviolet light from blue patches of sky. The fly uses visual motion to compute, in real time, how and when to land on a surface and how to alter its trajectory to intercept another fly. Day-old chicks discriminate spheres from pyramids, and peck preferentially at the spheres (most seeds are shaped like spheres, not pyramids). The praying mantis uses binocular vision to locate a fly in space and then, when the fly is at just the right distance, flicks out a foreleg to catch the fly in its tarsal-tibial joint. The mantis shrimp has ten color receptors, can find the range to a prey with just a single eye, and accurately stuns its prey with a quick strike of its raptorial appendage. Macaque monkeys see "structure from motion": with just one eye open they can construct the three-dimensional (3D) shape of a moving object. And the story that holds for our visual genius holds, in every case, for theirs as well: vision is construction.

Of course some visual constructions display less genius than others. For newly hatched goslings, whose first priority is to find Mom and safety, the first big moving object they see becomes "Mom." When Konrad Lorenz arranged to be that first big moving object, he instantly became "Mom" to several goslings, who faithfully followed him thereafter and, in adolescence, found him attractive as a possible mate.

The ethologist Niko Tinbergen found that for blackbird nestlings, "Mom" (or "parent") can be as simple as two adjacent disks, one having a diameter about a third that of the other. The absolute size of the disks matters little, but if the ratio of their diameters deviates much from one third, or if there are extra disks around, then they are not "Mom":

"Mom"

Not "Mom"

Not "Mom"

Hungry blackbird nestlings will gape to a cardboard copy of "Mom," but not to copies of the other two figures.

Tinbergen also found that for chickens and ducks, a harmless "goose" can be a cross moving in the direction of its long end, and a feared "hawk" can be a cross moving in the direction of its short end:

"Goose"   "Hawk"

A cardboard "hawk" flown overhead by mischievous ethologists sends chickens running for cover. A cardboard "goose" is ignored.

Jörg-Peter Ewert found that for the common toad *Bofu bofu*, a "prey" can be a stripe moving in the direction of its longer axis, and a "predator" can be a stripe moving along its shorter axis:

"Prey"   "Predator"

A cardboard "prey" moved around by other mischievous ethologists triggers the toad to orient, approach, fixate, snap, gulp, and wipe—only to find that cardboard just can't satisfy like a juicy slug or a crunchy beetle. Gary Larson catches the humor of all this in a cartoon showing a frog stuck to the bottom of a jumbo jet by its outstretched tongue.

What's so funny in each case is how easily the animal is duped. Simple figures trigger fantastic visual constructions. But as we laugh at these foibles we laugh at ourselves, for we too cannot help but create visual fantasies, as shown by the ripple, magic square, and devil's triangle. Perhaps we aren't taken in by our creations as badly as is the gosling. Yet, despite our better judgment, a simple figure triggers us to construct a ripple, just as a large moving object triggers a gosling to construct "Mom." In this respect there is no difference in principle between us and goslings. There is a difference in practice: we're not duped by some visual figures that dupe goslings. But then it's likely that they aren't duped by some figures that trigger visual fantasies in us.

So we share with all sighted animals a genius to construct and, in consequence, a chance to err. This raises questions. When should we trust what we see? If the ripple and magic square are false constructs, what further falsehoods might we see? And if our "genius" to construct can mislead, then why not dispense with it and just see the world as it is?

The sobering fact is that we cannot dispense with construction. To construct is the essence of vision. Dispense with construction and you dispense with vision. Everything you experience by sight is your construction.

From *Sensory Exotica: A World beyond Human Experience*

Howard C. Hughes

When we consider sensory perception, we naturally focus on the five "special" senses: vision, hearing, touch, taste, and smell. It is through these senses that we experience the world outside our bodies. There is also the world inside our bodies, and there are sensory organs that provide information crucial to internal body states. Our senses of balance, of body motion, and of posture, depend on sensory organs in the inner ear, in our joints, and in muscles. There are even organs that monitor such things as the levels of carbon dioxide in the blood, blood pressure, and blood glucose levels. These organs provide the brain with information essential to life, but they do not produce conscious sensory experiences (otherwise, people would be aware of the onset of hypertension, and it would less frequently go untreated).

Rather than ESP, perhaps we should call these internal sensory systems our sixth sense—a sense beyond the more familiar modalities of vision, hearing, touch, taste, and smell. If so, then this book is about the seventh, eighth, ninth and tenth senses. What are these new sensory modalities? Well, first of all, they are not new. Their possessors have been relying on them for millions of years. It's just that we've "discovered" them only since the 1970s and 1980s. But newness aside, they include such hi-tech systems as biological sonar systems, sophisticated navigational systems, and senses based on electrical fields.

These systems initially seemed so unlikely, so incredible, that many were reluctant to believe they existed. But they do. And in just a couple of decades we have learned a great deal about the detailed working of these remarkable sensory systems. In some respects, the mechanisms are not very different from the more familiar mechanisms of vision, hearing, or touch. In other ways, the differences are quite dramatic. They have one thing in common, however: they all provide vivid illustrations of the creative genius inherent in the process of evolution.

When we speak of sensory experiences beyond the realm of our five special senses, many may think of supernatural things like extrasensory perception: clairvoyance (the ability to see that which is not visible) or telepathy (the ability to sense the "thought waves" of others). Some have suggested that there may be a resurgence of mysticism in modern society, which is curious because there is not a single case of extrasensory perception that has withstood the tests of rational analysis and rigorous experimental control. But, as we shall soon see, the workings of biosonar, electroreception, and other exotic senses are far more interesting than bending spoons and reading unseen numbers on a stranger's driver's license.

Imagine a sonar system more sophisticated than that found in our most advanced submarines. Now imagine that system is used by a small bat that easily fits in the palm of your hand. All the computations that permit the bat to identify the distance, the speed, and even the particular species of insect target are performed by a brain that is smaller than your thumbnail! That is a truly remarkable device. But it is a device. It can be understood in mechanistic terms. Despite all the folklore associated with bats, no appeal to forces beyond natural laws is necessary. And that is what is truly remarkable about these most interesting creatures.

Each of our senses is a wondrous system of information processing. The events that culminate in perception begin with specialized receptor cells that convert a particular form of physical energy into bioelectric currents. Different receptors are sensitive to different types of energy, so the properties of the receptor cells determine the modality of a sensory system. Ionic currents are the currency of neural information processing, and current flows that begin in the receptors are transmitted through complex networks of interconnected neurons and, in the end, result in a pattern of brain activity we call perception. We can distinguish a red 1957 Chevy from a blue 1956 Ford because each car produces a different pattern of neural activity.

The percepts that result from all this brain activity usually provide us with an astonishingly accurate window through which we view the outside world. If that were not so, we couldn't hit a curve ball, or teach kids how to catch one (you've probably noticed they invariably need instruction). In short, our interactions with the world would not be possible. We interact with our environments so effectively and so effortlessly, it is difficult to appreciate the extensive computations that underlie even the simplest sensory experience. We become convinced that we see "what is really out there." But there are some refractive errors in our sensory windows to the world, some distortions. And our perceptual windows are not as transparent as we think.

For instance, our sense of vision depends upon wavelengths of light that range from about 430 to 700 billionths of a meter. But the entire electromagnetic spectrum covers a range that is approximately 300,000,000, 000,000,000,000,000,000,000,000,000 times larger than what we call the visible spectrum! Clearly, there is a (very large) portion of the electromagnetic spectrum that we cannot detect. That doesn't mean the energy isn't there, and it doesn't mean that other creatures cannot detect portions of it that to us are not visible. Our visual receptor cells are sensitive to an incredibly small range of wavelengths. Other animals are endowed with different types of receptors that render them sensitive to portions of the spectrum that we cannot see. Those wavelengths that are a little shorter than what we call blue light are called ultraviolet wavelengths, or UV light. We can't see UV light, but some insects can, and they use their UV sensitivity as an aid to navigation. In contrast, wavelengths that are a little longer than what we call red light are called the infrared wavelengths. Infrared (IR) radiation is emitted by warm objects. Have you seen the special night goggles that allow people to see in the dark? They work because they have detectors that are sensitive to the infrared part of the spectrum. Any object that is warmer than its surroundings will produce an IR "signature," and the goggles convert those infrared emissions to wavelengths of light that we are able to detect.

Certain snakes evolved their own form of IR night goggles: little pits that act like pinhole cameras for infrared radiation. Snakes use their infrared system to detect and localize their warm-blooded prey. The system was discovered when it was recognized that an agitated rattlesnake will produce accurate strikes at a warm soldering iron, even if its eyes are covered. All members of the family of venomous snakes known as pit vipers have these infrared detectors—it is the infrared-sensitive pits that give them their name. As far as we know, only two types of snakes have this infrared sensitivity—the pit vipers and some boid snakes (constrictors like the boa constrictor). It would probably be of no use to warm-blooded creatures. Their own body heat would produce so much noise in the system that detection of other objects would not be possible. For this system to work, the animal has to be a cold-

blooded hunter . . . as cold as the desert night. Rattlesnakes have been tracking their prey by the heat trail they leave behind for millions of years.

Analogous differences in the range of hearing exist for different animals. Dog whistles are one familiar example: we can't hear the whistle, but
dogs can. The reason is that they are sensitive to a higher range of sound frequencies than humans are. Yet the auditory abilities of dogs pales in comparison with that of bats or dolphins. Some bats can actually hear the foot-
steps of their insect prey!

Although dogs can hear higher auditory frequencies than humans,
they are most notable for their sense of smell. *U.S. News & World Report* recently had a story of a dog that apparently can detect the onset of its owner's
epileptic seizures—45 minutes before they occur! The pet's early warnings
allow the victim to prepare for the impending attack, for instance, by avoiding hazardous activities like driving. Family members say the accuracy rate is
as high as 97 percent. Clairvoyance? A case of canine precognition? Probably
not. It is much more likely that the dog can detect certain chemicals that may
be associated with the onset of an epileptic seizure.

Descriptive accounts of these remarkable feats of sensory perception
may be entertaining, but they are just the beginning of the story we wish to
tell. Our ultimate goal is and ought to be an understanding of the mechanisms that underlie these abilities. What anatomical and physiological principles permit the astonishing levels of sensitivity displayed by these sensory
receptors? How do these systems avoid the many sources of noise that would
otherwise degrade perceptual performance? How do the animals' brains
process the receptor responses, and how are these exotic modalities integrated with inputs from more conventional sensory systems? What conditions lead to the evolution of such systems, and what advantages are gained
by having them? These are the questions we hope to address in the following pages.

In every case, the initial evidence for a new sensory modality came
from behavioral experiments: from observations of what the animals actually *do*. The animal's behavior suggested they must possess some way of sensing environmental events that is different from our own. As early as the 18th
century, the bat's ability to avoid obstacles in complete darkness was a subject of scientific investigation, although the fact that they do this by using
echoes of calls they produce was not understood until the 1940s. Soon
thereafter, a similar system was discovered in dolphins. The auditory modal-

ity of these animals thus has two operating modes: a passive mode by which they detect externally produced sounds, and the active, biosonar mode that relies on reflections of self-produced sonar signals.

The sensory modality of electroreception also operates in an active mode and a passive mode: some fish passively sense electrical fields produced by potential prey, while others detect prey by analyzing the disturbances in an "electric halo" that they themselves produce. We hope to do more than produce a compendium of interesting facts that modern science has discovered about a variety of odd and curious creatures, however. These exotic senses illustrate alternative ways of experiencing our planet— ways that, without science and technology, would have forever remained invisible to us.

QUESTIONS

1. A famous essay by the philosopher Thomas Nagel asks, "What is it like to be a bat?" Can studies of echolocation and the like ever truly answer such a question? Why or why not?

2. Hoffman talks about vision by construction. Would the same hold true for other senses? Would it make sense, for example, to talk about hearing by construction?

CHAPTER SIX

LANGUAGE

Human beings are unique in many ways: we have unmatched capacities for acquiring culture (see Chapter 15), bizarre habits like wearing clothes and going to movies that are of no interest to any other species, not to mention an unprecedented level of control over our own environments. But perhaps nothing is more remarkable than our gift for language. No other system of animal communication approaches human language in its complexity, sophistication, or power. While most animals are limited to communicating about concrete things like immediate threats or their own current whereabouts, we human beings can converse about a virtually limitless range of topics, not just the here and now but the past, the future, our hopes, our dreams, our favorite television shows. From the sublime to the ridiculous, the human capacity for communication is unequaled.

In the first selection in this chapter, from *The Language Instinct* (1994), Steven Pinker makes the case that the human capacity for acquiring language is an instinct, built-in and automatic, as much a part of being human as web-spinning is part of being a garden spider. Drawing on evidence ranging from Hawaiian creoles to the language of the deaf, Pinker makes a convincing case that our linguistic capacity is not just universal—it is innate.

In the second selection, from *TheAtoms of Language* (2001), linguist Mark Baker explains a curious fact that motivates virtually all contemporary linguistic research: despite the many differences between the diverse languages of the world, even the most distantly related languages share a wide variety of subtle properties; in the words of the pioneering linguist Noam Chomsky, all languages are governed by a common "Universal Grammar." It is this surprising fact that makes the study of language so fascinating.

From *The Language Instinct:*
How the Mind Creates Language

Steven Pinker

The ubiquity of complex language among human beings is a gripping discovery and, for many observers, compelling proof that language is innate. But to tough-minded skeptics like the philosopher Hilary Putnam, it is no proof at all. Not everything that is universal is innate. Just as travelers in previous decades never encountered a tribe without a language, nowadays anthropologists have trouble finding a people beyond the reach of VCR's, Coca-Cola, and Bart Simpson T-shirts. Language was universal before Coca-Cola was, but then, language is more useful than Coca-Cola. It is more like eating with one's hands rather than one's feet, which is also universal, but we need not invoke a special hand-to-mouth instinct to explain why. Language is invaluable for all the activities of daily living in a community of people: preparing food and shelter, loving, arguing, negotiating, teaching. Necessity being the mother of invention, language could have been invented by resourceful people a number of times long ago. (Perhaps, as Lily Tomlin said, man invented language to satisfy his deep need to complain.) Universal grammar would simply reflect the universal exigencies of human experience and the universal limitations on human information processing. All languages have words for "water" and "foot" because all people need to refer to water and feet; no language has a word a million syllables long because no person would have time to say it. Once invented, language would entrench itself within a culture as parents taught their children and children imitated their parents. From cultures that had language, it would spread like wildfire to other, quieter cultures. At the heart of this process is wondrously flexible human intelligence, with its general multipurpose learning strategies.

So the universality of language does not lead to an innate language instinct as night follows day. To convince you that there is a language instinct, I will have to fill in an argument that leads from the jabbering of modern peoples to the putative genes for grammar. The crucial intervening steps come from my own professional specialty, the study of language development in children. The crux of the argument is that complex language is universal because *children actually reinvent it,* generation after generation—not because they are taught, not because they are generally smart, not because it is useful to them, but because they just can't help it. Let me now take you down this trail of evidence.

The trail begins with the study of how the particular languages we find in the world today arose. Here, one would think, linguistics runs into the problem of any historical science: no one recorded the crucial events at the time they happened. Although historical linguists can trace modern complex languages back to earlier ones, this just pushes the problem back a step; we need to see how people create a complex language from scratch. Amazingly, we can.

The first cases were wrung from two of the more sorrowful episodes of world history, the Atlantic slave trade and indentured servitude in the South Pacific. Perhaps mindful of the Tower of Babel, some of the masters of tobacco, cotton, coffee, and sugar plantations deliberately mixed slaves and laborers from different language backgrounds; others preferred specific ethnicities but had to accept mixtures because that was all that was available. When speakers of different languages have to communicate to carry out practical tasks but do not have the opportunity to learn one another's languages, they develop a makeshift jargon called a pidgin. Pidgins are choppy strings of words borrowed from the language of the colonizers or plantation owners, highly variable in order and with little in the way of grammar. Sometimes a pidgin can become a lingua franca and gradually increase in complexity over decades, as in the "Pidgin English" of the modern South Pacific. (Prince Philip was delighted to learn on a visit to New Guinea that he is referred to in that language as *fella belong Mrs. Queen.*)

But the linguist Derek Bickerton has presented evidence that in many cases a pidgin can be transmuted into a full complex language in one fell swoop: all it takes is for a group of children to be exposed to the pidgin at the age when they acquire their mother tongue. That happened, Bickerton has argued, when children were isolated from their parents and were tended collectively by a worker who spoke to them in the pidgin. Not content to reproduce the fragmentary word strings, the children injected grammatical complexity where none existed before, resulting in a brand-new, richly expressive language. The language that results when children make a pidgin their native tongue is called a creole.

Bickerton's main evidence comes from a unique historical circumstance. Though the slave plantations that spawned most creoles are, fortunately, a thing of the remote past, one episode of creolization occurred recently enough for us to study its principal players. Just before the turn of the century there was a boom in Hawaiian sugar plantations, whose demands for labor quickly outstripped the native pool. Workers were brought in from China, Japan, Korea, Portugal, the Philippines, and Puerto Rico, and a pidgin quickly developed. Many of the immigrant laborers who first developed that pidgin were alive when Bickerton interviewed them in the 1970s. Here are some typical examples of their speech:

Me capé buy, me check make.

Building—high place—wall pat—time—nowtime—an' den—a new tempecha eri time show you.

Good, dis one. Kaukau any-kin' dis one. Pilipine islan' no good. No mo money.

From the individual words and the context, it was possible for the listener to infer that the first speaker, a ninety-two-year-old Japanese immigrant talking about his earlier days as a coffee farmer, was trying to say "He bought my coffee; he made me out a check." But the utterance itself could just as easily have meant "I bought coffee; I made him out a check," which would have been appropriate if he had been referring to his current situation as a store owner. The second speaker, another elderly Japanese immigrant, had been introduced to the wonders of civilization in Los Angeles by one of his many children, and was saying that there was an electric sign high up on the wall of the building which displayed the time and temperature. The third speaker, a sixty-nine-year-old Filipino, was saying "It's better here than in the Philippines; here you can get all kinds of food, but over there there isn't any money to buy food with." (One of the kinds of food was "pfrawg," which he caught for himself in the marshes by the method of "kank da head.") In all these cases, the speaker's intentions had to be filled in by the listener. The pidgin did not offer the speakers the ordinary grammatical resources to convey these messages—no consistent word order, no prefixes or suffixes, no tense or other temporal and logical markers, no structure more complex than a simple clause, and no consistent way to indicate who did what to whom.

But the children who had grown up in Hawaii beginning in the 1890s and were exposed to the pidgin ended up speaking quite differently. Here are some sentences from the language they invented, Hawaiian Creole. The first two are from a Japanese papaya grower born in Maui; the next two, from a Japanese/Hawaiian ex-plantation laborer born on the Big Island; the last, from a Hawaiian motel manager, formerly a farmer, born in Kauai:

> *Da firs japani came ran away from japan come,*
> "The first Japanese who arrived ran away from Japan to here."

> *Some filipino wok o'he-ah dey wen' couple ye-ahs in filipin islan'.*
> "Some Filipinos who worked over here went back to the Philippines for a couple of years."

> *People no like t'come fo' go wok.*
> "People don't want to have him go to work [for them]."

> *One time when we go home inna night dis ting stay fly up.*
> "Once when we went home at night this thing was flying about."

> *One day had pleny of dis mountain fish come down.*
> "One day there were a lot of these fish from the mountains that came down [the river]."

Do not be misled by what look like crudely placed English verbs, such as *go*, *stay*, and *came*, or phrases like *one time*. They are not haphazard uses of English words but systematic uses of Hawaiian Creole grammar: the words have been converted by the creole speakers into auxiliaries, prepositions, case markers, and relative pronouns. In fact, this is probably how many of the grammatical prefixes and suffixes in established languages arose. For example, the English past-tense ending *-ed* may have evolved from the verb *do*: *He hammered* was originally something like *He hammer-did*. Indeed, creoles *are* bona fide languages, with standardized word orders and grammatical markers that were lacking in the pidgin of the immigrants and, aside from the sounds of words, not taken from the language of the colonizers.

Bickerton notes that if the grammar of a creole is largely the product of the minds of children, unadulterated by complex language input from their parents, it should provide a particularly clear window on the innate grammatical machinery of the brain. He argues that creoles from unrelated language mixtures exhibit uncanny resemblances—perhaps even the same basic grammar. This basic grammar also shows up, he suggests, in the errors children make when acquiring more established and embellished languages, like some underlying design bleeding through a veneer of whitewash. When English-speaking children say

> Why he is leaving?
>
> Nobody don't likes me.
>
> I'm gonna full Angela's bucket.
>
> Let Daddy hold it hit it,

they are unwittingly producing sentences that are grammatical in many of the world's creoles.

Bickerton's particular claims are controversial, depending as they do on his reconstruction of events that occurred decades or centuries in the past. But his basic idea has been stunningly corroborated by two recent natural experiments in which creolization by children can be observed in real time. These fascinating discoveries are among many that have come from the study of the sign languages of the deaf. Contrary to popular misconceptions, sign languages are not pantomimes and gestures, inventions of educators, or ciphers of the spoken language of the surrounding community. They are found wherever there is a community of deaf people, and each one is a distinct, full language, using the same kinds of grammatical machinery found worldwide in spoken languages. For example, American Sign Language, used by the deaf community in the United States, does not resemble English, or British Sign Language, but relies on agreement and gender systems in a way that is reminiscent of Navajo and Bantu.

Until recently there were no sign languages at all in Nicaragua, because its deaf people remained isolated from one another. When the Sandinista government took over in 1979 and reformed the educational system, the first schools for the deaf were created. The schools focused on drilling the children in lip reading and speech, and as in every case where that is tried, the results were dismal. But it did not matter. On the playgrounds and schoolbuses the children were inventing their own sign system, pooling the makeshift gestures that they used with their families at home. Before long the system congealed into what is now called the Lenguaje de Signos Nicaragüense (LSN). Today LSN is used, with varying degrees of fluency, by young deaf adults, aged seventeen to twenty-five, who developed it when they were ten or older.

Basically, it is a pidgin. Everyone uses it differently, and the signers depend on suggestive, elaborate circumlocutions rather than on a consistent grammar.

But children like Mayela, who joined the school around the age of four, when LSN was already around, and all the pupils younger than her, are quite different. Their signing is more fluid and compact, and the gestures are more stylized and less like a pantomime. In fact, when their signing is examined close up, it is so different from LSN that it is referred to by a different name, Idioma de Signos Nicaragüense (ISN). LSN and ISN are currently being studied by the psycholinguists Judy Kegl, Miriam Hebe Lopez, and Annie Senghas. ISN appears to be a creole, created in one leap when the younger children were exposed to the pidgin signing of the older children—just as Bickerton would have predicted. ISN has spontaneously standardized itself; all the young children sign it in the same way. The children have introduced many grammatical devices that were absent in LSN, and hence they rely far less on circumlocutions. For example, an LSN (pidgin) signer might make the sign for "talk to" and then point from the position of the talker to the position of the hearer. But an ISN (creole) signer modifies the sign itself, sweeping it in one motion from a point representing the talker to a point representing the hearer. This is a common device in sign languages, formally identical to inflecting a verb for agreement in spoken languages. Thanks to such consistent grammar, ISN is very expressive. A child can watch a surrealistic cartoon and describe its plot to another child. The children use it in jokes, poems, narratives, and life histories, and it is coming to serve as the glue that holds the community together. A language has been born before our eyes.

But ISN was the collective product of many children communicating with one another. If we are to attribute the richness of language to the mind of the child, we really want to see a single child adding some increment of grammatical complexity to the input the child has received. Once again the study of the deaf grants our wish.

When deaf infants are raised by signing parents, they learn sign language in the same way that hearing infants learn spoken language. But deaf children who are not born to deaf parents—the majority of deaf children—often have no access to sign language users as they grow up, and indeed are sometimes deliberately kept from them by educators in the "oralist" tradition who want to force them to master lip reading and speech. (Most deaf people deplore these authoritarian measures.) When deaf children become adults, they tend to seek out deaf communities and begin to acquire the sign language that takes proper advantage of the communicative media available to them. But by then it is usually too late; they must then struggle with sign language as a difficult intellectual puzzle, much as a hearing adult does in foreign language classes. Their proficiency is notably below that of deaf people who acquired sign language as infants, just as adult immigrants are often permanently burdened with accents and conspicuous grammatical errors. Indeed, because the deaf are virtually the only neurologically normal people who make it to adulthood without having acquired a language, their difficulties offer particularly good evidence that successful language acquisition must take place during a critical window of opportunity in childhood.

The psycholinguists Jenny Singleton and Elissa Newport have studied a nine-year-old profoundly deaf boy, to whom they gave the pseudonym Simon, and his parents, who are also deaf. Simon's parents did not acquire sign language until the late ages of fifteen and sixteen, and as a result they acquired it badly. In ASL, as in many languages, one can move a phrase to the front of a sentence and mark it with a prefix or suffix (in ASL, raised eyebrows and a lifted chin) to indicate that it is the topic of the sentence. The English sentence *Elvis I really like* is a rough equivalent. But Simon's parents rarely used this construction and mangled it when they did. For example, Simon's father once tried to sign the thought *My friend, he thought my second child was deaf.* It came out as *My friend thought, my second child, he thought he was deaf*—a bit of sign salad that violates not only ASL grammar but, according to Chomsky's theory, the Universal Grammar that governs all naturally acquired human languages (later in this chapter we will see why). Simon's parents had also failed to grasp the verb inflection system of ASL. In ASL, the verb *to blow* is signed by opening a fist held horizontally in front of the mouth (like a puff of air). Any verb in ASL can be modified to indicate that the action is being done continuously: the signer superimposes an arclike motion on the sign and repeats it quickly. A verb can also be modified to indicate that the action is being done to more than one object (for example, several candles): the signer terminates the sign in one location in space, then repeats it but terminates it at another location. These inflections can be combined in either of two orders: *blow* toward the left and then toward the right and repeat, or *blow* toward the left twice and then *blow* toward the right twice. The first order means "to blow out the candles on one cake, then another cake, then the first cake again, then the second cake again"; the second means "to blow out the candles on one cake continuously, and then blow out the candles on another cake continuously." This elegant set of rules was lost on Simon's parents. They used the inflections inconsistently and never combined them onto a verb two at a time, though they would occasionally use the inflections separately, crudely linked with signs like *then*. In many ways Simon's parents were like pidgin speakers.

Astoundingly, though Simon saw no ASL but his parents' defective version, his own signing was far better ASL than theirs. He understood sentences with moved topic phrases without difficulty, and when he had to describe complex videotaped events, he used the ASL verb inflections almost perfectly, even in sentences requiring two of them in particular orders. Simon must somehow have shut out his parents' ungrammatical "noise." He must have latched on to the inflections that his parents used inconsistently, and reinterpreted them as mandatory. And he must have seen the logic that was implicit, though never realized, in his parents' use of two kinds of verb inflection, and reinvented the ASL system of superimposing both of them onto a single verb in a specific order. Simon's superiority to his parents is an example of creolization by a single living child.

Actually, Simon's achievements are remarkable only because he is the first one who showed them to a psycholinguist. There must be thousands of Simons: ninety to ninety-five percent of deaf children are born to hearing parents. Children fortunate enough to be exposed to ASL at all often get it from hearing parents who themselves learned it, incompletely, to communicate with their children. Indeed, as the transition from LSN to ISN shows, sign languages themselves are surely products of creolization. Educators at various points in history have tried to invent sign systems, sometimes based on the surrounding spoken language. But these crude codes are always unlearnable, and when deaf children learn from them at all, they do so by converting them into much richer natural languages.

Extraordinary acts of creation by children do not require the extraordinary circumstances of deafness or plantation Babels. The same kind of linguistic genius is involved every time a child learns his or her mother tongue.

First, let us do away with the folklore that parents teach their children language. No one supposes that parents provide explicit grammar lessons, of course, but many parents (and some child psychologists who should know better) think that mothers provide children with implicit lessons. These lessons take the form of a special speech variety called Motherese (or, as the French call it, Mamanaise): Intensive sessions of conversational give-and-take, with repetitive drills and simplified grammar. ("Look at the *doggie!* See the *doggie?* There's a *doggie!*") In contemporary middle-class American culture, parenting is seen as an awesome responsibility, an unforgiving vigil to keep the helpless infant from falling behind in the great race of life. The belief that Motherese is essential to language development is part of the same mentality that sends yuppies to "learning centers" to buy little mittens with bull's-eyes to help their babies find their hands sooner.

One gets some perspective by examining the folk theories about parenting in other cultures. The !Kung San of the Kalahari Desert in southern Africa believe that children must be drilled to sit, stand, and walk. They carefully pile sand around their infants to prop them upright, and sure enough, every one of these infants soon sits up on its own. We find this amusing because we have observed the results of the experiment that the San are unwilling to chance: we don't teach our children to sit, stand, and walk, and they do it anyway, on their own schedule. But other groups enjoy the same condescension toward us. In many communities of the world, parents do not indulge their children in Motherese. In fact, they do not speak to their prelinguistic children at all, except for occasional demands and rebukes. This is not unreasonable. After all, young children plainly can't understand a word you say. So why waste your breath in soliloquies? Any sensible person would surely wait until a child has developed speech and more gratifying two-way conversations become possible. As Aunt Mae, a woman living in the South Carolina Piedmont, explained to the anthropologist Shirley Brice Heath: "Now just how crazy is dat? White folks uh hear dey kids say sump'n, dey say it back to 'em, dey aks 'em 'gain and 'gain 'bout things, like they 'posed to be born knowin'." Needless to say, the children in these communities, overhearing adults and other children, learn to talk, as we see in Aunt Mae's fully grammatical BEV.

Children deserve most of the credit for the language they acquire. In fact, we can show that they know things they could not have been taught. One of Chomsky's classic illustrations of the logic of language involves the process of moving words around to form questions. Consider how you might turn the declarative sentence *A unicorn is in the garden* into the corresponding question, *Is a unicorn in the garden?* You could scan the declarative sentence, take the auxiliary *is*, and move it to the front of the sentence:

a unicorn is in the garden. →

is a unicorn   in the garden?

Now take the sentence *A unicorn that is eating a flower is in the garden.* There are two *is*'s. Which gets moved? Obviously, not the first one hit by the scan; that would give you a very odd sentence:

a unicorn that is eating a flower is in the garden. →

is a unicorn that   eating a flower is in the garden?

But why can't you move that *is*? Where did the simple procedure go wrong? The answer, Chomsky noted, comes from the basic design of language. Though sentences are strings of words, our mental algorithms for grammar do not pick out words by their linear positions, such as "first word," "second word," and so on. Rather, the algorithms group words into phrases, and phrases into even bigger phrases, and give each one a mental label, like "subject noun phrase" or "verb phrase." The real rule for forming questions does not look for the first occurrence of the auxiliary word as one goes from left to right in the string; it looks for the auxiliary that comes after the phrase labeled as the subject. This phrase, containing the entire string of words *a unicorn that is eating a flower*, behaves as a single unit. The first *is* sits deeply buried in it, invisible to the question-forming rule. The second *is*, coming immediately after this subject noun phrase, is the one that is moved:

[a unicorn that is eating a flower] is in the garden. →

is [a unicorn that is eating a flower]   in the garden?

Chomsky reasoned that if the logic of language is wired into children, then the first time they are confronted with a sentence with two auxiliaries they should be capable of turning it into a question with the proper wording. This should be true even though the wrong rule, the one that scans the sentence as a linear string of words, is simpler and presumably easier to learn. And it should be true even though the sentences that would teach children that the linear rule is wrong and the structure-sensitive rule is right—

questions with a second auxiliary embedded inside the subject phrase—are so rare as to be nonexistent in Motherese. Surely not every child learning English has heard Mother say *Is the doggie that is eating the flower in the garden?* For Chomsky, this kind of reasoning, which he calls "the argument from the poverty of the input," is the primary justification for saying that the basic design of language is innate.

Chomsky's claim was tested in an experiment with three-, four-, and five-year-olds at a daycare center by the psycholinguists Stephen Crain and Mineharu Nakayama. One of the experimenters controlled a doll of Jabba the Hutt, of *Star Wars* fame. The other coaxed the child to ask a set of questions, by saying, for example, "Ask Jabba if the boy who is unhappy is watching Mickey Mouse." Jabba would inspect a picture and answer yes or no, but it was really the child who was being tested, not Jabba. The children cheerfully provided the appropriate questions, and, as Chomsky would have predicted, not a single one of them came up with an ungrammatical string like *Is the boy who unhappy is watching Mickey Mouse?*, which the simple linear rule would have produced.

From *The Atoms of Language: The Mind's Hidden Rules of Grammar*

Mark C. Baker

Deep mysteries of language are illustrated by an incident that occurred in 1943, when the Japanese military was firmly entrenched around the Bismarck Archipelago. American pilots had nicknamed the harbor of Rabaul "Dead End" because so many of them were shot down by antiaircraft guns placed in the surrounding hills. It became apparent that the Japanese could easily decode Allied messages and thus were forewarned about the time and place of each attack.

The Marine Corps responded by calling in one of their most effective secret weapons: eleven Navajo Indians. These were members of the famous Code Talkers, whose native language was the one cipher the Japanese cryptographers were never able to break. The Navajos quickly provided secure communications, and the area was soon taken with minimal further losses. Such incidents were repeated throughout the Pacific theater in World War II. Years after the end of the war, a U.S. president commended the Navajo Code Talkers with the following words: "Their resourcefulness, tenacity, integrity and courage saved the lives of countless men and women and sped the realization of peace for war-torn lands." But it was not only their resourcefulness, tenacity, integrity, and courage that made possible their remarkable contribution: It was also their language.

This incident vividly illustrates the fundamental puzzle of linguistics. On the one hand, Navajo must be extremely different from English (and Japanese), or the men listening to the Code Talkers' transmissions would eventually have been able to figure out what they were saying. On the other hand, Navajo must be extremely similar to English (and Japanese), or the Code Talkers could not have transmitted with precision the messages formulated by their English-speaking commanders. Navajo was effective as a code because it had both of these properties. But this seems like a contradiction: How can two languages be simultaneously so similar and so different? This paradox has beset the comparative study of human languages for centuries. Linguists are beginning to understand how the paradox can be dissolved, making it possible for the first time to chart out precisely the ways in which human languages can differ from one another and the ways in which they are all the same.

What was it about Navajo that made it so difficult to decode? As far as I know, no one has investigated what strategies the cryptographers tried and precisely why those strategies failed. But if one knows a little bit about Navajo, it is not hard to guess some of the reasons. Much of the difficulty in coming to grips with an unfamiliar language is that there are many layers of difference. Each layer might be understandable enough in its own terms, but the differences magnify each other until the total effect is overwhelming.

First, of course, there is the fact that the Navajos (to adapt an old Steve Martin joke about French) have a different word for everything. When an English speaker would say *girl*, a Navajo speaker would say *at'ééd*; for English *boy*, a Navajo would use *ashkii*; for English *horse*, Navajo has *lii*, and so on. Moreover, the things that English has specific words for and the things that Navajo has specific words for do not always match perfectly. For example, English is unusually rich in words for various modes of thought and feeling. In English, we can believe, know, wonder, opine, suppose, assume, presume, surmise, consider, maintain, and reckon. We can be furious, irritated, incensed, indignant, irate, mad, wrathful, cross, upset, infuriated, or enraged. In many other languages, this domain of meaning is covered with only two words, 'to think' and 'to be angry.' Navajo, for its part, has at least ten different verbs for different kinds of carrying, which depend on the shape and physical properties of the thing being carried: *'Aah* means to carry a solid roundish object, such as a ball, a rock, or a bottle; *kaah* means to carry an open container with its contents, such as a pot of soup or a basket of fruit; *lé* means to carry a slender flexible object like a belt, a snake, or a rope; and so on. For this reason, finding the right words to use in a translation to or from Navajo involves much more than simply substituting one string of letters for another. The "Replace All" command on your word processor will never be able to do it properly.

Second, there are important differences in the sounds that make up words in Navajo. As you surely noticed, the Navajo words listed above contain some strange-looking symbols: *l*'s with bars through them, vowels with accents over them and hooks under them, apostrophes in the middle of words. This reflects that the Navajo language is built around a different set of basic sounds than English is. For example, the *l* stands for a sound that is rather like that of the English *l* but made "whispering," without vibration of the vocal cords. (The same sound is indicated by the double *ll* in Welsh words like *Lloyd.*) Hooks under the vowels indicate that these sounds are pronounced nasally, with air passing through the nose as well as the mouth. The Navajo word są̨ 'old age' is pronounced much like the French word *sans* 'without.' To complicate matters further, the specific qualities of these sounds adjust in complex ways to the sounds around them. For example, Navajo has a prefix *bi-* that attaches to nouns and means 'his' or 'hers.' Thus, *gah* means 'rabbit' and *bigah* means 'his/her rabbit.' When this prefix attaches to certain words that begin with *s*, that *s* changes to a *z* sound. Thus, *séí* means 'sand,' but *bizéí* means 'his/her sand.' In the same context, the whispered *l* sound undergoes a similar change to become plain *l*: *lii'* is 'horse,' and *bilii* is 'his/her horse.'

These differences in sound are significant because it is notoriously difficult for people to recognize sounds that do not exist in their own languages. Japanese speakers have a terrible time distinguishing English *l* versus *r*, whereas English speakers have trouble recognizing the four different *l* sounds in Hindi. When added together, the many sound differences give Navajo speech a very distinctive, almost unearthly quality that speakers of Eurasian languages find difficult to grasp or remember.

Words in Navajo also change their form depending on their context in various ways. One of the most remarkable aspects of Navajo is its system of prefixes. Indeed, simple, invariant words are rare in Navajo. We just saw that a prefix can attach to a noun to show that the noun is possessed. The prefix system for verbs is even more elaborate. There are between 100 and 200 different prefixes that attach to Navajo verb stems, depending on the exact analysis. Even the simplest verbs in Navajo must take at least three prefixes, five or six are common, and a verb can have up to ten or twelve at one time. The total number of forms a Navajo verb can take is staggering. Nor can the language learner afford simply to overlook these prefixes and hope for the best. The subject of the sentence, for example, is often hidden inside the prefixes. 'The girl is crying' in Navajo is a fairly normal-looking combination of the word for 'girl' and (one form of) the word for 'cry.'

At'ééd	yicha.
Girl	crying

But 'I am crying' is expressed by a verb standing alone. That I am crying, not you or they, is expressed by a prefix *sh-* found before the verb root but after other prefixes.

Yishcha.   (yi + sh + cha)
'I am crying.'

(This ability of some languages to express subjects as changes on the verb plays a major role [later in the book]) Other Navajo prefixes elaborate on the basic meaning of the verb root in intricate ways. For example, the simple root *dlaad*, meaning 'to tear,' combines with six different prefixes to make the following word, meaning 'I am again plowing.'

Ninááhwiishdlaad.   (ni + náá + ho + hi + sh + l + dlaad)
'I am again plowing.'

These aspects of Navajo pose a major challenge to that great institution of Western civilization, the dictionary. Since Navajo has so many prefixes, the primary lexical meaning is rarely carried in the first part of a word. Thus, the basic idea of listing words in alphabetical order is not so practical for this language. Looking up a word in Navajo requires first identifying the prefixes, undoing the sound changes that they cause, and deleting them. Only then can one find the basic root of the word and calculate the changes in meaning caused by the prefixes. Dictionaries of Navajo do exist, but successfully using one is a major intellectual achievement—the way you prove you have mastered Navajo, not the way you learn it.

Navajo also has complexities at the level of syntax, how its words are put together to make phrases and sentences. The simplest subject-verb combinations, like 'the girl is crying' shown above, look innocent enough: The subject noun phrase comes first, as in English, and the verb that expresses the predicate comes second. But differences appear in more complex sentences. For example, consider a transitive sentence, one that contains a direct object noun phrase as well as a subject. In Navajo the direct object always comes before the verb, not after it as in English:

Ashkii   at'ééd   yiyiiltsá.
Boy   girl   saw
'The boy saw the girl.'

*Ashkii   yiyiiltsá   at'ééd.

Boy   saw   girl

(Linguists put an asterisk in front of an example to show that the way of combining words is impossible in the language under discussion. I use this convention frequently.) Other phrases have a distinctive word order, too. Whereas in English one says 'change into your clothes,' the Navajo would say the equivalent of 'clothes into change.' Whereas in English one says 'John believes that he is lying,' in Navajo one would say the equivalent of 'John he lying-is believes.' In fact, there is a systematic pattern to these Navajo word orders [...]. But systematic or no, it is confusing to an English speaker.

If the Japanese cryptographers had got this far, they might have breathed a sigh of relief at this point, because these word order patterns are actually the same as in Japanese. But their newfound confidence would have evaporated when they came across sentences like this:

Ashkii   at'ééd   biilstá

Boy   girl   saw

This sentence has almost the same words arranged in the same order as the one we saw above, and so we might reasonably guess that it has the same meaning: 'The boy saw the girl.' In fact, this sentence means the opposite, that the girl saw the boy. The crucial hint is once again in the prefixes attached to the verb: Here the verb starts with bi-, whereas the verb in the previous sentence started with yi-. This small difference indicates a large difference in sentence structure. Bi- tells the Navajo speaker roughly that the direct object of the sentence comes before the subject, rather than the other way around. Nor is it always easy to find these prefixes: Like any others in Navajo, they can be buried under other prefixes and disguised by sound changes. Furthermore, this option of choosing a sentence with yi- or a sentence with bi- is used in a culturally specific way in Navajo. The noun phrase that refers to a higher being always comes before a noun phrase that refers to a lower being, regardless of which is the subject and which is the object. (In the Navajo conception, humans count as higher than large and intelligent animals, which count as higher than smaller animals, which in turn count as higher than plants and inanimate objects.) Sentence structure and word structure thus are interdependent in Navajo, and both are influenced by the distinctive Navajo typology of creatures, which puts hawks below wildcats but on the same level as foxes. Not only is Navajo different from English at many levels, from single sounds to the arrangement of words in sentences, but those different levels interact with each other in various ways. There is a combinatorial explosion of difference, and it seems as if one cannot understand anything until one understands everything. The poor Japanese cryptographers didn't stand a chance.

Can even languages as different as English and Navajo be cut from the same cloth? Yes. We have already surveyed some of the salient features of Navajo, focusing on the differences. But even in that discussion there were signs of similarity as well. Some of the basic sounds of Navajo are different from English, but others are the same: Both languages have *p, t, m, n, w, y, a, e, i,* and *o.* Even the sounds that are different, such as *l,* can be described as being like an English sound with one feature of the pronunciation changed—in this case, the vibrating of the vocal cords. In both languages sounds adjust to their environments in comparable ways. For example, *s's* turn into *z's* in English, too, as you can see by listening carefully to yourself pronounce the word *dogs* (one actually says "dogz"). Like Navajo, English verbs also inflect to show tense and subject; compare the verb in *They walk* with *They walked* and *Chris walks.* It is true that Modern English has only a few of these inflections, and they are suffixes rather than prefixes. Its inflections are like a Ford Escort compared to Navajo's Lamborgini. Nevertheless, it has the rudiments of the kind of system that is so highly developed in Navajo. Direct objects come before the verb in Navajo and after the verb in English, but both languages have direct objects and verbs. More than that, they are similar in that in basic sentences the direct object appears right next to the verb, whereas the subject need not. In Navajo the object comes between the subject and the verb, whereas in English adverbs and tense auxiliaries can separate the two (e.g., *Chris will soon find a quarter*). This similarity foreshadows a very significant universal feature of human language important in subsequent chapters.

Perhaps the single most distinctive property of Navajo is that its word order changes when the verb contains the prefix *bi-* rather than *yi-.*

Ashkii	at'ééd	biilstá		At'ééd	ashkii	yiyiiltsą
Boy	girl	saw		Girl	boy	saw
'The girl saw the boy.'				'The girl saw the boy.'		

This is indeed a capstone of Navajo grammar and an endless source of fascination and controversy among the people who study this language and its relatives. Nevertheless, English does have something somewhat similar. In English, too, it is possible to permute the basic phrases of a sentence together with a change in the form of the verb. The English permutation is known as the passive voice:

> The girl saw the boy.
> The boy was seen by the girl.

QUESTIONS

1. Take a language you know other than English (or one you studied in school) and determine whether verbs typically precede their objects or follow them. Are there prepositions or postpositions? How do those relate to their objects? Compare the situation in the language you chose with the situation in English. (If you speak only English, interview a friend who speaks a different language, and meditate on the old joke: "What do you call someone who speaks two languages? A bilingual. What do you call someone who speaks three languages? A trilingual. What do you call someone who speaks one language? An American.")

2. Pinker argues that humans are born with an innate language instinct. How well might his arguments apply to other capacities, such as the ability to make intelligent guesses about other people's beliefs, desires, goals, emotions, and intentions? Do you think that humans are born with a "mind-reading instinct"? Why or why not?

LEARNING

"Give me a dozen healthy infants, well-formed, and my own specified world to bring them up and I'll guarantee to take any one at random and train him to become any type of specialist I might select—doctor, lawyer, merchant-chief, and yes, even beggarman and thief, regardless of his talents, penchants, tendencies, abilities, vocations, and race of his ancestors." With these words, reprinted dozens if not hundreds of times, the influential American psychologist John Watson denied that heredity had anything special to do with our fate. Watson may have overstated his case, and left too little room for genetics, but he is surely correct that no account of human mental life would be complete without a discussion of the mechanisms by which humans learn.

In the famous case study included below, Watson and his research assistant Rosalie Rayner describe their efforts to condition an infant to fear a white rabbit. Though the methodology was primitive (not to mention possibly inhumane), the paper, "Conditioned Emotional Reactions" (1920), was one of the first to study the capacities of human infants to learn from experience, and as such it is rightly famous.

Watson's influence on psychology reached its peak in the late 1950s, when Harvard learning theorist B. F. Skinner argued that simple laws of conditioning could capture not just the regularities of learning by pigeons but even the complexities of human language. No sooner did Skinner make that argument than the young Noam Chomsky wrote a devastating review (1959). Arguing that higher mental processes, such as human language learning, could not possibly be explained as a simple product of conditioning, Chomsky helped to launch the cognitive revolution. Whereas Skinner asserted that psychology could be understood purely in terms of external behavior, Chomsky argued that psychology could not be understood in terms of behavior alone. Instead, he claimed that internal representations—cognitive states—would play an important role in the scientific understanding of psychology. At the same time, Chomsky challenged Watson and Skinner's view that humans were born as blank slates—suggesting instead that significant portions of a person's psychology might be innate.

Ever since, psychologists have been struggling to come up with a more nuanced view of learning. As we saw from Pinker's selection in Chapter 6, Chomsky's view has only become more plausible over time. Capacities such as the human gift for acquiring language do indeed seem to require much more than simple conditioning. And, in fact, there may be no such thing as a single general mechanism for learning; different kinds of learning may each depend on different mental mechanisms. In place of a one-size-fits-all view in which simple conditioning is the motor of learning, psychologists and animal ethologists are working toward a new view, presented in the selection from Marc Hauser's *Wild Minds* (2000), in which each species has its own unique set of tools for learning.

Conditioned Emotional Reactions

John B. Watson and Rosalie Rayner

In recent literature various speculations have been entered into concerning the possibility of conditioning various types of emotional response, but direct experimental evidence in support of such a view has been lacking. If the theory advanced by Watson and Morgan to the effect that in infancy the original emotional reaction patterns are few, consisting so far as observed of fear, rage and love, then there must be some simple method by means of which the range of stimuli which can call out these emotions and their compounds is greatly increased. Otherwise, complexity in adult response could not be accounted for. These authors without adequate experimental evidence advanced the view that this range was increased by means of conditioned reflex factors. It was suggested there that the early home life of the child furnishes a laboratory situation for establishing conditioned emotional responses. The present authors have recently put the whole matter to an experimental test.

Experimental work had been done so far on only one child, Albert B. This infant was reared almost from birth in a hospital environment; his mother was a wet nurse in the Harriet Lane Home for Invalid Children. Albert's life was normal: he was healthy from birth and one of the best developed youngsters ever brought to the hospital, weighing twenty-one pounds at nine months of age. He was on the whole stolid and unemotional. His stability was one of the principal reasons for using him as a subject in this test. We felt that we could do him relatively little harm by carrying out such experiments as those outlined below.

At approximately nine months of age we ran him through the emotional tests that have become a part of our regular routine in determining whether fear reactions can be called out by other stimuli than sharp noises and the sudden removal of support. Tests of this type have been described by the senior author in another place. In brief, the infant was confronted suddenly and for the first time successively with a white rat, a rabbit, a dog, a monkey, with masks with and without hair, cotton wool, burning newspapers, etc. A permanent record of Albert's reactions to these objects and situations has been preserved in a motion picture study. Manipulation was the most usual reaction called out. *At no time did this infant ever show fear in any situation.* These experimental records were confirmed by the casual observations of the mother and hospital attendants. No one had ever seen him in a state of fear and rage. The infant practically never cried.

Up to approximately nine months of age we had not tested him with loud sounds. The test to determine whether a fear reaction could be called out by a loud sound was made when he was eight months, twenty-six days of age. The sound was that made by striking a hammer upon a suspended steel bar four feet in length and three-fourths of an inch in diameter. The laboratory notes are as follows:

One of the two experimenters caused the child to turn its head and fixate her moving hand; the other stationed back of the child, struck the steel bar a sharp blow. The child started violently, his breathing was checked and the arms were raised in a characteristic manner. On the second stimulation the same thing occurred, and in addition the lips began to pucker and tremble. On the third stimulation the child broke into a sudden crying fit. This is the first time an emotional situation in the laboratory has produced any fear or even crying in Albert.

We had expected just these results on account of our work with other infants brought up under similar conditions. It is worth while to call attention to the fact that removal of support (dropping and jerking the blanket upon which the infant was lying) was tried exhaustively upon this infant on the same occasion. It was not effective in producing the fear response. This stimulus is effective in younger children. At what age such stimuli lose their potency in producing fear is not known. Nor is it known whether less placid children ever lose their fear of them. This probably depends upon the training the child gets. It is well known that children eagerly run to be tossed into the air and caught. On the other hand it is equally well known that in the adult fear responses are called out quite clearly by the sudden removal of support, if the individual is walking across a bridge, walking out upon a beam, etc. There is a wide field of study here which is aside from our present point.

The sound stimulus, thus, at nine months of age, gives us the means of testing several important factors. I. Can we condition fear of an animal, *e.g.,* a white rat, by visually presenting it and simultaneously striking a steel bar?

II. If such a conditioned emotional response can be established, will there be a transfer to other animals or other objects? III. What is the effect of time upon such conditioned emotional responses? IV. If after a reasonable period such emotional responses have not died out, what laboratory methods can be devised for their removal?

I. The establishment of conditioned emotional responses.

At first there was considerable hesitation upon our part in making the attempt to set up fear reactions experimentally. A certain responsibility attaches to such a procedure. We decided finally to make the attempt, comforting ourselves by the reflection that such attachments would arise anyway as soon as the child left the sheltered environment of the nursery for the rough and tumble of the home. We did not begin this work until Albert was eleven months, three days of age. Before attempting to set up a conditioned response we, as before, put him through all of the regular emotional tests. *Not the slightest sign of a fear response was obtained in any situation.*

The steps taken to condition emotional responses are shown in our laboratory notes.

11 Months 3 Days

1. White rat suddenly taken from the basket and presented to Albert. He began to reach for rat with left hand. Just as his hand touched the animal the bar was struck immediately behind his head. The infant jumped violently and fell forward, burying his face in the mattress. He did not cry, however.
2. Just as the right hand touched the rat the bar was again struck. Again the infant jumped violently, fell forward and began to whimper.

In order not to disturb the child too seriously no further tests were given for one week.

11 Months 10 Days

1. Rat presented suddenly without sound. There was steady fixation but no tendency at first to reach for it. The rat was then placed nearer, whereupon tentative reaching movements began with the right hand. When the rat nosed the infant's left hand, the hand was immediately withdrawn. He started to reach for the head of the animal with the forefinger of the left hand, but withdrew it suddenly before contact. It

is thus seen that the two joint stimulations given the previous week
were not without effect. He was tested with his blocks immediately afterwards to see if they shared in the process of conditioning. He began
immediately to pick them up, dropping them, pounding them, etc. In
the remainder of the tests the blocks were given frequently to quiet him
and to test his general emotional state. They were always removed from
sight when the process of conditioning was under way.

2. Joint stimulation with rat and sound. Started, then fell over immediately to right side. No crying.

3. Joint stimulation. Fell to right side and rested upon hands, with head
   turned away from rat. No crying.

4. Joint stimulation. Same reaction.

5. Rat suddenly presented alone. Puckered face, whimpered and withdrew
   body sharply to the left.

6. Joint stimulation. Fell over immediately to right side and began to
   whimper.

7. Joint stimulation. Started violently and cried, but did not fall over.

8. Rat alone. *The instant the rat was shown the baby began to cry. Almost instantly he turned sharply to the left, fell over on left side, raised himself on all
   fours and began to crawl away so rapidly that he was caught with difficulty
   before reaching the edge of the table.*

This was as convincing a case of a completely conditioned fear response as
could have been theoretically pictured. In all seven joint stimulations were
given to bring about the complete reaction. It is not unlikely had the sound
been of greater intensity or of a more complex clang character that the number of joint stimulations might have been materially reduced. Experiments
designed to define the nature of the sounds that will serve best as emotional
stimuli are under way.

    II. When a conditioned emotional response has been established for
one object, is there a transfer? Five days later Albert was again brought back
into the laboratory and tested as follows:

11 Months 15 Days

1. Tested first with blocks. He reached readily for them, playing with them
   as usual. This shows that there has been no general transfer to the
   room, table, blocks, etc.

2. Rat alone. Whimpered immediately, withdrew right hand and turned head and trunk away.
3. Blocks again offered. Played readily with them, smiling and gurgling.
4. Rat alone. Leaned over to the left side as far away from the rat as possible, then fell over, getting up on all fours and scurrying away as rapidly as possible.
5. Blocks again offered. Reached immediately for them, smiling and laughing as before.

The above preliminary test shows that the conditioned response to the rat had carried over completely for the five days in which no tests were given. The question as to whether or not there is a transfer was next taken up.

6. Rabbit alone. The rabbit was suddenly placed on the mattress in front of him. The reaction was pronounced. Negative responses began at once. He leaned as far away from the animal as possible, whimpered, then burst into tears. When the rabbit was placed in contact with him he buried his face in the mattress, then got up on all fours and crawled away, crying as he went. This was a most convincing test.
7. The blocks were next given him, after an interval. He played with them as before. It was observed by four people that he played far more energetically with them than ever before. The blocks were raised high over his head and slammed down with a great deal of force.
8. Dog alone. The dog did not produce as violent a reaction as the rabbit. The moment fixation occurred the child shrank back and as the animal came nearer he attempted to get on all fours but did not cry at first. As soon as the dog passed out of his range of vision he became quiet. The dog was then made to approach the infant's head (he was lying down at the moment). Albert straightened up immediately, fell over to the opposite side and turned his head away. He then began to cry.
9. The blocks were again presented. He began immediately to play with them.
10. Fur coat (seal). Withdrew immediately to the left side and began to fret. Coat put close to him on the left side, he turned immediately, began to cry and tried to crawl away on all fours.
11. Cotton wool. The wool was presented in a paper package. At the end the cotton was not covered by the paper. It was placed first on his feet. He kicked it away but did not touch it with his hands. When his

hand was laid on the wool he immediately withdrew it but did not show the shock that the animals or fur coat produced in him. He then began to play with the paper, avoiding contact with the wool itself. He finally, under the impulse of the manipulative instinct, lost some of his negativism to the wool.

12. Just in play W. put his head down to see if Albert would play with his hair. Albert was completely negative. Two other observers did the same thing. He began immediately to play with their hair. W. then brought the Santa Claus mask and presented it to Albert. He was again pronouncedly negative.

11 Months 20 Days

1. Blocks alone. Played with them as usual.
2. Rat alone. Withdrawal of the whole body, bending over to left side, no crying. Fixation and following with eyes. The response was much less marked than on first presentation the previous week. It was thought best to freshen up the reaction by another joint stimulation.
3. Just as the rat was placed on his hand the rod was struck. Reaction violent.
4. Rat alone. Fell over at once to left side. Reaction practically as strong as on former occasion but no crying.
5. Rat alone. Fell over to left side, got up on all fours and started to crawl away. On this occasion there was no crying, but strange to say, as he started away he began to gurgle and coo, even while leaning far over to the left side to avoid the rat.
6. Rabbit alone. Leaned over to left side as far as possible. Did not fall over. Began to whimper but reaction not so violent as on former occasions.
7. Blocks again offered. He reached for them immediately and began to play.

All of these tests so far discussed were carried out upon a table supplied with a mattress, located in a small, well-lighted dark-room. We wished to test next whether conditioned fear responses so set up would appear if the situation were markedly altered. We thought it best before making this test to freshen the reaction both to the rabbit and to the dog by showing them at the moment the steel bar was struck. It will be recalled that this was the first time any effort had been made to directly condition response to the dog and rabbit. The experimental notes are as follows:

8. The rabbit at first was given alone. The reaction was exactly as given in test (6) above. When the rabbit was left on Albert's knees for a long time he began tentatively to reach out and manipulate its fur with forefingers. While doing this the steel rod was struck. A violent fear reaction resulted.

9. Rabbit alone. Reaction wholly similar to that on trial (6) above.

10. Rabbit alone. Started immediately to whimper, holding hands far up, but did not cry. Conflicting tendency to manipulate very evident.

11. Dog alone. Began to whimper, shaking head from side to side, holding hands as far away from the animal as possible.

12. Dog and sound. The rod was struck just as the animal touched him. A violent negative reaction appeared. He began to whimper, turned to one side, fell over and started to get up on all fours.

13. Blocks. Played with them immediately and readily.

On this same day and immediately after the above experiment Albert was taken into the large well-lighted lecture room belonging to the laboratory. He was placed on a table in the center of the room immediately under the skylight. Four people were present. The situation was thus very different from that which obtained in the small dark room.

1. Rat alone. No sudden fear reaction appeared at first. The hands, however, were held up and away from the animal. No positive manipulatory reactions appeared.

2. Rabbit alone. Fear reaction slight. Turned to left and kept face away from the animal but the reaction was never pronounced.

3. Dog alone. Turned away but did not fall over. Cried. Hands moved as far away from the animal as possible. Whimpered as long as the dog was present.

4. Rat alone. Slight negative reaction.

5. Rat and sound. It was thought best to freshen the reaction to the rat. The sound was given just as the rat was presented. Albert jumped violently but did not cry.

6. Rat alone. At first he did not show any negative reaction. When rat was placed nearer he began to show negative reaction by drawing back his body, raising his hands, whimpering, etc.

7. Blocks. Played with them immediately.

8. Rat alone. Pronounced withdrawal of body and whimpering.

9. Blocks. Played with them as before.

10. Rabbit alone. Pronounced reaction. Whimpered with arms held high, fell over backward and had to be caught.

11. Dog alone. At first the dog did not produce the pronounced reaction. The hands were held high over the head, breathing was checked, but there was no crying. Just at this moment the dog, which had not barked before, barked three times loudly when only about six inches from the baby's face. Albert immediately fell over and broke into a wail that continued until the dog was removed. The sudden barking of the hitherto quiet dog produced a marked fear response in the adult observers!

From the above results it would seem that emotional transfers do take place. Furthermore it would seem that the number of transfers resulting from an experimentally produced conditioned emotional reaction may be very large. In our observations we had no means of testing the complete number of transfers which may have resulted.

III. The effect of time upon conditioned emotional responses. We have already shown that the conditioned emotional response will continue for a period of one week. It was desired to make the time test longer. In view of the imminence of Albert's departure from the hospital we could not make the interval longer than one month. Accordingly no further emotional experimentation was entered into for thirty-one days after the above test. During the month, however, Albert was brought weekly to the laboratory for tests upon right and left-handedness, imitation, general development, etc. No emotional tests whatever were given and during the whole month his regular nursery routine was maintained in the Harriet Lane Home. The notes on the test given at the end of this period are as follows:

1 Year 21 Days

1. Santa Claus mask. Withdrawal, gurgling, then slapped at it without touching. When his hand was forced to touch it, he whimpered and

cried. His hand was forced to touch it two more times. He whimpered and cried on both tests. He finally cried at the mere visual stimulus of the mask.

2. Fur coat. Wrinkled his nose and withdrew both hands, drew back his whole body and began to whimper as the coat was put nearer. Again there was the strife between withdrawal and the tendency to manipulate. Reached tentatively with left hand but drew back before contact had been made. In moving his body to one side his hand accidentally touched the coat. He began to cry at once, nodding his head in a very peculiar manner (this reaction was an entirely new one). Both hands were withdrawn as far as possible from the coat. The coat was then laid on his lap and he continued nodding his head and whimpering, withdrawing his body as far as possible, pushing the while at the coat with his feet but never touching it with his hands.

3. Fur coat. The coat was taken out of his sight and presented again at the end of a minute. He began immediately to fret, withdrawing his body and nodding his head as before.

4. Blocks. He began to play with them as usual.

5. The rat. He allowed the rat to crawl towards him without withdrawing. He sat very still and fixated it intently. Rat then touched his hand. Albert withdrew it immediately, then leaned back as far as possible but did not cry. When the rat was placed on his arm he withdrew his body and began to fret, nodding his head. The rat was then allowed to crawl against his chest. He first began to fret and then covered his eyes with both hands.

6. Blocks. Reaction normal.

7. The rabbit. The animal was placed directly in front of him. It was very quiet. Albert showed no avoiding reactions at first. After a few seconds he puckered up his face, began to nod his head and to look intently at the experimenter. He next began to push the rabbit away with his feet, withdrawing his body at the same time. Then as the rabbit came nearer he began pulling his feet away, nodding his head, and wailing "da da". After about a minute he reached out tentatively and slowly touched the rabbit's ear with his right hand, finally manipulating it. The rabbit was again placed in his lap. Again he began to fret and withdrew his hands. He reached out tentatively with his left hand and touched the animal, shuddered and withdrew the whole body. The experimenter then took hold of his left hand and laid it on the rabbit's back. Albert immediately

withdrew his hand and began to suck his thumb. Again the rabbit was laid in his lap. He began to cry, covering his face with both hands.

8. Dog. The dog was very active. Albert fixated it intensely for a few seconds, sitting very still. He began to cry but did not fall over backwards as on his last contact with the dog. When the dog was pushed closer to him he at first sat motionless, then began to cry, putting both hands over his face.

These experiments would seem to show conclusively that directly conditioned emotional responses as well as those conditioned by transfer persist, although with a certain loss in the intensity of the reaction, for a longer period than one month. Our view is that they persist and modify personality throughout life. It should be recalled again that Albert was of an extremely phlegmatic type. Had he been emotionally unstable probably both the directly conditioned response and those transferred would have persisted throughout the month unchanged in form.

IV. "Detachment" or removal of conditioned emotional responses. Unfortunately Albert was taken from the hospital the day the above tests were made. Hence the opportunity of building up an experimental technique by means of which we could remove the conditioned emotional responses was denied us. Our own view, expressed above, which is possibly not very well grounded, is that these responses in the home environment are likely to persist indefinitely, unless an accidental method for removing them is hit upon. The importance of establishing some method must be apparent to all. Had the opportunity been at hand we should have tried out several methods, some of which we may mention. (1) Constantly confronting the child with those stimuli which called out the responses in the hopes that habituation would come in corresponding to "fatigue" of reflex when differential reactions are to be set up. (2) By trying to "recondition" by showing objects calling out fear responses (visual) and simultaneously stimulating the erogenous zones (tactual). We should try first the lips, then the nipples and as a final resort the sex organs. (3) By trying to "recondition" by feeding the subject candy or other food just as the animal is shown. This method calls for the food control of the subject. (4) By building up "constructive" activities around the object by imitation and by putting the hand through the motions of manipulation. At this age imitation of overt motor activity is strong, as our present but unpublished experimentation has shown.

Incidental Observations

(a) Thumb sucking as a compensatory device for blocking fear and noxious stimuli. During the course of these experiments, especially in the final test, it was noticed that whenever Albert was on the verge of tears or emotionally upset generally he would continually thrust his thumb into his mouth. The moment the hand reached the mouth he became impervious to the stimuli producing fear. Again and again while the motion pictures were being made at the end of the thirty-day period, we had to remove the thumb from his mouth before the conditioned response could be obtained. This method of blocking noxious and emotional stimuli (fear and rage) through erogenous stimulation seems to persist from birth onward. Very often in our experiments upon the work adders with infants under ten days of age the same reaction appeared. When at work upon the adders both of the infants arms are under slight restraint. Often rage appears. They begin to cry, thrashing their arms and legs about. If the finger gets into the mouth crying ceases at once. The organism thus apparently from birth, when under the influence of love stimuli is blocked to all others. This resort to sex stimulation when under the influence of noxious and emotional situations, or when the individual is restless and idle, persists throughout adolescent and adult life. Albert, at any rate, did not resort to thumb sucking except in the presence of such stimuli. Thumb sucking could immediately be checked by offering him his blocks. These invariably called out active manipulation instincts. It is worth while here to call attention to the fact that Freud's conception of the stimulation of erogenous zones as being the expression of an original "pleasure" seeking principle may be turned about and possibly better described as a compensatory (and often conditioned) device for the blockage of noxious and fear and rage producing stimuli.

(b) Equal primacy of fear, love and possibly rage. While in general the results of our experiment offer no particular points of conflict with Freudian concepts, one fact out of harmony with them should be emphasized. According to proper Freudians sex (or in our terminology, love) is the principal emotion in which conditioned responses arise which later limit and distort personality. We wish to take sharp issue with this view on the basis of the experimental evidence we have gathered. Fear is as primal a factor as love in influencing personality. Fear does not gather its potency in any derived manner from love. It belongs to the original and inherited nature of man. Probably the same may be true of rage although at present we are not so sure of this.

The Freudians twenty years from now, unless their hypotheses change, when they come to analyze Albert's fear of a seal skin coat—assuming that he comes to analysis at that age—will probably tease from him the recital of a dream which upon their analysis will show that Albert at three years of age attempted to play with the pubic hair of the mother and was scolded violently for it. (We are by no means denying that this might in some other case condition it.) If the analyst has sufficiently prepared Albert to accept such a dream when found as an explanation of his avoiding tendencies, and if the analyst has the authority and personality to put it over, Albert may be fully convinced that the dream was a true revealer of the factors which brought about the fear.

It is probable that many of the phobias in psychopathology are true conditioned emotional reactions either of the direct or the transferred type. One may possibly have to believe that such persistence of early conditioned responses will be found only in persons who are constitutionally inferior. Our argument is meant to be constructive. Emotional disturbances in adults cannot be traced back to sex alone. They must be retraced along at least three collateral lines—to conditioned and transferred responses set up in infancy and early youth in all three of the fundamental human emotions.

A Review of B. F. Skinner's *Verbal Behavior*

Noam Chomsky

I

A great many linguists and philosophers concerned with language have expressed the hope that their studies might ultimately be embedded in a framework provided by behaviorist psychology, and that refractory areas of investigation, particularly those in which meaning is involved, will in this way be opened up to fruitful exploration. Since this volume is the first large-scale attempt to incorporate the major aspects of linguistic behavior within a behaviorist framework, it merits and will undoubtedly receive careful attention. Skinner is noted for his contributions to the study of animal behavior. The book under review is the product of study of linguistic behavior extending over more than twenty years. Earlier versions of it have been fairly widely circulated, and there are quite a few references in the psychological literature to its major ideas.

The problem to which this book is addressed is that of giving a "functional analysis" of verbal behavior. By functional analysis, Skinner means identification of the variables that control this behavior and specification of how they interact to determine a particular verbal response. Furthermore, the controlling variables are to be described completely in terms of such notions as *stimulus, reinforcement, deprivation,* which have been given a reasonably clear meaning in animal experimentation. In other words, the goal of the book is to provide a way to predict and control verbal behavior by observing and manipulating the physical environment of the speaker.

Skinner feels that recent advances in the laboratory study of animal behavior permit us to approach this problem with a certain optimism, since "the basic processes and relations which give verbal behavior its special characteristics are now fairly well understood ... the results [of this experimental work] have been surprisingly free of species restrictions. Recent work has shown that the methods can be extended to human behavior without serious modification."

It is important to see clearly just what it is in Skinner's program and claims that makes them appear so bold and remarkable. It is not primarily the fact that he has set functional analysis as his problem, or that he limits himself to study of *observables*, i.e., input-output relations. What is so surprising is the particular limitations he has imposed on the way in which the observables of behavior are to be studied, and, above all, the particularly simple nature of the *function* which, he claims, describes the causation of behavior. One would naturally expect that prediction of the behavior of a complex organism (or machine) would require, in addition to information about external stimulation, knowledge of the internal structure of the organism, the ways in which it processes input information and organizes its own behavior. These characteristics of the organism are in general a complicated product of inborn structure, the genetically determined course of maturation, and past experience. Insofar as independent neurophysiological evidence is not available, it is obvious that inferences concerning the structure of the organism are based on observation of behavior and outside events.

Nevertheless, one's estimate of the relative importance of external factors and internal structure in the determination of behavior will have an important effect on the direction of research on linguistic (or any other) behavior, and on the kinds of analogies from animal behavior studies that will be considered relevant or suggestive.

Putting it differently, anyone who sets himself the problem of analyzing the causation of behavior will (in the absence of independent neurophysiological evidence) concern himself with the only data available, namely the record of inputs to the organism and the organism's present response, and will try to describe the function specifying the response in terms of the history of inputs. This is nothing more than the definition of his problem. There are no possible grounds for argument here, if one accepts the problem as legitimate, though Skinner has often advanced and defended this definition of a problem as if it were a thesis which other investigators reject. The differences that arise between those who affirm and those who deny the importance of the specific "contribution of the organism" to learning and performance concern the particular character and complexity of this function, and the kinds of observations and research necessary for arriving at a precise specification of it. If the contribution of the organism is complex, the only hope of predicting behavior even in a gross way will be through a very indirect program of research that begins by studying the detailed character of the behavior itself and the particular capacities of the organism involved.

Skinner's thesis is that external factors consisting of present stimulation and the history of reinforcement (in particular, the frequency, arrangement, and withholding of reinforcing stimuli) are of overwhelming importance, and that the general principles revealed in laboratory studies of these phenomena provide the basis for understanding the complexities of verbal behavior. He confidently and repeatedly voices his claim to have demonstrated that the contribution of the speaker is quite trivial and elementary, and that precise prediction of verbal behavior involves only specification of the few external factors that he has isolated experimentally with lower organisms.

Careful study of this book (and of the research on which it draws) reveals, however, that these astonishing claims are far from justified. It indicates, furthermore, that the insights that have been achieved in the laboratories of the reinforcement theorist, though quite genuine, can be applied to complex human behavior only in the most gross and superficial way, and that speculative attempts to discuss linguistic behavior in these terms alone omit from consideration factors of fundamental importance that are, no doubt, amenable to scientific study, although their specific character cannot at present be precisely formulated. Since Skinner's work is the most extensive attempt to accommodate human behavior involving higher mental faculties within a strict behaviorist schema of the type that has attracted many linguists and philosophers, as well as psychologists, a detailed documentation is of independent interest. The magnitude of the failure of this attempt to account for verbal behavior serves as a kind of measure of the importance of the factors omitted from consideration, and an indication of how little is really known about this remarkably complex phenomenon.

Consider first Skinner's use of the notions *stimulus* and *response*. In *Behavior of Organisms* (9) he commits himself to the narrow definitions for these terms. A part of the environment and a part of behavior are called *stimulus* (eliciting, discriminated, or reinforcing) and *response*, respectively, only if they are lawfully related; that is, if the *dynamic laws* relating them show smooth and reproducible curves. Evidently, stimuli and responses, so defined, have not been shown to figure very widely in ordinary human behavior. We can, in the face of presently available evidence, continue to maintain the lawfulness of the relation between stimulus and response only by depriving them of their objective character. A typical example of *stimulus control* for Skinner would be the response to a piece of music with the utterance *Mozart* or to a painting with the response *Dutch*. These responses are asserted to be "under the control of extremely subtle properties" of the physical object or event (108). Suppose instead of saying *Dutch* we had said *Clashes with the wallpaper, I thought you liked abstract work, Never saw it before, Tilted, Hanging too low, Beautiful, Hideous, Remember our camping trip last summer?*, or whatever else might come into our minds when looking at a picture (in Skinnerian translation, whatever other responses exist in sufficient strength). Skinner could only say that each of these responses is under the control of some other stimulus property of the physical object. If we look at a red chair and say *red*, the response is under the control of the stimulus *redness*; if we say *chair*, it is under the control of the collection of properties (for Skinner, the object) *chairness* (110), and similarly for any other response. This device is as simple as it is empty. Since properties are free for the asking (we have as many of them as we have nonsynonymous descriptive expressions in our language, whatever this means exactly), we can account for a wide class of responses in terms of Skinnerian functional analysis by identifying the *controlling stimuli*. But the word *stimulus* has lost all objectivity in this usage. Stimuli are no longer part of the outside physical world; they are driven back into the organism. We identify the stimulus when we hear the response. It is clear from such examples, which abound, that the talk of *stimulus control* simply disguises a complete retreat to mentalistic psychology. We cannot predict verbal behavior in terms of the stimuli in the speaker's environment, since we do not know what the current stimuli are until he responds. Furthermore, since we cannot control the property of a physical object to which an individual will respond, except in highly artificial cases, Skinner's claim that his system, as opposed to the traditional one, permits the practical control of verbal behavior is quite false.

Other examples of *stimulus control* merely add to the general mystification. Thus, a proper noun is held to be a response "under the control of a specific person or thing" (as controlling stimulus, 113). I have often used the words *Eisenhower* and *Moscow*, which I presume are proper nouns if any-thing is, but have never been *stimulated* by the corresponding objects. How can this fact be made compatible with this definition? Suppose that I use the name of a friend who is not present. Is this an instance of a proper noun un-der the control of the friend as stimulus? Elsewhere it is asserted that a stim-ulus controls a response in the sense that presence of the stimulus increases the probability of the response. But it is obviously untrue that the probabil-ity that a speaker will produce a full name is increased when its bearer faces the speaker. Furthermore, how can one's own name be a proper noun in this sense?

A multitude of similar questions arise immediately. It appears that the word *control* here is merely a misleading paraphrase for the traditional *denote* or *refer*. The assertion (115) that so far as the speaker is concerned, the relation of reference is "simply the probability that the speaker will emit a response of a given form in the presence of a stimulus having specified properties" is surely incorrect if we take the words *presence, stimulus,* and *probability* in their literal sense. That they are not intended to be taken literally is indicated by many examples, as when a response is said to be "controlled" by a situation or state of affairs as "stimulus." Thus, the expression *a needle in a haystack* "may be controlled as a unit by a particular type of situation" (116); the words in a single part of speech, e.g., all adjectives, are under the control of a single set of subtle properties of stimuli (121); "the sentence *The boy runs a store* is un-der the control of an extremely complex stimulus situation" (335); "*He is not at all well* may function as a standard response under the control of a state of affairs which might also control *He is ailing*" (325); when an envoy observes events in a foreign country and reports upon his return, his report is under "remote stimulus control" (416); the statement *This is war* may be a response to a "confusing international situation" (441); the suffix *-ed* is controlled by that "subtle property of stimuli which we speak of as action-in-the-past" (121) just as the *-s* in *The boy runs* is under the control of such specific features of the situation as its "currency" (332). No characterization of the notion *stimu-lus control* that is remotely related to the bar-pressing experiment (or that pre-serves the faintest objectivity) can be made to cover a set of examples like these, in which, for example, the controlling stimulus need not even impinge on the responding organism.

Consider now Skinner's use of the notion *response*. The problem of identifying units in verbal behavior has of course been a primary concern of linguists, and it seems very likely that experimental psychologists should be able to provide much-needed assistance in clearing up the many remaining difficulties in systematic identification. Skinner recognizes (20) the fundamental character of the problem of identification of a unit of verbal behavior, but is satisfied with an answer so vague and subjective that it does not really contribute to its solution. The unit of verbal behavior—the verbal operant—is defined as a class of responses of identifiable form functionally related to one or more controlling variables. No method is suggested for determining in a particular instance what are the controlling variables, how many such units have occurred, or where their boundaries are in the total response. Nor is any attempt made to specify how much or what kind of similarity in form or control is required for two physical events to be considered instances of the same operant. In short, no answers are suggested for the most elementary questions that must be asked of anyone proposing a method for description of behavior. Skinner is content with what he calls an *extrapolation* of the concept of operant developed in the laboratory to the verbal field. In the typical Skinnerian experiment, the problem of identifying the unit of behavior is not too crucial. It is defined, by fiat, as a recorded peck or bar-press, and systematic variations in the rate of this operant and its resistance to extinction are studied as a function of deprivation and scheduling of reinforcement (pellets). The operant is thus defined with respect to a particular experimental procedure. This is perfectly reasonable and has led to many interesting results. It is, however, completely meaningless to speak of extrapolating this concept of operant to ordinary verbal behavior. Such "extrapolation" leaves us with no way of justifying one or another decision about the units in the "verbal repertoire."

❋

The behavior of the speaker, listener, and learner of language constitutes, of course, the actual data for any study of language. The construction of a grammar which enumerates sentences in such a way that a meaningful structural description can be determined for each sentence does not in itself provide an account of this actual behavior. It merely characterizes abstractly the ability of one who has mastered the language to distinguish sentences from nonsentences, to understand new sentences (in part), to note certain ambiguities, etc. These are very remarkable abilities. We constantly read and hear new sequences of words, recognize them as sentences, and understand them. It is easy to show that the new events that we accept and understand as sentences are not related to those with which we are familiar by any simple notion of formal (or semantic or statistical) similarity or identity of grammatical frame. Talk of generalization in this case is entirely pointless and empty. It appears that we recognize a new item as a sentence not because it matches some familiar item in any simple way, but because it is generated by the grammar that each individual has somehow and in some form internalized. And we understand a new sentence, in part, because we are somehow capable of determining the process by which this sentence is derived in this grammar.

Suppose that we manage to construct grammars having the properties outlined above. We can then attempt to describe and study the achievement of the speaker, listener, and learner. The speaker and the listener, we must assume, have already acquired the capacities characterized abstractly by the grammar. The speaker's task is to select a particular compatible set of optional rules. If we know, from grammatical study, what choices are available to him and what conditions of compatibility the choices must meet, we can proceed meaningfully to investigate the factors that lead him to make one or another choice. The listener (or reader) must determine, from an exhibited utterance, what optional rules were chosen in the construction of the utterance. It must be admitted that the ability of a human being to do this far surpasses our present understanding. The child who learns a language has in some sense constructed the grammar for himself on the basis of his observation of sentences and nonsentences (i.e., corrections by the verbal community). Study of the actual observed ability of a speaker to distinguish sentences from nonsentences, detect ambiguities, etc., apparently forces us to the conclusion that this grammar is of an extremely complex and abstract character, and that the young child has succeeded in carrying out what from the formal point of view, at least, seems to be a remarkable type of theory construction. Furthermore, this task is accomplished in an astonishingly short time, to a large extent independently of intelligence, and in a comparable way by all children. Any theory of learning must cope with these facts.

It is not easy to accept the view that a child is capable of constructing an extremely complex mechanism for generating a set of sentences, some of which he has heard, or that an adult can instantaneously determine whether (and if so, how) a particular item is generated by this mechanism, which has many of the properties of an abstract deductive theory. Yet this appears to be a fair description of the performance of the speaker, listener, and learner. If this is correct, we can predict that a direct attempt to account for the actual behavior of speaker, listener, and learner, not based on a prior understanding of the structure of grammars, will achieve very limited success. The grammar must be regarded as a component in the behavior of the speaker and listener which can only be inferred, as Lashley has put it, from the resulting physical acts. The fact that all normal children acquire essentially comparable grammars of great complexity with remarkable rapidity suggests that human beings are somehow specially designed to do this, with data-handling or "hypothesis-formulating" ability of unknown character and complexity. The study of linguistic structure may ultimately lead to some significant insights into this matter. At the moment the question cannot be seriously posed, but in principle it may be possible to study the problem of determining what the built-in structure of an information-processing (hypothesis-forming) system must be to enable it to arrive at the grammar of a language from the available data in the available time. At any rate, just as the attempt to eliminate the contribution of the speaker leads to a "mentalistic" descriptive system that succeeds only in blurring important traditional distinctions, a refusal to study the contribution of the child to language learning permits only a superficial account of language acquisition, with a vast and unanalyzed contribution attributed to a step called *generalization* which in fact includes just about everything of interest in this process. If the study of language is limited in these ways, it seems inevitable that major aspects of verbal behavior will remain a mystery.

From *Wild Minds: What Animals Really Think*

Marc D. Hauser

A female Japanese macaque drops a heap of wheat and sand into the ocean, and then skims the wheat off the surface once the sand has settled to the bottom. Although this technique is now a tradition in the population of monkeys living on the Japanese island of Koshima, it was invented by a highly creative female and then acquired by other members of the population. Naïve blue tits, watching skilled birds remove foil from a milk bottle and then drink the rich cream from the top, will then operate the foil in the same way. Human infants, only one hour old, stick out their tongues after an adult has performed the same display. An unmated female guppy will copy the mating preferences of another female if she watches the model's selection of males. These observations, all well documented, suggest that in group living animals, an individual's actions are highly influenced by social interactions. But how do these social interactions help in solving the problems of extracting food, choosing a mate, or finding safe refuge from predators?

Assume you observed a Japanese macaque pick up a heap of wheat and sand, walk over to the water, drop the mixture in and then, as the sand drops down, skim the wheat off the surface and eat it. How did this monkey, or any of the others in the population, acquire the wheat-washing technique? One possibility is that a naïve individual walks over to the water without any group members in sight. Some wheat is floating in the water. She skims it off and eats it. All of a sudden she is struck by insight, and deduces the answer to this foraging problem. Like a contestant playing *Jeopardy*, she has been given the solution and must work out the question. The answer is, "The wheat floats, the sand sinks." The question is, "What happens when you bring wheat and sand over to the water and drop the mixture in?" In this scenario, deduction, not social learning, drives skill acquisition and thus knowledge. Here's a second, similarly asocial method of discovery: the animal walks over to the water for a drink and happens to have some sand and wheat on her hands. As she

137

bends over, she watches as the sand falls to the bottom and the wheat floats. She acquires the skill through luck. Now consider a more social situation: a naïve individual watches as Imo, the actual inventor of this technique, picks wheat flecks from the water. The information is similar to our *Jeopardy* example, but there is a social factor. The naïve individual has once again observed the solution and must fill in the preceding steps. Now imagine a naïve individual sitting and watching as Imo picks up a heap of wheat and sand, heads to the ocean, drops the mix, eats the wheat, and then moves off into a tree. Several minutes later, the naïve individual reproduces this precise sequence of actions. Here, we would be tempted to conclude that the wheat-washing technique was acquired by imitation, a kind of recollection of prior events, a mental replay of the sequence. Finally, consider a case where Imo carries her infant over to the water's edge while the infant holds a mixture of wheat and sand in one hand. The mother then takes her infant's hand and places it in the water, allowing the infant to watch as the sand falls and the wheat floats. In this case, we might be tempted to say that the mother has taught her infant the wheat-washing skill.

When a population of individuals perform the same actions—like using water to separate wheat from sand—we must not jump to the conclusion that they acquired the skill, technique, or gesture in the same exact way. Although *all* animals are equipped with a basic tool for learning, there are differences in the design of this basic tool. For some animals, knowledge is acquired through deduction or trial-and-error learning. For others, it is acquired through imitation and teaching. The challenge is to understand which variants of the basic learning tool are available to which species, in which domains of knowledge, and why.

❋

Teacher's Pets

A child reaches for the bright red glow of a stove-top burner; the mother shouts, "No!" and pulls the child's hand away. A tennis pro stands behind his pupil as they both hold onto the same racket and hit a stroke in unison. A university professor lectures to an audience of students taking down notes. A grandmother allows her granddaughter to continue a knitting project she has started.

In each of these cases, an individual with considerable knowledge and expertise conveys their wisdom to an ignorant individual, teaching them. By using such an umbrella term as *teaching*, however, we risk covering up important differences in the kinds of thoughts and motives underlying each action. Thus, for example, a mother may slap her child's hand as a reflex, an unconscious, automatic action that pays off precisely because it doesn't involve planning or forethought. Imagine what would happen if the mother, upon seeing her child reach for the stove, thought, "Hmmm, my daughter must be putting her hand next to the burning hot stove because she doesn't understand the significance of the red flame. I had better teach her a lesson so that she doesn't hurt herself now and in the future. I will run over and slap her hand away." Although this would certainly work in some cases, the situation is urgent, demanding a swift and nearly automatic response. Although such responses lack explicit planning, they can be functionally instructive. In contrast, the tennis pro's actions are clearly pedagogical instructions based on the recognition of ignorance. By standing behind the pupil and guiding her hand, the instructor molds the stroke, providing the requisite information for hitting a good forehand. The instructor's actions are intentional, designed to achieve a particular goal. If animals teach, therefore, we need to assess whether they do so reflexively or with foresight and planning.

Skilled use of a tool often requires several years of practice. One of the more striking examples of this among animals is the hammer and anvil technique employed by chimpanzees in western Africa and documented in the 1990s by the ethologist Christophe Boesch and the comparative psychologist Tetsuro Matsuzawa. The process starts with finding a functional hammer and anvil. The hammer is either a branch or a stone, configured with a thin grasping end and a thicker striking end. The anvil is either a flat stone or a log, one that will hold a palm nut in place while the hammer comes down and cracks it open. Chimpanzees begin cracking open nuts with some success at around three and a half years, but do not acquire the requisite competence for several more years. Given how long it takes to learn the nut-cracking skill, one might imagine that such pressures would set up the necessary conditions for teaching to evolve, for skilled adults to tutor their young in the art of hammer and anvil operation.

When mothers gather palm nuts and set up at a nut-cracking site, their young often sit around, watching. But the young do more than watch. They often steal nuts from the anvil or from the mother's general stash. Sometimes mothers leave their hammer and anvil set in the presence of young, thereby providing them with an opportunity to manipulate the tools. We certainly recognize such opportunities as invaluable to learning, though they represent only a weak form of teaching. Stronger, but extremely rare, are two cases where chimpanzee mothers have corrected their offspring's attempts at nut cracking. In one case, an infant picked up a branch, fat at one end and thin at the other. With her nut placed on the anvil, she held the fat end of the branch and attempted to crack the nut with the thin end. After the infant failed several times, her mother approached and reoriented the branch. On the next try, the infant held the thin end, struck with the fat end, and cracked the nut. In the second case, a mother helped her infant reposition the nut, placing it on a more secure part of the anvil. Her infant then successfully cracked the nut.

These observations suggest that chimpanzees have the *potential* to recognize inappropriate behavior in another and to respond in such a way that they can make corrections, behavioral fixes that presumably lead to greater competence. I say "presumably" because we actually don't know whether these two cases of instruction resulted in more efficient nut cracking over a longer period of time. So why are such cases of instruction rare, only two cases in more than 150 years of chimpanzee observations? Given the trivial costs incurred by the mother for this brief instruction, and the potentially significant benefits accrued from learning what to do, one would expect pedagogical interactions to be more frequent. Without knowing a great deal about the costs and benefits associated with chimpanzee instruction, we can only speculate here. But two additional factors may shed some light on the problem. Specifically, although young chimpanzees appear to learn from instruction, mortality rates are low during the juvenile years, and are rarely due to food shortages. Thus, although the technique requires years of experience to perfect, there may not be any pressure to learn the skill earlier in life. Also, although instruction helps with certain aspects of the nut-cracking skill, sufficient strength is also required, as well as an ability to find nuts and an appropriate hammer-anvil set. These motor and cognitive capacities develop slowly, and it is not clear how instruction would speed up the process. Before we puzzle over this problem any more, let us explore some additional terrain, attempting to identify other candidate examples.

The Serengeti National Park in Tanzania is populated with thousands of wildebeest and gazelles, as well as elephants, giraffe, buffalo, baboons, and of course, the big cats, leopards, lions, and cheetah. In contrast to lions, who hunt cooperatively, leopards and cheetah tend to hunt alone as adults. If hunting is a solitary affair, how do individuals acquire the requisite skills? Is it by trial and error, a kind of hit-or-miss operation? Or do young learn from their mothers?

Tim Caro, a wildlife biologist, has been studying the Serengeti cheetah since the 1980s, following their moves from the safety of a Land Rover. To understand how hunting skills develop, he started watching cubs, mothers, and females without cubs. When females without cubs chase after a Thompson's gazelle, they kill it by suffocation; if they are after a hare, they bite it through the skull. Mothers with one-and-a-half-month-old cubs hunt in the same way. But when the cubs are about three months old, mothers hunt with a different style. They chase after the prey, first maiming it and then carrying it back to the cubs so that they have the opportunity to first chase and then knock it over. Because cubs at this age rarely kill the prey, mothers intervene, finishing off the job. When the cubs are a few months older, mothers release only one-third of their prey in the presence of their cubs and allow them to finish the kill. At around eight months, cubs rip the prey apart while another member of the family bites into the esophagus to keep the prey from moving off. By ten months, the mother releases half of her prey and cubs are now almost completely successful in the final kill.

What these observations show is that cheetah mothers provide cubs with an opportunity to acquire hunting skills in a controlled environment, what one might call *opportunity teaching*. Their behavior appears sensitive to the cubs' developing abilities; the kind of opportunity presented changes as a function of current hunting skills. But in contrast to the chimpanzee case, cheetah mothers incur a significantly greater cost. Prey released to cubs are much more likely to escape, thereby forcing the mother to go out on another hunt. Hungry mothers therefore are less likely to repeatedly release prey than relatively satiated mothers. By doing the hunting themselves, hungry mothers insure a catch, but eliminate the opportunity for learning. Although we don't know whether cubs with fewer opportunities to hunt end up being less successful hunters later in life, it appears that such opportunities must be beneficial, given the kinds of costs that mothers are willing to incur.

The comparison between cheetah and chimpanzees allows us to make some predictions about the frequency of teaching in a population. Think of the problem in economic terms, where the teacher incurs certain costs of instruction and obtains certain benefits from the pupil acquiring a skill or some knowledge. Similarly, we can think about how the pupil benefits from instruction and the costs incurred if instruction is withheld. For chimpanzees, the costs to the teacher are low and the benefits to the pupil are relatively low; although infants appear to benefit from instruction, they clearly do not depend on instruction for survival, and mortality tends to be quite low during the juvenile years. In contrast, the costs of instruction are high for cheetah mothers and the benefits to cubs appear high as well.

Generalizing from chimpanzees and cheetah, we can make some specific predictions. When the benefits to the pupil are high, teaching should be common even if the costs to the teacher are high. When the benefits to the pupil are low, teaching should be infrequent when the costs to the teacher are low, and either rare or absent when the costs to the teacher are high.

In the late 1960s the zoologist Tom Struhsaker initiated a study of vervet monkeys living in Amboseli National Park, Kenya. Like many other primates, vervets face intense threats from predators. Amboseli is, however, particularly nasty since the vervets fall prey to a spectacular cadre of predators including cheetah, leopards, pythons, black mambas, green mambas, baboons, humans, martial eagles, and crowned hawk eagles. Twenty years of observation reveal that 70 percent of all infants fail to make it past their first birthday. The primary cause of mortality is predation.

Fortunately for vervets, the exceedingly strong pressure from predation has resulted in the evolution of a sophisticated system of alarm calls. Vervets have evolved a unique alarm call for each predator type confronted, calls that trigger the appropriate evasive action. Thus, when leopards are nearby, the best response for a vervet is to run up into a tree. Upon hearing a leopard alarm call, vervets run up into trees. When an eagle is swooping and an eagle alarm call has been sounded, the best response is to run out of a tree and under a bush. And if a snake has been detected or a snake alarm call heard, the best response is to stand bipedally and take a good look as to its whereabouts and possibly its direction of movement. Adults know these moves. Infants do not, at least not until they are about a year old or older. How do they learn?

When a vervet gives an alarm call, others often call as well. Consequently, when an infant spots a predator and gives an alarm call, repeat calls by adults function as positive reinforcement, functional pats on the back for a job well done. Although adults may not be intending to teach their young, their alarm calls provide positive feedback for the infant's vocal behavior. When infants under the age of one year were the first to call, follow-up alarm calls by adults occurred about half the time. Further, infants appeared to benefit from such experiences, as shown by their performance on subsequent encounters. Infants who received positive feedback from adults were more likely to produce an appropriate alarm on the next encounter than infants who either failed to receive such feedback or called to an inappropriate target. As in many other examples emerging from animals living under natural conditions, we cannot know if we have properly documented the infants' learning environment. Although thousands of hours were logged by the vervet research team, it was not possible to log all their experiences.

If we move away from these more detailed studies of teaching in animals, we are treated to an enticing catalog of onetime observations. For example, one vervet infant saw a mongoose (a nonpredator) and gave a leopard alarm call. Immediately she was picked up by her mother, who headed up into the trees. Upon seeing the mongoose, the mother turned to her offspring and slapped her, in what looked like punishment. Among birds, the juvenile yellow-eyed junco is perhaps one of the most inept foragers. In contrast to adults, juveniles pick up mealworms with an inappropriate orientation and, as a result, often drop them. Occasionally, adults approach juveniles and reorient the mealworm in their beak, thereby allowing them to eat their catch. Last, studies of human-reared chimpanzees reveal a few instances of sign language instruction. Thus, for example, while Washoe was anxiously waiting for food with her daughter Loulis, a chimpanzee raised without sign language instruction, she grabbed Loulis's hand and molded it into the sign for "food" repeatedly guiding her through the relevant actions.

Returning to our economic calculations, we find that many of our observations of teaching appear cheap from the perspective of time and energy invested by the teacher. In many of these cases, it would appear that the payoffs for the pupil are high. We are thus left to wonder why teaching is so rare in the animal kingdom, but so common among humans.

All animals enter the school of learning with a core tool for acquiring knowledge. This tool is sufficient for building associations, making deductions, and learning by trial and error. Many animals also learn through social interactions. Surprisingly, perhaps, humans may be the only species to have evolved the mental tools for imitation and teaching.

QUESTIONS

1. If you're reading this in tandem with an intro psych textbook, compare your textbook's version of Watson's study to what Watson and Rayner actually did, using Ben Harris's 1979 *American Psychologist* article, "Whatever happened to Little Albert?" (currently available online at *http://faculty.concord.edu/rockc/articles/albert.html*).

2. How important do you think conditioning is for what humans learn about the world? How much of our knowledge comes from conditioning? In what other ways might humans learn?

3. Which of Chomsky's points do you find most compelling? Least compelling?

4. Since Hauser's book came out, a team at Columbia University, Subiaul et al. (2004), published a paper arguing that macaque monkeys can learn by imitation. Read and evaluate Subiaul's argument (*Science* 305: 407–410).

CHAPTER EIGHT

COGNITIVE DEVELOPMENT

Watson's view (see Chapter 7) that children are born as blank slates is no longer tenable. From the moment babies are born, they know something about the world. They can recognize speech, distinguish a real face from a scrambled face, and use rhythmic clues to differentiate between languages from different families, such as Dutch versus Japanese.

Each of the two selections in this chapter reveals surprising sophistication on the part of infants and toddlers. In *The Scientist in the Crib* (1999), Alison Gopnik, Patricia Kuhl, and Andrew Meltzoff ask what newborns and toddlers know about the give and take between people that we call human social interaction. Whether or not you are convinced by the authors' analogies with flirting and romance, the studies they cite make amply clear that human beings are born to be social.

Paul Bloom's focus in the excerpt from *Descartes' Baby* (2004) is on what toddlers know about art, and in so doing touches on the subtle question of representation, of how young children understand that one thing can *stand* for another. "Would you eat a *picture* of an apple?" asks Bloom. If you were a child, how would you know the difference? Bloom argues that children do indeed seem to know the difference, but even more impressively, he suggests, they understand that the *intention* of an artist is an important component of art. Although it is unlikely that children have an "instinct" for art in the same sense that they do for language (see Chapter 6), such a sophisticated understanding shows that children realize that there is more to the world than what meets the eye.

From *The Scientist in the Crib:*
Minds, Brains, and How Children Learn

Alison Gopnik, Patricia Kuhl, and Andrew Meltzoff

What Newborns Know

You're lying in bed in the labor room of the hospital and you're about as exhausted, as utterly worn out, as you'll ever be. Giving birth is this peculiar combination of determination and compulsion. It's you pushing, and you push in a more concentrated, focused way than you've ever done anything, but in another sense you don't decide or try to push or even want to. You are just swept away by the action. It's like a cross between running a marathon and having the most enormous, shattering, irresistible orgasm of your life.

And then suddenly, in the midst of all this excitement and action, agitation and exhaustion, there is a small, warm body lying on your chest and a tranquil, quiet, wide-eyed face looking up at yours. Maybe it's just the natural endorphins flowing through you once the actual pain is gone, but instead of collapsing, as you might expect, you feel a kind of intensified alertness. You're preternaturally awake, and everything is clearer and sharper than usual. And through the next night or two, when the nurses have finally left you alone, and the helpful husband has gone home to get some sleep and tell the relatives, you lie with the baby in your arms and inhale that peculiar, sweet, animal, newborn smell, and you look, and look for an hour at a time, at the small, still somewhat squished face. And the baby, perhaps also under the spell of the endorphins, alert as he won't be for some days to come, looks at you. And then and there—before the sleepless nights and diapers and strollers and snowsuits have kicked in—that gaze seems to signify perfect mutual understanding, complete peace, absolute happiness.

That's the romance of it, anyway. The romance doesn't come, sadly, with every birth, just as the parallel romance of true love doesn't come with every sexual encounter. But, just as with true love, it is one of the great gifts of life and seems more than worth the risk of disappointment and the reality of pain.

How does this romance of instant understanding compare with the scientific reality? The recent research gives us a picture that is surprisingly in tune with the intuitions of new mothers. For many years "experts" who, in fact, knew nothing systematic about babies, took a certain perverse satisfaction in assuring parents that their new babies' minds were somewhat less sophisticated than that of the average garden slug. Babies couldn't really see; their smiles were "just gas"; the idea that they recognized familiar people was a fond maternal illusion. As this sentence is being written, a columnist in the day's paper talks about his son's new baby brother and comments pityingly on the child's conviction that the baby recognizes him, when, of course, babies can't tell people from dogs. It's as if there is a double layer of folk wisdom about babies. Nearly everyone who actually interacts with them immediately thinks babies have minds. And yet often there's an almost equally immediate cynicism, mixed with distorted echoes of medical legends. You hear new parents say things like "I could swear that she recognizes me, only I know that she can't."

But why should you believe us instead of those benighted experts who thought babies couldn't really see? How can we say we actually do know what babies think? With the help of videotape, scientists have developed ingenious experimental techniques to ask babies what they know. One whole set of techniques has been designed to answer two simple questions: Do babies think that two things are the same or different? And if they think they're different, do they prefer one to the other? You can present babies with pairs of carefully controlled events and see whether they can differentiate between them and which they prefer to look at or listen to. For instance, you can show babies a picture of a human face and a picture of a complicated object, like a checkerboard. Then an observer, who doesn't know what the babies are looking at, records their eye movements. By analyzing the babies' eye movements, you can see which picture they looked at longer. You can take the same idea a bit further by getting babies to suck on pacifiers that turn on different video- or audiotapes and determining which tapes they are willing to do some work for. You can see, for instance, if they will keep a tape of their own mother's voice playing longer than a tape of a stranger's voice.

Finally, you can exploit the fact that babies, like the rest of us, get bored. If you show babies the same old same old over and over, they stop looking and listening. Change the tape to something new, and they perk up and take notice. Developmental scientists call this boredom "habituation." So, for instance, you can show a series of different happy faces, and the babies will gradually lose interest; they'll habituate. Show them a new happy face, and they hardly look any longer. But show them a sad face, and they start to stare again. This means that babies somehow know that the happy faces are the same and the sad face is different.

Using these sorts of techniques we can show that at birth, babies can discriminate human faces and voices from other sights and sounds, and that they prefer them. Within a few days after they're born, they recognize familiar faces, voices, and even smells and prefer them to unfamiliar ones (it even looks as if they recognize their mother's voice at birth based on the muted but still audible sounds they hear in the womb). They'll turn toward a familiar face or voice and even toward a pad that has been held close to their mother's skin and turn away from other faces, voices, and smells.

Within the first nine months, before babies can walk or talk or even crawl, they can tell the difference between expressions of happiness and sadness and anger, and even can recognize that a happy-looking face, a face with a smile and crinkly eyes, goes with the chirp of a happy tone of voice. You can show them two films, side by side, one of a face with a happy expression and one of a face with a sad expression. If you turn on a sound track playing either a happy or sad voice, babies will look longer at the face displaying the emotional expression that matches the emotion they hear.

They even know how people move. You can tie small, bright lights to someone's elbows, knees, and shoulders and then film that person moving in the dark. In the resulting film, only the spots of moving light are visible. To an adult this pattern of lights is clearly human and can even convey emotions; it's like a kind of simple cartoon. It turns out that babies also are able to differentiate this abstract pattern of moving lights from patterns that aren't human, and they prefer it. They seem to be so tuned to other people that an abstractly human pattern of lights is riveting.

Even the limitations of babies' vision make them pay special attention to people. It's a myth that newborn babies can't see, but babies are very nearsighted by adult standards, and unlike adults, they have difficulty changing their focus to suit both near and far objects. What this means is that objects about a foot away are in sharp focus and objects nearer or farther are blurred. Of course, that's just the distance from a newborn's face to the face of the person who is holding him or her. Babies seem designed to see the people who love them more clearly than anything else.

The newborn's world seems to be a bit like the room full of Rembrandt portraits in the National Gallery of Art in Washington, D.C. Brightly lit faces, full of every nuance of movement, life, expression, and emotion, leap out from the background of gloomy obscurity, in a startling psychological chiaroscuro.

All this, though, is just appearances. Do babies have a deeper conception of what it is to be human? There is some reason to think that they do. Twenty years ago one of us, Andy, made a startling discovery. One-month-old babies imitate facial expressions. If you stick your tongue out at a baby, the baby will stick his tongue out at you; open your mouth, and the baby will open hers. How do we know that this is really imitation, that we aren't just reading it into the babies' endlessly mobile faces? Andy systematically showed babies either someone sticking out his tongue or someone opening his mouth. He videotaped the babies' faces. Then he showed the tapes of the babies' faces to someone else, someone who had no idea which gesture the babies had seen. This second person had to say whether each baby was sticking out his or her tongue or opening his or her mouth. It turned out there was a systematic relation between what the babies did, judged by this necessarily neutral and objective observer, and what the babies saw.

At first Andy did these experiments with three-week-olds. But to demonstrate that this ability was really innate, he had to show that newborn babies could imitate. So he set up a lab next to the labor room in the local hospital and arranged with parents to call him when the baby was about to arrive. For a year he would wake up in the middle of the night, or dash out of a lab meeting, and rush to the hospital, in almost as much of a hurry as the expectant parents themselves. But that meant he could test babies less than a day old; the youngest baby was only forty-two minutes old. The newborns imitated, too.

At first glance this ability to imitate might seem curious and cute but not deeply significant. But if you think about it a minute, it is actually amazing. There are no mirrors in the womb: newborns have never seen their own face. So how could they know whether their tongue is inside or outside their mouth? There is another way of knowing what your face is like. As you read this, you probably have a good idea of your facial expression (we hope intense concentration leavened by the occasional smile). Try sticking out your tongue (in a suitably private setting). The way you know you've succeeded is through kinesthesia, your internal feeling of your own body.

In order to imitate, newborn babies must somehow understand the similarity between that internal feeling and the external face they see, a round shape with a long pink thing at the bottom moving back and forth. Newborn babies not only distinguish and prefer faces, they also seem to recognize that those faces are like their own face. They recognize that other people are "like me." There is nothing more personal, more part of you, than this internal sense you have of your own body, your expressions and movements, your aches and tickles. And yet from the time we're born, we seem to link this deeply personal self to the bodily movements of other people, movements we can only see and not feel. Nature ingeniously gives us a jump start on the Other Minds problem. We know, quite directly, that we are like other people and they are like us.

There are other reasons to think that even very young babies are especially tuned to people. Babies flirt. One of the great pleasures in life is to hold a three-month-old in your arms and talk absolute nonsense. "My, my, my," you hear your usually sane, responsible, professional voice saying, "you *are* a pretty bunny, *aren't* you, aren't you, aren't you, sweetums, aren't you a pretty bunny?" You raise your eyebrows and purse your mouth and make ridiculous faces. But the even more striking thing is that that tiny baby responds to your absurdities. He coos in response to your coo, he answers your smile with a smile of his own, he gestures in rhythm with the intonation of your voice. It's as if the two of you are engaged in an intricate dance, a kind of wordless conversation, a silly love song, pillow talk. It's sheer heaven.

But aside from being sheer heaven, it's also more evidence that babies spontaneously coordinate their own expressions, gestures, and voices with the expressions, gestures, and voices of other people. Flirting is largely a matter of timing. If you look around at a party, you can tell who's flirting just by looking at them, without even hearing a word. What you see is the way two people time their gestures so they're in sync with each other and with nobody else in the crowded room. She brushes her hair off her face, and he puts his hand in his pocket; she leans forward eagerly and talks, and he leans back sympathetically and listens. It's the same way with babies. When you talk, the baby is still; when you pause, the baby takes her turn and there's a burst of coos and waving fists and kicking legs. Like imitation, baby flirtation suggests that babies not only know people when they see them but also that they are connected to people in a special way. Like grown-up flirtation, baby flirtation bypasses language and establishes a more direct link between people.

The Really Eternal Triangle

So even in the first few months of life babies understand that there's something special about other people and that they are linked to other people in a special way. That's the Martin Buber part of our everyday understanding of the mind. But life isn't, unfortunately, all mystic communion or, even more unfortunately, just pillow talk. Even college students may resort to meaningless baby talk in the Valentine's Day classifieds, but they will not do very well if their term papers are equally vacuous. There is a lot more we need to know about people.

One thing to know about people is what they think about *things*. People look at things, want them, act on them, and know about them. When babies are about a year old, there is a striking change in the way they interact with people. Suddenly, instead of just you and me insulated in our cocoon of infant romance, interlopers enter the picture: teddy bears, balls, keys, rattles, lamp cords, spoons, puppy dogs, telephones, porcelain vases, lipsticks, distant airplanes—a panoply of fascinating, seductive, irresistible objects. As babies become able to sit up and reach and crawl, these things, which were formerly mostly the objects of a fascinated but distant gaze, become objects of desire and danger. Fortunately, other people don't completely vanish from the babies' thoughts (though it may feel that way to parents). Instead, they become an essential part of a kind of cognitive triangle.

When babies are around a year old, they begin to point to things and they begin to look at things that other people point to. Like imitation, pointing is something so familiar we take it for granted. But also like imitation, pointing implies a deep understanding of yourself and of other people. To point to something, especially when you point again and again, looking back at the other person's face until he or she also looks at the object, implies that you think, at some level, that the other person should look at the same thing you are looking at. We can systematically record and measure where babies look as they watch a grown-up point to particular places. By the time they're a year old, the babies will look, quite precisely, at just the place the grown-up pointed to.

Other experiments also show that one-year-olds have a radically new understanding of people. What happens when you show a baby something new, something a little strange, maybe wonderful, maybe dangerous—say, a walking toy robot? The baby looks over at Mom quizzically and checks her out. What does she think? Is there a reassuring smile or an expression of shocked horror? One-year-olds will modify their own reactions accordingly. If there's a smile, they'll crawl forward to investigate, if there's horror, they'll stop dead in their tracks.

Again we can show this quite systematically. For instance, a grown-up can look into two boxes. She looks into one box with an expression of joy and into the other with an expression of complete disgust. Then she pushes the boxes toward the baby, who has never seen inside the boxes. Nevertheless, the baby figures out something about what is inside just by looking at the experimenter's face: the baby happily reaches into the box that made her happy but won't open the box that disgusted her. The baby doesn't just understand that the other person feels happy or disgusted, but also understands that she feels happy about some things and disgusted about others.

In a similar way, one-year-old babies can figure out what to do with objects by looking at what other people do with them. Andy used imitation to test this. He would show babies a completely unexpected way to use a new object—he would touch his forehead to the top of a box, and it would light up. The babies watched in fascination, but they weren't allowed to touch the box themselves. A week later the babies came back to the lab. This time Andy just gave them the box, without doing anything to it himself. But the babies immediately touched *their* foreheads to the top of the box. There's a common myth that babies have no memory. But all during that week the new information about what people do with this thing had been percolating away. Moreover, the babies seemed to assume that if other people do something special to an object, they should do the same thing. (You can see this in the way babies play with a toy telephone. Even though the toy telephone doesn't actually do anything, babies will mimic what grown-ups do with a real telephone; they push the buttons and hold the toy phone up to their ear and even babble into it.)

When babies are around a year old, then, they seem to discover that their initial emotional rapport with other people extends to a set of joint attitudes toward the world. We see the same objects, do the same things with those objects, even feel the same way about those objects. This insight adds a whole new dimension to the babies' understanding of other minds. But it also adds a whole new dimension to babies' understanding of the world. One-year-old babies know that they will see something by looking where other people point; they know what they should do to something by watching what other people do; they know how they should feel about something by seeing how other people feel.

The babies can use other people to figure out the world. In a very simple way, these one-year-olds are already participating in a culture. They already can take advantage of the discoveries of previous generations. They don't have to discover for themselves that there is something worth looking at in that corner or something disgusting in that box, or that the box lights up when you touch it with your forehead. Even without using language we can tell them all those things. Even babies who can't talk yet are naturally cultural beings.

This new understanding also lets babies use other people to get things done. A one-year-old can point to a toy that's out of reach and expect that the grown-up will get it for her, or put her hand on the grown-up's hand and get the grown-up to spoon out the applesauce. Even before babies can talk, they can communicate.

This particular triangular story has a happy ending. The babies' new interest in things also leads to a deeper commonality and communication with other people. After all, there is more to communication than communion. Even with grownups, pillow talk eventually gives way to the rather different delight of discovering that you both really do love Thai food and hate Quentin Tarantino movies. In the best romances, you face the world together; you don't just face each other. After twelve months or so the same thing happens in the romance between children and their parents.

From *Descartes' Baby: How the Science of Child Development Explains What Makes Us Human*

Paul Bloom

Baby Pictures

The earliest-emerging ability that bears a relationship to art is the ability to appreciate visual representations. Even babies can do this. If you let five-month-olds play with a doll and then take it away and show them pictures of dolls, they will look longer at a picture of a new doll than at one of the doll that they just played with, an indication that they appreciate that an object and a realistic depiction of it are very closely related. When children start to talk, they use words to name not only actual objects, but also objects portrayed in pictures. There is also some dramatic evidence that—contrary to some anthropological anecdotes—naming pictured objects does not require any prior experience with pictures. In 1962, the psychologists Julian Hochberg and Virginia Brooks reported a study where they took a child (presumably their own, though they did not say) and raised him without any access to pictures, television, or other visual representations. Then, when he was 19 months old, they showed him a series of photographs and line drawings of familiar objects and asked him to name them. He did so easily.

Who would have thought otherwise? After all, both Euclid and Leonardo da Vinci pointed out that a realistic painting works because it can impress upon the eye much the same visual array as the real world. A realistic picture of a dog looks to the eye much like a real dog. In fact, with *trompe l'oeil* ("fool the eye") artwork one actually cannot tell the difference between representation and reality. There is a story by O. Henry about a sickly woman who says that she will die when the last leaf falls. She stares out the window of her apartment, and after all the other leaves fall, one remains, even as the season changes. The leaf turns out to have been painted on the brick wall opposite by an elderly painter who wants to keep her alive. The ability to recognize realistic pictures is nothing more than a by-product of how vision works. Any creature that gets information through the senses—any creature that is not a deity—runs the risk of being confused by a clever enough representation.

(The opposite error—taking the real thing for a representation—is rare, but it does happen. At a masquerade ball in Monte Carlo there was a competition to decide which of the guests masquerading as Charlie Chaplin looked most like Chaplin. It so happened that Chaplin himself was there. He got third prize.)

It is possible, then, that babies might be able to recognize pictures without any understanding of their role as representations. And, in fact, children younger than about one and a half years of age do seem confused by pictures. Attentive adults have noticed certain weird behaviors such as a child trying to step into a picture of a shoe or scratching at a picture book as if trying to grasp the object depicted there. When experimenters plunk babies down in front of picture books and film their behavior, it turns out that they really do tend to treat depicted objects as if they were real, and try to lift them from the page. This is not limited to children living within representation-rich Western culture; those from impoverished and illiterate families in the Ivory Coast, where pictures are rare, do the same thing.

Babies can tell objects and pictures apart. When given the choice, they prefer to look at a doll than a picture of a doll; and they reach for real objects more often than they reach for pictures of objects. Also, when they try to pick up a depicted object and fail, they are not *that* upset; they seem somewhat resigned to their failure. It seems likely that they are confused about what pictures are; they are seen as bizarre things, as inferior objects—like real things in shape and color, but strangely flat. As the psychologist Judy DeLoache and her colleagues put it, "They treat a depiction as though it were an object, not because they firmly believe it is, but because they are unsure that it is not."

Adults are smarter than this; we know that pictures are representations and can be used as a medium to understand and talk about the things they represent. When someone shows you a picture of her child, she doesn't expect you to admire the *picture*; when she says "This is Emma," she is not naming regions of pixels or two-dimensional patterns of color. Much of what we know about the external world is not learned through seeing the things themselves, but by seeing pictures of them.

Indeed, most of us learn about specific artworks not by looking at the works but by looking at *pictures* of the works. (Almost everyone knows what the *Mona Lisa* looks like but only a small minority has actually seen it.) You might think, following Plato, that the original is always better than the representation, but this might not be true. One of Elkins's criers wept because of disappointment. Entranced by a film about Michelangelo's work, she flew to Florence and felt terribly let down by what she saw: "The statues were not as great as the *photographs* of them!"

Would You Eat a Picture of an Apple?

By the time children are about a year and a half, they no longer reach for pictures. Do they then appreciate their representational nature? To explore this, the psychologists Susan Carey and Melissa Allen Preissler did a simple but elegant study. They used pictures to teach children new words. For instance, they would take 18-month-olds who had never seen a whisk before, show them a line drawing of a whisk, and repeatedly use the word "whisk" to describe the drawing. Then they would give the children a choice between the very same picture they were trained on and a real whisk and ask them to find "the whisk." Children almost always go for the actual object. This is quite neat. It shows that they know that when a name is used for a picture, it does not refer to the picture itself; it refers to what the picture represents. Before children reach their second birthday, then, they know what pictures are.

I should admit that not all psychologists would agree with this. Some research purports to show that even older children are deeply confused about representations. Three-year-olds will sometimes say yes when asked, "Can you eat this picture of an apple?" They will sometimes agree that if you get close to a picture of a rose, you can smell it. Some of them will even agree that if you cut a picture of a rattle in half, something would happen to the real rattle! Other studies find that when asked to "point to things you can really eat," young children pointed not only to real foods, but also to pictures of food—even if they had previously agreed that the pictures are "just pictures."

Some researchers take this as showing a failure to distinguish reality from representation. I am skeptical. I think it just shows that children can be misled by weird questions. Adults are savvy enough about what goes on in a psychology experiment to focus on the literal form of what they are asked and to ignore normal rules of conversation. Imagine how strange it would be to be shown a picture of some food and be asked, "Can you eat it?" and assume that the person was asking about the *picture*. We do sometimes ask about pictures for their own sake, but this is typically if they are themselves of some artistic merit, as when a German officer once handed Picasso a postcard of his painting *Guernica*—inspired by the German bombing of the Basque village of that name—and asked, "Did you do that?" Picasso replied, "No, you did."

If these older children really didn't understand pictures, you would expect them to act oddly toward them in everyday life, but they don't. They might say that you can eat a picture of an apple, but if you ask them to go ahead and do so, they decline. Finally, children surely don't *really* think that what happens to a picture happens to the object. As the psychologist Norman Freeman pointed out, if you tell a three-year-old you are going to tear up a picture of her, she will not be struck with mortal terror.

This is not to say that young children are fully competent with representations. Some of their limitations are obvious: they cannot read maps, flowcharts, diagrams, and, most important, words. All this has to be learned.

Also, DeLoache and her colleagues have discovered that children have problems coping with the "dual nature" of representations—the fact that they are both concrete entities and abstract symbolic ones. For instance, two-and-a-half-year-olds can use a picture of a room to recover the location of a hidden toy. Once they see where the toy is in the picture, they know where to find it in the room itself. But they do much worse when shown the location of the toy in a three-dimensional model. This is surprising, because you might think that a model, being more realistic, would be easier to make sense of than a picture, and easier to use as a representation. But DeLoache argues that the model is so interesting (it is a tangible three-dimensional object) that children focus on it as a thing in itself, and this distracts them from its representational properties. When the model is made less interesting, children become better able to use it to find the hidden toy.

These findings have important practical implications. In cases of suspected sexual abuse, investigators often use anatomically correct dolls to try to elicit accurate reporting of what happened to the children. But there is some evidence that, at least with two- and three-year-olds, this is useless and misleading because dolls are sufficiently interesting in their own right that children fail to understand that they are supposed to serve as representations—in this case, of human bodies.

Adults shouldn't be too smug. We also do better when not distracted by extraneous properties of representations. And we can sometime confuse a change in representation with a change in reality, getting muddled about what happens when one shifts to and from daylight savings time or moves from one time zone to another. A dramatic example of this is when England adopted the Georgian calendar on September 3, 1752, which caused that date suddenly to become September 14. Farmers rioted because they worried that the lost 11 days would ruin the growing season!

Making and Naming Pictures

Every culture has some form of art, if only scratches on trees, markings on cave walls, or drawings in the sand. And all normal humans have some capacity to create art. Children love to draw, scribble, and mold with clay. There are plainly cultural and individual differences, but this should not obscure the universal tendency to make and appreciate art.

What can we learn from the earliest creations of children who have been raised in Western cultures? The most obvious fact is that these creations are not, to put it mildly, realistic. The psychologist Howard Gardner begins his book *Artful Scribbles* by giving us a tour of children's drawings and comparing each one to the work of a renowned adult artist. Here is Danny, whose minimalist creations are reminiscent of those of Theo van Doesburg; Kathy's painting looks much like the work of Jackson Pollock; this painting by Thomas could have well been done by Miró, Picasso, or Klee. These are all *abstract* artists; nobody says of children that they draw like Rembrandt, da Vinci, or Vermeer.

It might seem that even if these early creations are sensibly thought of as art, they are not representational art; they are not about anything in the world. But there is one wrinkle here: *Children name their creations.* They describe their scribbles, scrawls, and blotches using ordinary terms such as "Mommy," "truck," and so on. I first became interested in the psychology of art when my son Max, then a two-year-old, pointed to some smears of paint and proudly said that it was "an airplane."

What should we conclude from this behavior? Does Max believe that his paint blob represents an airplane? Do other children believe that their scribbles represent trucks, horses, their mothers? Gardner considers this issue, and raises several possibilities:

> Does the child really discern a resemblance that happens to be missed by everyone else? Does he seek to "wish" the form into being by so anointing it; might he even be performing some kind of magical or totemistic act? Does the child see labeling as a game in which the culture participates, or is it done simply to please adults who may well have been bombarding him with the inevitable "What is it? What are you drawing? Tell me what it is."

Although Gardner goes on to entertain the notion that there is *some* representational ability displayed here—perhaps the marks are "a primitive kind of notation standing for the object"—he is ultimately unsympathetic to this view and goes on to dub children's naming "romancing" because the child's names "promise representations which are not, however, delivered." If there is representational intent here, it is not successful.

But consider a different possibility, which is that children are representational artists from the moment they put crayon to paper. If so, then the child's perspective corresponds to that of the narrator of the classic children's book *The Little Prince*, which begins with his thinking about jungle adventures, and then creating a simple colored drawing, a brown shape that looks like a hat. He then shows it to adults and asks if they are frightened. They reply, "Why be scared of a hat?" The child writes, "My drawing was not a picture of a hat. It was a picture of a boa constrictor digesting an elephant." Later, discouraged, the narrator notes, "Grown-ups never understand anything by themselves, and it is exhausting for children to have to provide explanations over and over again."

What makes the brown shape a snake swallowing an elephant, presumably, is that the child intends it to be so. Perhaps, then, for a child, if something is *intended* to represent a thing, then it *does* represent that thing and can be given that name.

If this is true, it would follow that, at a minimum, children should be able to name pictures that do not resemble what they depict. This is what I explored in collaboration with the psychologist Lori Markson. In one study, three- and four-year-olds were told that they were going to be shown some pictures drawn by a child their own age who had a broken arm. To explain why the pictures were so unrealistic, they were informed that the child tried *really* hard to draw good pictures, but because of the broken arm, the pictures did not always come out looking like what the child wanted.

In the "size task," the children were shown a drawing that depicted two squiggles of unequal size and were told, "She drew a picture of a spider and a tree." In the "oddity task," they were shown a drawing of four ovals, one with a different orientation than the rest, and told, "She drew three pigs and one chicken." During testing, the experimenter pointed to each figure in the picture and asked the children to describe it. This is easy enough for an adult. For the size task, we take the relative sizes of the markings to correspond to the relative sizes of the objects in the world, and name the smaller object as the spider and the larger one as the tree. For the oddity task, we assume that the markings that look the same correspond to objects of the same kind, and the one that looks different corresponds to the object of a different kind, and so we correctly label the three pigs and the one chicken.

We found that even three-year-olds did better than chance on both tasks. They can name pictures on the basis of cues other than resemblance. This fits with the results of another study that used two yellow Ping-Pong balls of identical size, but one much heavier than the other. Children were told, "I have a daddy and a baby." On some trials they were asked to point to "the daddy"; on others they were asked to point to "the baby." By the age of about two and a half, children succeeded at picking the heavy one as the daddy.

The next step was to directly explore whether children of this age could actually use the intent of a person when making sense of drawings. To test this, we did a study where two similar objects, such as a fork and a spoon, were placed in front of the child, one to the left and one to the right. The experimenter looked intently at one of the objects and appeared to draw a picture of it. Unbeknownst to the child, the picture had actually been predrawn to look equally like both of the objects.

The picture was then placed between the two objects and the child was asked what it was a picture of. Almost always, the answer depended on what the child thought the experimenter was intending to draw. If she had been looking at the spoon while "drawing" it, they called it "a spoon"; if she was looking at the fork they called it "a fork." The very same picture got a different name according to how the child thought it had been created.

We then did a similar version with pictures that children themselves drew. Children were requested to draw four pictures on separate sheets of paper, each with a different-colored crayon. These were (1) a balloon, (2) a lollipop, (3) the child him- or herself, (4) the experimenter. After a pause of several minutes during which the child and the experimenter engaged in another activity, the experimenter "rediscovered" the drawings and asked the child to describe them.

The logic behind this study is that preschool children are notoriously unskilled artists. By having them draw different pictures of entities similar in appearance, we reasoned that their subsequent naming of these pictures could not be based on appearance, but would have to be determined, at least in part, by their memory of their own representational intent. It is important to note that, as expected, the drawings often did not look anything like balloons, lollipops, or people, and even when they did—mostly for the four-year-olds—one could not tell from its appearance whether a given drawing represented a lollipop or a balloon or the experimenter or the child. A typical example from a four-year-old is shown in figure 1 (on page 162).

As predicted, when later asked to name the drawings, both the three-year-olds and four-year-olds did so on the basis of what they had intended them to represent. If they created their drawing with the intent that it should represent a balloon, they would call it a balloon; if they wanted it to be a lollipop, they would call it a lollipop. This is not a subtle laboratory phenomenon: a good way to make a child cry is to take a picture that is described as "Mommy" and insist that it is a picture of someone else—the child's brother, say. Children resent this; they know it is a picture of Mommy because that is the person they intend it to depict.

If understanding pictures requires understanding people's goals and desires, it follows that autistic children should have problems understanding pictures.

They do. Melissa Allen Preissler gave autistic children the "whisk study" described earlier, where the experimenter named a picture of a novel object and then tested whether children would later extend the name to the same picture or the real object that the picture depicts. She found that unlike the normally developing children, autistic children would choose the picture.

What about much older and more adept autistic individuals? In some research that I did in collaboration with the psychologists Frances Abell, Francesca Happé, and Uta Frith, we explored whether they could use the intention of the artist when naming pictures. We tested older autistic children,

FIGURE 1——CHILDREN NAME THEIR DRAWINGS.
From Bloom and Markson, "Children's Naming of Representations,"
Psychological Science, April 1997, 4–6, by permission of Blackwell
Publishing.

of an average age of about 10 years old, and a verbal IQ of about 7 years old.
These were reasonably well functioning individuals; you could converse with
them, and they had no problem naming objects in realistic pictures which
actually resembled what they depicted. Our first effort was to duplicate the
study that Lori Markson and I had done with pictures of lollipops, balloons,
and the experimenter. We asked our autistic subjects to draw these things
and later asked them to name them, predicting that they would not be able
to tap their memory of their original intent to do so.

This experiment was a disaster. The problem was that the logic of the
study rested on the children creating pictures that could not be named on
the basis of appearance—and our subjects were just too adroit at drawing.
Their lollipops looked like lollipops; their pictures of me (when I was the experimenter) looked like me. In retrospect, this should not have been that

surprising, given that autistic children tend to be good artists. But it meant that the study could not be done, since our subjects could name their drawings without any appeal to intention, just by looking at them.

So we did something else. The child sat across from the experimenter, with either four toy cars or four toy planes spread in a line between them. The objects differed in color but were otherwise identical. The experimenter looked intently at one of the objects, drew it using a pencil, and then asked the child, "What is this a picture of?" In another task, using a different display of identical objects, the subjects were given a piece of paper and a pencil and asked to draw any one of the objects. Then the experimenter asked what their picture was of. Correct responses in both tasks entailed identifying the precise object that was attended to (by either the experimenter or by the subject) as the picture was being drawn. If a subject gave a vague answer, such as "A car" or "A plane," he or she was asked "Which car?" or "Which plane?" Note that because the only differentiating feature was color, the target of the drawing could not be identified by resemblance. The child would have to look at the drawing and remember the intention behind it.

For the sake of comparison, we also tested a group of normally developing children. These were younger than the autistic children, they had, on average, a lower verbal IQ, and they were nowhere near as good as drawing pictures. But they had no impairment in social reasoning.

We found that the children with autism performed significantly less well than the normally developing children, both when naming the picture drawn by the experimenter and when naming the picture that they themselves had drawn. These autistic children did not seem to have the same instinctive understanding about the relationship between what a picture was or how it should be named and the intent of the artist—even when they themselves were the artists.

QUESTIONS

1. What are some things that adults know about art that two-year-olds do not? How do they learn these things?

2. What are some things that adults know about human interaction that toddlers do not? How might children eventually attain a more sophisticated adult understanding?

CHAPTER NINE

MEMORY AND COGNITION

Humans are remarkably adept at thinking and reasoning about the world, but far from perfect. Moreover, as Freud anticipated, and as we read in Keith Stanovich's selection (Chapter 2), we're often unaware of our own internal mental processes. How do we think, reason, and remember? It is the burden of cognitive psychology to take us beyond our often unreliable intuitions about the operations of our own minds and into a genuine understanding of mind and behavior.

Each of the two selections here is drawn from a book that exposes cognitive limitations that we may not even realize we have. Daniel Schacter's *Searching for Memory* (1996) tells us something about the limits of recall, recollection, and remembrance; Daniel Wegner's *The Illusion of Conscious Will* (2002) explains how easily we can be fooled into thinking we control things that we do not (or, fooled into thinking that we are not in control when we really are, as with Ouija boards).

These studies call attention to the limitations of the human mind, but they also make a broader point. When it comes to understanding the mind and behavior, intuition alone is not enough. It is only through careful experimental research that we will ultimately be able to understand fully the inner workings of the human mind.

From *Searching for Memory: The Brain, the Mind, and the Past*

Daniel L. Schacter

December afternoons darken early in Boston. For most people, this is one of the more depressing features of the New England winter. I don't mind it much, because the early evenings allow me to enjoy the sunset from the windows of my office near the northern fringe of the Harvard campus. The stunning view of the entire Boston skyline is especially lovely in the fading light of dusk on a winter afternoon. At the close of one such afternoon in December 1993, I took a much-needed break and gazed out the windows. But my pleasant reverie was interrupted by the ring of a telephone.

The caller introduced himself as Rowan Wilson, an attorney with the prestigious New York firm of Cravath, Swaine, and Moore. His firm had been representing the computer giant IBM in a major lawsuit in which questions about memory seemed likely to play a role. I agreed to hear about the case and to consider becoming involved in it.

Wilson's first question struck an immediate chord: Is it possible, he wanted to know, for a person to retrieve information from a past experience without being aware that he is relying on memory? Most of my scientific efforts for the past decade had been directed toward precisely that issue. I had been conducting experiments investigating what my colleagues and I call *implicit memory:* when people are influenced by a past experience without any awareness that they are remembering. Yes, I responded, a person most definitely can make use of memory for a past experience without any awareness of remembering. But why on earth would an attorney have any interest in knowing that?

This one had excellent reasons: parts of his case hinged on the viability of the idea that memory can be manifested without awareness of remembering. Wilson's case entailed a dispute over intellectual property: Who owns the rights to the ideas and knowledge that an employee develops in the course of performing his duties? Much depended on the status of technical knowledge residing in the head of an electrical engineer who had once worked at IBM, Peter Bonyhard. Beginning in 1984, Bonyhard played a key role in IBM's development of a revolutionary new technology for reading information from a computer disk. He had helped to develop what is known in the industry as an MR (magneto-resistive) head. This almost unimaginably tiny, paper-thin device uses a magnetically based method for decoding information stored on a disk that allows computer manufacturers to pack much more information onto the disk than they could with previous technology. The technical and financial implications of MR head technology are enormous, and Bonyhard was a valued IBM employee. But his services were also coveted by others. In 1991 Bonyhard left IBM to join a rival company, Seagate, that specializes in manufacturing disk drives and heads.

IBM objected to the fact that Bonyhard was allowed to work on MR heads at Seagate. While at IBM, he had been exposed to a large amount of confidential, trade-secret information about the manufacture and function of MR heads, information he had promised not to disclose. IBM contended that because he was deeply involved in Seagate's attempt to develop its own MR head, it would be virtually impossible—despite his best intentions—for Bonyhard not to disclose trade-secret information. This was the heart of Rowan Wilson's case and the reason he was consulting me: he suspected that Bonyhard might unknowingly divulge trade-secret information in his new job.

Although I never had the opportunity to address the issues—IBM and Seagate settled their dispute and Bonyhard could no longer work directly on the development of MR heads—the case raises questions that are central to understanding memory's fragile power: To what extent can people show memory for previous experiences even when they are not aware of remembering them? What is the evidence for such implicit memories, and how do they influence what we do and what we think in our day-to-day lives? What does the existence of implicit memory tell us about the nature and organization of memory in mind and brain?

During the past fifteen years, psychology and neuroscience have made immense progress toward answering those questions. It is no exaggeration to say that research on implicit memory has revolutionized how we measure the effects of past experiences and how we think about the nature of memory. The path that led to implicit memory—both for me personally and for the field as a whole—can be traced back to events that unfolded some two decades earlier in the ancient town of Oxford.

Why Do Amnesic Patients Learn?

When I arrived in Oxford just after the New Year in 1978, it was the first time I had ever been to England. I was captivated immediately by the impressive towers and intricate spires of All Soul's College, the golden brown stones of the magnificent Bodleian library, and the narrow stone paths that lead to centuries-old stores and pubs. Enrolled as a graduate student at the University of Toronto, I had been blessed with a stroke of good fortune: my supervisor, Endel Tulving, had been awarded a visiting chair at Oxford for a year and I would be spending most of that year with him.

Tulving had arranged for me to meet weekly with Professor Lawrence Weiskrantz, one of the world's authorities on how the brain accomplishes perception and memory. Weiskrantz and his colleague, the London neuropsychologist Elizabeth Warrington, had recently published several articles about amnesic patients that intrigued and puzzled memory researchers. In their experiments, amnesics and a group of normal volunteers studied a list of common words, such as *table* or *garden*. When shown some of these words several minutes later, together with words that were not on the list, amnesic patients had great difficulty remembering which had been on the list and which hadn't. No surprise here: previous studies had already shown that amnesics have problems recognizing words from a recently presented study list. But Warrington and Weiskrantz gave another kind of memory test. They provided the first three letters of a word, such as tab___ or gar___, and asked people to supply the remaining letters. On this test, amnesic patients wrote down more words from the study list than would be expected if they were guessing randomly. Even more impressively, in some experiments they wrote down as many words as did people who had no memory problems. How is it possible to explain such a curious pattern?

Warrington and Weiskrantz suggested one reason why the three-letter cues might have been especially useful to amnesic patients: they help patients avoid being confused by irrelevant memories that ordinarily spring to mind and interfere with their recall of the correct answer. But something else was noteworthy about the amnesic patients' performance: they did not appear to be aware that they were recalling words from the study list when they provided them in response to the three-letter test cues. Instead, they often behaved as if they were in a guessing game. They were showing memory for the studied words, but they were not "remembering" in the ordinary sense of the term.

Weiskrantz noticed something even more extraordinary about a different type of brain-damaged patient. He started to study a man who had lost much of his vision as a result of damage to the occipital lobes, the structures in the rear of our brains that are necessary to perceive the external world around us. When a light was flashed in the part of visual space affected by his brain damage, the patient typically claimed to see nothing. But when asked to "guess" the location of the flash, he performed extremely accurately! The patient seemed capable of some form of unconscious perception. Weiskrantz called this remarkable ability *blindsight*, and suggested that it might be related in some way to memory without awareness in amnesic patients.

I was excited by these observations, which dovetailed with pioneering studies in the 1960s by Brenda Milner and her colleagues showing that the profoundly amnesic patient HM could learn new motor skills. When HM practiced tracking a moving target, his performance—just like that of people with intact memories—became increasingly accurate. HM, however, was not aware that he had ever performed the task before.

When first confronted with this surprising finding, memory researchers did not show much interest in it. The standard interpretation held that HM could learn new motor skills because motor learning is a special kind of memory that does not depend on the hippocampus and the other medial temporal lobe structures that were removed from HM's brain. Most memory researchers conceded that motor learning is different from other kinds of memory and pursued the matter no further. Yet Warrington and Weiskrantz's findings with amnesic patients, together with the demonstration of blindsight in vision, suggested that preserved motor learning in HM might have much broader implications. To me, these counterintuitive observations intimated the existence of a subterranean world of nonconscious memory and perception, normally concealed from the conscious mind.

Philosophers, physicians, and psychiatrists had already made sporadic observations about this intriguing hidden world. I was well aware that Freud and other psychoanalysts had theorized for decades about an unconscious mind that is a repository of repressed wishes, fantasies, and fears. But, as far as I could tell, retention without awareness in amnesic patients or perception without awareness in blindsight had nothing to do with repressed urges and desires. And there had been scant scientific progress in investigating or understanding the Freudian notion of the unconscious. Even before Freud, the British physician Robert Dunn reported in 1845 that a woman who had been rescued from a near-drowning incident seemed incapable of remembering anything (probably because of oxygen loss to the brain). Dunn wrote with some amazement how she learned to be a skilled dressmaker—even though she couldn't remember making any of the dresses! In 1911, the great French philosopher Henri Bergson distinguished conscious remembering of the past from learned habits that influence our behavior unconsciously. Bergson argued with great eloquence that the past survives in two fundamentally different forms, conscious and unconscious. It was exciting for me to contemplate using scientific techniques to study what Bergson and others had theorized about or observed in the clinic.

After returning to Toronto, I witnessed firsthand the peculiar kind of memory that others had described in amnesic patients. During the summer of 1980, Dr. Paul Wang, a clinical psychologist, invited me to test a patient who had sustained a serious head injury in an accident. The patient, whom I refer to as Mickey, remembered little or nothing of his recent experiences. I sat across a testing table from him and told him that I was going to try to teach him some interesting bits of trivia. I asked him about obscure facts that I had dredged up by rummaging through encyclopedias and similar sources, such as "Where was the first game of baseball played?" (Hoboken) and "Who holds the world's record for shaking hands?" (Theodore Roosevelt). When Mickey did not know the correct answer—and he almost never did—I told it to him. He was intrigued by these tidbits and enjoyed our trivia game. After I left the testing room and returned twenty minutes later, Mickey maintained only a dim memory that I had tested him. He did not recollect that I had mentioned any items of trivia. But when I asked him where the first game of baseball was played, he confidently answered "Hoboken," and when I inquired about the world's record for shaking hands, he felt certain that it was Theodore Roosevelt. He generally said that he had no idea how he had acquired this knowledge—the answer just "seemed reasonable" –although sometimes he proffered that he might have heard about it from his sister.

My encounter with Mickey dramatically confirmed what I had discussed with Professor Weiskrantz and read about in medical journals: amnesic patients could indeed be influenced by recent experiences that they fail to recollect consciously. At the same time, Tulving and I continued to mull over the Warrington and Weiskrantz experiments. Why did amnesic patients do so well when given letter cues as hints for recently studied words? If these cues tapped into some sort of nonconscious memory that is preserved in amnesic patients, shouldn't it be possible to uncover something similar in people without amnesia?

We designed an experiment to find out. Our reasoning was simple: if letter cues tap into a form of memory that is spared in amnesic patients, then we might be able to elicit such memory in healthy volunteers by giving them letters from a previously studied word and asking them to try to guess the answer. Weiskrantz had observed that amnesic patients treat the letter cue test as a guessing game. If young adults could also be induced to treat the test as a guessing game, we reasoned, then they might rely on the same kind of memory that Warrington and Weiskrantz had observed in amnesics.

We carried out our experiment in the summer of 1980. For you to get a feel for our procedure, you should study each of the following words carefully for five seconds: *assassin, octopus, avocado, mystery, sheriff,* and *climate.* Now imagine that you go about your business for an hour and then return to take a couple of tests. First I show you a series of words and ask whether you remember seeing any of them on the earlier list: *twilight, assassin, dinosaur,* and *mystery.* Presumably you had little difficulty here. Next I tell you that I am going to show you some words with missing letters. Your job is to fill in the blanks as best you can: ch_____nk, o_t__us, _og_y___, _l_m_te. You probably had a hard time coming up with a correct answer for two of the word fragments (*chipmunk* and *bogeyman*). But with the other two fragments, the correct answers probably jumped out at you. The reason these fragments are so easy to complete, of course, is that you just saw the words *octopus* and *climate* in our study list. This kind of memory is called *priming:* seeing the words on the list seems to prime your ability to come up with the correct solution when you try to complete a word fragment.

We tested people either one hour or one week after they studied the list. Conscious memory was, of course, much less accurate after a week than after an hour, but there was just as much priming on the word fragment-completion test after a week as there was after an hour. The implication of this finding is fascinating: something other than a conscious memory of seeing the word is responsible for priming on the word fragment-completion test. Equally intriguing, priming occurred even when people said they did not remember seeing a word during the study phase; in fact, the priming effect was just as strong for words that people did not remember seeing earlier as for words they did remember seeing. The results pushed us toward a strong, seemingly unavoidable conclusion: priming occurs independent of conscious memory.

These findings hit us with the force of an avalanche. We believed that we had been able to get a handle on the peculiar kind of memory that Warrington and Weiskrantz had documented in amnesic patients with the letter cueing task. This "other" kind of memory seemed to be lurking in the minds of healthy adults, and could be tapped by giving the word fragment-completion test. We felt a bit like astronomers must feel when discovering a new star or an entire galaxy whose existence had been only suspected: a whole new world of possibilities is suddenly open for exploration.

I also started to notice manifestations of priming in everyday life. It is likely involved in instances of unintentional plagiarism. Probably the best-known case in recent decades involved the former Beatle George Harrison and his 1970s hit "My Sweet Lord." Unfortunately for Harrison, his melody nearly duplicated the tune of a 1962 classic by The Chiffons, "He's So Fine." When a lawsuit was brought against him, Harrison conceded that he had heard "He's So Fine" prior to writing "My Sweet Lord," but denied that he had intentionally borrowed from the earlier song. Reasoning that the resemblance between the two was simply too strong to be the product of coincidence, the trial judge "held that Harrison's work did infringe through what the courts felt must have been unintentional copying of what was in Harrison's subconscious memory."

You may have encountered instances of this kind of priming, too. You propose an idea to a fellow employee or a friend, who seems unimpressed by it or even rejects it altogether. Weeks or months later, that person excitedly relates your idea as if he had just come up with it. When you draw this inconvenient fact to his attention—with an edge in your voice betraying exasperation—you may be faced with either heated denial or a sheepish apology born of a sudden dose of explicit memory. An incident from Sigmund Freud's life clearly illustrates this. Freud had maintained for years an intense and tumultuous friendship with the Berlin physician Wilhelm Fliess. He frequently confided his latest ideas and insights to Fliess, and was emotionally dependent on his approval of them. When Freud announced to Fliess a momentous new insight—that every person is fundamentally bisexual—he fully expected Fliess to be amazed by the idea. Instead, Fliess responded by reminding Freud that he himself had made exactly the same discovery two years earlier and told Freud all about it, and that Freud had rejected the idea. Freud eventually explicitly remembered the earlier incident, commenting that "[i]t is painful to have to surrender one's originality this way." Inspired by such observations, psychologists have recently been able to demonstrate a kind of unintentional plagiarism in the laboratory and tie it directly to priming.

Research into priming exploded during the early 1980s, as provocative new articles appeared in scientific journals. Priming occurred on a variety of tests in which people were instructed to identify a briefly flashed word or object, or guess an answer, rather than try explicitly to remember a word or an object from a list they had studied earlier. For example, Larry Jacoby and Mark Dallas found similar amounts of priming after deep encoding (focusing on a word's meanings and associations) and shallow encoding (focusing on the individual letters in the word)—a remarkable result, since deep encoding yields much higher levels of explicit memory than shallow encoding. Yet the priming effect could be easily eliminated. If people heard the target words on an audiotape during the study task but did not see a printed version of them, little or no priming was observed on a later visual test. Something about perceiving the actual word form was crucial for priming to occur.

Considered together with the results of our word fragment-completion experiment, these findings indicated that the new and mysterious phenomenon of priming obeys different rules than the kind of memory that researchers had been investigating for years. It became increasingly clear that part of the mystery could be traced to the instructions people are given when their memories are tested. For example, when amnesic patients are given word beginnings or other cues, and are instructed to think back to the study list to try to remember target words, they perform quite poorly. But when given the same test cues with instructions to guess or to provide the first word that pops to mind, they do just as well as people without memory problems. Likewise, depth of encoding influences later retention when normal volunteers try to remember the target items, yet has little effect when they respond with the first word that comes to mind.

Scientists love a good mystery, and many researchers tried to figure out what priming effects might mean. Tulving and I had already staked out a position: because priming seemed unrelated to conscious recollection, we reasoned that it does not depend on the episodic memory system that allows us to recollect specific incidents from the past. That system plays a key role in much of what I have discussed in the book so far: remembering what happened at last year's Thanksgiving dinner, remembering where you hit a tee shot during a round of golf, or remembering that you saw the word *octopus* in a study list. Amnesic patients have little or no episodic memory, but they often show normal priming. We concluded that the source of priming must lie outside the episodic system. But where?

Semantic memory—the intricate network of concepts, associations, and facts that constitutes our general knowledge of the world—seemed a reasonable place to look. When an amnesic patient such as Mickey learns that the first game of baseball was played in Hoboken but does not remember the episode in which he acquired that fact, semantic memory may be responsible. Likewise, in a priming experiment, exposure to a word such as *octopus* might result in a jolt to semantic memory, a kind of power surge that excites or activates the semantic representation of *octopus*. Perhaps amnesic patients benefit from such a jolt to semantic memory, even though their defective episodic memory prevents them from consciously recalling that they saw the word *octopus* during a recent study episode. The idea is reasonable enough, but we could see that it had problems. If priming depends on semantic memory, why doesn't deep, semantic processing of a word during the study task lead to more priming than shallow, nonsemantic processing? Why does priming depend on actually seeing the word during the study task? And since priming can be quite long-lasting, and we are constantly encountering words in our everyday lives, shouldn't just about all entries in semantic memory be chronically primed? We speculated that priming reflects "the operation of some other, as yet little understood, memory system."

We had postulated the existence of a new memory system, even though we didn't yet know what it was. The idea that the mind contains more than a single memory system had been around for a while. Bergson had come to this conclusion in 1911 when he distinguished conscious memory from habit, and other philosophers had made similar distinctions. In fact, during the early nineteenth century, a little-known French philosopher, Maine de Biran, had argued that memory can be subdivided into three different systems for ideas, feelings, and habits. But many experimental psychologists were reluctant to part with the idea of one all-purpose memory system. It is simpler and more parsimonious to assume a single memory system until and unless the evidence forces one to postulate multiple memory systems. During the 1960s and 1970s, they had fought a great battle about whether short-term memory (now called working memory) depends on a different system than long-term memory. I earlier mentioned evidence that it does, but not everyone was convinced. Tulving introduced the distinction between episodic and semantic memory in 1972, and some psychologists resisted this division of long-term memory into two further systems. Now we were proposing the addition of a third system—and this was simply unacceptable to some. Priming, these researchers believed, occurs within a single, undifferentiated memory system that can be investigated in different ways. Appealing to the operation of different memory systems seemed unparsimonious and just plain wrong.

A lively debate surrounded these questions. To fuel the fires, new evidence showed that amnesic patients could learn perceptual skills without remembering when and where they learned them. Neal Cohen and Larry Squire studied amnesic patients and healthy volunteers who read mirror-image versions of common words. Everyone has difficulty reading such images at first, but with practice people typically read them faster and faster. Amnesic patients showed a normal benefit of practice, yet they had problems consciously remembering which words they had read. The researchers suggested that such skill learning depends on a "procedural" memory system that is spared in amnesia. This system is selectively involved in "knowing how" to do things: ride a bicycle, type words on a keyboard, solve a jigsaw puzzle, or read words in mirror-image form. Could the procedural memory system also be involved in priming? Or does procedural memory constitute a fourth memory system, in addition to episodic memory, semantic memory, and the memory system Tulving and I had alluded to?

By the mid-1980s, the controversy over multiple memory systems had become so intense that it was difficult to talk about priming and skill learning without committing to one side of the quarrel or the other. The field needed terms that allowed researchers to talk about the exhilarating new phenomena of priming and learning without remembering, yet did not force them to side with one or the other warring faction in the memory systems debate. I decided to face this problem squarely in 1984, when my colleague Peter Graf and I were writing up the results of some new priming experiments. We recognized that new vocabulary was needed to talk about what we and others had been observing in our experiments.

We worked through several possibilities before settling on the contrast that seemed best to capture the distinction we wished to draw: *implicit* memory versus *explicit* memory. When amnesic patients showed priming or learned a skill, they were implicitly remembering some aspect of a recent experience, even though they had no explicit recollection of it. When a college student completed the fragment o_t__us with *octopus*, yet said that she did not remember seeing *octopus* on the list, she was showing the implicit influence of an experience she did not explicitly remember.

Soon I began to see that implicit memory might play a more prominent role in our everyday lives than anyone had suspected. For example, social psychologists who sought to understand why people prefer some things more than others had shown that a brief glimpse of a drawing—so brief that it was hardly possible to see it—led participants in an experiment later to say that they liked the flashed drawing more than one they had not seen. Yet people could not explicitly remember which drawings had been presented. These findings smacked of subliminal perception, illustrated by the apocryphal story about a sinister 1950s advertising ploy in which the words *Coca-Cola* and *popcorn* were flashed on a movie screen so briefly that nobody in the theater could see them. Supposedly, there would be a sudden mad dash to the concession stand to purchase these products. Although the effect turned out to be part of a publicity hoax, implicit memory was held to be reflected by an unexplained desire to drink Coke and eat popcorn.

By the mid-1980s a number of well-controlled studies had shown that preferences and feelings can be shaped by specific encounters and experiences that people do not remember explicitly. For instance, exposure to negative words that were flashed too quickly to register in conscious perception caused people later to feel hostility toward a fictional person. Some form of memory was responsible for their hostility, but participants had no idea that they were "remembering" any negative information. Likewise, studies of amnesic patients revealed implicit memory for emotional experiences they could not remember explicitly. For instance, the encephalitic patient Boswell, whose severe amnesia I mentioned in the previous chapter, took part in an experiment in which one researcher was designated a "good guy" (he gave Boswell special treats), another was designated a "bad guy" (he denied requests for treats), and a third behaved neutrally. Later, Boswell had no explicit memory for, or any sense of familiarity with, any of these people. Yet when pictures of them were each paired with pictures of unfamiliar people, and Boswell was asked to choose which one of the two he liked best, he selected the "good guy" most often and the "bad guy" least often.

There were also intriguing reports about people who had been given general anesthesia during surgical procedures. Received wisdom holds that patients cannot perceive or attend to anything that is said or done when they are unconscious during an operation. But in an experiment conducted during the 1960s, surgeons staged a mock crisis during surgery that included dire statements to the effect that the operation was in trouble and the patient might not pull through. Some of the patients who had been exposed to the mock crisis subsequently became extremely agitated when asked about it later, suggesting that they formed some sort of implicit memory while lying unconscious on the operating table.

On a more positive note, later studies showed that anesthetized patients who were given suggestions that they would make a quick recovery spent less time in the hospital postoperatively than patients who were not given any such suggestions. Yet none of the patients explicitly remembered the suggestions. My colleagues and I later demonstrated that patients who heard a list of spoken words during surgery showed priming for those words when tested during postoperative recovery. Not surprisingly, they had no explicit memory for the words.

Implicit memory may also be related to some of the memory distortions I considered earlier. When we forget the source of retrieved information—who said what, whether an incident actually occurred or was merely imagined—we may generate an inaccurate source and hence become prone to false recollections. Implicit memory, by definition, does not involve recollection of source information. Thus, we may generate plausible but incorrect sources in attempting to make sense of why a particular idea pops to mind or why we feel a certain emotion.

From *The Illusion of Conscious Will*

Daniel M. Wegner

All theory is against the freedom of the will; all experience is for it.
—Samuel Johnson, Boswell's Life of Johnson *(1791)*

So, here you are reading a book on conscious will. How could this have happened? One way to explain it would be to examine the causes of your behavior. A team of scientific psychologists could study your reported thoughts, emotions, and motives, your genetics and your history of learning, experience, and development, your social situation and culture, your memories and reaction times, your physiology and neuroanatomy, and lots of other things as well. If they somehow had access to all the information they could ever want, the assumption of psychology is that they could uncover the mechanisms that give rise to all your behavior and so could certainly explain why you picked up this book at this moment. However, another way to explain the fact of your reading this book is just to say that you decided to pick up the book and begin reading. You consciously willed what you are doing.

These two explanations are both appealing but in different ways. The scientific explanation accounts for behavior as a mechanism and appeals to that part of us that knows how useful science is for understanding the world. It would be wonderful if we could understand people in just the same way. The conscious will explanation, on the other hand, has a much deeper grip on our intuition. We each have a profound sense that we consciously will much of what we do, and we experience ourselves willing our actions many times a day. As William James put it, "The whole sting and excitement of our voluntary life ... depends on our sense that in it things are *really being decided* from one moment to another, and that it is not the dull rattling off of a chain that was forged innumerable ages ago" (1890). Quite apart from any resentment we might feel on being cast into the role of mechanisms or robots, we appreciate the notion of conscious will because we experience it so very acutely. We do things, and when we do them, we experience the action in such a way that it seems to flow seamlessly from our consciousness. We feel that *we cause ourselves to behave.*

The idea of conscious will and the idea of psychological mechanisms have an oil and water relationship, having never been properly reconciled. One way to put them together—the way this book explores—is to say that the mechanistic approach is the explanation preferred for scientific purposes but that the person's experience of conscious will is utterly convincing and important to the person and so must be understood scientifically as well. The mechanisms underlying the experience of will are themselves a fundamental topic of scientific study. We should be able to examine and understand what creates the experience of will and what makes it go away. This means, though, that conscious will is an illusion. It is an illusion in the sense that *the experience of consciously willing an action is not a direct indication that the conscious thought has caused the action.* Conscious will, viewed this way, may be an extraordinary illusion indeed—the equivalent of a magician's producing an elephant from the folds of his handkerchief. How could it seem so much like our wills cause our actions if this isn't actually happening? To grasp how this might be, we need to begin by examining what exactly is meant by conscious will. With any luck, we will discover a large expanse of the elephant protruding from the magician's pocket and so begin to understand how the trick works.

Lifting a Finger

At some arbitrary time in the next few seconds, please move your right index finger. That's correct, please perform a consciously willed action. Now, here's an interesting question: What was your brain up to at the time? In an elaborate experiment, Kornhuber and Deecke (1965) arranged to measure this event in a number of people by assessing the electrical potentials on the scalp just before and after such voluntary finger movements. Continuous recordings were made of electrical potentials at several scalp electrodes while the experimenter waited for the subject to lift that finger. The actual point when the finger moved was measured precisely by electromyography (EMG, a sensor to detect muscle movement), and this was repeated for as many as 1,000 movements per experiment with each subject. Then, using the movement onset as a reference point, the average scalp electrical potentials could be graphed for the time period surrounding all those voluntary actions.

Et voilà—the spark of will! Brain electrical activity was found to start increasing about 0.8 seconds before the voluntary finger movement. Kornhuber and Deecke dubbed this activity the *readiness potential* (RP). As shown in Figure 1, this RP occurs widely in the brain—in the left and right precentral regions (spots a bit above and forward of the ear, corresponding to the motor area) and in the midparietal region (top of the head), as shown in the upper three panels. This negative electrical impulse peaks about 90 milliseconds before the action and then drops a bit in the positive (downward) direction before the action. The ratio of the left to right potentials shown in the fourth panel also reveals a bit of a blip about 50 milliseconds before the action on the left side of the motor area of the brain. Just before the right finger moves, the finger and hand motor area contralateral to that finger—the area that controls the actual movement—is then activated. This blip has been called the *movement potential* (Deecke, Scheid, and Kornhuber 1969). It seems as though a general readiness for voluntary action resolves into a more localized activation of the area responsible for the specific action just as the action unfolds.

The discovery of the RP for voluntary action electrified a number of brains all over the world. The excitement at having found a brain correlate of conscious will was palpable, and a number of commentators exclaimed breathlessly that the science of mind had reached its Holy Grail. John Eccles (1976; 1982) applauded this research, for example, and suggested that these findings showed for the first time how the conscious self operates to produce movement. He proposed,

> Regions of the brain in liaison with the conscious self can function as extremely sensitive detectors of consciously willed influences. . . . As a consequence, the willing of a movement produces the gradual evolution of neuronal responses over a wide area of frontal and parietal cortices of both sides, so giving the readiness potential. Furthermore, the mental act that we call willing must guide or mold this unimaginably complex neuronal performance of the liaison cortex so that eventually it "homes in" on to the

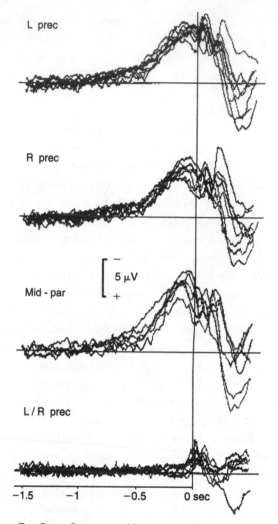

FIGURE 1——THE BRAIN POTENTIALS MEASURED BY DEECKE, GROZINGER, AND KORNHUBER (1976).

Each Graphic Curve Represents One Experiment. The Top Three Panels Show the Development of the Readiness Potential (RP) at Three Scalp Locations, and the Bottom Panel Shows the Movement Potential in the Difference Between Left and Right in the Precentral Motor Area Associated with Finger Movement. The RP Onset is about 800 Milliseconds Before the Voluntary Finger Movement, whereas the Movement Potential Onset is only 50 Milliseconds before the Movement.

appropriate modules of the motor cortex and brings about discharges of their motor pyramidal cells. (1976, 117)

What Eccles overlooked in his enthusiasm was that in this study the conscious self had in fact never been queried. The study simply showed that brain events occur reliably before voluntary action. When exactly in this sequence does the person experience *conscious will?* Benjamin Libet and colleagues (1983; Libet 1985; 1993) had the bright idea of asking people just this question and invented a way to time their answers. Like participants in the prior RP experiments, participants in these studies were also asked to move a finger spontaneously while wearing EMG electrodes on the finger and scalp EEG electrodes for RP measurement. And as in the prior studies the participants were asked to move the finger at will: "Let the urge to act appear on its own any time without any preplanning or concentration on when to act" (627). In this case, however, the participant was also seated before a visible clock. On the circular screen of an oscilloscope, a spot of light revolved in a clockwise path around the circumference of the screen, starting at the twelve o'clock position and revolving each 2.65 seconds—quite a bit faster than the second hand of a real clock. A circular scale with illuminated lines marked units around the edge, each of which corresponded to 107 milliseconds of real time. The participant's task was simply to report for each finger movement where the dot was on the clock when he experienced "*conscious awareness of 'wanting' to perform a given self-initiated movement*" (627).

The researchers called these measurements the W series (for wanting) and also took some other key measurements for comparison. For an M (movement) series, instead of asking the participant to report where the dot was when he became consciously aware of wanting to move, the participant was asked for the location of the dot when he became aware of actually moving. And in an S (stimulation) series, the participant was simply asked to report the clock position when a stimulus was applied to the back of his hand.

The results were truly noteworthy, although in some sense this is exactly what you would have to expect: The conscious willing of finger movement occurred at a significant interval *after* the onset of the RP but also at a significant interval *before* the actual finger movement (and also at a significant interval before the awareness of movement). The time line for the RP, W, M, and actual movement events is shown in Figure 2. These findings

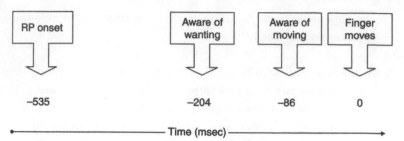

FIGURE 9.2——TIME LINE OF EVENTS PRIOR TO VOLUNTARY FINGER MOVE-
MENT, IN RESEARCH BY LIBET ET AL. (1983).

suggest that the brain starts doing something first (we don't know just what that is). Then the person becomes conscious of wanting to do the action. This would be where the conscious will kicks in, at least, in the sense that the person first becomes conscious of trying to act. Then, and still a bit *prior* to the movement, the person reports becoming aware of the finger actually moving. Finally, the finger moves.

Libet and colleagues suggested that the S series could be used as a guide to estimating how long any hand-to-brain activity might take. It took about 47 milliseconds for people to report being consciously aware of a stimulus to the hand, so Libet reasoned it might be useful to subtract this number from the W and M series values to adjust for this part of the process. This doesn't really change the overall conclusion; it just moves the "aware of wanting" time to −157 milliseconds and the "aware of moving" time to −39 milliseconds. One other quibble: You may have noticed that the RP in this study occurred later (−535 milliseconds) than the one in Kornhuber and Deecke's experiment (approximately −800 milliseconds). This is because Libet made a special point of asking participants to mention if they had done any preplanning of the finger movement and eliminated those instances from the analysis. In a separate study, Libet, Wright, and Gleason (1982) had learned that the RP occurred as much as a second or two earlier on trials when participants were allowed to plan for their movement, so the conscious will study avoided this by emphasizing spontaneous, unplanned movements.

The conclusion suggested by this research is that the experience of conscious will kicks in at some point *after* the brain has already started preparing for the action. Libet sums up these observations by saying that "the initiation of the voluntary act appears to be an unconscious cerebral process. Clearly, free will or free choice of whether *to act now* could not be the initiating agent, contrary to one widely held view. This is of course also contrary to each individual's own introspective feeling that he/she consciously initiates such voluntary acts; this provides an important empirical example of the possibility that the subjective experience of a mental causality need not necessarily reflect the actual causative relationship between mental and brain events" (Libet 1992, 269).

Recounting Libet's discovery has become a cottage industry among students of consciousness (Dennett 1991; Harth 1982; Nørretranders 1998; Spence 1996; Wegner and Bargh 1998), and for good reason. Although there have only been a few replications of the research itself, because this is difficult and painstaking science (Keller and Heckhausen 1990; Haggard and Eimer 1999), the basic phenomenon is so full of implications that it has aroused a wide range of comments, both supportive and critical (see the commentaries published following Libet 1985; also, Gomes 1998). Many commentators seem to agree that it is hard to envision conscious will happening well before anything in the brain starts clicking because that would truly be a case of a ghost in the machine. The common theme in several of the critiques, however, is the nagging suspicion that somehow conscious will might at least share its temporal inception with brain events. Some still hope, as did John Eccles, that conscious will and the RP leading to voluntary action would at least be synchronous. That way, although we might not be able to preserve the causal priority of conscious will, the conscious will might still be part of the brain train, all of which leaves the station at once. Yet this is not what was observed. In what happened, the brain started first, followed by the experience of conscious will, and finally followed by action.

We don't know what specific unconscious mental processes the RP might represent. These processes are likely to be relevant in some way to the ensuing events, of course, because they occur with precise regularity in advance of those events. Now, the ensuing events include both the experience of wanting to move *and* the voluntary movement. The RP could thus signal the occurrence of unconscious mental events that produce both the experience of wanting to move and the occurrence of actual movement. This possibility alerts us to the intriguing realization that conscious wanting, like voluntary action, is a mental event that is caused by prior events. It seems that conscious wanting is not the beginning of the process of making voluntary movement but rather is one of the events in a cascade that eventually yields such movement.

The position of conscious will in the time line suggests perhaps that the experience of will is a link in a causal chain leading to action, but in fact it might not even be that. It might just be a loose end—one of those things, like the action, that is caused by prior brain and mental events.

Acting Quickly

The odd sluggishness of consciousness becomes apparent in another way when people do fast things. When we react to a phone ringing, or take a swat at a fly, for example, we move so rapidly that we seem to leave consciousness behind. In fact, the consciousness of a stimulus that causes a reactive or triggered action of this kind typically *follows* much of the action, coming to mind several hundred milliseconds after the person has begun to respond to incoming signals (Rossetti 1998; Velmans 1991). Imagine, for example, being asked to press a button as soon as you feel a tap. It typically takes only about 100 milliseconds to react to such a stimulus, and sometimes much less, but it may take as much as 500 milliseconds to become conscious of having responded (Libet 1981). For example, in a study in which participants were tracking by hand an unexpectedly moving target, the change in their hand trajectory toward the target's movement happened as early as 100 milliseconds following the target jump. However, the vocal signal by which they reported their awareness of the jump (saying "Pah," which is apparently what you say in an experiment in France to signal something unexpected) did not occur on average until more than 300 milliseconds later (Castiello, Paulignan, and Jeannerod 1991).

Another illustration of the conscious delay is the finding that people can't gradually slow down their reaction times. Jensen (1979) asked people to try deliberately to lengthen their reaction time little by little and found that they could not do so. Rather, their reaction times jumped from the usual minimum values (in his study, about 250 milliseconds) to much higher values, which at a minimum were 500 to 1000 milliseconds. One cannot slow down one's reaction until one becomes conscious of the stimulus *and of having reacted*, and this takes lots of extra time. This discontinuity suggests that a response and a *conscious* response are two very different things, the first one typically far speedier than the second.

The slowness of consciousness prompted Posner and Snyder (1975) to draw a distinction between automatic processes and controlled (conscious) processes. They proposed that fast responses, such as hitting the accelerator when the light turns green, or pulling a finger away from the touch of a hot pan, could be understood as automatic. These automatic reactions take place in 200–300 milliseconds or even less and occur prior to reportable consciousness of the stimulus. They can include choices, such as picking which word to say in a given sentence or which soft drink to grab from the fridge, and they underlie the various fast and fluid skills of which people are capable. Playing tennis or reading or typing or walking are all skills that involve exceedingly fast reactions, many of which can be understood as automatic in this sense (Baars 1988; Bargh 1984; 1994; 1997; Bargh and Chartrand 2000; Wegner and Bargh 1998).

These automatic processes also are often uncontrollable in that once they have been launched, they continue until they are complete (Logan and Cowan 1984). Conscious processes are more flexible and strategic, but they also take more time—in the range of 500 milliseconds or beyond. Half a second doesn't seem like much, of course, but it can be an eternity when you're trying to do something fast. Consider that a skilled keyboarder might be able to type at the rate of 120 words per minute. That means *two words every second*, a phrase that itself would have taken me only 2 seconds to type if I were such a skilled keyboarder. So, a 500-millisecond interval would allow for the typing of an entire word. All the automatic keystrokes that go into typing that word are so fast that they are telescoped together into a sequence that takes only as long as it takes for something *once* to enter into a conscious response.

The slowness of consciousness suggests that much of what we see and do involves the operation of *preconscious* mental processes. That is, we may begin to react to a stimulus before we are aware of it. In fact, if our exposure to a target stimulus is cut short (by a masking stimulus that immediately follows the target and wipes out our visual image of it), we may have a cognitive response to the target without ever becoming aware of the target. People who are judging whether each of a series of letter strings is a word or not, for instance, are likely to judge a string correctly as a word more quickly if they have just been exposed to a related word at a very brief duration, followed by a masking stimulus (Marcel 1983).

Q U E S T I O N S

1. Textbooks in psychology often include a chapter on memory and cognition, but what is the relationship between the two? Can there be memory without cognition or cognition without memory? Or are the two necessarily intertwined?

2. Daniel Wegner is an experimental psychologist, and his approach to psychology may seem to be as far away from Freud as you can get, yet there is something the two of them share. What is it?

CHAPTER TEN

INTELLIGENCE

Some people are taller than others; some people are faster, skinnier, or better-looking than others—these are obvious facts that no one would deny. But do people also differ in how smart they are? Although it is not politically correct to say, the answer seems to be yes. Thousands of studies have confirmed again and again that there are reliable individual differences in intelligence. Richard Herrnstein and Charles Murray's much-maligned book *The Bell Curve* (1994) is one of the few to consider the implications. While I scarcely agree with all or even most of what Herrnstein and Murray wrote—especially when they stray into racial differences—I do think that they made a valuable point: intelligence is real, heritable, and increasingly reflected in the stratification of society.

IQ tests are not a perfect measure of intelligence, and intelligence itself is an ill-defined notion, but people who do better on these tests do tend, other things being equal, to be more successful in school and in their jobs. Those who do poorly on intelligence tests are more likely to wind up in jail, addicted to drugs, even more likely to have illegitimate children. To dismiss the test without recognizing this growing stratification is, as Herrnstein and Murray point out, to miss a forest for the trees.

A person's ability to blaze through the SAT or an IQ test is, however, scarcely the only measure of intelligence. The dictionary defines intelligence as an ability to learn and apply facts and skills, and in part because of the ways in which intelligence is traditionally measured, most people tend to think of intelligence as "rational thought," problem-solving, mathematical abilities, logic, reasoning, and the like. But another aspect of getting along in the world is getting along with people. The journalist Daniel Goleman has advocated a construct that he calls "emotional intelligence," well-illustrated in this excerpt from his 1995 book by the same name. Emotional intelligence, according to Goleman, is a collection of "abilities such as being able to motivate oneself and persist in the face of frustrations; to control impulse and delay gratification; to regulate one's moods and keep distress from swamping the ability to think; to empathize and to hope." Although none of these would count on a classic IQ test, there can be little doubt that such skills are an essential part of a happy and well-adjusted life.

187

From *The Bell Curve: Intelligence and Class Structure in American Life*

Richard J. Herrnstein and Charles Murray

Genetic Partitioning

Twenty years ago, one of us wrote a book that created a stir because it discussed the heritability of IQ and the relationship of intelligence to success in life, and foresaw a future in which socioeconomic status would increasingly be inherited. The logic of the argument was couched in a syllogism:

- If differences in mental abilities are inherited, and
- If success requires those abilities, and
- If earnings and prestige depend on success,
- Then social standing (which reflects earnings and prestige) will be based to some extent on inherited differences among people.

As stated, the syllogism is not fearsome. If intelligence is only trivially a matter of genes and if success in life is only trivially a matter of intelligence, then success may be only trivially inherited.

How Much Is IQ a Matter of Genes?

In fact, IQ is substantially heritable. The state of knowledge does not permit a precise estimate, but half a century of work, now amounting to hundreds of empirical and theoretical studies, permits a broad conclusion that the genetic component of IQ is unlikely to be smaller than 40 percent or higher than 80 percent. The most unambiguous direct estimates, based on identical twins raised apart, produce some of the highest estimates of heritability. For purposes of this discussion, we will adopt a middling estimate of 60 percent heritability, which, by extension, means that IQ is about 40 percent a matter of environment. The balance of the evidence suggests that 60 percent may err on the low side.

Because IQ and genes has been such a sensitive topic, it is worth a short digression to give some idea of where these estimates come from and how trustworthy they are.

First, consider the question that heads this section, not its answer. What we want to know is how much of the variation in IQ in a *population*—the aggregated differences among the individuals—is due to variations in genetic endowments and how much is due to variations in environment. If all the population variation in IQ is due to variations in environment, then the *heritability* is 0, if half is due to environmental variations, it is .5; if none is due to environmental variations, it is 1.0. Heritability, in other words, is a ratio that ranges between 0 and 1 and measures the relative contribution of genes to the variation observed in a trait.

Specialists have come up with dozens of procedures for estimating heritability. Nonspecialists need not concern themselves with nuts and bolts, but they may need to be reassured on a few basic points. First the heritability of any trait can be estimated as long as its variation in a population can be measured. IQ meets that criterion handily. There are, in fact, no other human traits—physical or psychological—that provide as many good data for the estimation of heritability as the IQ. Second, heritability describes something about a population of people, not an individual. It makes no more sense to talk about the heritability of an individual's IQ than it does to talk about his birthrate. A given individual's IQ may have been greatly affected by his special circumstances even though IQ is substantially heritable in the population as a whole. Third, the heritability of a trait may change when the conditions producing variation change. If, one hundred years ago, the variations in exposure to education were greater than they are now (as is no doubt the case), and if education is one source of variation in IQ, then, other things equal, the heritability of IQ was lower then than it is now.

This last point is especially important in the modern societies, with their intense efforts to equalize opportunity. As a general rule, *as environments become more uniform, heritability rises.* When heritability rises, children resemble their parents more, and siblings increasingly resemble each other; in general, family members become more similar to each other and more different from people in other families. It is the central irony of egalitarianism:

Uniformity in society makes the members of families more similar to each other and members of different families more different.

Now for the answer to the question, How much is IQ a matter of genes? Heritability is estimated from data on people with varying amounts of genetic overlap and varying amounts of shared environment. Broadly speaking, the estimates may be characterized as direct or indirect. Direct estimates are based on samples of blood relatives who were raised apart. Their genetic overlap can be estimated from basic genetic considerations. The direct methods assume that the correlations between them are due to the shared genes rather than shared environments because they do not, in fact, share environments, an assumption that is more or less plausible, given the particular conditions of the study. The purest of the direct comparisons is based on identical (monozygotic, MZ) twins reared apart, often not knowing of each other's existence. Identical twins share all their genes, and if they have been raised apart since birth, then the only environment they shared was that in the womb. Except for the effects on their IQs of the shared uterine environment, their IQ correlation directly estimates heritability. The most modern study of identical twins reared in separate homes suggests a heritability for general intelligence between .75 and .80, a value near the top of the range found in the contemporary technical literature. Other direct estimates use data on ordinary siblings who were raised apart or on parents and their adopted-away children. Usually, the heritability estimates from such data are lower but rarely below .4.

Indirect methods compare the IQ correlations between people with different levels of shared genes growing up in comparable environments— siblings versus half-siblings or versus cousins, for example, or MZ twins versus fraternal (dizygotic, DZ) twins, or nonadoptive siblings versus adoptive siblings. The underlying idea is that, for example, if full siblings raised in the same home and half-siblings raised in the same home differ in their IQ correlations, it is because they differ in the proportion of genes they share: full siblings share about 50 percent of genes, half siblings about 25 percent. Similarly, if siblings raised in unshared environments and cousins raised in unshared environments differ in their IQ correlations, it is because of the differing degrees of genetic overlap between cousins and siblings and not because of differing environmental influences, which are unshared by definition. And so on. Fleshed out in some sort of statistical model, this idea makes it possible to estimate the heritability, but the modeling can get complex. Some studies use mixtures of direct and indirect methods.

The technical literature is filled with varying estimates of the heritability of IQ, owing to the varying models being used for estimation and to the varying sets of data. Some people seem eager to throw up their hands and declare, "No one knows (or can know) how heritable IQ is." But that reaction is as unwarranted as it is hasty, if one is content, as we are, to accept a range of uncertainty about the heritability that specialists may find nerve-racking. We are content, in other words, to say that the heritability of IQ falls somewhere within a broad range and that, for purposes of our discussion, a value of .6±.2 does no violence to any of the competent and responsible recent estimates. The range of .4 to .8 includes virtually all recent (since 1980) estimates—competent, responsible, or otherwise.

Recent studies have uncovered other salient facts about the way IQ scores depend on genes. They have found, for example, that the more general the measure of intelligence—the closer it is to g—the higher is the heritability. Also, the evidence seems to say that the heritability of IQ rises as one ages, all the way from early childhood to late adulthood. This means that the variation in IQ among, say, youths ages 18 to 22 is less dependent on genes than that among people ages 40 to 44. Most of the traditional estimates of heritability have been based on youngsters, which means that they are likely to underestimate the role of genes later in life.

Finally, and most surprisingly, the evidence is growing that whatever variation is left over for the environment to explain (i.e., 40 percent of the total variation, if the heritability of IQ is taken to be .6), relatively little can be traced to the shared environments created by families. It is, rather, a set of environmental influences, mostly unknown at present, that are experienced by individuals as individuals. The fact that family members resemble each other in intelligence in adulthood as much as they do is very largely explained by the genes they share rather than the family environment they shared as children. These findings suggest deep roots indeed for the cognitive stratification of society.

The Syllogism in Practice

The heritability of IQ is substantial. [Earlier in the book] we presented evidence that the relationship of cognitive ability to success in life is far from trivial. Inasmuch as the syllogism's premises cannot be dismissed out of hand, neither can its conclusion that success in life will be based to some extent on inherited differences among people.

Furthermore, a variety of other scientific findings leads us to conclude that the heritability of success is going to increase rather than diminish. Begin with the limits that heritability puts on the ability to manipulate intelligence, by imagining a United States that has magically made good on the contemporary ideal of equality. Every child in this imaginary America experiences exactly the same environmental effects, for good or ill, on his or her intelligence. How much intellectual variation would remain? If the heritability of IQ is .6, the standard deviation of IQ in our magical world of identical environments would be 11.6 instead of 15—smaller, but still leaving a great deal of variation in intellectual talent that could not be reduced further by mere equalization. As we noted earlier, when a society makes good on the ideal of letting every youngster have equal access to the things that allow latent cognitive ability to develop, it is in effect driving the environmental component of IQ variation closer and closer to nil.

The United States is still very far from this state of affairs at the extremes. If one thinks of babies growing up in slums with crack-addicted mothers, at one extreme, compared to children growing up in affluent, culturally rich homes with parents dedicated to squeezing every last IQ point out of them, then even a heritability of .6 leaves room for considerable change if the changes in environment are commensurably large. We take up the evidence on that issue in detail [later in the book], when we consider the many educational and social interventions that have attempted to raise IQ. But those are, by definition, the extremes, the two tails of the distribution of environments. Moving a child from an environment that is the very worst to the very best may make a big difference. In reality, what most interventions accomplish is to move children from awful environments to ones that are merely below average, and such changes are limited in their potential consequences when heritability so constrains the limits of environmental effects.

So while we can look forward to a future in which science discovers how to foster intelligence environmentally and how to use the science humanely, inherited cognitive ability is now extremely important. In this sense, luck continues to matter in life's outcomes, but now it is more a matter of the IQ handed out in life's lottery than anything else about circumstances. High cognitive ability as of the 1990s means, more than even before, that the chances of success in life are good and getting better all the time, and these are *de-creasingly* affected by the social environment, which by extension indicates that they must be *increasingly* affected by genes. Holding these thoughts in mind, now consider the phenomenon known as *assortative mating.*

Love, Marriage, and IQ

The old saw notwithstanding, opposites do not really attract when it comes to love and marriage. Likes attract. In one of the classic papers, originally published in 1943, two sociologists studied 1,000 engaged couples in Chicago, expecting to find at least some traits in which opposites did indeed attract. But out of fifty-one social characteristics studied, the sign of the correlation was positive for every single one. For all but six of the fifty-one traits, the correlations were statistically significant. Modest but consistently positive correlations have been found for a wide variety of physical traits as well, ranging from stature (the correlations from many studies average about +.25) to eye color (also averaging about +.25, even within national populations).

Of the many correlations involving husbands and wives, one of the highest is for IQ. In most of the major studies, the correlation of husband and wife IQ has been in the region of .4, though estimates as low as .2 and as high as .6 have been observed. Jensen's review of the literature in the late 1970s found that the average correlation of forty-three spouse correlations for various tests of cognitive ability was +.45, almost as high as the typical correlation of IQs among siblings.

If the Propensity to Mate by Cognitive Ability Has Remained the Same:

When the propensity to mate by cognitive ability is combined with the educational and occupational stratification we have described, the impact on the next generation will be larger than on the previous one, *even if the underlying propensity to mate by cognitive ability remains the same.*

Consider 100 Harvard/Radcliffe marriages from the class of 1930 versus another 100 from the class of 1964. We stipulate that the propensity to marry people of similar intelligence has not changed in the intervening thirty-four years. Nonetheless, the ones who marry in 1964 will produce a set of children with considerably higher mean IQ than the ones who married in 1930, because the level of intelligence at Harvard and Radcliffe had risen so dramatically.

How much difference can it make? If the average Harvard man in the class of 1930 married the average Radcliffe woman in the same graduating class—as far as we can tell, both would have had IQs of about 117—then the expected mean IQ of their children, after taking regression to the mean into account, will be about 114, or at the 82d percentile. But average Harvard and Radcliffe newlyweds in the class of 1964 were likely to have children with a mean IQ of about 124, at the 95th percentile. In terms of distributions rather than averages, about a third of the children of the Harvard newlyweds of 1930 could be expected to have IQs of less than 110—not even college material by some definitions. In contrast, only 6 percent of the children of the Harvard newlyweds of 1965 could be expected to fall below this cutoff. Meanwhile, only about 22 percent of the children of the 1930 newlyweds could be expected to match or exceed the *average* of the children of the 1965 newlyweds. In such numbers lurk large social effects.

If the Propensity to Mate by Cognitive Ability Has Increased:

We have been assuming that the propensity to mate by IQ has remained the same. In reality, it has almost certainly increased and will continue to increase.

We hedge with "almost" because no quantitative studies tell whether assortative mating by intelligence has been increasing recently. But we do know from sociologist Robert Mare of the University of Wisconsin that assortative mating by educational level increased over the period from 1940 to 1987—an increase in "homogamy," in the sociologists' language. The increase in homogamy was most pronounced among college-educated persons. Specifically, the odds of a college graduate's marrying someone who was not a college graduate declined from 44 percent in 1940 to 35 percent in Mare's most recent data (for 1985 to 1987). The proportion hit a low of 33 percent in the 1980 data. Because educational attainment and IQ are so closely linked and became more closely linked in the postwar period, Mare's results suggest a substantial increase in assortative mating by IQ, with the greatest change occurring at the upper levels of IQ.

Mare identifies some of the reasons for increased homogamy in the trends involving educational attainment, age at leaving school, and age at marriage. But there are a variety of other potential explanations (some of which he notes) that involve cognitive ability specifically. For example, a smart wife in the 1990s has a much greater dollar payoff for a man than she did fifty years ago. The feminist movement has also increased the likelihood of marrying by cognitive ability.

First, the feminist revolution in practice (which began in the 1950s, antedating the revolution in rhetoric) drastically increased the odds that bright young women will be thrown in contact with bright young men during the years when people choose spouses. This is most obvious in college, where the proportion of women continuing to college surged from about half the proportion of men in 1950 to equality in 1975. It was not just the numbers, however. All of the elite men's colleges became coeducational, as did many of elite women's colleges. Strict parietal rules gave way to coeducational dorms. Intelligence has always been an important factor for sorting among prospective mates, but comparison shopping at single-sex colleges like Vassar or Yale was a struggle; the feminist revolution in the universities led to an explosion of information, as it were, that made it easier for the brightest to pair up.

The same phenomenon extended to the workplace. Large proportions of the cognitive elite delay marriage until the later twenties or even thirties. Only a few decades ago, delay tended to dilute the chances of assortative mating by IQ. In a world where the brightest women were usually not in the work force or were in a few restricted occupations, the pool from which a man in his late twenties found a bride were moderated primarily by socioeconomic status; he found his mate among the women he encountered in his neighborhood, church, social organizations, and other settings that were matched mostly by socioeconomic status. But today background status is less important than intelligence. The young man newly graduated from his elite law school joins his elite New York firm, thereupon encountering young women, just as highly selected for cognitive ability as he was, in the adjacent offices at his own firm, at business lunches, across the table in negotiations, on a daily basis. The opportunities for propinquity to work its magic were increased in the workplace too, and will continue to increase in the years to come.

The second effect of feminism is less ponderable but may be important anyway. Not so many years ago, the cliché was true: brains were not considered sexy in a woman, and many men undervalued brains as an asset in a prospective spouse or even felt threatened by smart women. Such attitudes may linger in some men, but feminism has surely weakened them and, to some degree, freed relationships among men and women so that a woman's potential for occupational success can take as dominant a place in the man's marriage calculus as it has traditionally taken in the woman's. We speculate that the effect has been most liberating among the brightest. If we are right, then the trends in educational homogamy that Mare has demonstrated are an understated reflection of what is really going on. Intermarriage among people in the top few percentiles of intelligence may be increasing far more rapidly than suspected.

The Limits of Churning

American society has historically been full of churning, as new groups came to this country, worked their way up, and joined the ranks of the rich and powerful. Meanwhile, some of the children of the rich and powerful, or their grandchildren, were descending the ladder. This process has made for a vibrant, self-renewing society. In depressing contrast, we have been envisioning a society that becomes increasingly quiescent at the top, as a cognitive elite moves toward the upper income brackets and runs most of the institutions of society, taking on some of the characteristics of a caste.

Is the situation really so extreme? To some extent, not yet. For example, national surveys still indicate that fewer than 60 percent in the top quartile of intelligence actually complete a bachelor's degree. This would seem to leave a lot of room for churning. But when we focus instead on the students in the top few centiles of cognitive ability (from which the nation's elite colleges pick almost exclusively), an extremely high proportion are already being swept into the comfortable precincts of the cognitive elite. In the NLSY, for example, 81 percent of those in the top 5 percent of IQ had obtained at least a bachelor's degree by 1990, when the youngest members of the sample were 25 years old.

When we examine the remaining 19 percent who had not obtained college degrees, the efficiency of American society in pushing the most talented to the top looks even more impressive. For example, only a small portion of that 19 percent were smart students who had been raised in a low-income family and did not get to college for lack of opportunity. Only 6 percent of persons in the top five IQ centiles did not have a college degree *and* came from families in the lower half of socioeconomic status.

If this 19 percent of high-IQ persons-without-B.A.s does not fit the stereotype of the deprived student, who were they? Some were becoming members of the cognitive elite even though they do not have a college degree.

Bill Gates, college dropout and founder of Microsoft, is the larger-than-life prototype. Five percentage points of the 19 percent were working in one of the high-IQ occupations, indicating that they were probably of the minor-league Bill Gates variety (corroborated by their incomes, which were high). Of the remaining 14 percent who were not working in high-IQ occupations, a quarter had family incomes in excess of $50,000 while they were still only in their late twenties and early thirties, putting them in the top 20 percent of family incomes for their age group. In total, roughly half of these smart non-college graduates are already taking their place among the smart college graduates, by virtue of their incomes, their occupations, or both. It seems a safe bet that the neighborhoods where they live and the way they socialize their children are going to be indistinguishable from those of most of their counterparts in the top five centiles who completed college.

There is doubtless some relatively small fraction of those in the top 5 percent intellectually who will never rise to successful positions, whether because of lack of motivation or objective barriers. But what a small percentage of the highly talented they are. And we may add a reminder that we are watching an ongoing process. Think back to [earlier in the book], and imagine the trend line from 1900 to 1990 stretched out to, say, 2020. Whatever the number of the cognitive elite who slip between the cracks now, it is a much smaller figure than it was in the 1950s, radically smaller than it was in the 1900s, and presumably it will get smaller still in the future.

These observations have several implications. At a practical policy level, the most obvious is that programs to expand opportunity for the disadvantaged are not going to make much difference in getting the most talented youths to college. An extremely high proportion of those who want to go are already going. The broader implication is that the funneling system is already functioning at a high level of efficiency, thereby promoting three interlocking phenomena:

1. The cognitive elite is getting richer, in an era when everybody else is having to struggle to stay even.
2. The cognitive elite is increasingly segregated physically from everyone else, in both the workplace and the neighborhood.

These phenomena are driven by forces that do not lend themselves to easy reconfiguration by politicians. As we leave Part I, here is a topic to keep in the back of your mind: What if the cognitive elite were to become not only richer than everyone else, increasingly segregated, and more genetically distinct as time goes on but were also to acquire common political interests? What might those interests be, and how congruent might they be with a free society? How decisively could the cognitive elite affect policy if it were to acquire such a common political interest?

From *Emotional Intelligence: Why It Can Matter More Than IQ*

Daniel Goleman

The Rudiments of Social Intelligence

It's recess at a preschool, and a band of boys is running across the grass. Reggie trips, hurts his knee, and starts crying, but the other boys keep right on running—save for Roger, who stops. As Reggie's sobs subside Roger reaches down and rubs his own knee, calling out, "I hurt my knee, too!"

Roger is cited as having exemplary interpersonal intelligence by Thomas Hatch, a colleague of Howard Gardner at Spectrum, the school based on the concept of multiple intelligences. Roger, it seems, is unusually adept at recognizing the feelings of his playmates and making rapid, smooth connections with them. It was only Roger who noticed Reggie's plight and pain, and only Roger who tried to provide some solace, even if all he could offer was rubbing his own knee. This small gesture bespeaks a talent for rapport, an emotional skill essential for the preservation of close relationships, whether in a marriage, a friendship, or a business partnership. Such skills in preschoolers are the buds of talents that ripen through life.

Roger's talent represents one of four separate abilities that Hatch and Gardner identify as components of interpersonal intelligence:

- *Organizing groups*—the essential skill of the leader, this involves initiating and coordinating the efforts of a network of people. This is the talent seen in theater directors or producers, in military officers, and in effective heads of organizations and units of all kinds. On the playground, this is the child who takes the lead in deciding what everyone will play, or becomes team captain.

- *Negotiating solutions*—the talent of the mediator, preventing conflicts or resolving those that flare up. People who have this ability excel in deal-making, in arbitrating or mediating disputes; they might have a career in diplomacy, in arbitration or law, or as middlemen or managers of takeovers. These are the kids who settle arguments on the playing field.

- *Personal connection*—Roger's talent, that of empathy and connecting. This makes it easy to enter into an encounter or to recognize and re-spond fittingly to people's feelings and concerns—the art of relation-ship. Such people make good "team players," dependable spouses, good friends or business partners; in the business world they do well as salespeople or managers, or can be excellent teachers. Children like Roger get along well with virtually everyone else, easily enter into play-ing with them, and are happy doing so. These children tend to be best at reading emotions from facial expressions and are most liked by their classmates.

- *Social analysis*—being able to detect and have insights about people's feelings, motives, and concerns. This knowledge of how others feel can lead to an easy intimacy or sense of rapport. At its best, this ability makes one a competent therapist or counselor—or, if combined with some literary talent, a gifted novelist or dramatist.

Taken together, these skills are the stuff of interpersonal polish, the necessary ingredients for charm, social success, even charisma. Those who are adept in social intelligence can connect with people quite smoothly, be astute in reading their reactions and feelings, lead and organize, and handle the disputes that are bound to flare up in any human activity. They are the natural leaders, the people who can express the unspoken collective senti-ment and articulate it so as to guide a group toward its goals. They are the kind of people others like to be with because they are emotionally nourish-ing—they leave other people in a good mood, and evoke the comment, "What a pleasure to be around someone like that."

These interpersonal abilities build on other emotional intelligences. People who make an excellent social impression, for example, are adept at monitoring their own expression of emotion, are keenly attuned to the ways others are reacting, and so are able to continually fine-tune their social per-formance, adjusting it to make sure they are having the desired effect. In that sense, they are like skilled actors.

However, if these interpersonal abilities are not balanced by an astute sense of one's own needs and feelings and how to fulfill them, they can lead to a hollow social success—a popularity won at the cost of one's true satisfaction. Such is the argument of Mark Snyder, a University of Minnesota psychologist who has studied people whose social skills make them first-rate social chameleons, champions at making a good impression. Their psychological credo might well be a remark by W. H. Auden, who said that his private image of himself "is very different from the image which I try to create in the minds of others in order that they may love me." That trade-off can be made if social skills outstrip the ability to know and honor one's own feelings: in order to be loved—or at least liked—the social chameleon will seem to be whatever those he is with seem to want. The sign that someone falls into this pattern, Snyder finds, is that they make an excellent impression, yet have few stable or satisfying intimate relationships. A more healthy pattern, of course, is to balance being true to oneself with social skills, using them with integrity.

Social chameleons, though, don't mind in the least saying one thing and doing another, if that will win them social approval. They simply live with the discrepancy between their public face and their private reality. Helena Deutsch, a psychoanalyst, called such people the "as-if personality," shifting personas with remarkable plasticity as they pick up signals from those around them. "For some people," Snyder told me, "the public and private person meshes well, while for others there seems to be only a kaleidoscope of changing appearances. They are like Woody Allen's character Zelig, madly trying to fit in with whomever they are with."

Such people try to scan someone for a hint as to what is wanted from them before they make a response, rather than simply saying what they truly feel. To get along and be liked, they are willing to make people they dislike think they are friendly with them. And they use their social abilities to mold their actions as disparate social situations demand, so that they may act like very different people depending on whom they are with, swinging from bubbly sociability, say, to reserved withdrawal. To be sure, to the extent that these traits lead to effective impression management, they are highly prized in certain professions, notably acting, trial law, sales, diplomacy, and politics.

Another, perhaps more crucial kind of self-monitoring seems to make the difference between those who end up as anchorless social chameleons, trying to impress everyone, and those who can use their social polish more

in keeping with their true feelings. That is the capacity to be true, as the saying has it, "to thine own self," which allows acting in accord with one's deepest feelings and values no matter what the social consequences. Such emotional integrity could well lead to, say, deliberately provoking a confrontation
in order to cut through duplicity or denial—a clearing of the air that a social
chameleon would never attempt.

The Making of a Social Incompetent

There was no doubt Cecil was bright; he was a college-trained expert in foreign languages, superb at translating. But there were crucial ways in which
he was completely inept. Cecil seemed to lack the simplest social skills. He
would muff a casual conversation over coffee, and fumble when having to
pass the time of day; in short, he seemed incapable of the most routine social exchange. Because his lack of social grace was most profound when he
was around women, Cecil came to therapy wondering if perhaps he had
"homosexual tendencies of an underlying nature," as he put it, though he
had no such fantasies.

The real problem, Cecil confided to his therapist, was that he feared that
nothing he could say would be of any interest to anybody. This underlying
fear only compounded a profound paucity of social graces. His nervousness
during encounters led him to snicker and laugh at the most awkward moments, even though he failed to laugh when someone said something genuinely funny. Cecil's awkwardness, he confided to his therapist, went back to
childhood; all his life he had felt socially at ease only when he was with his
older brother, who somehow helped ease things for him. But once he left
home, his ineptitude was overwhelming; he was socially paralyzed.

The tale is told by Lakin Phillips, a psychologist at George Washington
University, who proposes that Cecil's plight stems from a failure to learn in
childhood the most elementary lessons of social interaction:

> What could Cecil have been taught earlier? To speak directly to others when
> spoken to; to initiate social contact, not always wait for others; to carry on a
> conversation, not simply fall back on yes or no or other one-word replies; to
> express gratitude toward others, to let another person walk before one in
> passing through a door; to wait until one is served something . . . to thank

others, to say "please," to share, and all the other elementary interactions we begin to teach children from age 2 onward.

Whether Cecil's deficiency was due to another's failure to teach him such rudiments of social civility or to his own inability to learn is unclear. But whatever its roots, Cecil's story is instructive because it points up the crucial nature of the countless lessons children get in interaction synchrony and the unspoken rules of social harmony. The net effect of failing to follow these rules is to create waves, to make those around us uncomfortable. The function of these rules, of course, is to keep everyone involved in a social exchange at ease; awkwardness spawns anxiety. People who lack these skills are inept not just at social niceties, but at handling the emotions of those they encounter; they inevitably leave disturbance in their wake.

We all have known Cecils, people with an annoying lack of social graces—people who don't seem to know when to end a conversation or phone call and who keep on talking, oblivious to all cues and hints to say good-bye; people whose conversation centers on themselves all the time, without the least interest in anyone else, and who ignore tentative attempts to refocus on another topic; people who intrude or ask "nosy" questions. These derailments of a smooth social trajectory all bespeak a deficit in the rudimentary building blocks of interaction.

Psychologists have coined the term *dyssemia* (from the Greek *dys-* for "difficulty" and *semes* for "signal") for what amounts to a learning disability in the realm of nonverbal messages; about one in ten children has one or more problems in this realm. The problem can be in a poor sense of personal space, so that a child stands too close while talking or spreads their belongings into other people's territory; in interpreting or using body language poorly; in misinterpreting or misusing facial expressions by, say, failing to make eye contact; or in a poor sense of prosody, the emotional quality of speech so that they talk too shrilly or flatly.

Much research has focused on spotting children who show signs of social deficiency, children whose awkwardness makes them neglected or rejected by their playmates. Apart from children who are spurned because they are bullies, those whom other children avoid are invariably deficient in the rudiments of face-to-face interaction, particularly the unspoken rules that govern encounters. If children do poorly in language, people assume they are not very bright or poorly educated; but when they do poorly in the nonverbal rules of interaction, people—especially playmates—see them as "strange," and avoid them. These are the children who don't know how to join a game gracefully, who touch others in ways that make for discomfort rather than camaraderie—in short, who are "off." They are children who have failed to master the silent language of emotion, and who unwittingly send messages that create uneasiness.

As Stephen Nowicki, an Emory University psychologist who studies children's nonverbal abilities, put it, "Children who can't read or express emotions well constantly feel frustrated. In essence, they don't understand what's going on. This kind of communication is a constant subtext of everything you do; you can't stop showing your facial expression or posture, or hide your tone of voice. If you make mistakes in what emotional messages you send, you constantly experience that people react to you in funny ways—you get rebuffed and don't know why. If you're thinking you're acting happy but actually seem too hyper or angry, you find other kids getting angry at you in turn, and you don't realize why. Such kids end up feeling no sense of control over how other people treat them, that their actions have no impact on what happens to them. It leaves them feeling powerless, depressed, and apathetic."

Apart from becoming social isolates, such children also suffer academically. The classroom, of course, is as much a social situation as an academic one; the socially awkward child is as likely to misread and misrespond to a teacher as to another child. The resulting anxiety and bewilderment can themselves interfere with their ability to learn effectively. Indeed, as tests of children's nonverbal sensitivity have shown, those who misread emotional cues tend to do poorly in school compared to their academic potential as reflected in IQ tests.

"We Hate You": At the Threshold

Social ineptitude is perhaps most painful and explicit when it comes to one of the more perilous moments in the life of a young child: being on the edge of a group at play you want to join. It is a moment of peril, one when being liked or hated, belonging or not, is made all too public. For that reason that crucial moment has been the subject of intense scrutiny by students of child development, revealing a stark contrast in approach strategies used by popular children and by social outcasts. The findings highlight just how crucial it is for social competence to notice, interpret, and respond to emotional and interpersonal cues. While it is poignant to see a child hover on the edge of others at play, wanting to join in but being left out, it is a universal predicament. Even the most popular children are sometimes rejected—a study of second and third graders found that 26 percent of the time the most well liked children were rebuffed when they tried to enter a group already at play.

Young children are brutally candid about the emotional judgment implicit in such rejections. Witness the following dialogue from four-year-olds in a preschool. Linda wants to join Barbara, Nancy, and Bill, who are playing with toy animals and building blocks. She watches for a minute, then makes her approach, sitting next to Barbara and starting to play with the animals. Barbara turns to her and says, "You can't play!"

"Yes, I can," Linda counters. "I can have some animals, too."

"No, you can't," Barbara says bluntly. "We don't like you today."

When Bill protests on Linda's behalf, Nancy joins the attack: "We hate her today."

Because of the danger of being told, either explicitly or implicitly, "We hate you," all children are understandably cautious on the threshold of approaching a group. That anxiety, of course, is probably not much different from that felt by a grown-up at a cocktail party with strangers who hangs back from a happily chatting group who seem to be intimate friends. Because this moment at the threshold of a group is so momentous for a child, it is also, as one researcher put it, "highly diagnostic . . . quickly revealing differences in social skillfulness."

Typically, newcomers simply watch for a time, then join in very tentatively at first, being more assertive only in very cautious steps. What matters most for whether a child is accepted or not is how well he or she is able to enter into the group's frame of reference, sensing what kind of play is in flow, what out of place.

The two cardinal sins that almost always lead to rejection are trying to take the lead too soon and being out of synch with the frame of reference. But this is exactly what unpopular children tend to do: they push their way into a group, trying to change the subject too abruptly or too soon, or offering their own opinions, or simply disagreeing with the others right away—all apparent attempts to draw attention to themselves. Paradoxically, this results in their being ignored or rejected. By contrast, popular children spend time observing the group to understand what's going on before entering in, and then do something that shows they accept it; they wait to have their status in the group confirmed before taking initiative in suggesting what the group should do.

Let's return to Roger, the four-year-old whom Thomas Hatch spotted exhibiting a high level of interpersonal intelligence. Roger's tactic for entering a group was first to observe, then to imitate what another child was doing, and finally to talk to the child and fully join the activity—a winning strategy. Roger's skill was shown, for instance, when he and Warren were playing at putting "bombs" (actually pebbles) in their socks. Warren asks Roger if he wants to be in a helicopter or an airplane. Roger asks, before committing himself, "Are you in a helicopter?"

This seemingly innocuous moment reveals sensitivity to others' concerns, and the ability to act on that knowledge in a way that maintains the connection. Hatch comments about Roger, "He 'checks in' with his playmate so that they and their play remain connected. I have watched many other children who simply get in their own helicopters or planes and, literally and figuratively, fly away from each other."

Emotional Brilliance: A Case Report

If the test of social skill is the ability to calm distressing emotions in others, then handling someone at the peak of rage is perhaps the ultimate measure of mastery. The data on self-regulation of anger and emotional contagion suggest that one effective strategy might be to distract the angry person, empathize with his feelings and perspective, and then draw him into an alternative focus, one that attunes him with a more positive range of feeling—a kind of emotional judo.

Such refined skill in the fine art of emotional influence is perhaps best exemplified by a story told by an old friend, the late Terry Dobson, who in the 1950s was one of the first Americans ever to study the martial art aikido in Japan. One afternoon he was riding home on a suburban Tokyo train when a huge, bellicose, and very drunk and begrimed laborer got on. The man, staggering, began terrorizing the passengers: screaming curses, he took a swing at a woman holding a baby, sending her sprawling in the laps of an elderly couple, who then jumped up and joined a stampede to the other end of the car. The drunk, taking a few other swings (and, in his rage, missing), grabbed the metal pole in the middle of the car with a roar and tried to tear it out of its socket.

At that point Terry, who was in peak physical condition from daily eight-hour aikido workouts, felt called upon to intervene, lest someone get seriously hurt. But he recalled the words of his teacher: "Aikido is the art of reconciliation. Whoever has the mind to fight has broken his connection with the universe. If you try to dominate people you are already defeated. We study how to resolve conflict, not how to start it."

Indeed, Terry had agreed upon beginning lessons with his teacher never to pick a fight, and to use his martial-arts skills only in defense. Now, at last, he saw his chance to test his aikido abilities in real life, in what was clearly a legitimate opportunity. So, as all the other passengers sat frozen in their seats, Terry stood up, slowly and with deliberation.

Seeing him, the drunk roared, "Aha! A foreigner! You need a lesson in Japanese manners!" and began gathering himself to take on Terry.

But just as the drunk was on the verge of making his move, someone gave an earsplitting, oddly joyous shout: "Hey!"

The shout had the cheery tone of someone who has suddenly come upon a fond friend. The drunk, surprised, spun around to see a tiny Japanese man, probably in his seventies, sitting there in a kimono. The old man beamed with delight at the drunk, and beckoned him over with a light wave of his hand and a lilting "C'mere."

The drunk strode over with a belligerent, "Why the hell should I talk to you?" Meanwhile, Terry was ready to fell the drunk in a moment if he made the least violent move.

"What'cha been drinking?" the old man asked, his eyes beaming at the drunken laborer.

"I been drinking sake, and it's none of your business," the drunk bellowed.

"Oh, that's wonderful, absolutely wonderful," the old man replied in a warm tone. "You see, I love sake, too. Every night, me and my wife (she's seventy-six, you know), we warm up a little bottle of sake and take it out into the garden, and we sit on an old wooden bench . . ." He continued on about the persimmon tree in his backyard, the fortunes of his garden, enjoying sake in the evening.

The drunk's face began to soften as he listened to the old man; his fists unclenched. "Yeah ... I love persimmons, too ...," he said, his voice trailing off.

"Yes," the old man replied in a sprightly voice, "and I'm sure you have a wonderful wife."

"No," said the laborer. "My wife died...." Sobbing, he launched into a sad tale of losing his wife, his home, his job, of being ashamed of himself.

Just then the train came to Terry's stop, and as he was getting off he turned to hear the old man invite the drunk to join him and tell him all about it, and to see the drunk sprawl along the seat, his head in the old man's lap.

That is emotional brilliance.

QUESTIONS

1. What made *The Bell Curve* unpopular was not the selection excerpted here, but a different argument—about whether between-race differences in IQ could be attributed to genetics. Read and evaluate philosopher Ned Block's discussion of this in his article "How Heritability Misleads about Race" (1996), currently available online at www.nyu.edu/gsas/dept/philo/faculty/block/papers/Heritability.html.

2. Look for four examples of social intelligence in your life, actions that you, your friends, or your family have taken that might qualify as emotionally intelligent.

CHAPTER ELEVEN

MOTIVATION AND STRESS

The motto of my undergraduate alma mater is *non satis scire*, "to know is not enough." A creature that could reason perfectly about the world might still not *do* anything. Action requires not just knowledge but motivation. What motivates human beings? What gets an otherwise unmotivated couch potato off their duff and into the world? How can an army motivate its troops to risk their own lives? Of the many things in your daily agenda, why do you often seem to carry out some sorts of tasks and not others? According to Abraham Maslow's famous pyramid of needs, humans have a series of needs starting from the physiological (food and drink) and moving up through safety, belonging, and esteem before finally ascending to the most refined, what Maslow called self-actualization.

While Maslow's psychology was about determining what goals we set, Mihaly Csikszentmihalyi's work is about what it is like to be in the act of fulfilling those goals. When someone does something well, what does it feel like? In the excerpt from *Flow* (1990), Csikszentmihalyi asks what brings us pleasure: not just a sense of joy, but something beyond, a thoroughgoing positive sense of immersion in a pleasurable activity that he calls flow.

If pleasure is something we seek, stress is something we try to avoid. In this chapter's second selection, molecular biologist Robert Sapolsky steps into psychological territory, asking how mental factors mediate the experience of physiological stress. In an excerpt from his book *Why Zebras Don't Get Ulcers* (1994), Sapolsky explores the relationship between mind, brain, and body, showing how mental processes can influence physiological processes.

From *Flow: The Psychology of Optimal Experience*

Mihaly Csikszentmihalyi

Without enjoyment life can be endured, and it can even be pleasant. But it can be so only precariously, depending on luck and the cooperation of the external environment. To gain personal control over the quality of experience, however, one needs to learn how to build enjoyment into what happens day in, day out.

The rest of this chapter provides an overview of what makes experience enjoyable. This description is based on long interviews, questionnaires, and other data collected over a dozen years from several thousand respondents. Initially we interviewed only people who spent a great amount of time and effort in activities that were difficult, yet provided no obvious rewards, such as money or prestige: rock climbers, composers of music, chess players, amateur athletes. Our later studies included interviews with ordinary people, leading ordinary existences; we asked them to describe how it felt when their lives were at their fullest, when what they did was most enjoyable. These people included urban Americans—surgeons, professors, clerical and assembly-line workers, young mothers, retired people, and teenagers. They also included respondents from Korea, Japan, Thailand, Australia, various European cultures, and a Navajo reservation. On the basis of these interviews we can now describe what makes an experience enjoyable and thus provide examples that all of us can use to enhance the quality of life.

The Elements of Enjoyment

The first surprise we encountered in our study was how similarly very different activities were described when they were going especially well.

Apparently the way a long-distance swimmer felt when crossing the English Channel was almost identical to the way a chess player felt during a tournament or a climber progressing up a difficult rock face. All these feelings were shared, in important respects, by subjects ranging from musicians composing a new quartet to teenagers from the ghetto involved in a championship basketball game.

The second surprise was that, regardless of culture, stage of modernization, social class, age, or gender, the respondents described enjoyment in very much the same way. What they did to experience enjoyment varied enormously—the elderly Koreans liked to meditate, the teenage Japanese liked to swarm around in motorcycle gangs—but they described how it felt when they enjoyed themselves in almost identical terms. Moreover, the reasons the activity was enjoyed shared many more similarities than differences. In sum, optimal experience, and the psychological conditions that make it possible, seem to be the same the world over.

As our studies have suggested, the phenomenology of enjoyment has eight major components. When people reflect on how it feels when their experience is most positive, they mention at least one, and often all, of the following. First, the experience usually occurs when we confront tasks we have a chance of completing. Second, we must be able to concentrate on what we are doing. Third and fourth, the concentration is usually possible because the task undertaken has clear goals and provides immediate feedback. Fifth, one acts with a deep but effortless involvement that removes from awareness the worries and frustrations of everyday life. Sixth, enjoyable experiences allow people to exercise a sense of control over their actions. Seventh, concern for the self disappears, yet paradoxically the sense of self emerges stronger after the flow experience is over. Finally, the sense of the duration of time is altered; hours pass by in minutes, and minutes can stretch out to seem like hours. The combination of all these elements causes a sense of deep enjoyment that is so rewarding people feel that expending a great deal of energy is worthwhile simply to be able to feel it.

We shall take a closer look at each of these elements so that we may better understand what makes enjoyable activities so gratifying. With this knowledge, it is possible to achieve control of consciousness and turn even the most humdrum moments of everyday lives into events that help the self grow.

A Challenging Activity That Requires Skills

Sometimes a person reports having an experience of extreme joy, a feeling of ecstasy for no apparent good reason: a bar of haunting music may trigger it, or a wonderful view, or even less—just a spontaneous sense of well-being. But by far the overwhelming proportion of optimal experiences are reported to occur within sequences of activities that are goal-directed and bounded by rules—activities that require the investment of psychic energy, and that could not be done without the appropriate skills. Why this should be so will become clear as we go along; at this point it is sufficient to note that this seems to be universally the case.

It is important to clarify at the outset that an "activity" need not be active in the physical sense, and the "skill" necessary to engage in it need not be a physical skill. For instance, one of the most frequently mentioned enjoyable activities the world over is reading. Reading is an activity because it requires the concentration of attention and has a goal and to do it one must know the rules of written language. The skills involved in reading include not only literacy but also the ability to translate words into images, to empathize with fictional characters, to recognize historical and cultural contexts, to anticipate turns of the plot, to criticize and evaluate the author's style, and so on. In this broad sense, any capacity to manipulate symbolic information is a "skill," such as the skill of the mathematician to shape quantitative relationships in his head, or the skill of the musician in combining musical notes.

Another universally enjoyable activity is being with other people. Socializing might at first sight appear to be an exception to the statement that one needs to use skills to enjoy an activity, for it does not seem that gossiping or joking around with another person requires particular abilities. But of course, it does; as so many shy people know, if a person feels self-conscious, he or she will dread establishing informal contact and avoid company whenever possible.

Any activity contains a bundle of opportunities for action, "challenges," that require appropriate skills to realize. For those who don't have the right skills, the activity is not challenging; it is simply meaningless. Setting up a chessboard gets the juices of a chess player flowing, but leaves cold anyone who does not know the rules of the game. To most people, the sheer wall of El Capitan in Yosemite valley is just a huge chunk of featureless rock. But to the climber it is an area offering an endlessly complex symphony of mental and physical challenges.

One simple way to find challenges is to enter a competitive situation. Hence the great appeal of all games and sports that pit a person or team against another. In many ways, competition is a quick way of developing complexity: "He who wrestles with us," wrote Edmund Burke, "strengthens our nerves, and sharpens our skill. Our antagonist is our helper." The challenges of competition can be stimulating and enjoyable. But when beating the opponent takes precedence in the mind over performing as well as possible, enjoyment tends to disappear. Competition is enjoyable only when it is a means to perfect one's skills; when it becomes an end in itself, it ceases to be fun.

But challenges are by no means confined to competitive or physical activities. They are necessary to provide enjoyment even in situations where one would not expect them to be relevant. For example, here is a quote from one of our studies, of a statement made by an art expert describing the enjoyment he takes in looking at a painting, something most people would regard as an immediate, intuitive process. "A lot of pieces that you deal with are very straightforward... and you don't find anything exciting about them, you know, but there are other pieces that have some sort of challenge.... those are the pieces that stay in your mind, that are the most interesting." In other words, even the passive enjoyment one gets from looking at a painting or sculpture depends on the challenges that the work of art contains.

Activities that provide enjoyment are often those that have been designed for this very purpose. Games, sports, and artistic and literary forms were developed over the centuries for the express purpose of enriching life with enjoyable experiences. But it would be a mistake to assume that only art and leisure can provide optimal experiences. In a healthy culture, productive work and the necessary routines of everyday life are also satisfying. In fact, one purpose of this book is to explore ways in which even routine details can be transformed into personally meaningful games that provide optimal experiences. Mowing the lawn or waiting in a dentist's office can become enjoyable provided one restructures the activity by providing goals, rules, and the other elements of enjoyment to be reviewed below.

Heinz Maier-Leibnitz, the famous German experimental physicist and a descendant of the eighteenth-century philosopher and mathematician, provides an intriguing example of how one can take control of a boring situation and turn it into a mildly enjoyable one. Professor Maier-Leibnitz suffers from an occupational handicap common to academicians: having to sit through endless, often boring conferences. To alleviate this burden he invented a private activity that provides just enough challenges for him not to be completely bored during a dull lecture, but is so automated that it leaves enough attention free so that if something interesting is being said, it will register in his awareness.

What he does is this: Whenever a speaker begins to get tedious, he starts to tap his right thumb once, then the third finger of the right hand, then the index, then the fourth finger, then the third finger again, then the little finger of the right hand. Then he moves to the left hand and taps the little finger, the middle finger, the fourth finger, the index, and the middle finger again, and ends with the thumb of the left hand. Then the right hand reverses the sequence of fingering, followed by the reverse of the left hand's sequence. It turns out that by introducing full and half stops at regular intervals, there are 888 combinations one can move through without repeating the same pattern. By interspersing pauses among the taps at regular intervals, the pattern acquires an almost musical harmony, and in fact it is easily represented on a musical staff.

After inventing this innocent game, Professor Maier-Leibnitz found an interesting use for it: as a way of measuring the length of trains of thought. The pattern of 888 taps, repeated three times, provides a set of 2,664 taps that, with practice, takes almost exactly twelve minutes to perform. As soon as he starts tapping, by shifting attention to his fingers, Professor Maier-Leibnitz can tell exactly at what point he is in the sequence. So suppose that a thought concerning one of his physics experiments appears in his consciousness while he is tapping during a boring lecture. He immediately shifts attention to his fingers, and registers the fact that he is at the 300th tap of the second series; then in the same split second he returns to the train of thought about the experiment. At a certain point the thought is completed, and he has figured out the problem. How long did it take him to solve the problem? By shifting attention back to his fingers, he notices that he is about to finish the second series—the thought process has taken approximately two and a quarter minutes to play itself out.

Few people bother inventing quite such ingenious and complex diversions to improve the quality of their experiences. But all of us have more modest versions of the same. Everybody develops routines to fill in the boring gaps of the day, or to bring experience back on an even keel when anxiety threatens. Some people are compulsive doodlers, others chew on things or smoke, smooth their hair, hum a tune, or engage in more esoteric private rituals that have the same purpose: to impose order in consciousness through the performance of patterned action. These are the "microflow" activities that help us negotiate the doldrums of the day. But how enjoyable an activity is depends ultimately on its complexity. The small automatic games woven into the fabric of everyday life help reduce boredom, but add little to the positive quality of experience. For that one needs to face more demanding challenges, and use higher-level skills.

In all the activities people in our study reported engaging in, enjoyment comes at a very specific point: whenever the opportunities for action perceived by the individual are equal to his or her capabilities. Playing tennis, for instance, is not enjoyable if the two opponents are mismatched. The less skilled player will feel anxious, and the better player will feel bored. The same is true of every other activity: a piece of music that is too simple relative to one's listening skills will be boring, while music that is too complex will be frustrating. Enjoyment appears at the boundary between boredom and anxiety, when the challenges are just balanced with the person's capacity to act.

The golden ratio between challenges and skills does not only hold true for human activities. Whenever I took our hunting dog, Hussar, for a walk in the open fields he liked to play a very simple game—the prototype of the most culturally widespread game of human children, escape and pursuit. He would run circles around me at top speed, with his tongue hanging out and his eyes warily watching every move I made, daring me to catch him. Occasionally I would take a lunge, and if I was lucky I got to touch him. Now the interesting part is that whenever I was tired, and moved halfheartedly, Hussar would run much tighter circles, making it relatively easy for me to catch him; on the other hand, if I was in good shape and willing to extend myself, he would enlarge the diameter of his circle. In this way, the difficulty of the game was kept constant. With an uncanny sense for the fine balancing of challenges and skills, he would make sure that the game would yield the maximum of enjoyment for us both.

The Merging of Action and Awareness
When all a person's relevant skills are needed to cope with the challenges of a situation, that person's attention is completely absorbed by the activity. There is no excess psychic energy left over to process any information but what the activity offers. All the attention is concentrated on the relevant stimuli.

As a result, one of the most universal and distinctive features of optimal experience takes place: people become so involved in what they are doing that the activity becomes spontaneous, almost automatic; they stop being aware of themselves as separate from the actions they are performing.

A dancer describes how it feels when a performance is going well: "Your concentration is very complete. Your mind isn't wandering, you are not thinking of something else; you are totally involved in what you are doing. . . . Your energy is flowing very smoothly. You feel relaxed, comfortable, and energetic."

A rock climber explains how it feels when he is scaling a mountain: "You are so involved in what you are doing that you aren't thinking of yourself as separate from the immediate activity. . . . You don't see yourself as separate from what you are doing."

A mother who enjoys the time spent with her small daughter: "Her reading is the one thing that she's really into, and we read together. She reads to me, and I read to her, and that's a time when I sort of lose touch with the rest of the world, I'm totally absorbed in what I'm doing."

A chess player tells of playing in a tournament: ". . . the concentration is like breathing—you never think of it. The roof could fall in and, if it missed you, you would be unaware of it."

It is for this reason that we called the optimal experience "flow." The short and simple word describes well the sense of seemingly effortless movement. The following words from a poet and rock climber apply to all the thousands of interviews collected by us and by others over the years: "The mystique of rock climbing is climbing; you get to the top of a rock glad it's over but really wish it would go on forever. The justification of climbing is climbing, like the justification of poetry is writing; you don't conquer anything except things in yourself. . . . The act of writing justifies poetry. Climbing is the same: recognizing that you are a flow. The purpose of the flow is to keep on flowing, not looking for a peak or utopia but staying in the flow. It is not a moving up but a continuous flowing; you move up to keep the flow going. There is no possible reason for climbing except the climbing itself; it is a self-communication."

Although the flow experience appears to be effortless, it is far from being so. It often requires strenuous physical exertion, or highly disciplined mental activity. It does not happen without the application of skilled performance. Any lapse in concentration will erase it. And yet while it lasts consciousness works smoothly, action follows action seamlessly. In normal life, we keep interrupting what we do with doubts and questions. "Why am I doing this? Should I perhaps be doing something else?" Repeatedly we question the necessity of our actions, and evaluate critically the reasons for carrying them out. But in flow there is no need to reflect, because the action carries us forward as if by magic.

Clear Goals and Feedback

The reason it is possible to achieve such complete involvement in a flow experience is that goals are usually clear, and feedback immediate. A tennis player always knows what she has to do: return the ball into the opponent's court. And each time she hits the ball she knows whether she has done well or not. The chess player's goals are equally obvious: to mate the opponent's king before his own is mated. With each move, he can calculate whether he has come closer to this objective. The climber inching up a vertical wall of rock has a very simple goal in mind: to complete the climb without falling. Every second, hour after hour, he receives information that he is meeting that basic goal.

Of course, if one chooses a trivial goal, success in it does not provide enjoyment. If I set as my goal to remain alive while sitting on the living-room sofa, I also could spend days knowing that I was achieving it, just as the rock climber does. But this realization would not make me particularly happy, whereas the climber's knowledge brings exhilaration to his dangerous ascent.

Certain activities require a very long time to accomplish, yet the components of goals and feedback are still extremely important to them. One example was given by a sixty-two-year-old woman living in the Italian Alps, who said her most enjoyable experiences were taking care of the cows and tending the orchard: "I find special satisfaction in caring for the plants: I like to see them grow day by day. It is very beautiful." Although it involves a period of patient waiting, seeing the plants one has cared for grow provides a powerful feedback even in the urban apartments of American cities.

Another example is solo ocean cruising, in which a person alone might sail for weeks in a small boat without seeing land. Jim Macbeth, who did a study of flow in ocean cruising, comments on the excitement a sailor feels when, after days of anxiously scanning the empty reaches of water, he discerns the outline of the island he had been aiming for as it starts to rise over the horizon. One of the legendary cruisers describes this sensation as follows: "I ... experienced a sense of satisfaction coupled with some astonishment that my observations of the very distant sun from an unsteady platform and the use of some simple tables ... enable[d] a small island to be found with certainty after an ocean crossing." And another: "Each time, I feel the same mixture of astonishment, love, and pride as this new land is born which seems to have been created for me and by me."

The goals of an activity are not always as clear as those of tennis, and the feedback is often more ambiguous than the simple "I am not falling" information processed by the climber. A composer of music, for instance, may know that he wishes to write a song, or a flute concerto, but other than that, his goals are usually quite vague. And how does he know whether the notes he is writing down are "right" or "wrong"? The same situation holds true for the artist painting a picture, and for all activities that are creative or open-ended in nature. But these are all exceptions that prove the rule: unless a person learns to set goals and to recognize and gauge feedback in such activities, she will not enjoy them.

In some creative activities, where goals are not clearly set in advance, a person must develop a strong personal sense of what she intends to do. The artist might not have a visual image of what the finished painting should look like, but when the picture has progressed to a certain point, she should know whether this is what she wanted to achieve or not. And a painter who enjoys painting must have internalized criteria for "good" or "bad" so that after each brush stroke she can say: "Yes, this works; no, this doesn't." Without such internal guidelines, it is impossible to experience flow.

Sometimes the goals and the rules governing an activity are invented, or negotiated on the spot. For example, teenagers enjoy impromptu interactions in which they try to "gross each other out," or tell tall stories, or make fun of their teachers. The goal of such sessions emerges by trial and error, and is rarely made explicit; often it remains below the participants' level of awareness. Yet it is clear that these activities develop their own rules and that those who take part have a clear idea of what constitutes a successful "move," and of who is doing well. In many ways this is the pattern of a good jazz band, or any improvisational group. Scholars or debaters obtain similar satisfaction when the "moves" in their arguments mesh smoothly, and produce the desired result.

What constitutes feedback varies considerably in different activities. Some people are indifferent to things that others cannot get enough of. For instance, surgeons who love doing operations claim that they wouldn't switch to internal medicine even if they were paid ten times as much as they are for doing surgery, because an internist never knows exactly how well he is doing. In an operation, on the other hand, the status of the patient is almost always clear: as long as there is no blood in the incision, for example, a specific procedure has been successful. When the diseased organ is cut out, the surgeon's task is accomplished; after that there is the suture that gives a gratifying sense of closure to the activity. And the surgeon's disdain for psychiatry is even greater than that for internal medicine: to hear surgeons talk, the psychiatrist might spend ten years with a patient without knowing whether the cure is helping him.

Yet the psychiatrist who enjoys his trade is also receiving constant feedback: the way the patient holds himself, the expression on his face, the hesitation in his voice, the content of the material he brings up in the therapeutic hour—all these bits of information are important clues the psychiatrist uses to monitor the progress of the therapy. The difference between a surgeon and a psychiatrist is that the former considers blood and excision the only feedback worth attending to, whereas the latter considers the signals reflecting a patient's state of mind to be significant information. The surgeon judges the psychiatrist to be soft because he is interested in such ephemeral goals; the psychiatrist thinks the surgeon crude for his concentration on mechanics.

The *kind* of feedback we work toward is in and of itself often unimportant: What difference does it make if I hit the tennis ball between the white lines, if I immobilize the enemy king on the chessboard, or if I notice a glimmer of understanding in my patient's eyes at the end of the therapeutic hour? What makes this information valuable is the symbolic message it contains: that I have succeeded in my goal. Such knowledge creates order in consciousness, and strengthens the structure of the self.

Almost any kind of feedback can be enjoyable, provided it is logically related to a goal in which one has invested psychic energy. If I were to set myself up to balance a walking stick on my nose, then the sight of the stick wobbling upright above my face would provide a brief enjoyable interlude. But each of us is temperamentally sensitive to a certain range of information that we learn to value more than most other people do, and it is likely that we will consider feedback involving that information to be more relevant than others might.

For instance, some people are born with exceptional sensitivity to sound. They can discriminate among different tones and pitches, and recognize and remember combinations of sounds better than the general population. It is likely that such individuals will be attracted to playing with sounds; they will learn to control and shape auditory information. For them the most important feedback will consist in being able to combine sounds, to produce or reproduce rhythms and melodies. Composers, singers, performers, conductors, and music critics will develop from among them. In contrast, some are genetically predisposed to be unusually sensitive to other people, and they will learn to pay attention to the signals they send out. The feedback they will be looking for is the expression of human emotion. Some people have fragile selves that need constant reassurance, and for them the only information that counts is winning in a competitive situation. Others have invested so much in being liked that the only feedback they take into account is approval and admiration.

A good illustration of the importance of feedback is contained in the responses of a group of blind religious women interviewed by Professor Fausto Massimini's team of psychologists in Milan, Italy. Like the other respondents in our studies, they were asked to describe the most enjoyable experiences in their lives. For these women, many of whom had been sightless since birth, the most frequently mentioned flow experiences were the result of reading books in Braille, praying, doing handicrafts like knitting and binding books, and helping each other in case of sickness or other need. Of the over six hundred people interviewed by the Italian team, these blind women stressed more than anyone else the importance of receiving clear feedback as a condition for enjoying whatever they were doing. Unable to see what was going on around them, they needed to know even more than sighted people whether what they were trying to accomplish was actually coming to pass.

Concentration on the Task at Hand

One of the most frequently mentioned dimensions of the flow experience is that, while it lasts, one is able to forget all the unpleasant aspects of life. This feature of flow is an important by-product of the fact that enjoyable activities require a complete focusing of attention on the task at hand—thus leaving no room in the mind for irrelevant information.

In normal everyday existence, we are the prey of thoughts and worries intruding unwanted in consciousness. Because most jobs, and home life in general, lack the pressing demands of flow experiences, concentration is rarely so intense that preoccupations and anxieties can be automatically ruled out. Consequently the ordinary state of mind involves unexpected and frequent episodes of entropy interfering with the smooth run of psychic energy. This is one reason why flow improves the quality of experience: the clearly structured demands of the activity impose order, and exclude the interference of disorder in consciousness.

A professor of physics who was an avid rock climber described his state of mind while climbing as follows: "It is as if my memory input has been cut off. All I can remember is the last thirty seconds, and all I can think ahead is the next five minutes." In fact, any activity that requires concentration has a similarly narrow window of time.

But it is not only the temporal focus that counts. What is even more significant is that only a very select range of information can be allowed into awareness. Therefore all the troubling thoughts that ordinarily keep passing through the mind are temporarily kept in abeyance. As a young basketball player explains: "The court—that's all that matters.... Sometimes out on the court I think of a problem, like fighting with my steady girl, and I think that's nothing compared to the game. You can think about a problem all day but as soon as you get in the game, the hell with it!" And another: "Kids my age, they think a lot... but when you are playing basketball, that's all there is on your mind—just basketball.... Everything seems to follow right along."

A mountaineer expands on the same theme: "When you're [climbing] you're not aware of other problematic life situations. It becomes a world unto its own, significant only to itself. It's a concentration thing. Once you're into the situation, it's incredibly real, and you're very much in charge of it. It becomes your total world."

A similar sensation is reported by a dancer: "I get a feeling that I don't get anywhere else.... I have more confidence in myself than any other time. Maybe an effort to forget my problems. Dance is like therapy. If I am troubled about something, I leave it out of the door as I go in [the dance studio]."

On a larger time scale, ocean cruising provides an equivalent merciful oblivion: "But no matter how many little discomforts there may be at sea, one's real cares and worries seem to drop out of sight as the land slips behind the horizon. Once we were at sea there was no point in worrying, there was nothing we could do about our problems till we reached the next port.... Life was, for a while, stripped of its artificialities; [other problems] seemed quite unimportant compared with the state of the wind and the sea and the length of the day's run."

Edwin Moses, the great hurdler, has this to say in describing the concentration necessary for a race: "Your mind has to be absolutely clear. The fact that you have to cope with your opponent, jet lag, different foods, sleeping in hotels, and personal problems has to be erased from consciousness— as if they didn't exist."

Although Moses was talking about what it takes to win world-class sports events, he could have been describing the kind of concentration we achieve when we enjoy *any* activity. The concentration of the flow experience— together with clear goals and immediate feedback—provides order to consciousness, inducing the enjoyable condition of psychic negentropy.

From *Why Zebras Don't Get Ulcers: An Updated Guide to Stress, Stress-Related Diseases, and Coping*

Robert M. Sapolsky

Some people are born to biology. You can spot them instantly as kids—they're the ones comfortably lugging around the toy microscopes, stowing dead squirrels in the freezer, ostracized at school for their obsession with geckos.* But all sorts of folks migrate to biology from other fields—chemists, psychologists, physicists, mathematicians.

Several decades after stress physiology began, the discipline was inundated by people who had spent their formative years as engineers. Like physiologists, they thought there was a ferocious logic to how the body worked, but for bioengineers, that tended to mean viewing the body a bit like the circuitry diagram that you get with a new tape recorder: input-output ratios, impedance, feedback loops, servomechanisms. I shudder to even write such words, as I barely understand them; but the bioengineers did wonders for the field, adding a tremendous vigor.

Suppose you wonder how the brain knows when to stop glucocorticoid secretion—when enough is enough. In a vague sort of way, everyone knew that somehow the brain must be able to measure the amount of glucocorticoids in the circulation, compare that to some desired setpoint, and

*Personally, I used to collect the leftover chicken bones from everyone at the Friday night dinner table, clean them with my knife, and proudly display an articulated skeleton by the end of dessert. In retrospect, I think this was more to irritate my sister than to begin an anatomical quest. A biography of Teddy Roosevelt, however, recently helped me to appreciate that the world lost one of its great potential zoologists when he lapsed into politics. At age eighteen, he had already published professionally in ornithology; when he was half that age, he reacted to the news that his mother had thrown out his collection of field mice, stored in the family icebox, by moping around the house, proclaiming, "The loss to science! The loss to science!"

223

then decide whether to continue secreting CRF or turn off the faucet. The bioengineers came in and showed that the process was vastly more interesting and complicated than anyone had imagined. There are "multiple feedback domains"; some of the time the brain measures the *quantity* of glucocorticoids in the bloodstream, and sometimes how *fast* the level is changing. The bioengineers solved another critical issue: is the stress-response linear, or all-or-nothing? Epinephrine, glucocorticoids, prolactin, and other substances are all secreted during stress; but are they secreted to the same extent regardless of the intensity of the stressor (all-or-nothing responsiveness)? The system turns out, on the contrary, to be incredibly sensitive to the size of the stressor, demonstrating a linear relationship between the extent of blood pressure drop and the extent of epinephrine secretion, between the degree of hypoglycemia (drop in blood sugar) and glucagon release. The body not only can sense something stressful, but is amazingly accurate at measuring just how far and how fast that stressor is throwing the body out of homeostatic balance.

Beautiful stuff, and important. Selye loved the bioengineers, which makes perfect sense, since at his time the whole stress field must have still seemed a bit soft-headed to some mainstream physiologists. Those physiologists knew that the body does one set of things when it is too cold, and a diametrically opposite set when it is too hot, but here were Selye and his crew insisting that there were physiological mechanisms that... respond equally to cold *and* hot? *And* to injury *and* hypoglycemia *and* hypotension? The beleaguered stress experts welcomed the bioengineers with open arms. You see, it's for real; you can do math about stress, construct flow charts, feedback loops, formulas.... Golden days for the business. The system was turning out to be far more complicated than ever anticipated, but complicated in a way that was precise, logical, mechanistic. Soon it would be possible to model the body as one big input-output relationship: you tell me exactly to what degree a stressor impinges on an organism (how much it disrupts the homeostasis of blood sugar, fluid volume, optimal temperature, and so on), and I'll tell you exactly how much of a stress-response is going to occur.

This approach, fine for most of the ground that we've covered up until now, will probably allow us to estimate quite accurately what the pancreas of that zebra is doing when the organism is sprinting from a lion. But the approach is not going to tell us which of us will get an ulcer when the factory closes down. Starting in the late 1950s, a new style of experiments in stress physiology began to be conducted that burst that lucid, mechanistic bio-engineering bubble. A single example will suffice. An organism is subjected to a painful stimulus, and you are interested in how great a stress-response will be triggered. The bioengineers had been all over that one, mapping the relationship between the intensity and duration of the stimulus and the response. But this time, when the painful stimulus occurs, the organism under study can reach out for its Mommy and cry in her arms. And under these circumstances, this organism shows less of a stress-response.

Nothing in that clean, mechanistic world of the bioengineers could explain this phenomenon. The input was still the same; the same number of pain receptors should have been firing while the child underwent some painful procedure. Yet the output was completely different. A critical realization roared through the research community: the physiological stress-response can be modulated by psychological factors. Two identical stressors with the same extent of homeostatic disruption can be *perceived* differently, and the whole show changes from there.

Suddenly the stress-response could be made bigger or smaller, depending on psychological factors. In other words, psychological variables could *modulate* the stress-response. Inevitably, the next step was shown: in the absence of any change in physiological reality—any actual disruption of homeostasis—psychological variables alone could *trigger* the stress-response. Flushed with excitement, Yale physiologist John Mason, one of the leaders in this approach, even went so far as to proclaim that all stress-responses were psychological stress-responses.

The old guard was not amused. Just when the conception of stress was becoming systematized, rigorous, credible, along came this rabble of psychologists muddying up the picture. In a series of published exchanges in which they first praised each other's achievements and ancestors, Selye and Mason attempted to shred each other's work. Mason smugly pointed to the growing literature on psychological initiation and modulation of the stress-response. Selye, facing defeat, insisted that *all* stress-responses couldn't be psychological and perceptual: if an organism is anesthetized, it still gets a stress-response when a surgical incision is made.

The psychologists succeeded in getting a place at the table, and as they have acquired some table manners and a few gray hairs, they have been treated less like barbarians. We now have to consider which psychological variables are critical. Why is psychological stress stressful?

Psychological Stressors

You would expect key psychological variables to be mushy concepts to uncover, but in a series of elegant experiments, a physiologist at Rockefeller University named Jay Weiss demonstrated exactly what is involved. The subject of one experiment is a rat that receives mild electric shocks (roughly equivalent to the static shock you might get from scuffing your foot on a carpet). Over a series of these, the rat develops a prolonged stress-response: its heart rate and glucocorticoid secretion rate go up, for example. For convenience, we can express the long-term consequences by how likely the rat is to get an ulcer, and in this situation, the probability soars. In the next room, a different rat gets the same series of shocks—identical pattern and intensity; its homeostasis is challenged to exactly the same extent. But this time, whenever the rat gets a shock it can run over to a bar of wood and gnaw on it. The rat in this situation is far less likely to get an ulcer. You have given it an *outlet for its frustration*. Other types of outlets work as well—let the stressed rat eat something, drink water, or sprint on a running wheel, and it is less likely to develop an ulcer.

We humans also deal better with stressors when we have outlets for frustration—punch a wall, take a run, find solace in a hobby. We are even cerebral enough to *imagine* those outlets and derive some relief: consider the prisoner of war who spends hours imagining a golf game in tremendous detail. I have a friend who passed a prolonged and very stressful illness lying in bed with a mechanical pencil and a notepad, drawing topographic maps of imaginary mountain ranges and taking hikes through them.

A variant of Weiss's experiment uncovers a special feature of the outlet-for-frustration reaction. This time, when the rat gets the identical series of electric shocks and is upset, it can run across the cage, sit next to another rat and . . . bite the hell out of it. Stress-induced displacement of aggression: the practice works wonders at minimizing the stressfulness of a stressor. It's a real primate specialty as well. A male baboon loses a fight. Frustrated, he spins around and attacks a subordinate male who was minding his own business. The subadult lunges at an adult female, who bites a juvenile, who knocks an infant out of a tree. An extremely high percentage of primate aggression represents frustration displaced onto innocent bystanders. Humans are pretty good at it, too, and we have a technical way of describing the phenomenon in the context of stress-related disease: "He's one of those guys who doesn't get ulcers, he gives them." Taking it out on someone else—how well it works at minimizing the impact of a stressor.

There is an additional way in which we can interact with another organism to minimize the impact of a stressor on us, a way that is considerably more encouraging for the future of our planet than is displacement aggression. Rats rarely use it, but primates are great at it. Put an infant primate through something unpleasant: it gets a stress-response. Put it through the same stressor while in a room full of other primates and . . . it depends. If those primates are strangers, the stress-response gets worse. But if they are friends, the stress-response is decreased. *Social support networks*—it helps to have a shoulder to cry on, a hand to hold, an ear to listen to you, someone to cradle you and to tell you it will be okay.

Sometimes remarkably little social contact is sufficient. In one subtle demonstration, the hormonal stress-response was studied in people who were undergoing a painful and frightening cardiac catheterization. Those who talked to their doctors about their fear during the procedure had smaller glucocorticoid stress-responses than the stoics.

Some of my work has uncovered the importance of these social support networks. While I mostly do laboratory research on how stress and glucocorticoids affect the brain, I spend my summers in Kenya studying patterns of stress-related physiology and disease among wild baboons living in a national park. The social life of a male baboon can be pretty stressful—you get beaten up as a victim of displaced aggression; you carefully search for some tuber to eat and clean it off, only to have it stolen by someone of higher rank; and so on. Glucocorticoid levels are elevated among low-ranking baboons, and among the entire group if the dominance hierarchy is unstable or after a new, aggressive male has joined the troop. But if you are a male baboon with a lot of friends—you play with kids, or you have frequent nonsexual grooming bouts with females, for example—you have lower glucocorticoid concentrations than males of the same general rank who lack these outlets. (In a similar vein, for both primates and humans, holding hands or making physical contact lowers cardiovascular response to stress.)

As noted in the chapter on immunity, people with spouses and/or close friends have longer life expectancies. When the spouse dies, the risk of dying skyrockets. Recall also from that chapter the study of parents of Israeli soldiers killed in the Yom Kippur War: In the aftermath of this stressor, there was no notable increase in risk of diseases or mortality—except among those who were already divorced or widowed. A final example: in a study of patients with severe coronary heart disease, Redford Williams of Duke University and colleagues found that half of those lacking social supports were dead within five years—a rate three times higher than was seen in patients who had a spouse or close friend.

The rat studies also uncovered another variable modulating the stress-response. The rat gets the same pattern of electric shocks, but this time, just before each shock, it hears a warning bell. Fewer ulcers. *Unpredictability* makes stressors much more stressful. The rat with the warning gets two pieces of information. It learns when something dreadful is about to happen. And the rest of the time, it learns that something dreadful is *not* about to happen. It can relax. The rat without a warning always feels as if it is a half-second away from the shock. In effect, information that increases predictability tells you that there is bad news, but comforts you that it's not going to be worse—you are going to get shocked soon, but it's never going to be sprung on you without warning. As another variant on the helpfulness of predictability, organisms will eventually habituate to a stressor if it is applied over and over; it may knock physiological homeostasis equally out of balance the umpteenth time that it happens, but it is a familiar, predictable stressor by then and a smaller stress-response is triggered. I've never appreciated the importance of predictability as much as after living through the 1989 San Francisco earthquake. Now I think, "Those lucky people elsewhere, they know what time of year you don't have to worry much about tornadoes or hurricanes. But an earthquake, now that could be any second, maybe even while I'm sitting bumper-to-bumper beneath this highway overpass."

The power of loss of predictability as a psychological stressor is shown in an elegant, subtle study. A rat is going about its business in its cage, and at measured intervals the experimenter delivers a piece of food down a chute into the cage; rat eats happily. This is called an intermittent reinforcement schedule. Change the pattern of food delivery so that the rat gets *exactly* the same total amount of food over the course of an hour, but at a random rate. The rat receives just as much reward, but less predictably; and up go glucocorticoid levels. There is not a single physically stressful thing going on in the rat's world. It's not hungry, pained, running for its life—nothing is out of homeostatic balance. In the absence of any stressor, loss of predictability triggers a stress-response.

There are even circumstances in which stress-related disease can be *more* likely to occur among individuals with the lower rate of stressors. You can easily imagine how to design a rat experiment to demonstrate this, but the human version has already been done. During the onset of the Nazi blitzkrieg bombings of England, London was hit every night like clockwork. Lots of stressful negative reinforcement. In the suburbs the bombings were far more sporadic, occurring perhaps once a week. Fewer stressful negative reinforcers, but much less predictability. There was a significant increase in the incidence of ulcers during that time. Who developed more ulcers? The suburban population. (Another measure of the importance of unpredictability: by the third month of the bombing, ulcer rates in all the hospitals had dropped back to normal.) A similar anxious state has often been described by individuals awaiting execution at an uncertain date. For example Gary Gilmore, the multiple murderer who was executed in 1977 amid a media circus in Utah, expressed relief bordering on euphoria when all the appeals through various courts and the stays of execution were finally exhausted. In such cases, uncertainty can eventually appear even worse than death.

Rat studies also demonstrate a related facet of psychological stress. Give the rat the same series of shocks. This time, however, you study a rat that has been trained to press a lever to avoid electric shocks. Take away the lever, shock it, and it develops a massive stress-response. It's as if the rat were thinking, "I can't believe this. I know what to do about electric shocks; give me a goddamn lever and I could handle this. This isn't fair." Ulceration city. Give the trained rat a lever to press; even if it is disconnected from the shock mechanism, it still helps: down goes the stress-response. So long as the rat has been exposed to a higher rate of shocks previously, it will think that the lower rate now is due to it having control over the situation. This is an extraordinarily powerful variable in modulating the stress-response.

The identical style of experiment with humans yields the same results. Place a person in each of two adjoining rooms, and expose both to intermittent noxious, loud noises; the person who has a button and believes that pressing it decreases the likelihood of more noise is less hypertensive. In one variant on this experiment, subjects with the button who did not bother to press it did just as well as those who actually pressed the button—the *exercise* of control is not critical; rather, it is the *belief* that you have it. An everyday example:

airplanes are safer than cars, yet more of us are phobic about flying. Why? Because, despite the fact that we're at greater risk in a car, most of us in our heart of hearts believe that we are above-average drivers, thus more in control. In an airplane, we have no control at all. My wife and I, neither of us happy fliers, tease each other on flights, exchanging control: "Okay, you rest for awhile, I'll take over concentrating on keeping the pilot from having a stroke." The variable of control is extremely important; controlling the rewards that you get can be more desirable than getting them for nothing. As an extraordinary example, both pigeons and rats prefer to press a lever in order to obtain food (so long as the task is not too difficult) over having the food delivered freely—a theme found in the activities and statements of many scions of great fortunes, who regret the contingency-free nature of their lives, without purpose or striving.

Some researchers have emphasized that the stressfulness of loss of control and of loss of predictability share a common element. They subject an organism to novelty. You thought you knew how to manage things, you thought you knew what would happen next, and it turns out you are wrong in this novel situation. Others have emphasized that these types of stressors cause arousal and vigilance, as you search for the new rules of control and prediction. Both views are different aspects of the same issue.

Yet another critical psychological variable has been uncovered. A hypothetical example: two rats get a series of electric shocks. On the first day, one gets 10 shocks an hour, the other 50. Next day, both get 25 shocks an hour. Who becomes hypertensive? Obviously, the one going from 10 to 25. The other rat is thinking, "25!? Piece of cheese, no problem, I can handle that." Given the same degree of disruption of homeostasis, a perception that events are improving helps tremendously. I recently observed a version of this among the baboons I study in Kenya. In general, when dominance hierarchies are unstable, resting glucocorticoid levels rise. This makes sense, because such instabilities make for stressful times. Looking at individual baboons, however, shows a more subtle pattern: given the same degree of instability, males whose ranks are *dropping* have elevated glucocorticoid levels, while males whose ranks are *rising* amid the tumult don't show this endocrine trait. Similarly, in one classic human study, parents who were told that their children had, for example, a 25 percent chance of dying from cancer showed only a moderate rise in glucocorticoid levels in the bloodstream. How could that be? Because the children were all in remission after a period where the odds of death had been far higher. Twenty-five percent must have seemed like a miracle. Twenty-five shocks an hour, a certain degree of social instability, a one in four chance of your child dying—each can imply either good news or bad, and only the latter seems to stimulate a stress-response.

Thus there are some powerful psychologic factors that can trigger a stress-response on their own or make another stressor seem more stressful: loss of control or predictability, loss of outlets for frustration or sources of support, a perception that things are getting worse. These factors play a major role in explaining how we all go through lives full of stressors, yet differ so dramatically in our vulnerability to them. The final chapter of this book examines the bases of these individual differences in greater detail, serving as a blueprint so that we can analyze how to learn to exploit these psychological variables—how in effect, to manage stress better. As we'll see, many ideas about stress management revolve around issues of control and predictability. However, the answer will not be simply "Maximize control. Maximize predictability. Maximize outlets for frustration." It is considerably more complicated than that.

QUESTIONS

1. Does Csikszentmihalyi's discussion of flow fit with your own experience? Describe a situation in which you were pleasurably immersed in an experience and discuss your recollection of that experience in relation to Csikszentmihalyi's characterization.

2. How much of your own daily activity is driven by a desire to achieve a state of flow?

3. Think about the role of control in mediating your own stress. Describe an experience in which the loss of control led you to stress, and another in which you were not stressed despite the lack of control.

4. Do you think that stress plays a useful role? From the standpoint of evolution, what benefits might come to creatures that evolved mechanisms for measuring and responding to stress?

CHAPTER   TWELVE

EMOTION

If all of our mental life springs from our brain, and emotions are part of our mental life, it stands to reason that emotions emerge from our biology. The three selections in this chapter offer three different arguments in favor of this view.

In the first selection, from *The Emotional Brain* (1998), neuroscientist Joseph LeDoux recounts his journey to understand the basis of one of our most potent emotions—fear—and how those investigations led him to the almond-shaped piece of forebrain known as the amygdala. Although LeDoux is a neuroscientist rather than a psychologist, and his techniques have more to do with tracing tracts of neural fibers than characterizing the subtleties of complex human emotions, his style of research will come to play an increasingly significant role in our understanding of emotion. (The freezing and blood pressure measures that LeDoux mentions are two standard ways of experimentally assessing fear.)

In the second selection, from *Emotions Revealed* (2003), also autobiographical, psychologist Paul Ekman describes work that he did to understand facial expressions: the laughs and cries, smiles and smirks, scowls and grimaces that wordlessly communicate our moods. Like any aspect of human behavior, they are fodder for classic debates about nature and nurture, culture and biology. Must we learn what a smile means, or is that something we are born with? Like LeDoux, Ekman came to realize that our emotions emerge from a strong biological foundation. Here, Ekman, the world's leading expert on facial expressions, explains in his own words what led him to one of the most important psychological discoveries of the twentieth century.

In the final selection, from *Woman* (1999), Pulitzer Prize–winning science journalist Natalie Angier considers the subtle power and complexity of a single important hormone—estrogen—on sex and sexuality in humans and other animals. If Angier humbles us by showing the extent to which we, too, are driven by hormones, she draws a critical distinction between the nearly unadultered influence of hormones on desire and their more moderated influence on behavior. All emotion may be biological, but in humans, hormones are only one part of the equation. Our massive frontal lobes give us a way to resist the otherwise overwhelming messages carried by our hormones.

From *The Emotional Brain: The Mysterious Underpinnings of Emotional Life*

Joseph LeDoux

Highways and Byways

Imagine being in a unfamiliar land. You are handed a piece of paper on which the locations of a starting point and a destination are indicated. There are lots of other points marked on the paper. There are also some lines between some of the points, indicating possible ways to get from one to another. But you are told that the lines between the points may or may not indicate real roads, and also that not all of the roads that exist between points are marked. Your job is to get in your car at the starting point and find the best way to the destination, and to make an accurate map along the way.

This is essentially the problem that we faced when we began to try to figure out how networks in the brain make it possible for a novel acoustic stimulus to come to elicit defensive responses as a result of fear conditioning. We knew the starting point (the ear and its connections into the brain) and the end point (the behavioral defense responses and their autonomic concomitants), but the points that linked the inputs and outputs in the brain were unclear. Many of the relevant connections in the brain had been demonstrated with older techniques that were prone to lead to false results—identifying nonexistent connections between two points or failing to find real ones. Relatively little work on the neural basis of fear had used fear conditioning. And while research on fear using techniques other than fear conditioning had suggested some ideas about which brain areas might be involved, it wasn't clear whether these were essential way stations, interesting detours, or just plain wrong turns.

Go with the Flow: Much of the earlier work on the emotional brain had started in the middle of the brain, not surprisingly, in the limbic system. This work showed that lesions of limbic areas can interfere with some emotional behaviors, and that stimulation of limbic areas can elicit emotional responses. But these studies left unclear how the lesioned or stimulated area relates to the rest of the brain. Also, most of the earlier work used techniques that lacked a discrete eliciting stimulus and thus could not benefit from the advantages, described above, that a conditioned stimulus offers.

My approach was to let the natural flow of information through the brain be my guide. In other words, I started at the beginning, at the point that the auditory-conditioned stimulus enters the brain, and tried to trace the pathways forward from this system toward the final destinations that control the conditioned fear responses. I thought that this strategy would be the best and most direct way of figuring out the road map of fear. In retrospect, this strategy worked pretty well.

I began by asking a simple question: which parts of the auditory system are required for auditory fear conditioning (fear conditioning tasks in which an auditory stimulus serves the CS)? The auditory system, like other sensory systems, is organized such that the cortical component is the highest level; it is the culmination of a sequence of information processing steps that start with the peripheral sensory receptors, in this case, receptors located in the ear. I reasoned that damaging the ear would be uninteresting, since a deaf animal is obviously not going to be able to learn anything about a sound. So, instead, I started by damaging the highest part of the auditory pathway. If auditory cortex lesions interfered with fear conditioning, I would be able to conclude that the auditory stimulus had to go all the way through the system in order for conditioning to occur, and that the next step in the pathway should be an output connection of the auditory cortex. If, however, auditory cortex lesions did not disrupt conditioning, I would have to make lesions in lower stations to find the highest level that the auditory stimulus has to reach in order for conditioning to take place.

Damage to the auditory cortex, in fact, turned out to have no effect at all on the conditioning of either the freezing or the blood pressure responses. I then lesioned the next lower station, the auditory thalamus, and these lesions completely prevented fear conditioning. So did lesions of the next lower auditory station in the midbrain. On the basis of these studies I concluded that the auditory stimulus has to rise through the auditory pathway from the ear to the thalamus, but does not have to go the full distance to the auditory cortex. This presented me with a paradox.

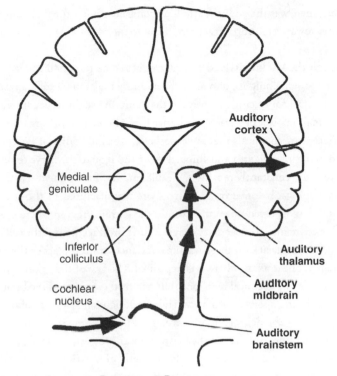

FIGURE 1——AUDITORY PROCESSING PATHWAYS.
This is a highly simplified depiction of auditory pathways in the human brain. A similar organization plan holds for other vertebrate species. Acoustic signals in the environment are picked up by special receptors in the ear (not shown) and transmitted into the brain by way of the auditory nerve (arrow at bottom left), which terminates in the auditory brainstem nuclei (cochlear nucleus and related regions). Axons from these regions then mostly cross over to the other side of the brain and ascend to the inferior colliculus of the midbrain. Inferior collicular axons then travel to the auditory thalamic relay nucleus, the medial geniculate body, which provides the major inputs to the auditory cortex. The auditory cortex is composed of a number of regions and subregions (not shown).

Traditionally, the sensory processing structures below the cortex are viewed as slaves to the cortical master. Their job is to get the information to the cortex, where all of the interesting things are done to the stimulus, like assembling neural bits and pieces of the input into the perceptions of the external world that we experience. According to neuroanatomy textbooks, the auditory cortex was the main if not the only target of the auditory thalamus.

Where, then, was the auditory stimulus going after it left the thalamus in its journey toward emotional reactivity, if not to the cortex?

Through the Looking Glass: In order to get some reasonable ideas about where the signal might go to after the auditory thalamus, I took advantage of techniques for tracing pathways in the brain. To use these, you have to inject a small amount of a tracer substance in the brain area you are interested in. Tracers are chemicals that are absorbed by the cell bodies of neurons located in the injected area and shipped down the axon to the nerve terminals. Neurons are constantly moving molecules around inside them—many important things, like neurotransmitters, are manufactured in the cell body and then transported down the axon to the terminal region where they are used in communication across synapses. After the tracer enters the cell body, it can ride piggyback on these mobile substances until it reaches the terminal region of the axon, where it is deposited. The fate of the tracer can then be visualized by chemical reactions that "stain" those parts of the brain that contain the transported substance. These techniques make it possible to figure out where the neurons in one area send their fibers. Since information can only get from one area of the brain to another by way of fibers, knowing the fiber connections of an area tells us where information processed in an area is sent next.

So we injected a tracer into the auditory thalamus. The substance injected sounds more like an ingredient of an exotic salad in a macrobiotic café than the chemical basis of a sophisticated neuroscience technique: wheat germ agglutinin conjugated horseradish peroxidase, or just WGA-HRP for short. The next day the brain was removed and sectioned, and the sections were stained by reacting them with a special chemical potion. We put the stained sections on slides and then looked at them with a microscope set up for dark-field optics, which involves shining indirect light onto the slide—this makes it easier to see the tracer reaction in the sections.

I'll never forget the first time I looked at WGA-HRP with dark-field optics. Bright orange particles formed streams and speckles against a dark blue-gray background. It was like looking into a strange world of inner space. It was incredibly beautiful and I stayed glued to the microscope for hours.

Once I got past the sheer beauty of the staining, I turned to the task at hand, which was to find out where, if anywhere, the auditory thalamus projected to besides the auditory cortex. I found four sub-cortical regions that

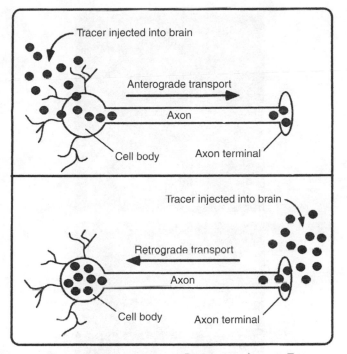

FIGURE 2——TRACING PATHWAYS IN THE BRAIN WITH AXONAL TRANSPORT.
In order to figure out whether neurons in two different brain regions are interconnected, tracers are injected into one of the regions. The tracer is then picked up by neurons that are bathed by the injection. Once the tracer is inside the neuron, it is transported through the axon. Some tracers are picked up by cell bodies and transported to axon terminals (anterograde transport), whereas other tracers are picked up by terminals and transported to cell bodies (retrograde transport).

contained heavy sprinkling with the tiny orange dots, suggesting that these regions receive projections from the auditory thalamus. This was surprising, given the well-received view that sensory areas of the thalamus project mainly, if not exclusively, to the cortex.

It seemed likely that one of the four labeled regions might be the crucial next step in the fear conditioning pathway—the place where the stimulus goes after the thalamus. So I designed a lesion study that would interrupt the flow of information from the auditory thalamus to each of these regions. Three of the lesions had absolutely no effect. But disconnection of auditory thalamus from the fourth area—the amygdala—prevented conditioning from taking place.

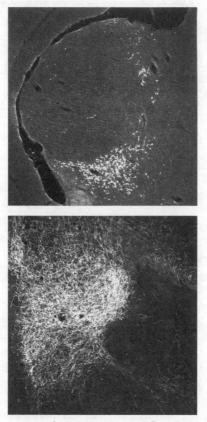

FIGURE 3——EXAMPLES OF ANTEROGRADE AND RETROGRADE TRANSPORT IN
THE THALAMO-AMYGDALA PATHWAY.

The top photograph shows anterograde labeling of terminals in the lateral amygdala
after an injection of a tracer in the auditory thalamus. These terminals in the lateral
amygdala thus originate from cell bodies in the auditory thalamus. Note the fine,
punctate nature of anterograde terminal labeling. The bottom photograph shows cell
bodies in the auditory thalamus that were retrogradely labeled by an injection of a
tracer in the lateral nucleus of the amygdala. The labeled cells are the bright white
structures that cluster together in a triangular region. The cells in the auditory thalamus thus send their axons to the lateral amygdala. Note the large size of the labeled
cell bodies, as compared to the terminals above. The two images are black-and-white
photographs of dark-field illuminated brain sections taken through a microscope.

Almond Joy: The amygdala is a small region in the forebrain, named by the
early anatomists for its almond shape (amygdala is the Latin word for almond). It was one of the areas of the limbic system and had long been
thought of as being important for various forms of emotional behavior—

earlier studies of the Klüver-Bucy syndrome had pointed to it, as had electrical stimulation studies (see below).

The discovery of a pathway that could transmit information directly to the amygdala from the thalamus suggested how a conditioned fear stimulus could elicit fear responses without the aid of the cortex. The direct thalamic input to the amygdala simply allowed the cortex to be bypassed. The brain is indeed a complex mesh of connections, but anatomical findings were taking us on a delightful journey of discovery through this neuronal maze.

I wasn't really looking for the amygdala in my work. The dissection of the brain's pathways just took me there. But my studies, when they first started coming out, fit nicely with a set of findings that Bruce Kapp had obtained concerning a subregion of the amygdala—the central nucleus. Noting that the central nucleus has connections with the brain stem areas involved in the control of heart rate and other autonomic nervous system responses, he proposed that this region might be a link in the neural system through which the autonomic responses elicited by a conditioned fear stim-

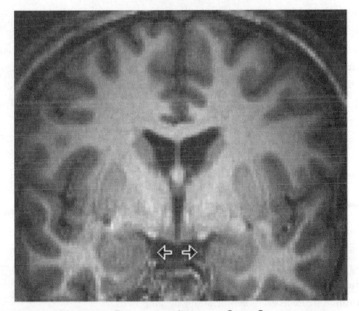

FIGURE 4——MAGNETIC RESONANCE IMAGING SCAN SHOWING THE LOCATION OF THE AMYGDALA IN THE HUMAN BRAIN.
The amygdala on each side of the brain is indicated by the arrows. (Image provided by E.A. Phelps of Yale University.)

ulus are expressed. And when he lesioned the central nucleus in the rabbit, his hypothesis was confirmed—the lesions dramatically interfered with the conditioning of heart rate responses to a tone paired with shock.

Kapp went on to show that stimulation of the central amygdala produced heart rate and other autonomic responses, strengthening his idea that the central nucleus was an important forebrain link in the control of autonomic responses by the brain stem. However, he also found that stimulation of the central nucleus elicited freezing responses, suggesting that the central amygdala might not just be involved in the control of autonomic responses, but might be part of a general-purpose defense response control network.

Indeed, subsequent research by several laboratories has shown that lesions of the central nucleus interfere with essentially every measure of conditioned fear, including freezing behavior, autonomic responses, suppression of pain, stress hormone release, and reflex potentiation. It was also found that each of these responses are mediated by different outputs of the central nucleus. For example, I demonstrated that lesions of different projections of the central nucleus separately interfered with freezing and blood pressure conditioned responses—lesions of one of the projections (the periaqueductal gray) interfered with freezing but not blood pressure responses, whereas lesions of another (the lateral hypothalamus) interfered with the blood pressure but not the freezing response. And while lesions of a third projection (the bed nucleus of the stria terminalis) had no effect on either of these responses, other scientists later showed that lesions of this region interfere with the elicitation of stress hormones by the CS.

Although no other creature has been studied as thoroughly with fear conditioning as the rat, and though no other technique has been used to study fear more extensively than fear conditioning, if we compile the evidence across species and experimental approaches we reach the inescapable conclusion that the basic brain mechanisms of fear are essentially the same through many levels of evolutionary development.

Let's start with our basic model of fear, fear conditioning. The effects of amygdala lesions on fear conditioning have been studied in birds, rats, rabbits, monkeys, and people using autonomic nervous system activity as the conditioned response. In each of these species, damage to the amygdala in-terferes with conditioned fear reactions—the CS fails to elicit the CR when the amygdala is damaged.

Pigeons are the only nonmammalian species in which the effects of amygdala lesions on fear conditioning have been examined. The similarity of the effects in pigeons and mammals means either that the amygdala was se-lected as a key component of the defense system of the vertebrate brain be-fore birds and mammals separated from reptiles, or that the amygdala evolved to perform this function separately in the two post-reptilian lines. The best way to resolve this issue would be to know whether amygdala le-sions interrupt fear conditioning in reptiles. Unfortunately, this experiment has not been performed. As a result, we need to turn to some other kind of evidence in search of an answer.

Another technique that has been used to map the brain pathways of fear or defensive behavior is brain stimulation. These techniques have been applied to reptiles as well as mammals and birds, and might thus be able to help us piece together an answer as to whether the amygdala has been involved in de-fense since at least the time when birds and mammals diverged from reptiles.

The first step we need to take, though, is to be certain that brain stim-ulation identifies the same pathways of fear reactivity that studies of fear conditioning have in the mammalian brain, where fear conditioning has been most clearly related to brain pathways. There is a long and interesting history to studies of brain stimulation in mammals, which we will only be able to touch on here. Our main concern is whether stimulation of the amyg-dala, the heart and soul of the fear system revealed by fear conditioning stud-ies, gives rise to defense responses in mammals. Clearly this occurs. It is well established that stimulation of the amygdala in anesthetized mammals elic-its autonomic nervous system responses and in awake mammals such stim-ulations elicit freezing, escape, and defensive attack responses, in addition to autonomic changes. These kinds of studies have been performed in rats, cats, dogs, rabbits, and monkeys, all with similar results. Further, defense re-sponses can be elicited from the central nucleus of the amygdala, the region by which the amygdala communicates with brain stem areas that control conditioned fear responses. And interruption of the pathways connecting the amygdala with these brain stem pathways interferes with the expression of the defense responses. Studies of fear conditioning and brain stimulation reveal similar output pathways in the expression of fear responses.

Let's now descend the phyletic tree and see what happens when we stimulate the amygdala of reptiles. It's tricky business to use living reptiles as examples of what reptiles might have been like when mammals diverged, as current reptiles themselves come from lines that have diverged from the ancestral lines. Nevertheless, since brain and behavior are not preserved in fossil records, this is the only way comparative studies of brain function can be conducted. Stimulation of the amygdala in lizards elicits the defensive behaviors these animals characteristically show when they are threatened by a predator, and lesions of the same regions reduce the expression of these behaviors in response to natural trigger stimuli.

Now going up the branching evolutionary tree, we can consider the effects of stimulation of the human amygdala. Such studies are performed in conjunction with brain surgery for otherwise untreatable epilepsy. Since the stimuli are delivered to the amygdala while the subjects are awake, it is possible to not only record expressive responses that are elicited, but also to ask the subjects to report on their experiences. Interestingly, the most common experience reported is a sense of foreboding danger, of fear. Fear is also the most commonly reported experience occurring in association with epileptic seizures, which are in essence spontaneous electrical stimulations that originate in the amygdala.

Recent studies of humans with amygdala damage also suggest that it plays a special role in fear. It is extremely rare to encounter patients with damage to only the amygdala, but it is not that rare to come across patients with damage that includes the amygdala. This is particularly common in patients who undergo surgery to remove epileptic regions of their temporal lobe. Kevin LaBar, Liz Phelps, and I conducted a study of fear conditioning in patients of this type. Because we were studying humans rather than rats, we chose to use a very loud obnoxious noise as the US instead of electric shock. This worked just fine for conditioning autonomic nervous system responses to a softer, non-noxious sound in the control subjects. Importantly, we found that autonomic conditioned responses were reduced in the temporal lobe lesioned group. Interestingly, the patients consciously "knew" the relationship between the CS and US: when asked what went on in the experiment, they typically said, "Oh, there was a sound followed by this other really loud sound." This knowledge was not enough to transform the meaningless sound into a trigger stimulus. Although the lesions included areas other than the amygdala, we know from the animal studies that of all the areas included in the lesion, damage to the amygdala is the likely cause of the deficit in fear conditioning. This is a good example of why animal studies are so important. Without the animal studies the human experiment would be uninterpretable.

Although damage restricted to the human amygdala is very rare, Antonio Damasio and his colleagues at the University of Iowa have come across such a patient. They have performed some extremely important and fascinating studies on her. For example, in one study they examined her ability to detect the emotional expression on faces. She was able to correctly identify most classes of expressions, except when the faces showed fear. And most importantly they have recently examined whether the capacity for fear conditioning is interfered with. Indeed, it was. Unlike the temporal lobe lesioned patients, this case unequivocally implicates the amygdala. Again, though, this study was inspired by the body of animal research that had already implicated the amygdala. If this study had been performed twenty years ago, before any of the animal conditioning studies had been done, we would have little understanding of the pathways through which the amygdala contributes to fear conditioning. In point of fact, though, the human studies might not have even been performed had the animal studies not set the stage for them—without the known effects of amygdala damage on conditioned fear in experimental animals, why would anyone consider doing such a study in humans with amygdala pathology?

The point of this discussion is to illustrate that the amygdala seems to do the same thing—take care of fear responses—in all species that have an amygdala. This is not the only function of the amygdala, but it is certainly an important one. The function seems to have been established eons ago, probably at least since dinosaurs ruled the earth, and to have been maintained through diverse branches of evolutionary development. Defense against danger is perhaps an organism's number one priority and it appears that in the major groups of vertebrate animals that have been studied (reptiles, birds, and mammals) the brain performs this function using a common architectural plan.

The remarkable fact is that at the level of behavior, defense against danger is achieved in many different ways in different species, yet the amygdala's role is constant. It is this neural correspondence across species that no doubt allows diverse behaviors to achieve the same evolutionary function in different animals. This functional equivalence and neural correspondence

applies to many vertebrate brains, including human brains. When it comes
to detecting and responding to danger, the brain just hasn't changed much.
In some ways we are emotional lizards. I am quite confident in telling you
that studies of fear reactions in rats tell us a great deal about how fear mechanisms work in our brains as well.

From *Emotions Revealed: Recognizing Faces and Feelings to Improve Communication and Emotional Life*

Paul Ekman

I began the project believing that expression and gesture were socially learned and culturally variable, and so did the initial group of people I asked for advice—Margaret Mead, Gregory Bateson, Edward Hall, Ray Bird-whistell, and Charles Osgood. I recalled that Charles Darwin had made the opposite claim, but I was so convinced that he was wrong that I didn't bother to read his book.

The second stroke of luck was meeting Silvan Tomkins. He had just written two books about emotion in which he claimed that facial expressions were innate and universal to our species, but he had no evidence to back up his claims. I don't think I would ever have read his books or met him if we hadn't both submitted articles on nonverbal behavior to the same journal at the same time—Silvan's a study of the face, mine a study of body movement.

I was very impressed with the depth and breadth of Silvan's thinking, but I thought he was probably wrong in his belief, like Darwin's, that expressions were innate and therefore universal. I was delighted that there were two sides to the argument, that it wasn't just Darwin, who had written a hundred years earlier, who opposed Mead, Bateson, Birdwhistell, and Hall. It wasn't a dead issue. There was a real argument between famous scientists, elder statesmen; and I, at the age of thirty, had the chance, and the funding, to try to settle it once and for all: Are expressions universal, or are they, like language, specific to each culture? Irresistible! I really didn't care who proved to be correct, although I didn't think it would be Silvan.

In my first study I showed photographs to people in five cultures— Chile, Argentina, Brazil, Japan, and the United States—and asked them to judge what emotion was shown in each facial expression. The majority in every culture agreed, suggesting that expressions might really be universal. Carrol Izard, another psychologist who had been advised by Silvan, and was working in other cultures, did nearly the same experiment and got the same results. Tomkins had not told either of us about the other, something that we initially resented when we found out we were not doing this work alone, but it was better for science that two independent researchers found the same thing. It seemed that Darwin was right.

There was a problem: How could we have found that people from many different cultures agreed about what emotion was shown in an expression when so many smart people thought just the opposite? It wasn't just the travelers who claimed that the expressions of the Japanese or the Chinese or some other cultural group had very different meanings. Birdwhistell, a respected anthropologist who specialized in the study of expression and gesture (a protégé of Margaret Mead), had written that he abandoned Darwin's ideas when he found that in many cultures people smiled when they were unhappy. Birdwhistell's claim fit the view that dominated cultural anthropology and most of psychology—anything socially important, such as emotional expressions, must be the product of learning, and therefore different in each culture.

I reconciled our findings that expressions are universal with Birdwhistell's observation of how they differ from one culture to another by coming up with the idea of *display rules*. These, I proposed, are socially learned, often culturally different, rules about the management of expression, about who can show which emotion to whom and when they can do so. It is why in most public sporting contests the loser doesn't show the sadness and disappointment he or she feels. Display rules are embodied in the parent's admonition—"Get that smirk off your face." These rules may dictate that we diminish, exaggerate, hide completely, or mask the expression of emotion we are feeling.

I tested this formulation in a series of studies that showed that when *alone* Japanese and Americans displayed the same facial expressions in response to seeing films of surgery and accidents, but when a scientist sat with them as they watched the films, the Japanese more than the Americans masked negative expressions with a smile. In private, innate expressions; in public, managed expressions. Since it is the public behavior that anthropologists and most travelers observe, I had my explanation and evidence of its operation. In contrast, symbolic gestures—such as the head nod yes, the head shake no, and the A-OK gesture—are indeed culture-specific. Here

Birdwhistell, Mead, and most other behavioral scientists were right, though they were wrong about the facial expressions of emotion.

There was a loophole, and if I could see it, so might Birdwhistell and Mead, who I knew would search for any way to dismiss my findings. All the people I (and Izard) had studied might have learned the meaning of Western facial expressions by watching Charlie Chaplin and John Wayne on the movie screen and television tube. Learning from the media or having contact with people from other cultures could explain why people from different cultures had agreed about the emotions shown in my photographs of Caucasians. I needed a visually isolated culture where the people had seen no movies, no television, no magazines, and few, if any, outsiders. If they thought the same emotions were shown in my set of facial expression photographs as the people in Chile, Argentina, Brazil, Japan, and the United States, I would have it nailed.

My entry to a Stone Age culture was Carleton Gajdusek, a neurologist who had been working for more than a decade in such isolated places in the highlands of Papua New Guinea. He was trying to find the cause of a strange disease, kuru, which was killing about half the people in one of these cultures. The people believed it was due to sorcery. When I arrived on the scene, Gajdusek already knew that it was due to a slow virus, a virus that incubates for many years before any symptoms become apparent (AIDS is such a virus). He didn't yet know how it was transmitted. (It turned out to be cannibalism. These people didn't eat their enemies, who would be more likely to be in good health if they died in combat. They are only their friends who died of some kind of disease, many of them from kuru. They didn't cook them before eating, so diseases were readily passed on. Gajdusek some years later won the Nobel Prize for the discovery of slow viruses.)

Fortunately, Gajdusek had realized that Stone Age cultures would soon disappear, so he took more than one hundred thousand feet of motion picture films of the daily lives of the people in each of two cultures. He had never looked at the films; it would have taken nearly six weeks to look just once at his films of these people. That's when I came along.

Delighted that someone had a scientific reason for wanting to examine his films, he lent me copies, and my colleague Wally Friesen and I spent six months carefully examining them. The films contained two very convincing proofs of the universality of facial expressions of emotion. First, we never saw an unfamiliar expression. If facial expressions are completely learned, then these isolated people should have shown novel expressions, ones we had never seen before. There were none.

It was still possible that these familiar expressions might be signals of very different emotions. But while the films didn't always reveal what happened before or after an expression, when they did, they confirmed our interpretations. If expressions signal different emotions in each culture, then total outsiders, with no familiarity with the culture, should not have been able to interpret the expressions correctly.

I tried to think how Birdwhistell and Mead would dispute this claim. I imagined they would say, "It doesn't matter that there aren't any new expressions; the ones you did see really had different meanings. You got them right because you were tipped off by the social context in which they occurred. You never saw an expression removed from what was happening before, afterward, or at the same time. If you had, you wouldn't have known what the expressions meant." To close this loophole, we brought Silvan from the East Coast to spend a week at my lab.

Before he came we edited the films so he would see only the expression itself, removed from its social context, just close-up shots of a face. Silvan had no trouble at all. Every one of his interpretations fit the social context he hadn't seen. What's more, he knew exactly how he got the information. Wally and I could sense what emotional message was conveyed by each expression, but our judgments were intuitively based; we usually could not specify exactly what in the face carried the message unless it was a smile. Silvan walked up to the movie screen and pointed out exactly which specific muscular movements signaled the emotion.

We also asked him for his overall impression of these two cultures. One group he said seemed quite friendly. The other was explosive in their anger, highly suspicious if not paranoid in character, and homosexual. It was the Anga that he was describing. His account fit what we had been told by Gajdusek, who had worked with them. They had repeatedly attacked Australian officials who tried to maintain a government station there. They were known by their neighbors for their fierce suspiciousness. And the men led homosexual lives until the time of marriage. A few years later the ethologist Irenäus Eibl-Eibesfeldt literally had to run for his life when he attempted to work with them.

After that meeting I decided to devote myself to the study of facial expression. I would go to New Guinea and try to get evidence to support what

I then knew to be true—that at least some facial expressions of emotion are universal. And I would work to develop an objective way to measure facial behavior so that any scientist could objectively derive from facial movement what Silvan could see so keenly.

Late in 1967 I went to the South East Highlands to do research on the Fore people, who lived in small scattered villages at an elevation of seven thousand feet. I did not know the Fore language, but with the help of a few boys who had learned Pidgin from a missionary school, I could go from English to Pidgin to Fore and back again. I brought with me pictures of facial expressions, mostly the pictures I had been given by Silvan for my studies of literate cultures. (Following, on page 251, are three examples.) I also brought photographs of some Fore people I had selected from the motion picture film, thinking they might have trouble interpreting the expressions shown by Caucasians. I even worried that they might not be able to understand photographs at all, never having seen any before. Some anthropologists had earlier claimed that people who hadn't seen photographs had to learn how to interpret them. The Fore had no such problem, though; they immediately understood the photographs, and it didn't seem to make much of a difference what nationality the person was, Fore or American. The problem was what I asked them to do.

They had no written language, so I couldn't ask them to pick a word from a list that fit the emotion shown. If I were to read them a list of emotion words, I would have to worry about whether they remembered the list, and whether the order in which the words were read influenced their choice. Instead I asked them to make up a story about each facial expression. "Tell me what is happening now, what happened before to make this person show this expression, and what is going to happen next." It was like pulling teeth. I am not certain whether it was the translation process, or the fact that they had no idea what it was I wanted to hear or why I wanted them to do this. Perhaps making up stories about strangers was just something the Fore didn't do.

I did get my stories, but it took each person a lot of time to give me each story. They and I were exhausted after each session. Nevertheless, I had no shortage of volunteers, even though I suspect the word was out that what I was asking wasn't easy to do. There was a powerful incentive to look at my photographs: I gave each person either a bar of soap or a pack of cigarettes for helping me. They had no soap, so it was highly valued. They grew their own tobacco, which they smoked in pipes, but they seemed to like my cigarettes better.

Most of their stories fit the emotion each photograph supposedly depicted. For example, when looking at a picture depicting what people in literate cultures judged as sadness, the New Guineans most often said that the person's child had died. But the storytelling procedure was awkward, and proving that the different stories fit a particular emotion would not be an easy task. I knew I had to do it differently, but I didn't know how.

I also filmed spontaneous expressions and was able to catch the look of joy when people from another nearby village met their friends. I arranged situations to provoke emotions. I recorded two men playing their musical instruments, and then I filmed their surprise and delight when for the first time they heard their voices and music come out of a tape recorder. I even stabbed a boy with a rubber knife I had brought with me, as my movie camera recorded his response and the reactions of his friends. They thought it was a good joke. (I had the good sense not to try this trick with one of the men.) Such film clips could not serve as my evidence, for those committed to the view that expressions differ in each culture could always argue I had selected only those few occasions when universal expressions were shown.

I left New Guinea after a few months—not a hard decision because I was hungry for conversation, something I couldn't have with any of these people, and for food, since I had made the mistake of thinking I would enjoy eating the local cuisine. Yams and something resembling the part of the asparagus we discard grew pretty tiresome. It was an adventure, the most exciting one of my life, but I was still worried that I had not been able to get definitive evidence. I knew this culture would not stay isolated much longer, and there were not many others like it still left in the world.

Back home I came across a technique that psychologist John Dashiel had used in the 1930s to study how well young children could interpret facial expressions. They were too young to read, so he couldn't give them a list of words from which to choose. Instead of asking them to make up a story— as I had done in New Guinea—Dashiel cleverly read them a story and showed them a set of pictures. All they had to do was pick the one that fit the story. I knew that would work for me. I went over the stories the New Guineans had made up, picking the story that had been given most often for each type of emotional expression. They were pretty simple: "His/her friends have come and s/he is happy; s/he is angry and about to fight; his/her child has died and s/he feels very sad; s/he is looking at something s/he dislikes, or s/he is looking at something that smells bad; he/she is just now looking at something new and unexpected."

There was a problem with the most frequent story for fear, about the danger posed by a wild pig. I had to change it to reduce the chance that it would be relevant to surprise or anger. It went like this: "S/he is sitting in her/his house all alone, and there is no one else in the village. There is no knife, axe, or bow and arrow in the house. A wild pig is standing in the door of the house, and the man (woman) is looking at the pig and is very afraid of it. The pig has been standing in the doorway for a few minutes and the person is looking at it very afraid, and the pig won't move away from the door and s/he is afraid the pig will bite him/her."

I made up sets of three pictures, which would be shown while one of the stories was read (an example appears below). The subject would only have to point to the picture. I made up many sets of pictures, I didn't want any picture to appear more than once, so the person's choice wouldn't be made by exclusion: "Oh, that was the one where the child died, and that was the one where I said she was about to fight, so this one must be the one about the pig."

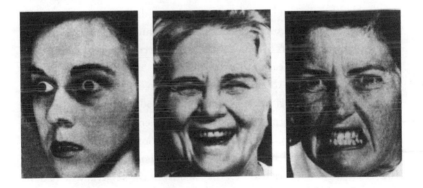

I returned to New Guinea late in 1968 with my stories and pictures and a team of colleagues to help gather the data. (This time I also brought canned food.) Our return was heralded, I suppose, because apart from Gajdusek and his filmmaker, Richard Sorenson (who was of great help to me in the prior year), very few outsiders ever visited, and even fewer returned. We did travel to some villages, but once the word got out that what we were asking was very easy to do, people from villages far away started coming to us. They liked the task and were again delighted with the soap and cigarettes.

I took special care to ensure that no one in our group would unwittingly tip off the subjects as to which picture was the correct one. The sets of pictures were mounted onto transparent pages, with a code number written on the back of each picture that could be seen from the backside of the page. We did not know, and made a point of not finding out, which codes went with each expression. Instead a page would be turned toward the subject, arranged so that the person writing down the answers would not be able to see the front of the page. The story would be read, the subject would point to the picture, and one of us would write down the code number for the picture the subject had chosen.

In the space of just a few weeks we saw more than three hundred people, about 3 percent of this culture, and more than enough to analyze statistically. The results were very clear-cut for happiness, anger, disgust, and sadness. Fear and surprise were not distinguished from each other—when people heard the fear story, they just as often picked a surprise as a fear expression, and the same was true when they heard the surprise story. But fear and surprise were distinguished from anger, disgust, sadness, and happiness. To this day I do not know why fear and surprise were not distinguished from each other. It could have been a problem with the stories, or it could have been that these two emotions are so often intermingled in these people's lives that they aren't distinguished. In literate cultures fear and surprise are distinguished from each other.

All except twenty-three of our subjects had seen no movies, television, or photographs; they neither spoke nor understood English or Pidgin, had not lived in any Western settlement or government town, and had never worked for a Caucasian. The twenty-three exceptions had all seen movies, spoke English, and had attended a missionary school for more than a year. There were no differences between the majority of the subjects who had little contact with the outside world and the few who had, nor were there any differences between males and females.

We did one more experiment, which was not as easy for our subjects. One of the Pidgin speakers read them one of the stories and asked them to show what their face would look like if they were the person in the story. I videotaped nine men doing this, none of whom had participated in the first study. The unedited videotapes were shown to college students in America.

If the expressions were culture-specific, then these college students would not be able to interpret correctly the expressions. But the Americans correctly identified the emotion except for the fear and surprise poses, where they were equally likely to call the pose fear or surprise, just like the New Guineans. Here are four examples of the New Guineans' poses of emotion.

ENJOYMENT

SADNESS

ANGER

DISGUST

I announced our findings at the annual anthropology national conference in 1969. Many were unhappy with what we had found. They were firmly convinced that human behavior is all nurture and no nature; expressions must be different in each culture, despite my evidence. The fact that I had actually found cultural differences in the *management* of facial expressions in my Japanese American study was not good enough.

The best way to dispel their doubts would be to repeat the entire study in another preliterate, isolated culture. Ideally, someone else should do it, preferably someone who wanted to prove me wrong. If such a person found what I found, that would enormously strengthen our case. Because of another stroke of luck, the anthropologist Karl Heider did just that.

Heider had recently come back from spending a few years studying the Dani, another isolated group in what is now called West Irian, part of Indonesia. Heider told me there must be something wrong with my research because the Dani didn't even have words for emotions. I offered to give him all of my research materials and teach him how to run the experiment the next time he went back to the Dani. His results perfectly replicated my findings, even down to the failure to distinguish between fear and surprise.

Nevertheless, not all anthropologists are convinced, even today. And there are a few psychologists, primarily those concerned with language, who complain that our work in literate cultures, where we asked people to identify the emotion word that fit the expressions, does not support universals since the words for each emotion don't have perfect translations. How emotions are represented in language is, of course, the product of culture rather than evolution. But in studies of now more than twenty literate Western and Eastern cultures, the judgment made by the majority in each culture about what emotion is shown in an expression is the same. Despite the translation problems, there has never been an instance in which the majority in two cultures ascribes a different emotion to the same expression.

From *Woman: An Intimate Biography*

Natalie Angier

A female rat can't mate if she is not in estrus. I don't mean that she doesn't want to mate, or that she won't find a partner if she's not in heat and sending forth the appropriate spectrum of olfactory and auditory enticements. I mean that she is physically incapable of copulating. Unless she is in estrus, her ovaries do not secrete estrogen and progesterone, and without hormonal stimulation, the rat can't assume the mating position known as lordosis, in which she arches her back and flicks aside her tail. The lordosis posture changes the angle and aperture of the vagina, making it accessible to the male rat's penis once he has mounted her from behind. There is no rat's version of the *Kama Sutra*. An ovariectomized female won't assume lordosis, and hence she can't mate— unless, that is, she is given hormone shots to compensate for the loss of the natural ablutions of the ovarian follicle.

In a female guinea pig, a membrane normally covers the vaginal opening. It takes the release of sex hormones during ovulation to open up the membrane and allow the guinea pig to have sex.

For both the rat and the guinea pig, as well as for many other female animals, mechanics and motivation are intertwined. Only when she is in heat is the female driven to seek a mate, and only when she is in heat can her body oblige her. Estrogen controls her sexual appetite and sexual physics alike.

A female primate can copulate whenever she pleases, whether she is ovulating or not. There is no connection between the mechanics of her reproductive tract and the status of her hormones. Estrogen does not control the nerves and muscles that would impel her to hoist her rear end in the air, angle her genitals just so, and whip her tail out of the way, if she has one. A female primate does not have to be capable of becoming pregnant in order to partake of sex. She can have sex every day, and if she's a bonobo, she will have sex more than once a day, or once an hour. A female primate has been

unshackled from the tyranny of hormones. In an almost literal sense, the key
to her door has been taken away from her ovaries and placed in her hands.

Yet she still cycles. Her blood bears estrogen from place to place, including to the portions of the brain where desire and emotion and libido
dwell, in the limbic system, the hypothalamus, the amygdala. The female
primate has been freed from the rigidity of hormonal control. Now she can
take the sex steroid and apply it subtly, to integrate, modulate, and interpret a wealth of sensory and psychological cues. For rats, hormones are
thumpish, unmistakable, the world in black and white; for primates, they
act like a box of crayons, the sixty-four pack, with a color for every occasion and at least three names for every color. Do you want it in pink, blush,
or fuchsia?

"In primates, all the effects of hormones on sexual behavior have
become focused on psychological mechanisms, not physical ones," Kim
Wallen, of Emory University, says to me. "The decoupling of physical from
psychological allows primates to use sex in different contexts, for economic
reasons or political reasons." Or emotional reasons, or to keep from getting
bored. As Wallen speaks, we watch a group of five rhesus monkeys at the
Yerkes Primate Research Center chase two other rhesus monkeys around and
around in their enclosure, all seven swearing back and forth at each other in
rhesusese, as you can tell because the more they scream, the faster everybody
runs. In a primate, Wallen continues, hormone pulses may not make the female bow down in lordosis, but they clearly influence her sexual motivation.
He points at the group of rhesus monkeys. The seven samurai are still
screaming and running. Several other monkeys look on with rapt anxiety,
like bettors at a racetrack. One large, scruffy male ignores everything and
picks his teeth. None is doing anything remotely sexual. Rhesus monkeys are
Calvinists, Wallen says, prudish and autocratic in matters of sex. When a female rhesus is alone with a familiar male and no other monkeys are there to
spy on her, she will mate with the male regardless of where she is in her
breeding cycle. But a female under the constraints of the social group does
not have the luxury of freewheeling carnality. If she sidles up to a male and
begins engaging in a bit of heavy petting, other group members strive to intervene, raucously and snappishly. A female rhesus doesn't often bother de-
fying convention. What does she look like, a bonobo?

Hormones change everything. They tint her judgment and sweep her
from Kansas to Oz. When she is ovulating and her estrogen levels soar, her

craving overcomes her political instincts and she will mate madly and profligately, all the while out-snarling those who would dare to interfere.

When we think about motivation, desire, and behavior, we accord the neocortex and the thinking brain the greater share of credit. We believe in free will, and we must. Free will, of a sort, is a hallmark of human nature. This is not to say that we start each morning afresh, with an infinity of possible selves awaiting us—that is a figment, alas, and a durable one. Nevertheless, we have what Roy Baumeister, of Case Western Reserve University, calls an "executive function," the dimension of the self that exercises volition, choice, self-control. The human capacity for self-control must be counted among our species' great strengths, the source of our adaptability and suppleness. Very little of our conduct is genuinely automatic. Even when we think we're operating on automatic pilot, the executive function keeps an eye out, checks, edits, corrects the course. If you know how to touch-type, you know that the executive brain is never far removed from the drone brain. When all is well, you type along automatically, your fingers so familiar with the keys that it's as though each digit has a RAM chip embedded in its tip. But the moment you make a mistake, the automaton stops and the executive function kicks in, even before you're quite aware of what went wrong. With its guidance, your finger reaches for the backspace key to correct the error, and you see what happened and you fix things, and a moment later your hands have returned to robot mode. Athletes, surgeons, and musicians perform similar exchanges between intentional and programmatic behaviors hundreds of times a minute; such commerce is the soul of mastery. The human capacity for self-control is limited, and we get into trouble when we overestimate it and embrace the caustic ethos of perfectionism, but volition still deserves our gratitude.

At the same time, we know that there's a macaque darting about in the genomic background and that we feel like monkeys and can act like them too. The moment a young girl enters adolescence, she begins dwelling on sex, consciously, unconsciously, in her dreams, alone in the bath—however or wherever it happens, it happens. Her desire is aroused. The changes of puberty are largely hormonal changes. The shifting of the chemical setting stirs desire. Intellectually, we accept the idea that sexuality is a hormonally inflected experience, but we still resent the connection. If hormones count, we worry that they count too much and that therefore we have no free will, and so we deny that they count, all the while knowing that they count, because we see it in our teenage children and we remember, please goddess, our teenage greed.

Rather than denying the obvious, we should try to appreciate the ways in which estrogen and other hormones affect behavior. Granted, our knowledge of neurobiology is primitive, presimian. We don't understand how estrogen or any other substance works on the brain to elicit desire, or feed a fantasy, or muffle an impulse. But there are enough indirect strands of evidence to knit a serviceable thinking cap with which to mull over estrogen's meaning.

Desires and emotions can be fleeting, mayflies in the brain. They're born and they're gone. But they can also be persistent. They can change from whims to obsessions. If an emotion or drive is going to persist and resonate, a hormone is a useful object to turn to for the task. In the brain, steroid hormones generally work together with one or more of the neuropeptides. A neuropeptide is quick and transient. A steroid hormone is resilient and insistent. They work synergistically on neural circuits that subserve motive and behavior, integrating psyche with body. Take the sensation of thirst. When your body is low in water and salt, it reacts vigorously, because we all once dwelled in the sea and our cells still must be bathed in salty water to survive. Among the responses is the activation of the adrenal glands, which secrete steroid hormones such as aldosterone. Aldosterone is a practical hormone, and it seeks to conserve the supplies that exist—for instance, by reabsorbing salt from urine or gastric juice and returning it to the fluid between cells. Aldosterone also infiltrates the brain, where it galvanizes the activity of a neuropeptide, angiotensin. The neuropeptide in turn arouses the brain's circuitry of thirst. You feel thirsty. You have an urge to drink. The sensation can usually be satisfied with ease, with a glass of water, and the adrenals and the thirst locus settle down. But if your requirements for fluid and sodium are unusually large, as they are during breastfeeding, you will be awash in aldosterone and very efficient in your use of water and salt, but you will also feel chronically parched, and you will wonder if the Nile itself is large enough to slake you, and you will love salty foods as you never did before.

An emotion is a piece of information. It is a signal of need, of a temporary lapse in homeostasis. It is the body's way of encouraging or inhibiting behaviors, which the body hopes will fulfill the need and restore balance. We don't usually think of thirst as an emotion, but that's what it is, an emotion of the body's interstitial spaces. As an emotion, thirst can be disregarded or overruled by competing demands. If you are running a race in the heat and feel thirsty, you might ignore the desire rather than stop to drink and lose precious time and weigh your belly down with fluids. Panic can bring on enormous thirst, in part because the adrenal activity that comes with fear unleashes the flow of angiotensin in the brain; but panic can also clench the throat and stomach and make the thought of drink or food repulsive. Still, thirst gives you a comparatively short leash. You can only ignore it so long—a week without water, and you will die of dehydration. The synergistic impact of neuropeptide and steroid hormone on the circuitry overseeing the behavior of fluid acquisition is therefore quite extreme. The longer you refuse to engage in the requested behavior, drinking, the more exaggerated your adrenal output becomes and the more overwhelming the desire is. At some point, as you near death, you will drink anything—poisoned water, sea water that is too salty for your body to use. Even Jesus could not conquer thirst, and died with vinegar moistening his lips.

If, however, you don't reproduce during a particular cycle, it won't kill you. Humans are long-lived creatures who operate on the implicit assumption that they will have many opportunities to breed and can afford to override the whims and impulses of Eros for months, years, decades, and, oops, a lifetime if conditions of the moment are not quite optimal. Animals in whom reproductive drives are as relentless as thirst are short-lived species who may have only one or two breeding seasons in which to leave their Mendelian badge on the world. A corollary of longevity is a rich emotional life and a complex sexuality. We mistakenly equate emotionality with the primitive and rationality with the advanced, but in fact the more intelligent the animal, the deeper its passions. The greater the intelligence, the greater the demand on the emotions, the portmanteaus of information, to expand their capacity and multiply their zippers and compartments.

We impugn emotions, but we are lucky to be so thick with them. They give us something to think about and decode. We are brilliant because of them, not in spite of them. Hormones are part of the suitcase, and they are part of the contents. They relay information about themselves, and they carry information about others. They do not make us do anything, but they may make the doing of something easier or more pleasurable when all else conspires in favor of it.

Estrogen, puckish estrogen, works through many intermediaries in the brain, many neuropeptides and neurotransmitters. It works through nerve growth factor, and it works through serotonin, a neuropeptide best known for its role in depression. It works through natural opiates and it works through oxytocin. It may be thought of as a conjoiner or a facilitator, or as leavening, like yeast or baking soda. Estrogen has no particular emotion in mind, yet it permits emoting. For years researchers have sought to link estrogen levels to women's sexual behavior. The assumption is logical. Estrogen concentrations rise steadily as the egg follicle grows each month, peaking with the moment of ovulation, when the egg is released into the fallopian tube. If the egg has a need, a desire to be fertilized, in theory it could make the need known to the brain through estrogen, and estrogen would then stimulate a neuropeptide to encourage a particular behavior—to wit, seeking a sexual partner like a thirsty pedestrian seeks a water fountain.

The difficulties of correlating estrogen to human sexual behavior are considerable. What sort of behavior are you looking at? What are the relevant data points? Frequency of intercourse? Frequency of orgasm? Frequency of masturbation or sexual fantasy? The sudden urge to buy *Cosmopolitan*? Here is what we know. There is no association between rate of intercourse and where a woman is in her ovulatory cycle. Women do not have sex more often during ovulation than they do at any other time of the month, unless they're consciously on the fertility quest. But the completion of a behavior tells you little about the subliminal provocations of that behavior. If you plot the incidence of intercourse among couples, you'll see an amazing statistical high point, and it's called the weekend—not because people necessarily feel sexy each Sunday, but because people have sex when it's convenient, when they're not exhausted by work, and when they have the whole day to toy with. A hormone may lead you to water, but it can't make you drink.

There is also no correlation between estrogen levels and physical arousability—the tendency of the genitals to swell and lubricate in response to an overt sexual stimulus, such as a lovemaking scene in a movie. Women have been shown to be fairly invariate in their display of physiological arousal, regardless of their cycle. But physiological arousal says little about meaningful sexual motivation or hunger, for some women will lubricate during rape, and Ellen Laan, of the University of Amsterdam, has shown that women's genitals congest robustly when they watch pornography that the women later describe as stupid, trite, and distinctly unerotic.

We get a somewhat better kinship between hormones and sexuality when we look at desire rather than at genital performance. Some studies have taken female initiation of sex as the marker of desire. The results have varied considerably, depending on the type of birth control used, but they list in the predicted direction. Women on oral contraceptives, which interfere with normal hormonal oscillations, are no more likely to come on to their partners at the middle of the cycle than they are at other times. When the birth control method is reliable but nonhormonal—a vasectomized husband, for example—women show a tendency to be the initiators of sex at the peak of ovulation more than they are during other times of the month, suggesting that the estrogen high is beckoning to them. Add in the complicating factor of a less trustworthy barrier, such as a diaphragm or condom, and the likelihood of midpeak propositioning subsides. No great enigma there: if you don't want to get pregnant, you might not be eager to fool around when you think you're at your most fertile. In a study of lesbian couples, who have no fear of pregnancy, don't use birth control, and are free of supposedly confounding factors of male expectations and manipulations, psychologists found that women were about 25 percent more likely to initiate sex and had twice as many orgasms during the midpoint of their cycle than at other times of the month.

The strongest correlations between hormones and sexuality are seen when pure, disembodied desire is the object of scrutiny. In one large study, five hundred women were asked to take their basal temperatures every day for several months and to mark down the day of the month when they first noticed the stirrings of sexual desire. The pooled results show an extraordinary concordance between the onset of sexual hunger and the time that basal temperature readings suggest the women were at or nearing ovulation. Women may even express desire through unconscious body language. In a study of young women who spent a lot of time dancing in nightclubs, the scientists found that as the women approached the day of ovulation, their outfits became progressively skimpier, more flaunting of flesh: the hemlines rose with estrogen levels as if with a bull market.

1. LeDoux convincingly and elegantly shows the role of the amygdala in fear, but says (in the excerpt included here) little about the neural basis of other emotions. Choose one of the other emotions that Ekman discusses, and see (a) whether the amygdala plays a role in that emotion and (b) what other parts of the brain play an active role in interpreting or expressing that emotion.

2. Compare Ekman's perspective on culture to those in Chapter 15. (Don't forget to consider the role of "display rules.")

3. Relate Ekman's observations to John Watson's perspective on psychology (Chapter 7).

4. Angier's emphasis is on estrogen, but that doesn't mean that women are more influenced by hormones than men are. For balance, look up some of the effects of testosterone on male cognition. (As a start, try Googling *testosterone* and *sports*, and see what happens to a man if his favorite team wins—or loses.)

5. Angier distinguishes between the effects of hormones on behavior and the effects of hormones on desire. Relate this distinction to Richerson and Boyd's discussion of hormones and the Southern America "Culture of Honor" (Chapter 15).

CHAPTER THIRTEEN

SOCIAL PSYCHOLOGY

If cognition is about how we think and reason about the world, social psychology is about how we think and reason about people. How do we persuade them? Show empathy? When do we do what is asked of us, and when do we rebel? How do we form first impressions? Are first impressions truly long-lasting? How vulnerable are we to stereotyping? To what extent is our behavior driven by our personalities as opposed to by the situations in which we are in?

Some of the most famous early results in social psychology are far from comforting. Darley and Latané showed that we are unlikely to take responsibility for treating a stranger in need if there are other people around who could help—whether or not anybody else actually does help. Stanley Milgram showed that ordinary people were willing to administer severe electrical shocks to strangers merely because lab-coated Yale scientists asked them to. Solomon Asch showed that you can get someone to override their own best judgments just by putting them in a room full of lying confederates.

In the first selection in this chapter, from *Influence* (1993), Robert Cialdini shows that our foibles continue to this day. Starting with the way in which savvy salespeople can sometimes sell their wares more quickly by pricing them *higher*, Cialdini paints a somewhat dark picture of human reasoning capacities. But it's not all bleak. As Cialdini notes, much of this slipshod social reasoning comes from split-second decisions made on too little information. But the human mind is also endowed with abilities for careful, considered reflection. Wisdom lies in knowing the difference between the two, and in knowing when to use deliberation reflection as an antidote to hasty decisions that may not be optimal.

Shelley Taylor takes on a different aspect of social psychology: bonds. Not the kind of bond that accrues interest, but the kind that forms between two people, a mother and a child, a brother and a sister, or a leader and a follower. In *The Tending Instinct* (2002), Taylor focuses particularly on the bond that women form with each other and with their children. (Yes, that's *women* and their children, not *parents* and their children. Although this may seem sexist, as Taylor notes, even today, in the most liberated societies, that's still

where most of the bonding action is. Like it or not, the behavior—and psychology—of male parents and female parents continues to differ.) Bonds
between human beings may be invisible and untouchable, but their importance in human interaction can scarcely be overstated. By exploring the psychology of how and why we form our most intimate connections, we can't
help but gain valuable insight into the human condition.

From *Influence:*
The Psychology of Persuasion

Robert B. Cialdini

Everything should be made as simple as possible, but not simpler.

—Albert Einstein

I got a phone call one day from a friend who had recently opened an Indian jewelry store in Arizona. She was giddy with a curious piece of news. Something fascinating had just happened, and she thought that, as a psychologist, I might be able to explain it to her. The story involved a certain allotment of turquoise jewelry she had been having trouble selling. It was the peak of the tourist season, the store was unusually full of customers, the turquoise pieces were of good quality for the prices she was asking; yet they had not sold. My friend had attempted a couple of standard sales tricks to get them moving. She tried calling attention to them by shifting their location to a more central display area; no luck. She even told her sales staff to "push" the items hard, again without success.

Finally, the night before leaving on an out-of-town buying trip, she scribbled an exasperated note to her head saleswoman, "Everything in this display case, price ×$\frac{1}{2}$," hoping just to be rid of the offending pieces, even if at a loss. When she returned a few days later, she was not surprised to find that every article had been sold. She was shocked, though, to discover that, because the employee had read the "$\frac{1}{2}$" in her scrawled message as a "2," the entire allotment had sold out at twice the original price!

That's when she called me. I thought I knew what had happened but told her that, if I were to explain things properly, she would have to listen to a story of mine. Actually, it isn't my story; it's about mother turkeys, and it belongs to the relatively new science of ethology—the study of animals in their natural settings. Turkey mothers are good mothers—loving, watchful, and protective. They spend much of their time tending, warming, cleaning, and huddling the young beneath them. But there *is* something odd about their method. Virtually all of this mothering is triggered by one thing: the "cheep-cheep" sound of young turkey chicks. Other identifying features of the chicks, such as their smell, touch, or appearance, seem to play minor roles in the mothering process. If a chick makes the "cheep-cheep" noise, its mother will care for it; if not, the mother will ignore or sometimes kill it.

The extreme reliance of maternal turkeys upon this one sound was dramatically illustrated by animal behaviorist M. W. Fox in his description of an experiment involving a mother turkey and a stuffed polecat. For a mother turkey, a polecat is a natural enemy whose approach is to be greeted with squawking, pecking, clawing rage. Indeed, the experimenters found that even a stuffed model of a polecat, when drawn by a string toward a mother turkey, received an immediate and furious attack. When, however, the same stuffed replica carried inside it a small recorder that played the "cheep-cheep" sound of baby turkeys, the mother not only accepted the oncoming polecat but gathered it underneath her. When the machine was turned off, the polecat model again drew a vicious attack.

How ridiculous a female turkey seems under these circumstances: She will embrace a natural enemy just because it goes "cheep-cheep," and she will mistreat or murder one of her own chicks just because it does not. She looks like an automaton whose maternal instincts are under the automatic control of that single sound. The ethologists tell us that this sort of thing is far from unique to the turkey. They have begun to identify regular, blindly mechanical patterns of action in a wide variety of species.

Called *fixed-action patterns*, they can involve intricate sequences of behavior, such as entire courtship or mating rituals. A fundamental characteristic of these patterns is that the behaviors that compose them occur in virtually the same fashion and in the same order every time. It is almost as if the patterns were recorded on tapes within the animals. When the situation calls for courtship, the courtship tape gets played; when the situation calls for mothering, the maternal-behavior tape gets played. *Click* and the appropriate tape is activated; *whirr* and out rolls the standard sequence of behaviors.

The most interesting thing about all this is the way the tapes are activated. When a male animal acts to defend his territory, for instance, it is the intrusion of another male of the same species that cues the territorial-defense tape of rigid vigilance, threat, and, if need be, combat behaviors. But there is a quirk in the system. It is not the rival male as a whole that is the trigger; it is some specific feature of him, the *trigger feature*. Often the trigger feature will be just one tiny aspect of the totality that is the approaching intruder. Sometimes a shade of color is the trigger feature. The experiments of ethologists have shown, for instance, that a male robin, acting as if a rival robin had entered its territory, will vigorously attack nothing more than a clump of robin-redbreast feathers placed there. At the same time, it will virtually ignore a perfect stuffed replica of a male robin *without* red breast feathers; similar results have been found in another species of bird, the bluethroat, where it appears that the trigger for territorial defense is a specific shade of blue breast feathers.

Before we enjoy too smugly the ease with which lower animals can be tricked by trigger features into reacting in ways wholly inappropriate to the situation, we might realize two things. First, the automatic, fixed-action patterns of these animals work very well the great majority of the time. For example, because only healthy, normal turkey chicks make the peculiar sound of baby turkeys, it makes sense for mother turkeys to respond maternally to that single "cheep-cheep" noise. By reacting to just that one stimulus, the average mother turkey will nearly always behave correctly. It takes a trickster like a scientist to make her tapelike response seem silly. The second important thing to understand is that we, too, have our preprogrammed tapes; and, although they usually work to our advantage, the trigger features that activate them can be used to dupe *us* into playing them at the wrong times.

This parallel form of human automatic action is aptly demonstrated in an experiment by Harvard social psychologist Ellen Langer. A well-known principle of human behavior says that when we ask someone to do us a favor *we will be more successful if we provide a reason*. People simply like to have reasons for what they do. Langer demonstrated this unsurprising fact by asking a small favor of people waiting in line to use a library copying machine: *Excuse me, I have five pages. May I use the Xerox machine because I'm in a rush?* The effectiveness of this request-plus-reason was nearly total: *Ninety-four percent* of those asked let her skip ahead of them in line. Compare this success rate to the results when she made the request only: *Excuse me, I have five pages. May I use the Xerox machine?* Under those circumstances, only 60 percent of those asked complied. At first glance, it appears that the crucial difference between the two requests was the additional information provided by the words "because I'm in a rush." But a third type of request tried by Langer showed that this was not the case. It seems that it was not the whole series of words, but the first one, "because," that made the difference. Instead of including a real reason for compliance, Langer's third type of request used the word "because" and then, adding nothing new, merely restated the obvious: *Excuse me, I have five pages. May I use the Xerox machine because I have to make some copies?* The result was that once again nearly all (*93 percent*) agreed, even though no real reason, no new information, was added to justify their compliance. Just as the "cheep-cheep" sound of turkey chicks triggered an automatic mothering response from maternal turkeys—even when it emanated from a stuffed polecat—so, too, did the word "because" trigger an automatic compliance response from Langer's subjects, even when they were given no subsequent reason to comply. *Click, whirr!*

Although some of Langer's additional findings show that there are many situations in which human behavior does not work in a mechanical, tape-activated way, what is astonishing is how often it does. For instance, consider the strange behavior of those jewelry-store customers who swooped down on an allotment of turquoise pieces only after the items had been mistakenly offered at double their original price. I can make no sense of their behavior, unless it is viewed in *click, whirr* terms.

The customers, mostly well-to-do vacationers with little knowledge of turquoise, were using a standard principle—a stereotype—to guide their buying: "*expensive = good*." Thus the vacationers, who wanted "good" jewelry, saw the turquoise pieces as decidedly more valuable and desirable when nothing about them was enhanced but the price. Price alone had become a trigger feature for quality; and a dramatic increase in price alone had led to a dramatic increase in sales among the quality-hungry buyers. *Click, whirr!*

It is easy to fault the tourists for their foolish purchase decisions. But a close look offers a kinder view. These were people who had been brought up on the rule "You get what you pay for" and who had seen that rule borne out over and over in their lives. Before long, they had translated the rule to mean "expensive = good." The "expensive = good" stereotype had worked quite well for them in the past, since normally the price of an item increases along with its worth; a higher price typically reflects higher quality. So when they found themselves in the position of wanting good turquoise jewelry without much knowledge of turquoise, they understandably relied on the old standby feature of cost to determine the jewelry's merits.

Although they probably did not realize it, by reacting solely to the price feature of the turquoise, they were playing a shortcut version of betting the odds. Instead of stacking all the odds in their favor by trying painstakingly to master each of the things that indicate the worth of turquoise jewelry, they were counting on just one—the one they knew to be usually associated with the quality of any item. They were betting that price alone would tell them all they needed to know. This time, because someone mistook a "$^1/_2$" for a "2," they bet wrong. But in the long run, over all the past and future situations of their lives, betting those shortcut odds may represent the most rational approach possible.

In fact, automatic, stereotyped behavior is prevalent in much of human action, because in many cases it is the most efficient form of behaving, and in other cases it is simply necessary. You and I exist in an extraordinarily complicated stimulus environment, easily the most rapidly moving and complex that has ever existed on this planet. To deal with it, we *need* shortcuts. We can't be expected to recognize and analyze all the aspects in each person, event, and situation we encounter in even one day. We haven't the time, energy, or capacity for it. Instead, we must very often use our stereotypes, our rules of thumb to classify things according to a few key features and then to respond mindlessly when one or another of these trigger features is present.

Sometimes the behavior that unrolls will not be appropriate for the situation, because not even the best stereotypes and trigger features work every time. But we accept their imperfection, since there is really no other choice. Without them we would stand frozen—cataloging, appraising, and calibrating—as the time for action sped by and away. And from all indications, we will be relying on them to an even greater extent in the future. As the stimuli saturating our lives continue to grow more intricate and variable, we will have to depend increasingly on our shortcuts to handle them all.

The renowned British philosopher Alfred North Whitehead recognized this inescapable quality of modern life when he asserted that "civilization advances by extending the number of operations we can perform without thinking about them." Take, for example, the "advance" offered to civilization by the discount coupon, which allows consumers to assume that they will receive a reduced purchase price by presenting the coupon. The extent to which we have learned to operate mechanically on that assumption is illustrated in the experience of one automobile-tire company. *Mailed-out coupons that—because of a printing error—offered no savings to recipients produced just as much customer response as did error-free coupons that offered substantial savings.* The obvious but instructive point here is that we expect discount coupons to do double duty. Not only do we expect them to save us money, we also expect them to save us the time and mental energy required to think about how to do it. In today's world, we need the first advantage to handle pocketbook strain; but we need the second advantage to handle something potentially more important—brain strain.

It is odd that despite their current widespread use and looming future importance, most of us know very little about our automatic behavior patterns. Perhaps that is so precisely because of the mechanistic, unthinking manner in which they occur. Whatever the reason, it is vital that we clearly recognize one of their properties: They make us terribly vulnerable to anyone who does know how they work.

Epilogue

Primitive Consent for an Automatic Age

Every day in every way, I'm getting better.

—*Emile Coué*

Every day in every way, I'm getting busier.

—*Robert Cialdini*

Back in the 1960s a man named Joe Pine hosted a rather remarkable TV talk show that was syndicated from California. The program was made distinctive by Pine's caustic and confrontational style with his guests—for the most part, a collection of exposure-hungry entertainers, would-be celebrities, and representatives of fringe political or social organizations. The host's abrasive approach was designed to provoke his guests into arguments, to fluster them into embarrassing admissions, and generally to make them look foolish. It was not uncommon for Pine to introduce a visitor and launch immediately into an attack on the individual's beliefs, talent, or appearance. Some people claimed that Pine's acid personal style was partially caused by a leg amputation that had embittered him to life; others said no, that he was just vituperous by nature.

One evening rock musician Frank Zappa was a guest on the show. This was at a time in the sixties when very long hair on men was still unusual and controversial. As soon as Zappa had been introduced and seated, the following exchange occurred:

> Pine: I guess your long hair makes you a girl.
> Zappa: I guess your wooden leg makes you a table.

Aside from containing what may be my favorite ad-lib, the above dialogue illustrates a fundamental theme of this book: Very often in making a decision about someone or something, we don't use all the relevant available information; we use, instead, only a single, highly representative piece of the total. And an isolated piece of information, even though it normally counsels us correctly, can lead us to clearly stupid mistakes—mistakes that, when exploited by clever others, leave us looking silly or worse.

At the same time, a complicating companion theme has been present throughout this book: Despite the susceptibility to stupid decisions that accompanies a reliance on a single feature of the available data, the pace of modern life demands that we frequently use this shortcut. Recall that [earlier] our shortcut approach was likened to the automatic responding of lower animals whose elaborate behavior patterns could be triggered by the presence of a lone stimulus feature—a "cheep-cheep" sound, a shade of red breast feather, or a specific sequence of light flashes. The reason infrahumans must often rely on such solitary stimulus features is their restricted mental capability. Their small brains cannot begin to register and process all the relevant information in their environments. So these species have evolved special sensitivities to certain aspects of the information. Because those selected aspects of information are normally enough to cue a correct response, the system is usually very efficient: Whenever a female turkey hears "cheep-cheep," *click, whirr,* out rolls the proper maternal behavior in a mechanical fashion that conserves much of her limited brainpower for dealing with the variety of other situations and choices she must face in her day.

We, of course, have vastly more effective brain mechanisms than mother turkeys, or any other animal group, for that matter. We are unchallenged in the ability to take into account a multitude of relevant facts and, consequently, to make good decisions. Indeed, it is this information-processing advantage over other species that has helped make us the dominant form of life on the planet.

Still, we have our capacity limitations, too; and, for the sake of efficiency, we must sometimes retreat from the time-consuming, sophisticated, fully informed brand of decision making to a more automatic, primitive, single-feature type of responding. For instance, in deciding whether to say yes or no to a requester, it is clear that we frequently pay attention to but one piece of the relevant information in the situation. We have been exploring several of the most popular of the single pieces of information that we use to prompt our compliance decisions. They are the most popular prompts precisely because they are the most reliable ones, those that normally point us toward the correct choice. That is why we employ the factors of reciprocation, consistency, social proof, liking, authority, and scarcity so often and so automatically in making our compliance decisions. Each, by itself, provides a highly reliable cue as to when we will be better off saying yes than no.

We are likely to use these lone cues when we don't have the inclination, time, energy, or cognitive resources to undertake a complete analysis of the situation. Where we are rushed, stressed, uncertain, indifferent, distracted, or fatigued, we tend to focus on less of the information available to us. When making decisions under these circumstances, we often revert to the rather primitive but necessary single-piece-of-good-evidence approach. All this leads to a jarring insight: With the sophisticated mental apparatus we have used to build world eminence as a species, we have created an environment so complex, fast-paced, and information-laden that we must increasingly deal with it in the fashion of the animals we long ago transcended.

From *The Tending Instinct: How Nurturing Is Essential to Who We Are and How We Live*

Shelley Taylor

Women's preferences for one another's company may come not only from the rewarding companionship that other women provide, but also from an evolutionary heritage that has selected for female friendship. Women and children have literally stayed alive over the centuries because women form friendships. Our most insistent needs—for food and safety—and our most vital tasks—the care of children and the sustenance of the social group— have been met through these ties. This is a new and potentially controversial view of women's friendships, but one that, I think, is amply supported.

Women have formed bonds with other women for hundreds of thousands, perhaps millions, of years. We know very little about these early ties. What knowledge we have comes from how we think early people may have lived, and from the hunter-and-gatherer societies that have survived to the present time. We know that early women were foragers, who combed the land in search of roots, tubers, and other nutritious foods. We believe that they may have coordinated their foraging activity so that no isolate would be picked off by a predator and so that conflict over food sources could be kept low. From current-day foraging societies we can infer that some food sharing among women also took place and that shared child-care arrangements, especially with kin, probably helped to free each woman to do her foraging.

As humans began to cultivate the land, women farmed together talking, singing, and laughing, as they still do in many countries, to let would-be predators know that they were there in numbers. From the Dogon women of Upper Volta who clean millet in village circles to the boisterous female relatives and friends who get Thanksgiving dinner on to the table, women prepare food together to nourish themselves and others. And they sew, knit, darn, and quilt while they talk through events of their lives and what they mean.

Would our prehistoric ancestors recognize the women's groups of the present? Certainly some of the forms they now assume would be unfamiliar. Women join book clubs to discuss a current bestseller, investment clubs to manage their money, and theater groups when their partners eschew cultural activities. But other groups would be readily recognizable, especially the sewing and mending circles and the most common of women's groups, the Mommy and Me toddler get-togethers. Our ancestors would probably also understand the spirit of such groups, even without knowing one word of our language, for women's groups have a distinctive style.

Throughout life, women seek more close friends than men do. Beginning in early childhood, girls develop more intimate friendships than boys do and create larger social networks for themselves. Groups of women share more secrets, disclose more details about their lives, and express more empathy and affection for one another than do members of men's groups. They sit closer together and touch one another more than men in groups do. Women confide their problems to one another, seeking help and understanding. Men do so much more rarely.

This inclination of women to bond together may be far older than we imagine, for the comfort that females enjoy in one another's company is not confined to humans; it is evident in animals as well. Psychologist Martha McClintock, who studies female reproductive hormones in animals, noticed a curious phenomenon in her Norway rats. When too few individual cages necessitated housing the females together in groups of about five, the rats lived 40 percent longer than when they were housed alone. This surprising finding led McClintock to rethink how to house her animals, since the convention of one rat to a cage originally developed to prevent male rats from attacking one another.

Biologist Sue Carter, a pioneer in investigations of social affiliation in animals, noticed a similar curiosity. Carter studies prairie voles, the small rodent best known for its tendency to form strong, lifelong male-female pairs, as humans often do. When conditions become stressful for the voles, males seek contact with their mates. Under the same stressful conditions, however, female voles turn not to their mates, but to their female "friends"—that is, the other females with whom they have previously been housed.

Intrigued by observations like these, primatologist Sally Mendoza and her colleagues at the Regional Primate Center in Davis, California, conducted an experimental study in which they took female squirrel monkeys out of their familiar cages and placed them in an unfamiliar environment, a move that usually distresses monkeys and leaves them agitated. Half the females were put in the strange environment alone, and the other half were put there in the company of their female cage mates. Those who had the company of their cage mates showed less distress than those who were put there alone, suggesting that these familiar females protected them against the stress of the new environment.

My interest in women's groups was initially piqued not by my own experiences but by these animal studies. For many years I have studied how people cope with stress; turning to the social group for safety and support, as I've noted, is one of the most common ways to do so. The fact that one can see a similar pattern in animals suggests that turning to others may have quite old biological origins. What particularly intrigued me, though, was how, in females, this desire for social contact seems to include a preference for female company. I began to look at women's groups with a new perspective and wondered whether they might represent more than the informal, pleasant social sororities they seem to be on the surface. Specifically, I began to think of them as possible buffers against stress.

I shared my interest with an anthropologist friend, a prominent investigator of social relationships. His immediate response was, "Women don't form groups." When I told him about the kinds of groups I was interested in—mother and toddler groups, fireside food preparation groups, and the like—his response was "Oh, those kinds of groups. Of course, women form those kinds of groups. They just don't form groups that matter."

I contend that these groups matter a great deal, not only to the women who participate in them, but to the networks and communities in which they are embedded. Women's networks form an inner core of social life that may be barely visible in nonstressful times, but that leap to prominence when life becomes more difficult. These bonds may be based on kinship—with mothers, sisters, aunts, or nieces or on simple friendship, but regardless, the needs they meet are fundamental ones: raising children, getting food, protecting against violence, and coping with stress.

Turning to the social group in times of stress is beneficial to both men and women, of course. Historically, however, the social group has probably been especially important to women because it provides safety for each woman and her children. For many centuries, women spent much of their adolescent and adult lives pregnant, nursing, or caring for their young. Unlike men, who could readily attack an invader or flee from a predator, women, as I've already noted, had to develop ways of managing stress that included protection for their young as well as themselves, and group life affords such protection. But why would a specific preference for the company of other females develop? And what needs would that preference for female company meet?

Our primate heritage provides a good place to look for answers to these questions. Although bonds among females may be almost invisible in human societies some of the time, they are starkly evident in other primate groups, most notably the Old World monkeys—gorillas, orangutans, baboons, macaque monkeys, chimpanzees, and bonobos—who are our closest relatives.

First, a bit of background: Each primate society is organized somewhat differently, but most feature a hierarchical structure with dominant animals at the top, who commandeer resources for themselves, and subordinates further down, whose resources are few. How important the dominance hierarchy is varies a lot among the species. Macaque monkeys are very dominance-oriented, for example, whereas bonobos are quite egalitarian. Males, for the most part, are more dominance-oriented than females, aggressively attempting to ascend the hierarchy and defend their position against other males. Dominance in females is often based on kinship—a daughter's position in the hierarchy is determined by who her mother is—and female-dominance hierarchies are usually more stable and somewhat less rancorous than their male counterparts.

In many primate societies, females stay in the troop in which they were born and males emigrate, which is one reason why kinship is the primary basis for female ties. But when females do emigrate, as is true among bonobos, friendships may actually be more important. Once settled in their new troops, female bonobos form intense, long-lasting bonds with other females. And even where bonds among females are based on kinship, unrelated females in several primate species form strong "friendships" as well.

How are these bonds expressed? Grooming, the practice of picking through the coat of one's companion to remove parasites, is one important way. Primatologist Robin Dunbar calls it the primate equivalent of talking on the phone. Depending on who grooms whom for how long and under what circumstances, grooming can communicate very complex messages such as solace, solidarity, amends making, or, by its absence, rejection. Grooming keeps a friend's coat clean and attractive, and it is also a very soothing, comforting activity. Mothers groom daughters, and sisters and friends groom one another, an activity that can consume up to 10 to 20 percent of an animal's waking time. When you consider that as much as 70 percent of a female primate's waking time may go to foraging for food, this means that grooming fills much of what remains, making it a primary leisure-time activity. Grooming of males by other males, on the other hand, is less common in most primate species, and nearly unheard of in some.

Female bonds among primates, then, are common, usually based on kin, sometimes based on "friendship," and maintained, in part, by grooming. What are the purposes of these alliances? Like mothers everywhere, female primates need to gather food and care for their young, and their female friends and relatives help them with these tasks. Indeed, primatologist Richard Wrangham believes that females' relationships with one another may have evolved primarily to manage food collection and distribution, with females sharing information about where the good food is, harvesting food collectively, and driving off rival groups of females from good food patches. Males need food, too, of course, but if they are providing primarily for their own needs, their food-gathering strategies don't have to take infants' needs into account to the same extent as mothers' strategies do. For females, getting enough food for everyone is vital.

Just as coordinating food allocation is a major task for females, so is child care, and sharing this responsibility benefits mothers and offspring alike. Like human mothers, primate mothers often sit on the outskirts of a group of youngsters, seemingly interested primarily in communicating with (grooming) one another or resting, but usually keeping one eye on the group, ready to intervene if the boisterous play gets out of hand. Not surprisingly, when all the females are watching out for them, infants benefit. They are less likely to wander into harm's way and be killed or die from neglect.

Sometimes females trade off child care as well, with kin, with "friends," or with younger female "baby-sitters." The benefits of these exchanges are not confined to convenience. When care of infants is shared among females, they grow faster, whether because their mothers are more free to forage for food, or because their sitters help feed them, or both. It's a good arrangement all around, and it has a significant by-product as well: younger females who have not yet given birth learn how to be mothers, which is vital to how well they care for their own infants later on.

All things considered, the female primate network can be an amazing little social system. Food gets distributed, babies are cared for, the mothers of the future get training, and everyone gets groomed and comforted in the process. This is the ideal situation, of course. Just as is true in groups of women, groups of female primates can go off in some unpleasant directions as well. Other females sometimes kill or eat babies rather than nurture them, and squabbles over food, friendships, or males can turn ugly. On the whole, though, if this system seems eerily familiar to many mothers, it is probably because, for the most part, it has been successful and has consequently made its way into our own genes and lives as well.

Bonds with other females also provide protection. If you know how often a female is groomed by others, and by whom, you can predict pretty well who will come to her aid if she is attacked by a female outside her group, the male in her own group, or an outside predator. Robin Dunbar describes such an encounter in Gelada baboons when the male head of a "harem" becomes too aggressive in his efforts to control the females:

> The male's attempts to ride herd on his females when they stray too far from him often backfire. The luckless victim's grooming partners invariably come to her aid. Standing shoulder-to-shoulder, they outface the male with outraged threats and furious barks of their own. The male will usually back off, and walk huffily away, endeavoring to maintain an air of ruffled dignity. However, occasionally, the male will persist, feeling, perhaps, unusually sensitive about his honor and security. This only leads to more of the group's females racing in to support their embattled sisters. The male invariably ends up being chased 'round the mountainside by his irate females in an impressive display of sisterly solidarity.

When strong female bonds are absent, males are often aggressive, even abusive, toward females. For example, although chimpanzees and bonobos are very closely related, male chimps take out their frustrations on females much more often than male bonobos do to female bonobos. This is in large part because bonds among female chimps are not as strong as they are among bonobos. Even among chimpanzees, however, when the environment becomes especially stressful or threatening, female bonds may strengthen to meet the challenge.

> It is not unusual for females in a captive chimpanzee colony to band together to protect themselves against an abusive male. Given that such female coalitions can deliver quite a beating, the male is in an understandable hurry to get out of their way. He watches the other sex from a safe distance if he has been lucky enough to escape. Because none of the females matches him in strength and speed, their solidarity is crucial.

Primatologist Sue Boinski found that female squirrel monkeys' ties to other females change in this fashion to cope with extreme stress. Like chimpanzees, female squirrel monkeys are typically lone foragers with relatively weak ties to other females. But during the period in which the females give birth, a plentiful supply of delicious little squirrel monkeys suddenly appears, attracting birds of prey. To reduce this threat, the previously solitary mothers begin traveling in close-knit groups. They often sit together, staring into the sky, swiveling their heads in search of the birds. Each time a falcon swoops down to pluck away a baby, it is mobbed by the vigilant females and driven off. Then, once the infants are mature enough to fend for themselves, the mothers return to their solitary foraging style. These intriguing animal studies suggest that female ties may be loose and variable in normal times but flexible enough to promote shared defense in stressful times.

This is the picture of female bonds that we get from primates: Together, females provide food, groom one another, take care of offspring, hold hostile males at bay, and come to one another's aid when threats appear. On the whole, this is a pretty fair characterization of women's bonds as well.

We'll start with food. Women seem to have a special relationship with food. It's not just that women are the ones who buy it, although they are, by a large margin, the food shoppers of the world. And it's not just that women prepare it, although this task, too, is more commonly a woman's province than a man's. Food seems to have a special meaning for women. When women want to celebrate a special occasion, they think of food. When they get together, eating is commonly the activity. "Having lunch" means something special to women that it doesn't necessarily mean to men. When women want to send a message of caring or affection to someone, they often cook for them. Men don't typically try new dishes out on one another or exchange recipes, as women do. And women's pathologies often revolve around food as well. Women are by no small margin the dieters, the anorexics, and the bulimics of the world. Women come by their interest—even obsession—with food quite honestly. Just as female primates did, early foraging women had the important job of ensuring that they and their offspring got fed. And the foraging mother faced a daunting task.

The human infant is vulnerable and matures slowly, requiring almost continuous care for the first few years of life, as every weary mother knows. Even after infancy, almost continual monitoring is needed to ensure the child's safety. Moreover, infants have an enormous need for food, estimated by one expert to be between 3 million and 10 million calories over the course of time it takes to bring an infant to maturity. Attempting to meet both her own and her offspring's nutritional needs by herself would have posed almost impossible demands on the foraging mother. She must have had help.

In many cases, that help would have come from the baby's father or from the woman's partner—sometimes, but not always, the same person. For a variety of reasons, however, this would not have been a reliable source of help, so much as an occasional one. Relationships with partners do not always last, and so fathers may have abandoned their responsibilities to an old family as they assumed obligations to a new one. Paternity may have been uncertain, and a man may have been unwilling to provide food for a child he doubted was his. Hunts were not always successful, and even when they were, the food might not have found its way to the hunter's offspring. So to whom did women turn to get the food they needed to bring their offspring to maturity? They relied heavily on ties with other women.

Sometimes they gave offspring to baby-sitters, typically girls who did not yet have children of their own, so they could forage more easily. Foraging is hard work. You have to move rocks and underbrush aside and then dig to get stubborn tubers out of the ground; trying to do so with an infant in tow makes the process even more difficult. Moreover, women foragers typically covered a lot of territory—an estimated 1,500 miles a year by some accounts—and to do so accompanied by an infant or child would have been difficult.

But baby-sitters solve only the problem of freeing the mother to find food more efficiently. They don't address the problem of how the mother was able to provide the sheer amount of food required to satisfy the caloric needs of both herself and her offspring. What may have solved this caloric conundrum was food sharing with female kin and friends. Closest kin are most likely to have helped—a mother, sister, grandmother, or aunt—but other women with whom a mother had forged ties may also have provided food as well. Friends or relatives with infants of their own may have helped out by suckling the hungry baby of a mother who was off foraging. This kind of milk sharing is still found in some present-day foraging groups. Older women who had already had their children but who were able to obtain more food than they needed probably shared food with mothers of young offspring as well. Indeed, in present-day African foraging societies, such as the Hadza and the !Kung, where grandmothers contribute to the care and feeding of their grandchildren, those children who have a living grandmother are more likely to survive.

Food gathering and child care were intimately tied to each other in early human existence. To some degree, that remains so today. Most women don't forage anymore, but they do other things to provide for their families—work, errands, chores—and the arrangements they make for child care with women friends and kin are similar, often startlingly so, to those that early women likely created for one another.

In particular, women continue to play the primary role in child care. I made this statement in a scientific paper recently, and a reviewer solemnly wagged a finger at me, pronouncing that with more egalitarian sex roles this is now much less true. I raced to the library to make sure I wasn't living on a different planet, and, yes, by a large margin, women continue to be the primary players in child care, both for their own children and for one another's. Women are more likely than men to stay home with children, and they do more child care than their husbands do, even when they work full-time. Baby-sitters are more commonly girls than boys, and child-care workers are more often women than men. The preferred form of child care continues to be care by a female relative.

Just as early humans did, modern women also exchange child care. Your kids come to our house where I watch them, and my kids go to your house where you watch them. It isn't that men can't or shouldn't care for kids. Men just don't do so to the degree that women do. So, as was true for our early ancestors, women get food and care for children with the help of the women around them.

QUESTIONS

1. Are the mental mechanisms that underlie pair-bonding conscious or unconscious?

2. Do you think hormones are likely to play an important role in male-female differences in bonding (see the selection by Angier in Chapter 12)? How could you test this possibility?

3. Cialdini explains how decisions about what to buy are easily influenced by superficial and irrelevant information. Do you think that our decisions about possible mates are as easily influenced by superficial or irrelevant information?

PERSONALITY

No two snowflakes are alike—and nor are any two human beings, not even "identical" twins. The science of personality aims, more perhaps than any other field of psychology, to understand "individual differences": what makes different human beings behave in different ways. Why is one person shy, another outgoing? Why are some people more obedient, others more rebellious?

In the film *28 UP*, a documentary about a group of British children, recorded at intervals of seven years, director Michael Apted used a series of real-life case studies to investigate the truth of an old Jesuit saying: "Give me a child until he is seven, and I will show you the man." In *Galen's Prophecy* (1994), psychologist Jerome Kagan goes one step farther, using the scientific method to investigate this very question systematically. By tracking children from infancy to adulthood, measuring everything from cortisol levels to how children interact with strangers, Kagan has developed a robust picture of the ways in which temperament does and does not change over time, proving once and for all that temperament is neither a pure product of our experience (as John Watson might have held) nor a fixed and immutable quality.

Judith Harris's selection from *The Nurture Assumption* (1998) starts in part with the remarkable finding (from studies of identical twins) that parenting style influences children's personality less than most people would have expected. In technical terms, being raised in the same family predicts very little. But this is not because nurture doesn't matter, it's because some of the biggest influences of the environment come from *outside* the home. Kids don't just grow up with their parents; they grow up with other kids. Harris challenges the "nurture assumption" not by arguing that children are genetically programmed automatons that pay no heed to their environment, but rather by emphasizing that children's natures lead them to be influenced by *other children*. If we are ever to understand how our children form their preferences, tastes, and values, we will need to understand more than just what happens at home.

Finally, in his article "Personality Plus," which originally appeared in the *New Yorker* (2004), journalist Malcom Gladwell discusses some of the most popular techniques researchers use to assess personality, noting how widely they are used in the workplace, yet also questioning whether personality is really something that can be reliably measured.

From *Galen's Prophecy: Temperament in Human Nature*

Jerome Kagan

Coll's strategy was straightforward.* She filmed 117 twenty-one-month-old Caucasian children—first- and later-born—as they encountered unfamiliar people, objects, and situations. After being greeted, the mother and infant were taken to a playroom with toys arranged on the rug. After five minutes of play, the examiner and mother joined the child on the floor, and the examiner modeled some acts that varied in complexity (for example, a doll talking on a telephone, three animals walking together through a rainstorm and then hiding under a cloth).

The examiner then withdrew without giving any special instructions to the child. Some children cried as the examiner moved away. We interpreted the distress as occasioned by the child's uncertainty about the implied obligation to imitate the examiner. After an additional period of play, an unfamiliar woman entered the room and sat on a chair for thirty seconds. Some children retreated to the mother; most stared. The woman then called the child by name and invited him to join her in performing some simple acts taken from a popular mental development assessment. Some children withdrew to the mother and would not approach. The unfamiliar woman then left, and the examiner returned to open up a set of curtains in a corner of the room, revealing a metal robot. The examiner encouraged the child to approach and touch the robot; some children refused and stood by their mothers. Finally, the examiner left and, upon a signal, the mother left the room, leaving the child alone. Some children cried as the mother left; others became distressed as the door closed.

Coll used fretting, crying, withdrawal, absence of spontaneous interactions with the examiner, and prolonged hesitation in approaching the

*Cynthia Garcia-Coll began this study in 1979.

robot or the stranger as signs of fear. The thirty-three children who displayed these behavioral signs of fear in a majority of the situations were classified as inhibited. The thirty-eight children who approached the unfamiliar woman and the robot, did not cry after the examiner modeled the acts, and did not stay close to the mother during the play period or retreat to her when unfamiliarity occurred were classified as uninhibited. The behaviors of the remaining forty-seven children were inconsistent, and these children were not followed longitudinally.

Most of the children (80 percent) who had been classified as either inhibited or uninhibited returned to the same room several weeks later and were taken through the same unfamiliar procedures in order to guarantee that their initial behavior was stable and not a temporary reaction. Fortunately each group retained the style displayed earlier (the correlation across the two sessions was .63). Incidentally, the mothers were asked to rate their children on shyness, fearfulness, and sociability. Even though Coll had selected extreme groups of inhibited and uninhibited children, the correlation between the behavior observed in the laboratory and the parents' descriptions of their children was only 0.5, supporting the claim . . . that parents are not perfect observers of these qualities.

The children were also brought to a small laboratory room where heart rate and heart rate variability in response to a set of varied stimuli were measured. The inhibited children had a less variable heart rate than the uninhibited children, replicating the results with the Fels adults and with the Chinese children in the day care study.

Nancy Snidman, who joined the laboratory soon after the selection of this first cohort, was interested in applying the techniques of spectral analysis of heart rate to these two temperament groups, because spectral analysis is a more sensitive index of sympathetic reactivity than the simpler measures of heart rate or heart rate variability. Snidman chose to study slightly older children—thirty-one months old—because spectral analysis requires the child to remain very still and twenty-one-month-olds find it difficult to inhibit movement. An added motivation for selecting a second sample was the modest size of Coll's groups (thirty-three inhibited and thirty-eight uninhibited children), which might become even smaller through attrition. Snidman assumed that if a thirty-one-month-old was extremely inhibited or uninhibited it was likely that these behaviors were the product of temperamental biases we would have seen earlier. We have learned that this assumption is not completely warranted.

Further, Snidman had to use a different assessment because Coll's procedures were not sufficiently novel to provoke much fear in two-and-a-half-year-olds. Earlier research had revealed that encountering an unfamiliar child of the same age and sex was a powerful way to produce variation in inhibited behavior. Snidman filmed a large number of pairs of thirty-one-month-olds of the same sex as they played together in a large room with both mothers present. She coded the amount of time the child remained close to the mother, hesitation in initiating play, spontaneous speech, and social approaches to the unfamiliar peer. At the end of half an hour of play a woman dressed in an unusual costume—a plastic cover over her head and torso—entered and, after a period of silence, invited the two children to approach her. Some did approach within the first thirty seconds; others retreated to their mothers and never came close to the intruder. About 15 percent of the total sample were unusually shy and timid with both the unfamiliar child and the adult stranger; another 15 percent were sociable and bold. Thus, twenty-six children were classified as inhibited and twenty-three as uninhibited.

Both cohorts of children—Coll's as well as Snidman's—were assessed again when they were approximately four, five-and-a-half, seven-and-a-half, and thirteen years of age in order to answer three questions: (1) How many children in each of the two temperamental groups retained their characteristic behavioral style? (2) Did these styles correlate with other theoretically relevant characteristics? (3) Did the two groups differ on peripheral physiological measures of limbic excitability?

The indexes of inhibited and uninhibited behavior at four years of age were based on reactions with an unfamiliar child of the same age and sex. The primary variables were hesitation to approach the other child, time staring at the other child, and time spent near the mother.

The assessment at five-and-a-half years was made in several situations on different days. One index of inhibited behavior was based on reluctance to explore three novel objects in a small, unfamiliar room. A second index, based on observations in the child's own kindergarten classroom, was derived from the total time the child was alone, staring at another child, or not engaged in any social interaction. A third index of inhibition was based on the amount of spontaneous conversation with, as well as glances at, the examiner during a one-hour battery in which a variety of cognitive tasks were administered. A final source of evidence was behavior with an unfamiliar peer of the same age and sex in a thirty-minute play session. These four separate sources of information on each child were combined into an aggregate index of inhibited behavior.

The evaluation at seven-and-a-half years was also conducted on different days. One index was derived from behavior with seven to ten unfamiliar children of the same age and sex who played for ninety minutes in a large room. Initially the children played alone for about ten minutes. Two women then entered and told the children that the plan for the session was team competitions across a series of games. There were five- to seven-minute intervals between games during which no adult was in the room. The index of inhibition was based on the total time the child was spatially distant from all other children during the free-play intervals, as well as the lack of spontaneous conversation with the other children and the adult examiners across the entire session. The second situation, a laboratory battery with an unfamiliar female examiner, produced an index of inhibition based on the elapsed time until the child had made six spontaneous comments to the examiner as well as the total number of spontaneous comments. As at four and five-and-a-half years, an aggregate index of inhibited behavior at seven-and-a-half years was created by averaging the standard scores derived from the separate assessments.

Ideally, all the evaluations should have been equally sensitive assessments of the two temperamental styles. That is unlikely. We are relatively certain that the assessment at five-and-a-half years was not as sensitive as the others, because one source of evidence came from observation of the child with a single unfamiliar peer. We have since learned that a single unfamiliar child does not generate as much uncertainty in a five-year-old as it does in a two-, three-, or four-year-old.

Preservation of Temperament

We consider first the preservation of the two temperamental profiles from the original classification at twenty-one or thirty-one months to seven-and-a-half years. Over three-fourths (77 percent) of the children classified originally as inhibited (from both the Coll and the Snidman cohorts) had an aggregate index above the mean value, reflecting an inhibited style, while three-fourths (73 percent) of those classified as uninhibited had an aggregate score below the mean. We also applied a more rigorous criterion. To be classified as inhibited (or uninhibited), a child's aggregate index at age seven-and-a-half had to be at least 0.6 standard deviations above (or below) the mean. This analysis revealed that 25 percent of the originally inhibited children met this stiffer criterion for inhibition, while only 5 percent (two children) were uninhibited; 42 percent of the original uninhibited group were uninhibited, and only one child was inhibited (see Figure 1). Thus, one-third of the children had preserved their original temperamental style, whereas only three children had changed from one category to the other. Because the children classified originally as inhibited made up about 20 percent of the total population sampled, we estimate that between 5 and 10 percent of a typical population of school-age children are very inhibited in their public behavior. This figure matches Kenneth Rubin's claim that 10 percent Toronto of second-graders are extreme social isolates.

A typical inhibited seven-and-a-half-year-old stayed at the periphery of the large group of peers, reading a book, painting at an easel, or standing in a corner quietly watching another child. This vigilant staring is also seen in timid primates. Among a small group of macaque monkeys who were observed regularly from infancy to old age (twenty years in the monkey), the most stable individual behavior—a "personality" trait—was staring at another animal from a distance ($r = 0.9$). In contrast to the inhibited child, who remained apart from others, the uninhibited child was talkative, initiated

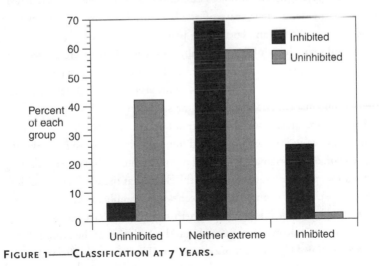

FIGURE 1——CLASSIFICATION AT 7 YEARS.

interaction, often with smiling and laughter, and showed a vitality that was missing from the demeanor of the inhibited child.

Spontaneous speech with children or adults was an unusually sensitive index of each type. Each animal species has a favored, biologically prepared reaction to novelty. Rabbits freeze, rhesus monkeys display a retraction of the muscles of the lower face called a grimace, cats arch their back. In children, silence is a common reaction to uncertainty. The inhibited children were very quiet with unfamiliar peers and adults at every age, although the absence of speech distinguished the two groups most clearly at seven years. About 90 percent of the seven-year-old inhibited children either uttered less than thirty spontaneous comments with the examiner during the long individual testing session or took longer than five minutes to offer their sixth spontaneous comment. Two-thirds of the uninhibited children spoke more than thirty times, and their first six comments occurred in the first five minutes of the session.

Steven Reznick studied an independent group of one hundred children who had backgrounds similar to these inhibited and uninhibited children but were not selected originally on any behavioral criteria. These children were observed at fourteen, twenty, thirty-two, and forty-eight months in unfamiliar rooms with unfamiliar objects, people, and events. The usual criteria of hesitancy in approaching unfamiliar objects and time proximal to the mother were applied to the children's behaviors in response to these unfamiliar incentives, creating a continuous index of behavioral inhibition. There was preservation of inhibited and uninhibited behavior from fourteen or twenty months to four years of age but only for those children whose scores were in the top and bottom 20 percent of the index of inhibition in the second year. These inhibited and uninhibited children were observed at five-and-a-half years as they interacted with an unfamiliar female examiner and participated in a peer play session with seven to nine unfamiliar children of the same sex and age—the same situation described for the seven-and-a-half-year-olds. Once again, restraint on spontaneous speech with the adult examiner and the unfamiliar children provided the most sensitive differentiation of the originally inhibited or uninhibited children. This finding with an independent group supports the claim that there is a powerful link between restraint of spontaneous speech with unfamiliar people and a temperamental bias to be inhibited, as other psychologists have noted.

Terrence Deacon has suggested that the evolution of the primate brain was accompanied by a rich set of connections between the prefrontal cortex and the limbic area, which gave the primate frontal lobe increased control of the emotionally based vocalizations mediated by limbic sites. Perhaps cessation of speech is a sensitive sign of fear to novelty because of activation of an inhibitory circuit that involves the frontal cortex, anterior cingulate, central gray, and amygdala.

Inhibited and uninhibited children differ at home as well as at school. When the children in cohort one were thirty-one months old and those in cohort two forty-three months, they were visited at home by an unfamiliar woman who coded how long it took the child to approach her and play with toys she had brought and the duration of time the child spent close to the mother. The children classified earlier as inhibited took several minutes before initiating contact with the examiner; many retreated to the mother and remained quiet. Most of the uninhibited children approached the stranger within several seconds and were quite vocal.

We noted earlier that when the children were five years old they were observed in their kindergarten classrooms by Michelle Gersten. The inhibited children were clearly more subdued and isolated. One inhibited boy seemed to be in his own world at school. Most of the day he stared at other children from the periphery of the room, and often he ran and hid behind a tree. One inhibited girl, who spent most of the time alone, was easily intimidated by the boys in the room and froze when a boy intruded into her space. A second inhibited girl usually failed to respond when another child spoke to her, and she spent much of the time staring at other children. Another inhibited girl displayed an unusual response following a quarrel with a peer. She left the scene, sat on a chair with her arms folded, and screamed when anyone approached. After several minutes in this posture she crawled under a table and stared at the other children. These very unusual actions were never observed in any uninhibited child. Kenneth Rubin, who studies school children in Canada, has noted that inhibited eight-year-olds are not always unpopular with peers, but they are often perceived as sensitive, shy, and withdrawn.

The Adolescent Profile

The children in Coll's and Snidman's samples were seen last when they were between twelve and fourteen years old; thirty-six inhibited and twenty-eight uninhibited youth came to the laboratory for a two-hour assessment with an unfamiliar female examiner and, on a separate occasion, for a long interview with Carl Schwartz, a child psychiatrist, who was responsible for the adolescent assessment. The most striking result was that the external demeanor of most children had changed little since their assessment at age seven. Spontaneous speech and smiling during the lengthy session with the examiner were the most distinguishing features. The adolescents who had been classed as inhibited eleven years earlier were quieter and smiled much less often than the uninhibited children. Many inhibited youth answered only the questions posed and neither elaborated nor asked any questions. The difference between the groups in spontaneous smiling was more striking. Uninhibited children smiled as they greeted the examiner, and many smiled as they failed a difficult test item, as if they were laughing at themselves. Inhibited children rarely smiled following failure, and most remained dour throughout the battery.

When ratings of spontaneous conversation and smiling were combined to create indexes of an inhibited or uninhibited style, two-thirds of the children who had remained inhibited from the second to the seventh year were quiet and serious. Only five were as lively and affectively spontaneous as the typical uninhibited child. Among the youth who had been uninhibited from the second to the seventh year, 40 percent had preserved that style from age seven to age thirteen; only two had become unusually subdued and quiet. Thus about one-half of the adolescents retained their expected behavioral demeanor, while only 15 percent had changed in a major way.

These data represent remarkable *stability* over an eleven-year interval. A one-hour laboratory observation of children at twenty-one or thirty-one months detected the two temperamental types with sufficient sensitivity that over one-half were still displaying some of the salient features of their category, while only seven children had seriously changed their style. This result should quiet those psychologists who claim that laboratory observations cannot be as revealing as parental report. No longitudinal study of the relation between parental descriptions of two-year-olds and the behavior of adolescents has come close to revealing this degree of preservation of two such complex psychological qualities.

From *The Nurture Assumption:*
Why Children Turn Out the Way They Do

Judith Rich Harris

> They fuck you up, your mum and dad.
> They may not mean to, but they do.
> They fill you with the faults they had
> And add some extra, just for you.
> —*Philip Larkin*

Poor old Mum and Dad: publicly accused by their son, the poet, and never given a chance to reply to his charges. They shall have one now, if I may take the liberty of speaking for them.

> How sharper than a serpent's tooth
> To hear your child make such a fuss.
> It isn't fair—it's not the truth—
> He's fucked up, yes, but not by us.

Philip's mum and dad are not on trial here, however. The defendant is the nurture assumption itself, which their son summed up so succinctly in his four lines of doggerel. Ladies and gentlemen of the jury, I ask you to find the defendant guilty of fraud and grand larceny. The people have been robbed of the truth and the nurture assumption is the perpetrator.

Fooling the People All of the Time

Philip Larkin isn't the only one who blames his failings on his parents. Everybody does (even, in my weaker moments, me). It sure beats blaming yourself. But self-interest alone cannot account for the way the nurture assumption has worked itself so deeply into our culture. Nor is the explanation I gave [earlier]—that it's a product of the combined influence of psychoanalytic theory (Freud) and behaviorism (Watson and Skinner)—enough to account for its pervasiveness. What started out as part of academic psychology has long since spread beyond its ivory tower origins. Talk-show hosts and talk-show guests, poets and potato farmers, your accountant and your kids—they all blame their parents for their own failings and themselves for their kids'.

Parenting has been oversold. You have been led to believe that you have more of an influence on your child's personality than you really do. At the beginning of the book I quoted the science journalist who said we don't have to wait for the day when parents can choose their children's genes because parents already have a good deal of power to determine how their children will turn out. "Parents play the largest and most important role in shaping their children's sense of themselves," said another science journalist in the pages of the *New York Times*. You are expected to give them a positive sense of themselves by showering them with praise and physical affection. The professional advice-giver who calls herself "Dr. Mom" tells you to make sure to give your child "daily nonverbal messages of love and acceptance." All children need touching and hugging, she says, no matter how old they get. If you do the job right, your child will emerge happy and self-confident, according to Penelope Leach, another professional advice-giver. "His foundations are laid in his relationship with you and all that you have taught him." Physical punishment and verbal criticism are outlawed by the advice-givers. You don't tell the child that he was bad, you tell him that what he did was bad. No, better not go even that far: tell him that what he did made you feel bad.

Kids are not that fragile. They are tougher than you think. They have to be, because the world out there does not handle them with kid gloves. At home they might hear "What you did made me feel bad," but out on the playground it's "You shithead!"

The nurture assumption is the product of a culture that has as its motto, We can overcome. With our dazzling electronic devices, our magical biochemical elixirs, we can overcome nature. Sure, children are born different, but that's no problem. Just put them through this marvelous machine here—step right up, ladies and gentlemen!—and add our special patented mixture of love, limits, time-outs, and educational toys. Voilá! A happy, smart, well-adjusted, self-confident person!

Perhaps it's a fin-de-siècle phenomenon: the tendency to carry things to extreme, to push ideas beyond their logical limits. The nurture assumption has become so overblown, so oppressive in the demands it makes upon parents, that it looks to be past ripe and well on its way to rot.

First of All, Do No Harm

I wouldn't feel so strongly about it if I thought it was a harmless fantasy. After all, the nurture assumption might have some beneficial side effects. At least in theory, it should make parents kinder. If they think that any mistake they make could mark their kids for life, shouldn't that encourage them to be more careful? To bite back those mean words? To spare the rod? It's a nice thought, but there are no signs of a decline in parental abusiveness. Nor are there any signs that children are happier today than they were two or three generations ago.

There is no evidence that the nurture assumption has done any real good. But it has done some real harm. It has put a terrible burden of guilt on parents unfortunate enough to have a child whose pass through the marvelous machine has for some reason failed to produce a happy, smart, well-adjusted, self-confident person. Not only must these parents suffer the pain of having a child who is difficult to live with or who fails in some other way to live up to the community's standards: they must also bear the community's opprobrium. Sometimes it's more than mere opprobrium: sometimes they are held legally responsible. Fined. Threatened with jail sentences.

The nurture assumption has turned children into objects of anxiety. Parents are nervous about doing the wrong thing, fearful that a stray word or glance might ruin their child's chances forever. Not only have they become servants to their children: they have been declared unsatisfactory servants, because the standards set by the promulgators of the nurture assumption are so high that no one can meet them. Parents who lack the time to get a full night's sleep are being told that they're not giving their kids enough quality time. Parents are being made to feel that they've fallen short. They try to make it up to their kids by buying them lots of toys. The modern American child owns an astonishing quantity of toys.

The nurture assumption has introduced an element of phoniness to family life. It has made sincere expressions of love meaningless because they are drowned out by the obligatory, feigned expressions of love.

The nurture assumption has also held back the progress of scientific inquiry. The proliferation of meaningless research—one more dreary study showing a correlation between parents' sighs and children's yawns—has been substituted for useful investigation. Here are some of the things that researchers *should* be looking at, a few of the questions they *should* be asking. How can we keep a classroom of children from splitting up into two dichotomous groups, pro-school and anti-school? How do some teachers, some schools, some cultures, manage to prevent this split and keep the kids united and motivated? How can we keep kids who start out with disadvantageous personality characteristics from getting worse? How can we step in and break the vicious cycle of aggressive kids becoming more aggressive because in childhood they are rejected by their peers and in adolescence they get together with others like themselves? Is there any way to influence the norms of children's groups for the better? Is there any way to keep the larger culture from having deleterious effects on the norms of teenagers' groups? How many does it take to make a group?

I have been unable, in this book, to give you answers to these questions because the research has not yet been done.

The Case for the Defense

According to the nurture assumption, parents have important effects on the way their children turn out. *Important* effects. We are not talking about an IQ point here or there, or one more "yes" on a questionnaire of a hundred items. We are talking about popular versus friendless, college graduate versus high school dropout, neurotic versus well-adjusted, virgin versus pregnant. We are talking about psychological characteristics that affect how you behave and how well you do in life—characteristics that are noticeable to you and to the people you live and work with. Characteristics that will remain with you for the rest of your days. That's what people think, isn't it? That parents have big effects on their children, lasting effects.

But if they do have effects, it must be a different effect for each child, because children raised by the same parents do not turn out alike, once you skim off the similarities due to shared genes. Two adopted children reared in the same home are no more similar in personality than two adopted children reared in separate homes. A pair of identical twins reared in the same home are no more alike than a pair reared in separate homes. Whatever the home is doing to the children who grow up in it, it is not making them more conscientious, or less sociable, or more aggressive, or less anxious, or more likely to have a happy marriage. At least, it's not doing any of these things to all of them.

The behavioral geneticists were the ones who made this discovery and it put them in a pickle, because most of them do believe in the importance of the home environment, just like everyone else. So they came up with the idea that what matters in the home are the things that *differ* for each child who lives there. The things that two siblings have in common had been shown not to matter—or at least to have no predictable effects—so the things the siblings *don't* have in common were left to bear the full weight of supporting the nurture assumption.

This is not quite as far-fetched as it sounds. After all, there's no reason to expect parents to treat their children all alike. Shouldn't good parents want each of their children to be unique, each to do whatever he or she does best? It's the Marxist view of parenting: from each according to his abilities, to each according to his needs.

And it's true, to a point. Yes, parents should want their children to be different, at least in some ways. If the first child is active and talkative, a quiet one would be a welcome change. If the first is a pianist, they might be perfectly happy to have the second one take up the tuba. But that doesn't mean they would be equally happy to have the second one become a prizefighter or a drug dealer. When our second child came along, my husband and I didn't say, "Well, we have one academic achiever, no point doing *that* again. Let's make the second one into something else." On the contrary, we could have put up quite nicely with the boredom of having two academic achievers. There are certain qualities parents would like to see in all their children—kindness, conscientiousness, intelligence—and other qualities they are willing to let vary within reasonable limits. But the findings for the universally desired qualities are the same as for the optional ones: no evidence of a long-term effect of the home environment.

Parents treat each of their children differently and the children *are* different—these two facts are indisputable. But for the behavioral geneticists to hold on to the nurture assumption, it is necessary for them to show that the differences in parental behavior are producing or contributing to the differences among the children and are not just a response to preexisting differences. That has not been shown. In fact, there is evidence that parental treatment is actually more uniform than the children themselves—that there is more variation in the way two siblings behave than in the way their parents treat them.

One thing that could have worked in favor of the nurture assumption, but didn't, is birth order. Parents treat firstborns and laterborns differently, and the differential treatment isn't just a response to characteristics the kids were born with. But researchers have been trying for more than half a century to find convincing proof that birth order leaves lasting marks on personality and their efforts have not panned out. Nor have efforts to show differences in personality between only children and children with siblings. If parents have major effects on their children, how come they don't mess up the personality of the only child?

These two disappointments—no birth order effects, no only-child effect—should knock the last remaining prop from under the nurture assumption.

Hmm, it hasn't fallen down yet; something still seems to be holding it up. Ah yes, I see it. It is the claim that the behavioral genetic evidence—the data showing that the overall home environment has no predictable effects—does not cover a wide enough range of home environments. The trouble is that all the subjects came from "good-enough" homes—homes within the normal range. Some theoreticians are now willing to admit in public that it doesn't matter which home a child grows up in, as long as it is within the range of normal, good-enough homes. But they still think it is possible that homes *outside* the normal range—that is, exceptionally bad homes—have an effect on the child.

What they're saying is that there's no relationship between the goodness of the home and the goodness of the offspring over the entire range of homes for which they have data, the range that begins at "excellent" and extends through "bad" but stops short of "terrible." The relationship holds only for the small proportion of homes for which they do not have data. All the evidence they've collected so far—and they've collected a great deal of it—either is irrelevant or indicates that the nurture assumption is wrong. But there is a little bit of evidence they haven't collected yet, and *that*, they believe, will prove that the nurture assumption is right.

It's an awfully thin prop. The idea is that ordinary, run-of-the-mill parents like you and me don't have any distinctive effects on our children: we are interchangeable, like factory workers. The only parents who do have distinctive effects are the super-bad ones who abuse their kids so severely they wind up in the hospital, or who leave them unattended in cold apartments stinking with unchanged diapers and rotted food. It's the nurture assumption's last slim hope: that a home environment can be bad enough to inflict permanent damage on the children who grow up in it.

I will leave the proponents of the nurture assumption clinging to their last slim hope, that their assumption might hold true for the small proportion of families that qualify as super-bad. It does not hold true for the vast majority of families. It does not hold for families like yours and mine. There is no justification for using it as a weapon against ordinary parents whose children are not turning out quite the way we hoped they would.

Where Did They Go Wrong?

How are children shaped by the experiences they have while they are growing up? That is the question the nurture assumption was designed to answer. The answer is wrong because it is based on a number of mistaken ideas about children.

The first mistake has to do with the child's environment. The natural environment of the child was assumed to be the nuclear family—the arrangement that was so popular during the first half of this century. Mother, father, two or three kids, living cozily together in a private house. But there is nothing particularly natural about this arrangement. The separateness of the nuclear family—its ability to carry on its activities free from the prying eyes of neighbors—is a modern invention, only a few hundred years old. The monogamous bond between one man and one woman is also something of a novelty. In 80 percent of the cultures known to anthropologists, men who could afford them have been allowed extra wives. Polygyny is ancient and widespread in our species. Children have often been required to share their fathers with the children of their father's other wives. Or they've had to grow up without a father or without a mother, because parental death was as prevalent in the past as parental divorce is today.

The second mistake has to do with the nature of socialization. A child's job is not to learn how to behave like all the other people in his or her society, because all the other people in the society do not behave alike. In every society, acceptable behavior depends on whether you're a child or an adult, a male or a female. Children have to learn how to behave like the other people in their own social category. In most cases they do this willingly. Socialization is not something that grownups do to kids—it is something kids do to themselves.

The third mistake has to do with the nature of learning. It was assumed that learned behavior is carried along like a backpack from one place to another—from the home to the schoolyard, for example—even though it has always been clear that people of every age behave differently in different social contexts. They behave differently because they have had different experiences—in one place they are praised, in another they are laughed at—and because different behaviors are called for. It was also assumed, also incorrectly, that if children behave one way at home and in a different way in the schoolyard, it must be the home behavior that matters most.

The fourth mistake has to do with the nature of nature—of heredity. The power of the genes has still not been given its due, even though everybody has heard the stories about the separated identical twins who meet in adulthood and find they are both wearing blue shirts with pockets on both sides and epaulets on the shoulders. Philip Larkin noticed that he shared many of his faults with his parents, but that did not give him the idea that he inherited them: he thought it was something his parents did to him after he was born.

The fifth mistake is to ignore our evolutionary history and the fact that, for millions of years, our ancestors lived in groups. It was the group that enabled those delicate creatures, unequipped with fangs or claws, to survive in an environment that did have fangs and claws. But animal predators were not their greatest threat: the most dangerous creatures in their world were the members of other groups. That is still true today.

The Alternative: Group Socialization Theory

The group is the natural environment of the child. Starting with that assumption takes us in a different direction. Think of childhood as the time when young humans turn themselves into accepted and valued members of their group, because that is what they needed to do in ancestral times.

During childhood, children learn to behave the way people of their age and sex are expected to behave in their society. Socialization is the process of adapting one's behavior to that of the other members of one's social category. In the novel *The Shipping News*, a father is counseled by his aunt to put off worrying about his young daughter's peculiarities:

> "Why don't you just wait, Nephew. See how it goes. She starts school in September... I agree with you that she's different, you might say she is a bit strange sometimes, but you know, we're all different though we may pretend otherwise. We're all strange inside. We learn how to disguise our differentness as we grow up. Bunny doesn't do that yet."

We learn how to disguise our differentness; socialization makes us less strange. But the disguise tends to wear thin later in life. I see socialization as a sort of hourglass: you start out with a bunch of disparate individuals and as they are squeezed together the pressure of the group makes them more alike. Then in adulthood the pressure gradually lets up and individual differences reassert themselves. People get more peculiar as they grow older because they stop bothering to disguise their differentness. The penalties for being different are not so severe.

Children identify with a group of others like themselves and take on the norms of the group. They don't identify with their parents because parents are not people like themselves—parents are grownups. Children think of themselves as kids, or, if there are enough of them, as girls and boys, and these are the groups in which they are socialized. Most socialization occurs today in same-age, same-sex groups because developed societies make it possible for children to form such groups. In the past, when humans were spread thinly across the planet, children were socialized in mixed-age, mixed-sex groups.

There has always been a bond between parents and their children, but the intense, guilt-ridden form of parenting we see today is unprecedented. In societies that don't send their kids to school and have not yet been penetrated by the advice-givers, children learn most of what they need to know from other children. Although parenting styles differ drastically from one culture to another—too hard in some places, too soft in others—children's groups are pretty much the same around the world. That is why children get socialized in every society, even though their parents don't read Dr. Spock. Their brains develop normally in every society too, even though their parents don't read *Goodnight Moon*.

Modern children do learn things from their parents; they bring to the group what they learned at home. The language their parents taught them is retained if it turns out that the other kids speak the same language, and the same is true for other aspects of the culture. Since most children grow up in culturally homogeneous neighborhoods—their parents speak the same language and have the same culture as the parents of their peers—most children are able to retain a good deal of what they learned at home. This makes it look as though the parents are the conveyers of the culture, but they are not: the peer group is. If the peer group's culture differs from the parents', the peer group's always wins. The child of immigrant parents or deaf parents invariably learns the language of her peers and favors it over the language her parents taught her. It becomes her native language.

You can see it happening as early as nursery school, when three-year-olds start bringing home the accents of their peers. Perhaps it begins even earlier than that. Psychologists Susan Savage and Terry Kit-fong Au tell this story in a recent issue of the journal *Child Development:*

> A baby we know had to face a dilemma very early on. From the age of about 12 months on, she was quite successful in requesting a bottle by saying "Nai nai!" (the Chinese term for milk) to her parents. Meanwhile, she noticed that other babies at her day-care center got their bottles by saying "Ba ba!" and followed suit at age 15 months. The demands of leading a double life apparently were too great for her to bear. A day or two later, when her mother asked "Nai nai?" she shook her head vigorously and said emphatically "Ba ba!"

Even when their parents belong to the same culture as the parents of their peers, children cannot count on being able to export the behaviors they acquired at home. A boy can whine and complain with impunity at home; he can express anxiety and affection. But in the peer group he is expected to be tough and cool. It is the tough, cool persona that will become his public personality and that he will carry with him to adulthood. The personality acquired at home won't be lost completely, however: it will turn up at Christmas dinners like the Ghost of Christmas Past.

In the peer groups of childhood and adolescence, kids take on the behaviors and attitudes of their peers and contrast themselves with the members of other groups—groups that differ in sex or race or social class or in their propensities and interests. The differences between these groups widen because the members of each group like their own group best and are at pains to distinguish themselves from the others. Differences *within* the group widen, too, especially when the group is not actively engaged in competing with another group. At the same time that children are becoming more similar to their peers in some ways, they are becoming more distinctive in other ways. Children learn about themselves by comparing themselves to their groupmates. They vie for status within the group; they win or lose. They are typecast by their peers; they choose or are chosen for different niches. Identical twins do not end up with identical personalities, even if they are members of the same peer group, because they have different experiences within the group.

Experiences in childhood and adolescent peer groups modify children's personalities in ways they will carry with them to adulthood. Group socialization theory makes this prediction: that children would develop into the same sort of adults if we left their lives outside the home unchanged—left them in their schools and their neighborhoods—but switched all the parents around.

A Penny for Your Thoughts

Arguments based on scientific evidence are not enough to change your mind. Your belief in the nurture assumption is not based on cold science but on feelings, thoughts, and memories. If your parents weren't important in your personal history—if they didn't have a powerful influence on you—why is it that your memories of childhood, along with so many of the memories you've stored away since then, have your parents playing leading roles? Why are they so often in your thoughts?

In his book *How the Mind Works*, evolutionary psychologist Steven Pinker discusses the fact that the conscious mind has access to some kinds of information and not to others.

> I ask, "A penny for your thoughts?" You reply by telling me the content of your daydreams, your plans for the day, your aches and itches, and the colors, shapes, and sounds in front of you. But you cannot tell me about the enzymes secreted by your stomach, the current settings of your heart and breathing rate, the computations in your brain that recover 3-D shapes from the 2-D retinas, the rules of syntax that order the words as you speak, or the sequence of muscle contractions that allow you to pick up a glass.

It isn't that your daydreams and itches are more important than the computations in your brain that enable you to see three-dimensional objects or speak grammatical sentences or pick up a glass. It's just that some of these things are accessible to consciousness and some of them aren't.

The other thing about the way the mind works (as Pinker and his fellow evolutionary psychologists have pointed out) is that it's modular. The mind is composed of a number of specialized departments, each collecting its own data and issuing its own reports or orders. Just as the body is organized into physical organs that each do one specific job—the lungs oxygenate the blood, the heart pumps it around the body—so the mind is organized into mental organs or modules or departments. One department lets you see the world in three dimensions, another enables you to pick up the glass. Some of the mind's departments issue reports that are accessible to consciousness; others do not.

I believe the human mind has at least two different departments for dealing with social behavior. One has to do with personal relationships, the other has to do with groups.

The group department has a long history and is found in many species. Fish, for example, swim around in schools. They have to adapt their behavior to the group's but they don't have to recognize their schoolmates. Though they may distinguish between males and females, between bigger fish and smaller ones, between kin and nonkin, they don't remember individuals, not even their own children.

The social life of primates is more complex. Primates, too, have to adapt their behavior to the group's, but they also have to keep track of the individuals in their lives. They must learn which members of their community they can count on for support and which they'd better keep away from. It's a talent that has flowered in our species. Humans remember who did them a favor and who owes them one. They know—both from personal experience and by word of mouth—who can be trusted and who cannot be. They hold grudges, sometimes forever, against those who did them wrong, and they look for opportunities to take revenge. And those who did the wrongs had better not forget who their victims were. We have very good memories for people. Our brains have a special area devoted to recognizing faces.

The department of the brain that keeps track of relationships is accessible to the conscious mind. The department of the brain that adapts your behavior to that of your group is no less important but it is less accessible to consciousness. A lot of its work goes on at an automatic level, like the muscle movements that enable you to pick up the glass.

Much of the information we collect about the world is collected unconsciously. We don't know how we know many of the things we know; we just know them. Children learn that red fruits are sweeter than green ones and if you give them a choice they'll pick the red one, but they can't tell you why. The gathering of data, the construction of categories, and the averaging of data within categories was all carried out below the level of consciousness.

The processes that I have been talking about in this book generally go on below the level of consciousness. We identify with a group of people. We learn to speak and behave like these people; we take on their attitudes. We adapt our speech and behavior to different social contexts. We develop stereotypes of our own group and of other groups. These things can be brought into consciousness but that's not where they live. In this book I have been talking about things that children do without noticing them, without having to exert conscious effort. It leaves the tops of their minds free to do other things.

Groups and relationships: they are both important to us but in different ways. Our childhood experiences with peers and our experiences at home with our parents are important to us in different ways.

The bond between parent and child lasts a lifetime. We kiss our parents goodbye not once but many times; we do not lose track of them. Each visit home gives us opportunities to take out family memories and look at them again. Meanwhile, our childhood friends have scattered to the winds and we've forgotten what happened on the playground.

When you think about childhood you think about your parents. Blame it on the relationship department of your mind, which has usurped more than its rightful share of your thoughts and memories.

As for what's wrong with you: don't blame it on your parents.

Personality Plus

Malcolm Gladwell

1.

When Alexander (Sandy) Nininger was twenty-three, and newly commissioned as a lieutenant in the United States Army, he was sent to the South Pacific to serve with the 57th Infantry of the Philippine Scouts. It was January, 1942. The Japanese had just seized Philippine ports at Vigan, Legazpi, Lamon Bay, and Lingayen, and forced the American and Philippine forces to retreat into Bataan, a rugged peninsula on the South China Sea. There, besieged and outnumbered, the Americans set to work building a defensive line, digging foxholes and constructing dikes and clearing underbrush to provide unobstructed sight lines for rifles and machine guns. Nininger's men were on the line's right flank. They labored day and night. The heat and the mosquitoes were nearly unbearable.

Quiet by nature, Nininger was tall and slender, with wavy blond hair. As Franklin M. Reck recounts in "Beyond the Call of Duty," Nininger had graduated near the top of his class at West Point, where he chaired the lecture-and-entertainment committee. He had spent many hours with a friend, discussing everything from history to the theory of relativity. He loved the theatre. In the evenings, he could often be found sitting by the fireplace in the living room of his commanding officer, sipping tea and listening to Tchaikovsky. As a boy, he once saw his father kill a hawk and had been repulsed. When he went into active service, he wrote a friend to say that he had no feelings of hate, and did not think he could ever kill anyone out of hatred. He had none of the swagger of the natural warrior. He worked hard and had a strong sense of duty.

In the second week of January, the Japanese attacked, slipping hundreds of snipers through the American lines, climbing into trees, turning the battlefield into what Reck calls a "gigantic possum hunt." On the morning of January 12th, Nininger went to his commanding officer. He wanted, he said, to be assigned to another company, one that was in the thick of the action, so he could go hunting for Japanese snipers.

He took several grenades and ammunition belts, slung a Garand rifle over his shoulder, and grabbed a submachine gun. Starting at the point where the fighting was heaviest—near the position of the battalion's K Company— he crawled through the jungle and shot a Japanese soldier out of a tree. He shot and killed snipers. He threw grenades into enemy positions. He was wounded in the leg, but he kept going, clearing out Japanese positions for the other members of K Company, behind him. He soon ran out of grenades and switched to his rifle, and then, when he ran out of ammunition, used only his bayonet. He was wounded a second time, but when a medic crawled toward him to help bring him back behind the lines Nininger waved him off. He saw a Japanese bunker up ahead. As he leaped out of a shell hole, he was spun around by a bullet to the shoulder, but he kept charging at the bunker, where a Japanese officer and two enlisted men were dug in. He dispatched one soldier with a double thrust of his bayonet, clubbed down the other, and bayonetted the officer. Then, with outstretched arms, he collapsed face down. For his heroism, Nininger was posthumously awarded the Medal of Honor, the first American soldier so decorated in the Second World War.

2.

Suppose that you were a senior Army officer in the early days of the Second World War and were trying to put together a crack team of fearless and ferocious fighters. Sandy Nininger, it now appears, had exactly the right kind of personality for that assignment, but is there any way you could have known this beforehand? It clearly wouldn't have helped to ask Nininger if he was fearless and ferocious, because he didn't know that he was fearless and ferocious. Nor would it have worked to talk to people who spent time with him. His friend would have told you only that Nininger was quiet and thoughtful and loved the theatre, and his commanding officer would have talked about the evenings of tea and Tchaikovsky. With the exception, perhaps, of the Scarlet Pimpernel, a love of music, theatre, and long afternoons in front of a teapot is not a known predictor of great valor. What you need is some kind of sophisticated psychological instrument, capable of getting to the heart of his personality.

Over the course of the past century, psychology has been consumed with the search for this kind of magical instrument. Hermann Rorschach proposed that great meaning lay in the way that people described inkblots. The creators of the Minnesota Multiphasic Personality Inventory believed in the revelatory power of true-false items such as "I have never had any black, tarry-looking bowel movements" or "If the money were right, I would like to work for a circus or a carnival." Today, Annie Murphy Paul tells us in her fascinating new book, *The Cult of Personality*, that there are twenty-five hundred kinds of personality tests. Testing is a four-hundred-million-dollar-a-year industry. A hefty percentage of American corporations use personality tests as part of the hiring and promotion process. The tests figure in custody battles and in sentencing and parole decisions. "Yet despite their prevalence—and the importance of the matters they are called upon to decide—personality tests have received surprisingly little scrutiny," Paul writes. We can call in the psychologists. We can give Sandy Nininger a battery of tests. But will any of it help?

One of the most popular personality tests in the world is the Myers-Briggs Type Indicator (M.B.T.I.), a psychological-assessment system based on Carl Jung's notion that people make sense of the world through a series of psychological frames. Some people are extroverts, some are introverts. Some process information through logical thought. Some are directed by their feelings. Some make sense of the world through intuitive leaps. Others collect data through their senses. To these three categories—(I)ntroversion/(E)xtroversion, i(N)tuition/(S)ensing, (T)hinking/(F)eeling—the Myers-Briggs test adds a fourth: (J)udging/(P)erceiving. Judgers "like to live in a planned, orderly way, seeking to regulate and manage their lives," according to an M.B.T.I. guide, whereas Perceivers "like to live in a flexible, spontaneous way, seeking to experience and understand life, rather than control it." The M.B.T.I. asks the test-taker to answer a series of "forced-choice" questions, where one choice identifies you as belonging to one of these paired traits. The basic test takes twenty minutes, and at the end you are presented with a precise, multidimensional summary of your personality—your type might be INTJ or ESFP, or some other combination. Two and a half million Americans a year take the Myers-Briggs. Eighty-nine companies out of the Fortune 100 make use of it, for things like hiring or training sessions to help employees "understand" themselves or their colleagues. Annie Murphy Paul says that at the eminent consulting firm McKinsey, "'associates' often know their colleagues' four-letter M.B.T.I. types by heart," the way they might know their own weight or (this being McKinsey) their S.A.T. scores.

It is tempting to think, then, that we could figure out the Myers-Briggs type that corresponds best to commando work, and then test to see whether Sandy Nininger fits the profile. Unfortunately, the notion of personality type is not nearly as straightforward as it appears. For example, the Myers-Briggs poses a series of items grouped around the issue of whether you—the test-taker—are someone who likes to plan your day or evening beforehand or someone who prefers to be spontaneous. The idea is obviously to determine whether you belong to the Judger or Perceiver camp, but the basic question here is surprisingly hard to answer. I think I'm someone who likes to be spontaneous. On the other hand, I have embarked on too many spontaneous evenings that ended up with my friends and me standing on the sidewalk, looking at each other and wondering what to do next. So I guess I'm a spontaneous person who recognizes that life usually goes more smoothly if I plan first, or, rather, I'm a person who prefers to be spontaneous only if there's someone around me who isn't. Does that make me spontaneous or not? I'm not sure. I suppose it means that I'm somewhere in the middle.

This is the first problem with the Myers-Briggs. It assumes that we are either one thing or another—Intuitive or Sensing, Introverted or Extroverted. But personality doesn't fit into neat binary categories: we fall somewhere along a continuum.

Here's another question: Would you rather work under a boss (or a teacher) who is good-natured but often inconsistent, or sharp-tongued but always logical?

On the Myers-Briggs, this is one of a series of questions intended to establish whether you are a Thinker or a Feeler. But I'm not sure I know how to answer this one, either. I once had a good-natured boss whose inconsistency bothered me, because he exerted a great deal of day-to-day control over my work. Then I had a boss who was quite consistent and very sharp-tongued—but at that point I was in a job where day-to-day dealings with my boss were minimal, so his sharp tongue didn't matter that much. So what do I want in a boss? As far as I can tell, the only plausible answer is: It depends. The Myers-Briggs assumes that who we are is consistent from one situation to another. But surely what we want in a boss, and how we behave toward our boss, is affected by what kind of job we have.

This is the gist of the now famous critique that the psychologist Walter Mischel has made of personality testing. One of Mischel's studies involved watching children interact with one another at a summer camp. Aggressiveness was among the traits that he was interested in, so he watched the children in five different situations: how they behaved when approached by a peer, when teased by a peer, when praised by an adult, when punished by an adult, and when warned by an adult. He found that how aggressively a child responded in one of those situations wasn't a good predictor of how that same child responded in another situation. Just because a boy was aggressive in the face of being teased by another boy didn't mean that he would be aggressive in the face of being warned by an adult. On the other hand, if a child responded aggressively to being teased by a peer one day, it was a pretty good indicator that he'd respond aggressively to being teased by a peer the next day. We have a personality in the sense that we have a consistent pattern of behavior. But that pattern is complex and that personality is contingent: it represents an interaction between our internal disposition and tendencies and the situations that we find ourselves in.

It's not surprising, then, that the Myers-Briggs has a large problem with consistency: according to some studies, more than half of those who take the test a second time end up with a different score than when they took it the first time. Since personality is continuous, not dichotomous, clearly some people who are borderline Introverts or Feelers one week slide over to Extroversion or Thinking the next week. And since personality is contingent, not stable, how we answer is affected by which circumstances are foremost in our minds when we take the test. If I happen to remember my first boss, then I come out as a Thinker. If my mind is on my second boss, I come out as a Feeler. When I took the Myers-Briggs, I scored as an INTJ. But, if odds are that I'm going to be something else if I take the test again, what good is it?

Once, for fun, a friend and I devised our own personality test. Like the M.B.T.I., it has four dimensions. The first is Canine/Feline. In romantic relationships, are you the pursuer, who runs happily to the door, tail wagging? Or are you the pursued? The second is More/Different. Is it your intellectual style to gather and master as much information as you can or to make imaginative use of a discrete amount of information? The third is Insider/Outsider. Do you get along with your parents or do you define yourself outside your relationship with your mother and father? And, finally, there is Nibbler/Gobbler. Do you work steadily, in small increments, or do everything at once, in a big gulp? I'm quite pleased with the personality inventory we devised. It directly touches on four aspects of life and temperament—romance, cognition, family, and work style—that are only hinted at by Myers-Briggs. And it can be completed in under a minute, nineteen minutes faster than Myers-Briggs, an advantage not to be dismissed in today's fast-paced business environment. Of course, the four traits it measures are utterly arbitrary, based on what my friend and I came up with over the course of a phone call. But then again surely all universal dichotomous typing systems are arbitrary.

Where did the Myers-Briggs come from, after all? As Paul tells us, it began with a housewife from Washington, D.C., named Katharine Briggs, at the turn of the last century. Briggs had a daughter, Isabel, an only child for whom (as one relative put it) she did "everything but breathe." When Isabel was still in her teens, Katharine wrote a book-length manuscript about her daughter's remarkable childhood, calling her a "genius" and "a little Shakespeare." When Isabel went off to Swarthmore College, in 1915, the two exchanged letters nearly every day. Then, one day, Isabel brought home her college boyfriend and announced that they were to be married. His name was Clarence (Chief) Myers. He was tall and handsome and studying to be a lawyer, and he could not have been more different from the Briggs women. Katharine and Isabel were bold and imaginative and intuitive. Myers was practical and logical and detail-oriented. Katharine could not understand her future son-in-law. "When the blissful young couple returned to Swarthmore," Paul writes, "Katharine retreated to her study, intent on 'figuring out Chief.'" She began to read widely in psychology and philosophy. Then, in 1923, she came across the first English translation of Carl Jung's *Psychological Types*. "This is it!" Katharine told her daughter. Paul recounts, "In a dramatic display of conviction she burned all her own research and adopted Jung's book as her 'Bible,' as she gushed in a letter to the man himself. His system explained it all: Lyman [Katharine's husband], Katharine, Isabel, and Chief were introverts; the two men were thinkers, while the women were feelers; and of course the Briggses were intuitives, while Chief was a senser." Encouraged by her mother, Isabel—who was living in Swarthmore and writing mystery novels—devised a paper-and-pencil test to help people identify which of the Jungian categories they belonged to, and then spent the rest of her life tirelessly and brilliantly promoting her creation.

The problem, as Paul points out, is that Myers and her mother did not actually understand Jung at all. Jung didn't believe that types were easily identifiable, and he didn't believe that people could be permanently slotted into one category or another. "Every individual is an exception to the rule," he wrote; to "stick labels on people at first sight," in his view, was "nothing but a childish parlor game." Why is a parlor game based on my desire to entertain my friends any less valid than a parlor game based on Katharine Briggs's obsession with her son-in-law?

3.

The problems with the Myers-Briggs suggest that we need a test that is responsive to the complexity and variability of the human personality.

And that is why, not long ago, I found myself in the office of a psychologist from New Jersey named Lon Gieser. He is among the country's leading experts on what is called the Thematic Apperception Test (T.A.T.), an assessment tool developed in the nineteen-thirties by Henry Murray, one of the most influential psychologists of the twentieth century.

I sat in a chair facing Gieser, as if I were his patient. He had in his hand two dozen or so pictures—mostly black-and-white drawings—on legal-sized cards, all of which had been chosen by Murray years before. "These pictures present a series of scenes," Gieser said to me. "What I want you to do with each scene is tell a story with a beginning, a middle, and an end." He handed me the first card. It was of a young boy looking at a violin. I had imagined, as Gieser was describing the test to me, that it would be hard to come up with stories to match the pictures. As I quickly discovered, though, the exercise was relatively effortless: the stories just tumbled out.

"This is a young boy," I began. "His parents want him to take up the violin, and they've been encouraging him. I think he is uncertain whether he wants to be a violin player, and maybe even resents the imposition of having to play this instrument, which doesn't seem to have any appeal for him. He's not excited or thrilled about this. He'd rather be somewhere else. He's just sitting there looking at it, and dreading having to fulfill this parental obligation."

I continued in that vein for a few more minutes. Gieser gave me another card, this one of a muscular man clinging to a rope and looking off into the distance. "He's climbing up, not climbing down," I said, and went on:

It's out in public. It's some kind of big square, in Europe, and there is some kind of spectacle going on. It's the seventeenth or eighteenth century.

The King is coming by in a carriage, and this man is shimmying up, so he can see over everyone else and get a better view of the King. I don't get the sense that he's any kind of highborn person. I think he aspires to be more than he is. And he's kind of getting a glimpse of the King as a way of giving himself a sense of what he could be, or what his own future could be like.

We went on like this for the better part of an hour, as I responded to twelve cards—each of people in various kinds of ambiguous situations. One picture showed a woman slumped on the ground, with some small object next to her; another showed an attractive couple in a kind of angry embrace, apparently having an argument. (I said that the fight they were having was staged, that each was simply playing a role.) As I talked, Gieser took notes. Later, he called me and gave me his impressions. "What came out was the way you deal with emotion," he said. "Even when you recognized the emotion, you distanced yourself from it. The underlying motive is this desire to avoid conflict. The other thing is that when there are opportunities to go to someone else and work stuff out, your character is always going off alone. There is a real avoidance of emotion and dealing with other people, and everyone goes to their own corners and works things out on their own."

How could Gieser make such a confident reading of my personality after listening to me for such a short time? I was baffled by this, at first, because I felt that I had told a series of random and idiosyncratic stories. When I listened to the tape I had made of the session, though, I saw what Gieser had picked up on: my stories were exceedingly repetitive in just the way that he had identified. The final card that Gieser gave me was blank, and he asked me to imagine my own picture and tell a story about it. For some reason, what came to mind was Andrew Wyeth's famous painting Christina's World, of a woman alone in a field, her hair being blown by the wind. She was from the city, I said, and had come home to see her family in the country: "I think she is taking a walk. She is pondering some piece of important news. She has gone off from the rest of the people to think about it." Only later did I realize that in the actual painting the woman is not strolling through the field. She is crawling, desperately, on her hands and knees. How obvious could my aversion to strong emotion be?

The T.A.T. has a number of cards that are used to assess achievement—that is, how interested someone is in getting ahead and succeeding in life. One is the card of the man on the rope; another is the boy looking at his violin. Gieser, in listening to my stories, concluded that I was very low in achievement:

Some people say this kid is dreaming about being a great violinist, and he's going to make it. With you, it wasn't what he wanted to do at all. His parents were making him do it. With the rope climbing, some people do this Tarzan thing. They climb the pole and get to the top and feel this great achievement. You have him going up the rope—and why is he feeling the pleasure? Because he's seeing the King. He's still a nobody in the public square, looking at the King.

Now, this is a little strange. I consider myself quite ambitious. On a questionnaire, if you asked me to rank how important getting ahead and being successful was to me, I'd check the "very important" box. But Gieser is suggesting that the T.A.T. allowed him to glimpse another dimension of my personality.

This idea—that our personality can hold contradictory elements—is at the heart of *Strangers to Ourselves*, by the social psychologist Timothy D. Wilson. He is one of the discipline's most prominent researchers, and his book is what popular psychology ought to be (and rarely is): thoughtful, beautifully written, and full of unexpected insights. Wilson's interest is in what he calls the "adaptive unconscious" (not to be confused with the Freudian unconscious). The adaptive unconscious, in Wilson's description, is a big computer in our brain which sits below the surface and evaluates, filters, and looks for patterns in the mountain of data that come in through our senses. That system, Wilson argues, has a personality: it has a set of patterns and responses and tendencies that are laid down by our genes and our early-childhood experiences. These patterns are stable and hard to change, and we are only dimly aware of them. On top of that, in his schema we have another personality: it's the conscious identity that we create for ourselves with the choices we make, the stories we tell about ourselves, and the formal reasons we come up with to explain our motives and feelings. Yet this "constructed self" has no particular connection with the personality of our adaptive unconscious. In fact, they could easily be at odds. Wilson writes:

> The adaptive unconscious is more likely to influence people's uncontrolled, implicit responses, whereas the constructed self is more likely to influence people's deliberative, explicit responses. For example, the quick, spontaneous decision of whether to argue with a co-worker is likely to be under the control

of one's nonconscious needs for power and affiliation. A more thoughtful decision about whether to invite a coworker over for dinner is more likely to be under the control of one's conscious, self-attributed motives.

When Gieser said that he thought I was low in achievement, then, he presumably saw in my stories an unconscious ambivalence toward success. The T.A.T., he believes, allowed him to go beyond the way I viewed myself and arrive at a reading with greater depth and nuance.

Even if he's right, though, does this help us pick commandos? I'm not so sure. Clearly, underneath Sandy Nininger's peaceful façade there was another Nininger capable of great bravery and ferocity, and a T.A.T. of Nininger might have given us a glimpse of that part of who he was. But let's not forget that he volunteered for the front lines: he made a conscious decision to put himself in the heat of the action. What we really need is an understanding of how those two sides of his personality interact in critical situations. When is Sandy Nininger's commitment to peacefulness more, or less, important than some unconscious ferocity? The other problem with the T.A.T., of course, is that it's a subjective instrument. You could say that my story about the man climbing the rope is evidence that I'm low in achievement or you could say that it shows a strong desire for social mobility. The climber wants to look down—not up—at the King in order to get a sense "of what he could be." You could say that my interpretation that the couple's fighting was staged was evidence of my aversion to strong emotion. Or you could say that it was evidence of my delight in deception and role-playing. This isn't to question Gieser's skill or experience as a diagnostician. The T.A.T. is supposed to do no more than identify themes and problem areas, and I'm sure Gieser would be happy to put me on the couch for a year to explore those themes and see which of his initial hypotheses had any validity. But the reason employers want a magical instrument for measuring personality is that they don't have a year to work through the ambiguities. They need an answer now.

4.

A larger limitation of both Myers-Briggs and the T.A.T. is that they are indirect. Tests of this kind require us first to identify a personality trait that corresponds to the behavior we're interested in, and then to figure out how to

measure that trait—but by then we're two steps removed from what we're after. And each of those steps represents an opportunity for error and distortion. Shouldn't we try, instead, to test directly for the behavior we're interested in? This is the idea that lies behind what's known as the Assessment
Center, and the leading practitioner of this approach is a company called
Development Dimensions International, or D.D.I.

Companies trying to evaluate job applicants send them to D.D.I.'s head-
quarters, outside Pittsburgh, where they spend the day role-playing as business
executives. When I contacted D.D.I., I was told that I was going to be Terry
Turner, the head of the robotics division of a company called Global Solutions.

I arrived early in the morning, and was led to an office. On the desk
was a computer, a phone, and a tape recorder. In the corner of the room was
a video camera, and on my desk was an agenda for the day. I had a long telephone conversation with a business partner from France. There were labor
difficulties at an overseas plant. A new product—a robot for the home—had
run into a series of technical glitches. I answered e-mails. I prepared and
recorded a talk for a product-launch meeting. I gave a live interview to a local television reporter. In the afternoon, I met with another senior Global
Solutions manager, and presented a strategic plan for the future of the robotics division. It was a long, demanding day at the office, and when I left, a
team of D.D.I. specialists combed through copies of my e-mails, the audiotapes of my phone calls and my speech, and the videotapes of my interviews,
and analyzed me across four dimensions: interpersonal skills, leadership
skills, business-management skills, and personal attributes. A few weeks
later, I was given my report. Some of it was positive: I was a quick learner. I
had good ideas. I expressed myself well, and—I was relieved to hear—wrote
clearly. But, as the assessment of my performance made plain, I was something less than top management material:

> Although you did a remarkable job addressing matters, you tended to handle
> issues from a fairly lofty perch, pitching good ideas somewhat unilaterally
> while lobbing supporting rationale down to the team below. . . . Had you
> brought your team closer to decisions by vesting them with greater accounta-
> bility, responsibility and decision-making authority, they would have un-
> doubtedly felt more engaged, satisfied and valued. . . . In a somewhat similar
> vein, but on a slightly more interpersonal level, while you seemed to recognize
> the value of collaboration and building positive working relationships with

people, you tended to take a purely businesslike approach to forging partnerships. You spoke of win/win solutions from a business perspective and your rationale for partnering and collaboration seemed to be based solely on business logic. Additionally, at times you did not respond to some of the softer, subtler cues that spoke to people's real frustrations, more personal feelings, or true point of view.

Ouch! Of course, when the D.D.I. analysts said that I did not respond to "some of the softer, subtler cues that spoke to people's real frustrations, more personal feelings, or true point of view," they didn't mean that I was an insensitive person. They meant that I was insensitive in the role of manager. The T.A.T. and M.B.T.I. aimed to make global assessments of the different aspects of my personality. My day as Terry Turner was meant to find out only what I'm like when I'm the head of the robotics division of Global Solutions. That's an important difference. It respects the role of situation and contingency in personality. It sidesteps the difficulty of integrating my unconscious self with my constructed self by looking at the way that my various selves interact in the real world. Most important, it offers the hope that with experience and attention I can construct a more appropriate executive "self." The Assessment Center is probably the best method that employers have for evaluating personality.

But could an Assessment Center help us identify the Sandy Niningers of the world? The center makes a behavioral prediction, and, as solid and specific as that prediction is, people are least predictable at those critical moments when prediction would be most valuable. The answer to the question of whether my Terry Turner would be a good executive is, once again: It depends. It depends on what kind of company Global Solutions is, and on what kind of respect my co-workers have for me, and on how quickly I manage to correct my shortcomings, and on all kinds of other things that cannot be anticipated. The quality of being a good manager is, in the end, as irreducible as the quality of being a good friend. We think that a friend has to be loyal and nice and interesting—and that's certainly a good start. But people whom we don't find loyal, nice, or interesting have friends, too, because loyalty, niceness, and interestingness are emergent traits. They arise out of the interaction of two people, and all we really mean when we say that someone is interesting or nice is that they are interesting or nice to us.

All these difficulties do not mean that we should give up on the task of trying to understand and categorize one another. We could certainly send Sandy Nininger to an Assessment Center, and find out whether, in a make-believe battle, he plays the role of commando with verve and discipline. We could talk to his friends and discover his love of music and theatre. We could find out how he responded to the picture of the man on a rope. We could sit him down and have him do the Myers-Briggs and dutifully note that he is an Introverted, Intuitive, Thinking Judger, and, for good measure, take an extra minute to run him through my own favorite personality inventory and type him as a Canine, Different, Insider Gobbler. We will know all kinds of things about him then. His personnel file will be as thick as a phone book, and we can consult our findings whenever we make decisions about his future. We just have to acknowledge that his file will tell us little about the thing we're most interested in. For that, we have to join him in the jungles of Bataan.

———————

QUESTIONS

1. Kagan discusses (in the selection here) just one aspect of personality—how we deal with new situations and new people—but one could ask the same sorts of questions about many other aspects of personality. What are some aspects of personality that you would expect to be stable over time, from infancy to adulthood? What aspects of personality would you expect to change more radically over time?

2. Watch the film *28 Up* (or one of its sequels, *35 Up* or *42 Up*). Pick two aspects of personality development that are illustrated and say whether what is depicted in the film matches Kagan's results.

3. Reflect on Harris's claim with respect to your own development. What are some ways in which you feel that you were more influenced by your parents than by your peers? And in what ways do you think that you were influenced more by your peers than by your parents?

4. Drawing on Gladwell's "parlor game," make up your own four-question personality test, doing the best you can to create questions that you think would elicit reliable answers. Compare what you've produced to Samuel Gosling's Ten-Item Personality Measure (TIPI) (currently available at http://homepage.psy.utexas.edu/homepage/faculty/gosling/scales_we.htm).

CHAPTER FIFTEEN

CULTURE

Does a chapter on culture belong in a psychology reader? Few textbooks in psychology do more than mention the topic, but in my view this is a mistake. Culture should not be the exclusive province of anthropologists. Like the ability to walk or talk, culture is a product of the mind and brain; only if you have the right sort of mind or brain can you have culture at all. Worms don't, plants don't, but people do, in spades. If culture is a set of collected traditions, it's the mind and brain that allow us to collect them.

In many anthropology classes, the emphasis is on how cultures differ— on the exotic beliefs and practices of human beings who live in very different circumstances than our own. Although this is both fun and interesting, it may be a bit misleading, because it overlooks what we as a species share. In the selection from *Human Universals* (1991), Donald Brown courageously breaks from that tradition and asks whether there is in fact a universal culture. Cultures may vary from one place to the next, but as the pychotherapist Harry Stack Sullivan put it, "We are all more human than otherwise." Brown's vivid description of what we all share reminds us why.

Even if Brown is correct in stating that there are great similarities between human cultures, there could still be important differences. Are the differences all at the level of specific practices, such as in which deity (or deities) a given culture believes, or the exact nature of its coming-of-age ceremony? Or are there deeper ways in which culture influences our basic ways of thinking? In his comparison of Asian and Western cultures, excerpted from *The Geography of Thought* (2003), Richard Nisbett aims to understand how and whether culture affects cognition.

In *Not by Genes Alone* (2004), Peter Richerson and Robert Boyd pull off the neat trick of mediating between cultural anthropologists who typically value cultural difference but ignore evolution, and evolutionary psychologists who value evolution but give little attention to culture. As such, Boyd and Richerson's effort to synthesize the two is a most welcome harbinger of a more unified science of mind and behavior.

From *Human Universals*

Donald E. Brown

What do all people, all societies, all cultures, and all languages have in common? In the following pages I attempt to provide answers, in the form of a description of what I will call the Universal People (UP). Theirs is a description of every people or of people in general. Bear in mind the tentative nature of this chapter: as surely as it leaves out some universals it includes some that will prove in the long run not to be universal, and even more surely it divides up traits and complexes in ways that in time will give way to more accurate or meaningful divisions. At the end of the chapter I will discuss how it was put together and the ways in which it will change in the future.

Although humans are not unique in their possession of culture—patterns of doing and thinking that are passed on within and between generations by learning—they certainly are unique in the extent to which their thought and action are shaped by such patterns. The UP are aware of this uniqueness and posit a difference between their way—culture—and the way of nature.

A very significant portion of UP culture is embodied in their language, a system of communication without which their culture would necessarily be very much simpler. With language the UP think about and discuss both their internal states and the world external to each individual (this is not to deny that they also think without language—surely they do). With language, the UP organize, respond to, and manipulate the behavior of their fellows. UP language is of strategic importance for those who wish to study the UP. This is so because their language is, if not precisely a mirror of, then at least a window into, their culture and into their minds and actions. Their language is not a perfect mirror or window, for there are often discrepancies between what the UP say, think, and do. But we would be very hard pressed to understand many aspects of the UP without access to their thinking through their language. Because their language is not a simple reflex of the way the world is, we need to distinguish their (emic) conceptualization of it from objective (etic) conceptualizations of the world.

The UP's language allows them to think and speak in abstractions, and about things or processes not physically present. If one of them is proficient in the use of language—particularly if it is a male—it gains him prestige, in part because good speech allows him to more effectively manipulate, for better or worse, the behavior of his fellows. An important means of verbal manipulation among the UP is gossip.

In their conversations the UP manage in many ways to express more than their mere words indicate. For example, shifts in tone, timing, and other features of speech indicate that one person is or is not ready for another to take a turn at speaking. UP speech is used to misinform as well as inform. Even if an individual among the UP does not tell lies, he understands the concept and watches for it in others. For some UP do lie, and they dissimulate and mislead in other ways too. UP use of language includes ways to be funny and ways to insult.

UP speech is highly symbolic. Let me explain how this is different from animal communication. Many bird species vocalize a danger warning. The vocalization is substantially the same for the species from one location to another. Indeed, it is somewhat similar from one species to another. Humans have cries of fright and warning that are in some ways analogous to these bird calls, but between many, many members of our species our routine vocalizations are meaningless. This is so because speech sounds and the things they signify have very little intrinsic connection. Sound and sense, as a rule, are only arbitrarily associated. Equally arbitrary is the way units of speech that are equivalent to our words get strung together to make sentences. But in spite of this arbitrariness there are features of language at all basic levels—phonemic, grammatical, and semantic—that are found in all languages.

Thus UP phonemes—their basic speech sounds—include a contrast between vocalics (sounds produced in or channeled through the oral cavity) and nonvocalics (e.g., nasals). UP language has contrasts between vowels and contrasts between stops and nonstops (a stop, e.g., English p or b, stops the flow of air during speech). The phonemes of UP speech form a system of contrasts, and the number of their phonemes goes neither above 70 nor below 10.

In time, their language undergoes change. So it follows that the UP do not speak the language of their more remote ancestors, though it may be quite similar.

However much grammar varies from language to language, some things are always present. For example, UP language includes a series of contrasting terms that theoretically could be phrased in three different ways, but that are only phrased two ways. To illustrate, they could talk about the "good" and the "bad" (two contrasting terms, neither with a marker added to express negation); or they could talk about the "good" and the "not good" (i.e., not having the word "bad" at all but expressing its meaning with a marked version of its opposite, the marking in this case to negate), or they could talk about the "bad" and the "not bad" (i.e., not having the word "good," etc.). Logically, these alternatives are identical: each arrangement conveys the same information. Similar possibilities exist for "deep" and "shallow," "wide" and "narrow," etc. But in each case the third possibility never occurs as the obligatory or common way of talking. So the UP are never forced to express, for lack of an alternative, the ideas of "good," "wide," "deep," and so on as negated versions of their opposites.

By virtue of its grammar UP language conveys some information redundantly. In English, for example, both subject and verb indicate number, while in Spanish both noun and adjective indicate gender.

Two final points about UP grammar are that it contains nouns and verbs, and the possessive. The latter is used both for what have been called the "intimate" or "inalienable" possessions, i.e., to talk about their fingers, your hands, and her thoughts, and for "loose" or "alienable" possessions too, e.g., my axe.

The UP have special forms of speech for special occasions. Thus they have poetic or rhetorical standards deemed appropriate to speech in particular settings. They use narrative to explain how things came to be and to tell stories. Their language includes figurative speech: metaphor is particularly prominent, and metonymy (the use of a word for that with which it is associated, e.g., crown for king) is always included too. The UP can speak onomatopoeically (using words that imitate sound, like "bowwow"), and from time to time they do. They have poetry in which lines, demarcated by pauses, are about 3 seconds in duration. The poetic lines are characterized by the repetition of some structural, semantic, or auditory elements but by free variation too.

Most of the specific elementary units of meaning in UP language— units that are sometimes but not always equivalent to words—are not found in all the rest of the languages of the world. This does not prevent us from translating much of the UP speech into our own or any other particular language; centimeters and inches are not the same entities, but we can translate one to another quite precisely; people who lack a word for "chin" and thus call it the "end of the jaw" still make sense.

A few words or meanings cut across all cultural boundaries and hence form a part of UP language. I am not saying, of course, that the UP make the same speech sounds as we English speakers do for these words, but rather that the meanings for these terms are expressed by the UP in their terms. For example, the UP have terms for black and white (equivalent to dark and light when no other basic colors are encoded) and for face, hand, and so on.

Certain semantic components are found in UP language, even if the terms in which they are employed are not. For example, UP kin terminology includes terms that distinguish male from female (and thus indicate the semantic component of sex) and some generations from others. If not explicit, durational time is semantically implicit in their language, and they have units of time—such as days, months, seasons, and years. In various ways there is a temporal cyclicity or rhythmicity to UP lives. The UP can distinguish past, present, and future.

UP language also classifies parts of the body, inner states (such as emotions, sensations, or thoughts), behavioral propensities, flora, fauna, weather conditions, tools, space (by which they give directions), and many other definite topics, though each of them does not necessarily constitute an emically distinct lexical domain. The UP language refers to such semantic categories as motion, speed, location, dimension, and other physical properties; to giving (including analogous actions, such as lending); and to affecting things or people.

As is implied in their use of metaphor and metonymy, UP words (or word equivalents) are sometimes polysemous, having more than one meaning. Their antonyms and synonyms are numerous. The words or word equivalents that the UP use more frequently are generally shorter, while those they use less frequently are longer.

UP language contains both proper names and pronouns. The latter include at least three persons and two categories of number. Their language contains numerals, though they may be as few as "one, two, and many."

The UP have separate terms for kin categories that include mother and father. That is, whereas some peoples include father and father's brothers in a single kin category, and lump mother with her sisters—so that it is obligatory or normal to refer to each of one's parents with terms that lump them with others—it is not obligatory among the UP to refer to their actual parents in ways that lump mother with father.

UP kinship terms are partially or wholly translatable by reference to the relationships inherent in procreation: mother, father, son, daughter. The UP have an age terminology that includes age grades in a linear sequence similar to the sequence child, adolescent, adult, etc. Our first reflex is to think that it could not be otherwise, but it could: an elderly person can be "like a child"; an age classification that had a term indicating "dependent age" could break from the normal pattern of linearity.

The UP have a sex terminology that is fundamentally dualistic, even when it comprises three or four categories. When there are three, one is a combination of the two basic sexes (e.g., a hermaphrodite), or one is a crossover sex (e.g., a man acting as a woman). When there are four there are then two normal sexes and two crossover sexes.

Naming and taxonomy are fundamental to UP cognition. Prominent elements in UP taxonomy and other aspects of their speech and thought are binary discriminations, forming contrasting terms or semantic components (a number of which have already been mentioned—black and white, nature and culture, male and female, good and bad, etc.). But the UP also can order continua, so they can indicate not only contrasts but polar extremes with gradations between them. Thus there are middles between their opposites, or ranked orders in their classifications. The UP are able to express the measure of things and distances, though not necessarily with uniform units.

The UP employ such elementary logical notions as "not," "and," "same," "equivalent," and "opposite." They distinguish the general from the particular and parts from wholes. Unfortunately, the UP overestimate the objectivity of their mode of thought (it is particularly unobjective when they compare their in-group with out-groups).

The UP use what has been called "conjectural" reasoning to, for example, deduce from minute clues the identification, presence, and behavior of animals, or from miscellaneous symptoms the presence of a particular disease that cannot in itself be observed and is a wholly abstract conception.

Language is not the only means of symbolic communication employed by the UP. They employ gestures too, especially with their hands and arms. Some of their nonverbal communication is somewhat one-sided, in that the message is received consciously but may be sent more or less spontaneously. For example, the squeals of children, cries of fright, and the like all send messages that UP watch closely or listen to carefully, even though the sender did not consciously intend them to communicate. The UP do not merely listen and watch what is on the surface, they interpret external behavior to grasp interior intention.

Communication with their faces is particularly complex among the UP, and some of their facial expressions are recognized everywhere. Thus UP faces show happiness, sadness, anger, fear, surprise, disgust, and contempt, in a manner entirely familiar from one society to another. When they smile while greeting persons it signifies friendly intentions. UP cry when they feel unhappiness or pain. A young woman acting coy or flirting with her eyes does it in a way you would recognize quite clearly. Although some facial communication is spontaneous, as noted earlier, the UP can mask, modify, and mimic otherwise spontaneous expressions. Whether by face, words, gesture, or otherwise, the UP can show affection as well as feel it.

The UP have a concept of the person in the psychological sense. They distinguish self from others, and they can see the self both as subject and object. They do not see the person as a wholly passive recipient of external action, nor do they see the self as wholly autonomous. To some degree, they see the person as responsible for his or her actions. They distinguish actions that are under control from those that are not. They understand the concept of intention. They know that people have a private inner life, have memories, make plans, choose between alternatives, and otherwise make decisions (not without ambivalent feeling sometimes). They know that people can feel pain and other emotions. They distinguish normal from abnormal mental states. The UP personality theory allows them to think of individuals departing from the pattern of behavior associated with whatever status(es) they occupy, and they can explain these departures in terms of the individual's character. The UP are spontaneously and intuitively able to, so to say, get in the minds of others to imagine how they are thinking and feeling.

In addition to the emotions that have already been mentioned, the UP are moved by sexual attraction; sometimes they are deeply disturbed by sexual jealousy. They also have childhood fears, including fear of loud noises and—particularly toward the end of the first year of life—of strangers (this is the apparent counterpart of a strong attachment to their caretaker at this time). The UP react emotionally—generally with fear—to snakes. With effort, the UP can overcome some of their fears. Because there is normally a man present to make a claim on a boy's mother, the Oedipus complex—in the sense of a little boy's possessiveness toward his mother and coolness toward her consort—is a part of male UP psychology.

The UP recognize individuals by their faces, and in this sense they most certainly have an implicit concept of the individual (however little they may explicitly conceptualize the individual apart from social statuses). They recognize individuals in other ways too.

The UP are quintessential tool makers; not simply because they make tools—some other animals do too—but because they make so many, so many different kinds of them, and are so dependent upon them. Unlike the other animals, the UP use tools to make tools. They make cutters that improve upon what they can do with their teeth or by tearing with their hands. They make pounders that improve upon what they can do with their teeth, fists, feet, knees, shoulders, elbows, and head. They make containers that allow them to hold more things at one time, to hold them more comfortably or continuously, and to hold them when they otherwise couldn't, as over a fire. Whether it be string, cord, sinew, vine, wire, or whatever, the UP have something to use to tie things together and make interlaced materials. They know and use the lever. Some of their tools are weapons, including the spear. The UP make many of their tools with such permanence that they can use them over and over again. They also make some of their tools in uniform patterns that are more or less arbitrary—thus we can often tell one people's tools from another's. Such patterns persist beyond any one person's lifetime. Since tools are so closely related to human hands, we might note in passing that most people among the UP are right-handed.

The UP may not know how to make fire, but they know how to use it. They use fire to cook food but for other purposes too. Tools and fire do much to make them more comfortable and secure. The UP have other ways to make themselves feel better (or different). These include substances they can take to alter their moods or feelings: stimulants, narcotics, or intoxicants. These are in addition to what they take for mere sustenance.

The UP always have some form of shelter from the elements. Further ways in which they attend to their material needs will be discussed later.

The UP have distinct patterns of preparation for birth, for giving birth, and for postnatal care. They also have a more or less standard pattern and time for weaning infants.

The UP are not solitary dwellers. They live part of their lives, if not the whole of them, in groups. One of their most important groups is the family, but it is not the only group among them. One or more of the UP groups maintains a unity even though the members are dispersed.

The UP have groups defined by locality or claiming a certain territory, even if they happen to live almost their entire lives as wanderers upon the sea. They are materially, cognitively, and emotionally adjusted to the environment in which they normally live (particularly with respect to some of its flora and fauna). A sense of being a distinct people characterizes the UP, and they judge other people in their own terms.

The core of a normal UP family is composed of a mother and children. The biological mother is usually expected to be the social mother and usually is. On a more or less permanent basis there is usually a man (or men) involved, too, and he (or they) serve minimally to give the children a status in the community and/or to be a consort to the mother. Marriage, in the sense of a "person" having a publicly recognized right or sexual access to a woman deemed eligible for childbearing, is institutionalized among the UP. While the person is almost always a male, it need not necessarily be a single individual, nor even a male.*

The UP have a pattern of socialization: children aren't just left to grow up on their own. Senior kin are expected to contribute substantially to socialization. One of the ways children learn among the UP is by watching elders and copying them. The socialization of UP children includes toilet training. Through practice, children and adults perfect what they learn. The UP learn some things by trial and error.

One's own children and other close kin are distinguished from more distant relatives or nonrelatives among the UP, and the UP favor their close kin in various contexts.

UP families and the relationships of their family members to each other and to outsiders are affected by their sexual regulations, which sharply delimit, if not eliminate, mating between the genetically close kin. Mating between mother and son, in particular, is unthinkable or taboo. Sex is a topic of great interest to the UP, though there may be contexts in which they will not discuss it.

*Among some peoples, for example, a woman *A* may assume the status of a man, take a woman *B* as wife, and then arrange for the wife *B* to bear children to which *A* will be the social father.

Some groups among the UP achieve some of their order by division into socially significant categories or subgroups on the basis of kinship, sex, and age. Since the UP have kinship, sex, and age statuses, it follows, of course, that they have statuses and roles and hence a social structure. But they have statuses beyond those of sex, age, and kinship categories. And while these are largely ascribed statuses, they have achieved statuses too. There are rules of succession to some of their statuses.

Although it may be only another way of saying that they have statuses and roles, the UP recognize social personhood: social identities, including collective identities, that are distinguishable from the individuals who bear them. The distinction between persons and individuals involves the entification of the former; i.e., the UP speak of statuses as though they were entities that can act and be acted upon, such as we do when we say, for example, that "the legislature" (a social entity) "punished the university" (another social entity).

Prestige is differentially distributed among the UP, and the members of UP society are not all economically equal. They acknowledge inequalities of various sorts, but we cannot specify whether they approve or disapprove.

The UP have a division of labor, minimally based on the sex and age statuses already mentioned. For example, their women have more direct child-care duties than do their men. Children are not expected to, and typically do not, engage in the same activities in the same way that adults do. Related to this division of labor, men and women and adults and children are seen by the UP as having different natures. Their men are in fact on the average more physically aggressive than women and are more likely to commit lethal violence than women are.

In the public political sphere men form the dominant element among the UP. Women and children are correspondingly submissive or acquiescent, particularly, again, in the public political sphere.

In addition to their division of labor, whereby different kinds of people do different things, the UP have customs of cooperative labor, in which people jointly undertake essentially similar tasks. They use reciprocal exchanges, whether of labor, or goods, or services, in a variety of settings. Reciprocity—including its negative or retaliatory forms—is an important element in the conduct of their lives. The UP also engage in trade, that is, in nonreciprocal exchanges of goods and services (i.e., one kind of good or service for another). Whether reciprocally or not, they give gifts to one another too. In certain contexts they share food.

Whether in the conduct of family life, of subsistence activities, or other matters, the UP attempt to predict and plan for the future. Some of their plans involve the maintenance or manipulation of social relations. In this context it is important to note that the UP possess "triangular awareness," the ability to think not only of their own relationships to others but of the relationships between others in relation to themselves. Without such an ability they would be unable to form their ubiquitous coalitions.

The UP have government, in the sense that they have public affairs and these affairs are regulated, and in the sense that decisions binding on a collectivity are made. Some of the regulation takes place in a framework of corporate statuses (statuses with orderly procedures for perpetuating membership in them).

The UP have leaders, though they may be ephemeral or situational. The UP admire, or profess to admire, generosity, and this is particularly desired in a leader. No leader of the UP ever has complete power lodged in himself alone. UP leaders go beyond the limits of UP reason and morality. Since the UP never have complete democracy, and never have complete autocracy, they always have a de facto oligarchy.

The UP have law, at least in the sense of rules of membership in perpetual social units and in the sense of rights and obligations attached to persons or other statuses. Among the UP's laws are those that in certain situations proscribe violence and rape. Their laws also proscribe murder—unjustified taking of human life (though they may justify taking lives in some contexts). They have sanctions for infractions, and these sanctions include removal of offenders from the social unit—whether by expulsion, incarceration, ostracism, or execution. They punish (or otherwise censure or condemn) certain acts that threaten the group or are alleged to do so.

Conflict is more familiar to the UP than they wish it were, and they have customary, though far from perfect, ways of dealing with it (their proscription of rape and other forms of violence, for example, does not eliminate them). They understand that wronged parties may seek redress. They employ consultation and mediation in some conflict cases.

Important conflicts are structured around in-group–out-group antagonisms that characterize the UP. These antagonisms both divide the UP as an ethnic group as well as set them off from other ethnic groups. An ethical dualism distinguishes the in-group from the out-group, so that, for example, cooperation is more expectable in the former than with the latter.

The UP distinguish right from wrong, and at least implicitly, as noted earlier, recognize responsibility and intentionality. They recognize and employ promises. Reciprocity, also mentioned earlier, is a key element in their morality. So, too, is their ability to empathize. Envy is ubiquitous among the UP, and they have symbolic means for coping with its unfortunate consequences.

Etiquette and hospitality are among UP ideals. They have customary greetings and customs of visiting kin or others who dwell elsewhere. They have standardized, preferred, or typical times of day to eat, and they have occasions on which to feast. In other ways, too, they have normal daily routines of activities and are fundamentally diurnal.

They have standards of sexual modesty—even though they might customarily go about naked. People, adults in particular, do not normally copulate in public, nor do they relieve themselves without some attempt to do it modestly. Among their other taboos are taboos on certain utterances and certain kinds of food. On the other hand, there are some kinds of food— sweets in particular—that they relish.

The UP have religious or supernatural beliefs in that they believe in something beyond the visible and palpable. They anthropomorphize and (some if not all of them) believe things that are demonstrably false. They also practice magic, and their magic is designed to do such things as to sustain and increase life and to win the attention of the opposite sex. They have theories of fortune and misfortune. They have ideas about how to explain disease and death. They see a connection between sickness and death. They try to heal the sick and have medicines for this purpose. The UP practice divination. And they try to control the weather.

The UP have rituals, and these include rites of passage that demarcate the transfer of an individual from one status to another. They mourn their dead.

Their ideas include a worldview—an understanding or conception of the world about them and their place in it. In some ways their worldview is structured by features of their minds. For example, from early infancy they have the ability to identify items that they know by one sense with the same items perceived in another sense, and so they see the world as a unity, not as different worlds imposed by our different sense modalities. Their worldview is a part of their supernatural and mythological beliefs. They have folklore too. The UP dream and attempt to interpret their dreams.

However spiritual they may be, the UP are materialists also. As indicated by their language having the possessive for use on "loose property," the UP have concepts of property, distinguishing what belongs—minimal though it may be—to the individual, or group, from what belongs to others. They also have rules for the inheritance of property.

In addition to their use of speech in poetic or polished ways, the UP have further aesthetic standards. However little clothing they wear they nonetheless adorn their bodies in one way or another, including a distinctive way of maintaining or shaping their hair. They have standards of sexual attractiveness (including, for example, signs of good health and a clear male preference for the signs of early nubility rather than those of the postmenopausal state). Their decorative art is not confined to the body alone, for the UP apply it to their artifacts too. In addition to their patterns of grooming for essentially aesthetic reasons, they also have patterns of hygienic care.

The UP know how to dance and have music. At least some of their dance (and at least some of their religious activity) is accompanied by music. They include melody, rhythm, repetition, redundancy, and variation in their music, which is always seen as an art, a creation. Their music includes vocals, and the vocals include words—i.e., a conjunction of music and poetry. The UP have children's music.

The UP, particularly their youngsters, play and playfight. Their play besides being fun, provides training in skills that will be useful in adulthood.

From *The Geography of Thought: How Asians and Westerners Think Differently... and Why*

Richard E. Nisbett

In 1991 a Chinese physics student at the University of Iowa named Gang Lu lost an award competition. He appealed the decision unsuccessfully and he subsequently failed to obtain an academic job. On October 31, he entered the physics department and shot his adviser, the person who had handled his appeal, several fellow students and bystanders, and then himself.

Michael Morris, a graduate student at Michigan at the time, noticed that the explanations for Gang Lu's behavior in the campus newspapers focused almost entirely on Lu's presumed qualities—the murderer's psychological foibles ("very bad temper," "sinister edge to his character"), attitudes ("personal belief that guns were an important means to redress grievances"), and psychological problems ("a darkly disturbed man who drove himself to success and destruction," "a psychological problem with being challenged"). He asked his fellow student Kaiping Peng what kinds of accounts of the murder were being given in Chinese newpapers. They could scarcely have been more different. Chinese reporters emphasized causes that had to do with the context in which Lu operated. Explanations centered on Lu's relationships ("did not get along with his adviser," "rivalry with slain student," "isolation from Chinese community"), pressures in Chinese society ("victim of Chinese 'Top Student' educational policy") and aspects of the American context ("availability of guns in the U.S.").

In order to be sure that their impressions were accurate, Morris and Peng carried out a systematic content analysis of reports in the *New York Times* and the Chinese-language newspaper the *World Journal*. This objective procedure showed that their initial observations were correct. Should the different causal attributions be regarded as mere chauvinism? The American reporters blamed the perpetrator, who happened to be Chinese, whereas the Chinese reporters, perhaps protecting one of their own, blamed situational factors. As it happens, a "control" mass murder allows us to see whether it was chauvinism or worldview that produced the differences in explanation patterns.

In the same year that Gang Lu committed his murders and suicide, an American postal worker in Royal Oak, Michigan, named Thomas McIlvane lost his job. He appealed the decision unsuccessfully to his union and subsequently failed to find a full-time replacement job. On November 14, he entered the post office where he had previously worked and shot his supervisor, the person who handled his appeal, several fellow workers and bystanders, and then himself.

Morris and Peng performed the same kind of content analysis on the *New York Times* and *World Journal* reports of the McIlvane mass murder that they did for the Gang Lu mass murder. They found exactly the same trends as for the Chinese murderer. American reporters focused on McIlvane's personal dispositions—attitudes and traits inferred from past behavior ("repeatedly threatened violence," "had a short fuse," "was a martial arts enthusiast," "mentally unstable"). Chinese reporters emphasized situational factors influencing McIlvane ("gunman had been recently fired," "post office supervisor was his enemy," "influenced by example of a recent mass slaying in Texas").

Morris and Peng gave descriptions of the murders to American and Chinese college students and asked them to rate the importance of a large number of presumed personal attributes and situational factors culled from the newspaper reports. American students, whether explaining the American mass murder or the Chinese one, placed more emphasis on the murderer's presumed dispositions. Chinese students stressed situational factors for both mass murders. Even more impressively, Morris and Peng listed a number of situational factors and asked participants to judge whether, if circumstances had been different, the murder might not have occurred. They asked, for example, if the tragedies might have been averted "if Lu had received a job" or "if McIlvane had had many friends or relatives in Royal Oak." Americans and Chinese participants responded very differently. The Chinese thought that, in many cases, the murders might very well not have occurred. But the Americans, because of their conviction that it was the murderer's long-established dispositions that were the key to his rampage, felt it was likely that the killings would have occurred regardless of whether circumstances had been different.

❉

Avoiding the Fundamental Attribution Error

It appears that Easterners and Westerners don't seem to differ that much in the personality dimensions they use. Why is it then that Westerners rely so much more heavily on personality traits in explaining behavior? The answer seems to be that Easterners are more likely to notice important situational factors and to realize that they play a role in producing behavior. As a consequence, East Asians are less susceptible to what social psychologist Lee Ross labeled the "Fundamental Attribution Error" (or FAE for short).

Imagine that you see a college student being asked to show possible donors around the campus for a day and that for this service the student is offered only a small amount of money—less than the minimum wage— and imagine that the student refuses. Do you suppose you would think it is likely that the student would volunteer to help in an upcoming Red Cross blood drive? Probably not very likely. But suppose a friend of yours had seen another student offered a reasonable amount of money—say, 50 percent above the minimum wage—to show the donors around and the student had agreed to do so. Do you suppose the friend would think it is likely that the student would help in the blood drive? Probably more likely than you thought your student would be. If so, both you and your friend would be showing a version of the FAE: attributing behavior to a presumed disposition of the person rather than to an important situational factor—namely money—that was the primary driving force behind the behavior.

This error—ignoring the situation and inventing strong dispositional explanations for behavior—is a highly pervasive one. It makes people mistakenly confident that a person they see being interviewed for an important job is rather nervous by nature, that a person they see being withdrawn at a particular party (where the person happens to know no one) is rather shy in general, that a person who gives a good talk on a subject they know well, to a familiar audience, is a polished speaker and a confident person to boot.

The first solid experimental demonstration of the error was by the noted social psychologist Edward E. Jones and his colleagues. In a study published in 1967, they asked college students to read a speech or essay allegedly written by another student. This other student will be called the "target." It was made clear that the target had been required to write the speech or essay upholding a particular side of a particular issue. For example, the target had been told to write an essay in a political science class favoring Castro's Cuba or to give a speech in a debate class opposing the legalization of marijuana. Participants were asked to indicate what they thought was the actual opinion of the target student who wrote the essay or gave the speech. The sharp situational constraints should have made the participants recognize that they had learned nothing about the target's real views, but in fact they were heavily influenced by what the target said. If the target said he was in favor of Castro's handling of Cuba, participants assumed he was actually inclined toward that opinion; if the target said he was opposed to the legalization of marijuana, participants tended to assume he was of that view.

As it turns out, this illusion is sufficiently powerful that even East Asians are susceptible. Chinese, Japanese, and Koreans have all participated in versions of this experiment and have been found to infer that the targets actually have attitudes corresponding to the views they read in the essay. But there is a difference between East Asian and American susceptibility: East Asians do not make the error if they are first placed in the target's shoes. Incheol Choi and I placed participants themselves into the situation of being required to write an essay on a particular topic, taking a particular stance, and using a particular set of four arguments in writing their essay. Then they read an essay by a person who, they knew, had been in the same situation they themselves had been. This had precisely no effect on Americans: Their dispositional inferences about others were as strong as if they had not themselves experienced exactly the target person's situation. But the experience rendered Koreans almost impervious to the error.

Other evidence indicates that making situational factors salient has a greater effect on Asians than on Westerners. Ara Norenzayan, Incheol Choi, and I asked American and Korean college students to read one of two scenarios and then to guess whether a target person would give someone bus fare. Both scenarios began in the following way:

You just met a new neighbor, Jim. As you and Jim are taking a walk in the neighborhood, a well-dressed man approaches Jim and explains that his car is broken down and he needs to call a mechanic. Then with a somewhat embarrassed voice, the man asks Jim for a quarter to make the phone call. You find that Jim searches his pocket and, after finding a quarter, gives it to the man. On another day Jim is walking toward the bus stop to catch the bus to work. As he is walking, a teenager carrying some books approaches Jim and politely asks him if he can borrow a dollar for a bus ride, explaining that he forgot his wallet at home and needs to get a ride to school.

In a version of the scenario read by one group of participants, Jim searches his pocket and discovers that he has several dollars; in a version read by other participants he discovers that he has only enough money for his own bus fare. Korean participants were more likely to recognize that Jim would be inclined to give the teenager the money if he finds he has several dollars than if he finds he has only one.

We gave participants a total of six different scenarios, each having their two different versions, and found that for each one the Koreans were more responsive to the situational information than the Americans were, predicting that a given behavior was more likely if situational factors facilitated it than if situational factors discouraged it.

So the evidence on causal attribution dovetails with the evidence on perception. Westerners attend primarily to the focal object or person and Asians attend more broadly to the field and to the relations between the object and the field. Westerners tend to assume that events are caused by the object and Asians are inclined to assign greater importance to the context.

From *Not by Genes Alone: How Culture Transformed Human Evolution*

Peter J. Richerson and Robert Boyd

The American South has long been more violent than the North. Colorful descriptions of duels, feuds, bushwhackings, and lynchings feature prominently in visitors' accounts, newspaper articles, and autobiographies from the eighteenth century onward. Statistics bear out these impressions. For example, over the period 1865–1915, the homicide rate in the South was ten times the current rate for the whole United States, and twice the rate in our most violent cities. Modern homicide statistics tell the same story.

In their book, *Culture of Honor*, psychologists Richard Nisbett and Dov Cohen argue that the South is more violent than the North because southern people have culturally acquired beliefs about personal honor that are different from their northern counterparts. Southerners, they argue, believe more strongly than Northerners that a person's reputation is important and worth defending even at great cost. As a consequence, arguments and confrontations that lead to harsh words or minor scuffles in Amherst or Ann Arbor often escalate to lethal violence in Asheville or Austin.

What else could explain these differences? Some feature of the southern environment, such as its greater warmth, could explain why Southerners are more violent. Such hypotheses are plausible, and Nisbett and Cohen are at pains to test them. Northerners and Southerners might differ genetically, but this hypothesis is not very plausible. The settlers of the North and South came mostly from the British Isles and adjacent areas of northwestern Europe. Human populations are quite well mixed on this scale.

Nisbett and Cohen support their hypothesis with an impressive range of evidence. Let's start with statistical patterns of violence. In the rural and small-town South, murder rates are elevated for arguments among friends and acquaintances, but not for killings committed in the course of other felonies. In other words, in the South men are more likely than Northerners to kill an acquaintance when an argument breaks out in a bar, but they are no more likely to kill the guy behind the counter when they knock off a liquor store. Thus, Southerners seem to be more violent than other Americans only in situations that involve personal honor. Competing hypotheses don't do so well: neither white per-capita income nor hot climate nor history of slavery explain this variation in homicide.

Differences in what people say about violence also support the "culture of honor" hypothesis. For example, Nisbett and Cohen asked people to read vignettes in which a man's honor was challenged—sometimes trivially (for example, by insults to his wife), and in other cases seriously (for example, by stealing his wife). Southern respondents were more likely than Northerners to say that violent responses were justified in all cases, and that one would "not be much of a man" unless he responded violently to insults. In the case of more serious affronts, southern respondents were almost twice as likely to say that shooting the perpetrator was justified.

Interestingly, this difference in behavior is not just talk; it can also be observed under the controlled conditions of the psychology laboratory. Working at the University of Michigan, Nisbett and Cohen recruited participants from northern and southern backgrounds, ostensibly to participate in an experiment on perception. As part of the procedure, an experimenter's confederate bumped some participants and muttered "Asshole!" at them. This insult had very different effects on southern and northern participants, as revealed by the next part of the experiment. Sometime after being bumped, participants encountered another confederate walking toward them down the middle of a narrow hall, setting up a little game of chicken. This confederate, a six-foot, three-inch, 250-pound linebacker on the UM football squad, was much bigger and stronger than any participant, and had been instructed to keep walking until either the participant stepped aside and let him pass or a collision was immanent. Northerners stepped aside when the confederate was six feet away, whether or not they had been insulted. Southerners who had not been insulted stepped aside when they were nine feet away from the confederate, while previously insulted Southerners continued walking until they were just three feet away. Polite, but prepared to be violent, uninsulted Southerners take more care, presumably because they attribute a sense of honor to the football player and are careful not to test it. When their own honor is challenged, however, they are willing to challenge someone at considerable risk to their own safety. These behavioral differences have physiological correlates. In a similar confederate-insulter experiment, Nisbett and Cohen measured levels of two hormones, cortisol and testosterone, in participants before and after they had been insulted. Physiologists know that cortisol levels increase in response to stress, and testosterone levels rise in preparation for violence. Insulted Southerners showed much bigger jumps in cortisol and testosterone than insulted Northerners.

Nisbett and Cohen argue that the difference in beliefs between northern and southern people can be understood in terms of their cultural and economic histories. Scots-Irish livestock herders were the main settlers of the South, while English, German, and Dutch peasant farmers populated the North. States historically have had considerable difficulty imposing the rule of law in the sparsely settled regions where herding is the dominant occupation, and livestock are easy to steal. Hence in herding societies a culture of honor often arises out of necessity as men seek to cultivate reputations for willingly resorting to violence as a deterrent to theft and other predatory behavior. Of course, bad men may also subscribe to the same code, the better to intimidate their victims. As this arms race escalates, arguments over trivial acts can rapidly get out of hand if a man thinks his honor is at stake. This account is supported by the fact that Southern white homicide rates are unusually high in poor regions with low population density and a historically weak presence of state institutions, not in the richer, more densely settled, historically slave-plantation districts. In such an environment the Scots-Irish honor system remained adaptive until recent times.

This fascinating study illustrates the two main points we want to make in this book.

Culture is crucial for understanding human behavior. People acquire beliefs and values from the people around them, and you can't explain human behavior without taking this reality into account. Murder is more common in the South than in the North. If Nisbett and Cohen are right, this difference can't be explained in terms of contemporary economics, climate, or any other external factor. Their explanation is that people in the South have acquired a complex set of beliefs and attitudes about personal honor that make them more polite, but also more quick to take offense than people in the North. This complex persists because the beliefs of one generation are learned by the next. This is not an isolated example. We will present several other similar well-studied examples demonstrating that culture plays an important role in human behavior. These are only the tip of the iceberg—a complete scholarly rehearsal of the evidence would try the patience of all but the most dedicated reader. Culturally acquired ideas are crucially important for explaining a wide range of human behavior—opinions, beliefs, and attitudes, habits of thought, language, artistic styles, tools and technology, and social rules and political institutions.

Culture is part of biology. An insult that has trivial effects in a Northerner sets off a cascade of physiological changes in a southern male that prepare him to harm the insulter and cope with the likelihood that the insulter is prepared to retaliate violently. This example is merely one strand in a skein of connections that enmesh culturally acquired information in other aspects of human biology. Much evidence suggests that we have an evolved psychology that shapes what we learn and how we think, and that this in turn influences the kind of beliefs and attitudes that spread and persist. Theories that ignore these connections cannot adequately account for much of human behavior. At the same time, culture and cultural change cannot be understood solely in terms of innate psychology. Culture affects the success and survival of individuals and groups; as a result, some cultural variants spread and others diminish, leading to evolutionary processes that are every bit as real and important as those that shape genetic variation. These culturally evolved environments then affect which genes are favored by natural selection. Over the evolutionary long haul, culture has shaped our innate psychology as much as the other way around.

Few who have thought much about the problem would dispute either of these claims *in principle*. Beliefs and practices that we learn from one another are clearly important, and like all human behavior, culture must in some way be rooted in human biology. However, *in practice* most social scientists ignore at least one of them. Some scholars, including most economists, many psychologists, and many social scientists influenced by evolutionary biology, place little emphasis on culture as a cause of human behavior. Others, especially anthropologists, sociologists, and historians, stress the importance of culture and institutions in shaping human affairs, but usually fail to consider their connection to biology. The success of all these disciplines suggests that many questions can be answered by ignoring culture or its connection to biology. However, the most fundamental questions of how humans came to be the kind of animal we are can *only* be answered by a theory in which culture has its proper role *and* in which it is intimately inter-twined with other aspects of human biology. In this book we outline such a theory.

Humans are much more variable than any other species of animal. Other animals do vary. Consider baboons as an example. Many biologists classify most baboons in a single species, *Papio cynocephalus*. These animals occupy a range that includes many different habitats: hot lowland forest, cool highland forest, savannah, scrub, and true desert. Within this range, ba-boons vary physically, especially in size and color. All baboons feed mainly on plant materials, and supplement their diet with insects, eggs, and small animal prey. However, across their range, the exact composition of their di-ets varies. The baboons in Amboseli, Kenya, dig up grass corms and crack open acacia pods, while the baboons of the Okavango delta eat figs and water-lily bulbs. Most savanna baboons live in multimale, multifemale groups of about thirty to seventy individuals. Females remain in these groups throughout their lives. However, in the highlands of southern Africa, ba-boons form much smaller, one-male groups, and females sometimes disperse between groups; in the forests of West Africa, baboons aggregate in enor-mous hordes that may number several hundred individuals. Social behavior also varies to some extent. In East Africa, males form coalitions with other males to compete for access to receptive females; these kinds of coalitions are never seen in southern Africa.

Now compare the amount of human variation that we see among peo-ple who occupy the same range of African environments. Like baboons, hu-mans vary physically, mainly in size and color. Unlike baboons, the people in these regions get their daily bread and organize their social lives in very dif-ferent ways. Until about ten thousand years ago, all people were foragers who lived in small, flexible bands, gathering plants and hunting mammals. However, even among hunter-gatherers there was great variation. !Kung bushmen have a simple system of kinship in which male and female rela-tions are treated the same, while their neighbors, the !Xo, who live a few hundred miles to the south, have an elaborate system of clans based on rela-tionship through the male line. The !Kung and the !Xo both hunt the game of the Kalahari with small bows, while the Kxoe bushmen live mainly by fishing in the nearby swamps of the Okavango. Some pygmies of the central African forest rely on large-scale cooperative hunting using nets, while the Hadza of the East African savannah hunt big game with great bows.

Of course, today most people in Africa are not hunter-gatherers. There are nomadic pastoralists like the Maasai of East Africa who live on the products of their cattle, moving from place to place in search of good grazing. Maasai political organization is based on cooperation and loyalty among age sets, groups of men who were circumcised at the same time. Among other nomadic pastoralists loyalties are based on kinship—male kinship in the case of the Somalis and female kinship for the Himba of Namibia. Farming peoples grow a wide range of crops: millet and sorghum in the seasonally parched Sahel, peanuts, corn, and cassava in the forests of the Congo. They exhibit an equally wide range of social and political organizations: small family groups without any ranks or offices, elaborate kin-based clans, and great cities with full-time soldiers, priests, and rulers.

The behavioral variation within human groups is also much greater than the behavioral variation within groups of other animals. Again compare humans with baboons. The baboons living in a group do vary in their behavior. Male baboons are more likely to hunt than females; dominant females eat more of the most preferred foods, have the safest sleeping sites, and are harassed less than subordinate females; juveniles play more than adults; some females are more sociable than others; and so on. But all baboons must find their own food, keep a lookout for predators, and take care of their own infants. By comparison, even hunter-gather societies have part-time specialists in tool production, ritual activity, and food gathering. In complex farming societies the amount of variation explodes—there are butchers, bakers, candlestick makers, serfs, soldiers, sheriffs, kings, and clergy, who all have different knowledge, behavior, obligations, and subsistence tasks.

The difference between the range of human variation and that of other animals like baboons demands an evolutionary explanation. Ten million years ago (or thereabouts), our ancestors were an apelike species living in the forests and (perhaps) the savannahs of Africa whose range of variation was comparable with that of present-day baboons. Over the next ten million years, the processes of Darwinian evolution transformed that lineage into modern humans. Any theory that hopes to explain the behavior of contemporary humans *must* tell us what it is that causes humans to be so much more variable than any other species and why this peculiar capacity for variation was favored by natural selection. This burden falls particularly hard on models that try to account for human behavior invoking only individual learning mechanisms that also apply to other animals.

We think that the answer to the ultimate question about the magnitude of human variation is the same as the answer to the proximate question about its causes—culture.

QUESTIONS

1. Do nonhuman primates have culture? Read and evaluate papers on the topic by Whiten et al. (*Nature*, 1999, 399, 682–85) and van Schaik et al. (*Science*, 2003, 299, 102–5).

2. How strong are the differences that Nisbett describes? Can Westerners think like Asians? Can Asians think like Westerners? Are the differences matters of habit or something deeper that cannot easily be overcome?

3. Do the universals proposed by Brown ring true? Pick three of Brown's universals that seem implausible to you, and explain why. Try to come up with one that you think he might have missed.

CHAPTER SIXTEEN

DISORDERS

Like any part of the body, the brain is vulnerable. It can be injured, by stroke or gunshot wound, through the ingestion of toxins or narcotics; it may be malformed in development; it may degenerate later in life. Anything from an imbalance of neurotransmitters to damage to neural tissue can disrupt brain and mind function. When one reflects on the complexity of the brain, it is amazing that things don't go wrong more often.

Rather than aiming to be comprehensive, I've chosen here to be vivid. The selections in this chapter illustrate three common disorders: schizophrenia, bipolar disorder (manic depression), and autism. The passage on schizophrenia is from *A Beautiful Mind* (1998), Sylvia Nasar's moving portrait of John Nash, Nobel Laureate in Economics. The other two are first-hand accounts by exceptional individuals. Kay Redfield Jamison is not just one of the world's leading authorities on manic depression, she is also one of its most visible victims, as narrated in *An Unquiet Mind* (1995), Temple Grandin, author of *Thinking in Pictures* (1996), is a highly successful academic and inventor who has thrived despite having autism.

From *A Beautiful Mind: The Life of Mathematical Genius and Nobel Laureate John Nash*

Sylvia Nasar

By his late twenties, Nash's insights and discoveries had won him recognition, respect, and autonomy. He had carved out a brilliant career at the apex of the mathematics profession, traveled, lectured, taught, met the most famous mathematicians of his day, and become famous himself. His genius also won him love. He had married a beautiful young physics student who adored him, and fathered a child. It was a brilliant strategy, this genius, this life. A seemingly perfect adaptation.

Many great scientists and philosophers, among them René Descartes, Ludwig Wittgenstein, Immanuel Kant, Thorstein Veblen, Isaac Newton, and Albert Einstein, have had similarly strange and solitary personalities. An emotionally detached, inward-looking temperament can be especially conducive to scientific creativity, psychiatrists and biographers have long observed, just as fiery fluctuations in mood may sometimes be linked to artistic expression. In *The Dynamics of Creation*, Anthony Storr, the British psychiatrist, contends that an individual who "fears love almost as much as he fears hatred" may turn to creative activity not only out of an impulse to experience aesthetic pleasure, or the delight of exercising an active mind, but also to defend himself against anxiety stimulated by conflicting demands for detachment and human contact. In the same vein, Jean-Paul Sartre, the French philosopher and writer, called genius "the brilliant invention of someone who is looking for a way out." Posing the question of why people often are willing to endure frustration and misery in order to create something, even in the absence of large rewards. Storr speculates:

> Some creative people . . . of predominately schizoid or depressive temperaments . . . use their creative capacities in a defensive way. If creative work protects a man from mental illness, it is small wonder that he pursues it with

avidity. The schizoid state . . . is characterized by a sense of meaninglessness and futility. For most people, interaction with others provides most of what they require to find meaning and significance in life. For the schizoid person, however, this is not the case. Creative activity is a particularly apt way to express himself . . . the activity is solitary . . . [but] the ability to create and the productions which result from such ability are generally regarded as possessing value by our society.

Of course, very few people who exhibit "a lifelong pattern of social isolation" and "indifference to the attitudes and feelings of others"—the hallmarks of a so-called schizoid personality—possess great scientific or other creative talent. And the vast majority of people with such strange and solitary temperaments never succumb to severe mental illness. Instead, according to John G. Gunderson, a psychiatrist at Harvard, they tend "to engage in solitary activities which often involve mechanical, scientific, futuristic and other non-human subjects . . . [and] are likely to appear increasingly comfortable over a period of time by forming a stable but distant network of relationships with people around work tasks." Men of scientific genius, however eccentric, rarely become truly insane—the strongest evidence for the potentially protective nature of creativity.

Nash proved a tragic exception. Underneath the brilliant surface of his life, all was chaos and contradiction: his involvements with other men; a secret mistress and a neglected illegitimate son; a deep ambivalence toward the wife who adored him, the university that nurtured him, even his country; and, increasingly, a haunting fear of failure. And the chaos eventually welled up, spilled over, and swept away the fragile edifice of his carefully constructed life.

The first visible signs of Nash's slide from eccentricity into madness appeared when he was thirty and was about to be made a full professor at MIT. The episodes were so cryptic and fleeting that some of Nash's younger colleagues at that institution thought that he was indulging a private joke at their expense. He walked into the common room one winter morning in 1959 carrying *The New York Times* and remarked, to no one in particular, that the story in the upper lefthand corner of the front page contained an encrypted message from inhabitants of another galaxy that only he could decipher. Even months later, after he had stopped teaching, had angrily resigned his professorship, and was incarcerated at a private psychiatric hospital in suburban Boston, one of the nation's leading forensic psychiatrists, an expert who testified in the case of Sacco and Vanzetti, insisted that Nash was perfectly sane. Only a few of those who witnessed the uncanny metamorphosis, Norbert Wiener among them, grasped its true significance.

At thirty years of age, Nash suffered the first shattering episode of paranoid schizophrenia, the most catastrophic, protean, and mysterious of mental illnesses. For the next three decades, Nash suffered from severe delusions, hallucinations, disordered thought and feeling, and a broken will. In the grip of this "cancer of the mind," as the universally dreaded condition is sometimes called. Nash abandoned mathematics, embraced numerology and religious prophecy, and believed himself to be a "messianic figure of great but secret importance." He fled to Europe several times, was hospitalized involuntarily half a dozen times for periods up to a year and a half, was subjected to all sorts of drug and shock treatments, experienced brief remissions and episodes of hope that lasted only a few months, and finally became a sad phantom who haunted the Princeton University campus where he had once been a brilliant graduate student, oddly dressed, muttering to himself, writing mysterious messages on blackboards, year after year.

The origins of schizophrenia are mysterious. The condition was first described in 1806, but no one is certain whether the illness—or, more likely, group of illnesses—existed long before then but had escaped definition or, on the other hand, appeared as an AIDS-like scourge at the start of the industrial age. Roughly 1 percent of the population in all countries succumbs to it. Why it strikes one individual and not another is not known, although the suspicion is that it results from a tangle of inherited vulnerability and life stresses. No element of environment—war, imprisonment, drugs, or upbringing—has ever been proved to cause, by itself, a single instance of the illness. There is now a consensus that schizophrenia has a tendency to run in families, but heredity alone apparently cannot explain why a specific individual develops the full-blown illness.

Eugen Bleuler, who coined the term *schizophrenia* in 1908, describes a "specific type of alteration of thinking, feeling and relation to the external world." The term refers to a splitting of psychic functions, "a peculiar destruction of the inner cohesiveness of the psychic personality." To the person experiencing early symptoms, there is a dislocation of every faculty, of time, space, and body. None of its symptoms—hearing voices, bizarre delusions, extreme apathy or agitation, coldness toward others—is, taken singly, unique to the illness. And symptoms vary so much between individuals and over time for the same individual that the notion of a "typical case" is virtually nonexistent. Even the degree of disability—far more severe, on average, for men—varies wildly. The symptoms can be "slightly, moderately, severely, or absolutely disabling," according to Irving Gottesman, a leading contemporary researcher. Though Nash succumbed at age thirty, the illness can appear at any time from adolescence to advanced middle age. The first episode can last a few weeks or months or several years. The life history of someone with the disease can include only one or two episodes. Isaac Newton, always an eccentric and solitary soul, apparently suffered a psychotic breakdown with paranoid delusions at age fifty-one. The episode, which may have been precipitated by an unhappy attachment to a younger man and the failure of his alchemy experiments, marked the end of Newton's academic career. But, after a year or so, Newton recovered and went on to hold a series of high public positions and to receive many honors. More often, as happened in Nash's case, people with the disease suffer many, progressively more severe episodes that occur at ever shorter intervals. Recovery, almost never complete, runs the gamut from a level tolerable to society to one that may not require permanent hospitalization but in fact does not allow even the semblance of a normal life.

More than any symptom, the defining characteristic of the illness is the profound feeling of incomprehensibility and inaccessibility that sufferers provoke in other people. Psychiatrists describe the person's sense of being separated by a "gulf which defies description" from individuals who seem "totally strange, puzzling, inconceivable, uncanny and incapable of empathy, even to the point of being sinister and frightening." For Nash, the onset of the illness dramatically intensified a pre-existing feeling, on the part of many who knew him, that he was essentially disconnected from them and deeply unknowable. As Storr writes:

> However melancholy a depressive may be, the observer generally feels there is some possibility of emotional contact. The schizoid person, on the other hand, appears withdrawn and inaccessible. His remoteness from human contact makes his state of mind less humanly comprehensible, since his feelings are not communicated. If such a person becomes psychotic (schizophrenic) this lack of connection with people and the external world becomes more obvious; with the result that the sufferer's behavior and utterances appear inconsequential and unpredictable.

Schizophrenia contradicts popular but incorrect views of madness as consisting solely of wild gyrations of mood, or fevered delirium. Someone with schizophrenia is not permanently disoriented or confused, for example, the way that an individual with a brain injury or Alzheimer's might be. He may have, indeed usually does have, a firm grip on certain aspects of present reality. While he was ill, Nash traveled all over Europe and America, got legal help, and learned to write sophisticated computer programs. Schizophrenia is also distinct from manic depressive illness (currently known as bipolar disorder), the illness with which it has most often been confounded in the past.

If anything, schizophrenia can be a ratiocinating illness, particularly in its early phases. From the turn of the century, the great students of schizophrenia noted that its sufferers included people with fine minds and that the delusions which often, though not always, come with the disorder involve subtle, sophisticated, complex flights of thought. Emil Kraepelin, who defined the disorder for the first time in 1896, described "dementia praecox," as he called the illness, not as the shattering of reason but as causing "predominant damage to the emotional life and the will." Louis A. Sass, a psychologist at Rutgers University, calls it "not an escape from reason but an exacerbation of that thoroughgoing illness. Dostoevsky imagined ... at least in some of its forms ... a heightening rather than a dimming of conscious awareness and an alienation not from reason but from emotion, instincts and the will."

Nash's mood in the early days of his illness can be described, not as manic or melancholic, but rather as one of heightened awareness, insomniac wakefulness and watchfulness. He began to believe that a great many things that he saw—a telephone number, a red necktie, a dog trotting along the sidewalk, a Hebrew letter, a birthplace, a sentence in *The New York Times*—had a hidden significance, apparent only to him. He found such signs increasingly compelling, so much so that they drove from his consciousness his usual concerns and preoccupations. At the same time, he believed he was on the brink of cosmic insights. He claimed he had found a solution to the greatest unsolved problem in pure mathematics, the so-called Riemann Hypothesis. Later he said he was engaged in an effort to "rewrite the foundations of quantum physics." Still later, he claimed, in a torrent of letters to former colleagues, to have discovered vast conspiracies and the secret meaning of numbers and biblical texts. In a letter to the algebraist Emil Artin, whom he addressed as "a great necromancer and numerologist," Nash wrote:

> I have been considering Algerbiac [sic] questions and have noticed some interesting things that might also interest you ... I, a while ago, was seized with the concept that numerological calculations dependent on the decimal

system might not be sufficiently intrinsic also that language and alphabet structure might contain ancient cultural stereotypes interfering with clear understands [sic] or unbiased thinking. . . . I quickly wrote down a new sequence of symbols. . . . These were associated with (in fact natural, but perhaps not computationally ideal but suited for mystical rituals, incantations and such) system for representing the integers via symbols, based on the products of successive primes.

A predisposition to schizophrenia was probably integral to Nash's exotic style of thought as a mathematician, but the full-blown disease devastated his ability to do creative work. His once-illuminating visions became increasingly obscure, self-contradictory, and full of purely private meanings, accessible only to himself. His longstanding conviction that the universe was rational evolved into a caricature of itself, turning into an unshakable belief that everything had meaning, everything had a reason, nothing was random or coincidental. For much of the time, his grandiose delusions insulated him from the painful reality of all that he had lost. But then would come terrible flashes of awareness. He complained bitterly from time to time of his inability to concentrate and to remember mathematics, which he attributed to shock treatments. He sometimes told others that his enforced idleness made him feel ashamed of himself, worthless. More often, he expressed his suffering wordlessly. On one occasion, sometime during the 1970s, he was sitting at a table in the dining hall at the Institute for Advanced Study—the scholarly haven where he had once discussed his ideas with the likes of Einstein, von Neumann, and Robert Oppenheimer—alone as usual. That morning, an institute staff member recalled, Nash got up, walked over to a wall, and stood there for many minutes, banging his head against the wall, slowly, over and over, eyes tightly shut, fists clenched, his face contorted with anguish.

From *An Unquiet Mind:*
A Memoir of Moods and Madness

Kay Redfield Jamison

When it's two o'clock in the morning, and you're manic, even the UCLA Medical Center has a certain appeal. The hospital—ordinarily a cold clotting of uninteresting buildings—became for me, that fall morning not quite twenty years ago, a focus of my finely wired, exquisitely alert nervous system. With vibrissae twinging, antennae perked, eyes fast-forwarding and fly faceted, I took in everything around me. I was on the run. Not just on the run but fast and furious on the run, darting back and forth across the hospital parking lot trying to use up a boundless, restless, manic energy. I was running fast, but slowly going mad.

The man I was with, a colleague from the medical school, had stopped running an hour earlier and was, he said impatiently, exhausted. This, to a saner mind, would not have been surprising: the usual distinction between day and night had long since disappeared for the two of us, and the endless hours of scotch, brawling, and fallings about in laughter had taken an obvious, if not final, toll. We should have been sleeping or working, publishing not perishing, reading journals, writing in charts, or drawing tedious scientific graphs that no one would read.

Suddenly a police car pulled up. Even in my less-than-totally-lucid state of mind I could see that the officer had his hand on his gun as he got out of the car. "What in the hell are you doing running around the parking lot at this hour?" he asked. A not unreasonable question. My few remaining islets of judgment reached out to one another and linked up long enough to conclude that this particular situation was going to be hard to explain. My colleague, fortunately, was thinking far better than I was and managed to reach down into some deeply intuitive part of his own and the world's collective unconscious and said, "We're both on the faculty in the psychiatry department." The policeman looked at us, smiled, went back to his squad car, and drove away.

Being professors of psychiatry explained everything.

Within a month of signing my appointment papers to become an assistant professor of psychiatry at the University of California, Los Angeles, I was well on my way to madness; it was 1974, and I was twenty-eight years old. Within three months I was manic beyond recognition and just beginning a long, costly personal war against a medication that I would, in a few years' time, be strongly encouraging others to take. My illness, and my struggles against the drug that ultimately saved my life and restored my sanity, had been years in the making.

For as long as I can remember I was frighteningly, although often wonderfully, beholden to moods. Intensely emotional as a child, mercurial as a young girl, first severely depressed as an adolescent, and then unrelentingly caught up in the cycles of manic-depressive illness by the time I began my professional life, I became, both by necessity and intellectual inclination, a student of moods. It has been the only way I know to understand, indeed to accept, the illness I have; it also has been the only way I know to try and make a difference in the lives of others who also suffer from mood disorders. The disease that has, on several occasions, nearly killed me does kill tens of thousands of people every year: most are young, most die unnecessarily, and many are among the most imaginative and gifted that we as a society have.

The Chinese believe that before you can conquer a beast you first must make it beautiful. In some strange way, I have tried to do that with manic-depressive illness. It has been a fascinating, albeit deadly, enemy and companion; I have found it to be seductively complicated, a distillation both of what is finest in our natures, and of what is most dangerous. In order to contend with it, I first had to know it in all of its moods and infinite disguises, understand its real and imagined powers. Because my illness seemed at first simply to be an extension of myself—that is to say, of my ordinarily changeable moods, energies, and enthusiasms—I perhaps gave it at times too much quarter. And, because I thought I ought to be able to handle my increasingly violent mood swings by myself, for the first ten years I did not seek any kind of treatment. Even after my condition became a medical emergency, I still intermittently resisted the medications that both my training and clinical research expertise told me were the only sensible way to deal with the illness I had.

My manias, at least in their early and mild forms, were absolutely intoxicating states that gave rise to great personal pleasure, an incomparable flow of thoughts, and a ceaseless energy that allowed the translation of new ideas into papers and projects. Medications not only cut into these fast-flowing, high-flying times, they also brought with them seemingly intolerable side effects. It took me far too long to realize that lost years and relationships cannot be recovered, that damage done to oneself and others cannot always be put right again, and that freedom from the control imposed by medication loses its meaning when the only alternatives are death and insanity.

The war that I waged against myself is not an uncommon one. The major clinical problem in treating manic-depressive illness is not that there are not effective medications—there are—but that patients so often refuse to take them. Worse yet, because of a lack of information, poor medical advice, stigma, or fear of personal and professional reprisals, they do not seek treatment at all. Manic-depression distorts moods and thoughts, incites dreadful behaviors, destroys the basis of rational thought, and too often erodes the desire and will to live. It is an illness that is biological in its origins, yet one that feels psychological in the experience of it; an illness that is unique in conferring advantage and pleasure, yet one that brings in its wake almost unendurable suffering and, not infrequently, suicide.

I am fortunate that I have not died from my illness, fortunate in having received the best medical care available, and fortunate in having the friends, colleagues, and family that I do. Because of this, I have in turn tried, as best I could, to use my own experiences of the disease to inform my research, teaching, clinical practice, and advocacy work. Through writing and teaching I have hoped to persuade my colleagues of the paradoxical core of this quicksilver illness that can both kill and create; and, along with many others, have tried to change public attitudes about psychiatric illnesses in general and manic-depressive illness in particular. It has been difficult at times to weave together the scientific discipline of my intellectual field with the more compelling realities of my own emotional experiences. And yet it has been from this binding of raw emotion to the more distanced eye of clinical science that I feel I have obtained the freedom to live the kind of life I want, and the human experiences necessary to try and make a difference in public awareness and clinical practice.

I kept on with my life at a frightening pace. I worked ridiculously long hours and slept next to not at all. When I went home at night it was to a place of increasing chaos: Books, many of them newly purchased, were strewn everywhere. Clothes were piled up in mounds in every room, and there were unwrapped packages and unemptied shopping bags as far as the eye could see. My apartment looked like it had been inhabited and then abandoned by a colony of moles. There were hundreds of scraps of paper as well; they cluttered the top of my desk and kitchen counters, forming their own little mounds on the floor. One scrap contained an incoherent and rambling poem; I found it weeks later in my refrigerator, apparently triggered by my spice collection, which, needless to say, had grown by leaps and bounds during my mania. I had titled it, for reasons that I am sure made sense at the time, "God Is a Herbivore." There were many such poems and fragments, and they were everywhere. Weeks after I finally cleaned up my apartment, I still was coming across bits and pieces of paper—filled to the edges with writing—in unimaginably unlikely places.

My awareness and experience of sounds in general and music in particular were intense. Individual notes from a horn, an oboe, or a cello became exquisitely poignant. I heard each note alone, all notes together, and then each and all with piercing beauty and clarity. I felt as though I were standing in the orchestra pit; soon, the intensity and sadness of classical music became unbearable to me. I became impatient with the pace, as well as overwhelmed by the emotion. I switched abruptly to rock music, pulled out my Rolling Stones albums, and played them as loud as possible. I went from cut to cut, album to album, matching mood to music, music to mood. Soon my rooms were further strewn with records, tapes, and album jackets as I went on my way in search of the perfect sound. The chaos in my mind began to mirror the chaos of my rooms; I could no longer process what I was hearing; I became confused, scared, and disoriented. I could not listen for more than a few minutes to any particular piece of music; my behavior was frenetic, and my mind more so.

Slowly the darkness began to weave its way into my mind, and before long I was hopelessly out of control. I could not follow the path of my own thoughts. Sentences flew around in my head and fragmented first into phrases and then words; finally, only sounds remained. One evening I stood in the middle of my living room and looked out at a blood-red sunset spreading out over the horizon of the Pacific. Suddenly I felt a strange sense of light at the back of my eyes and almost immediately saw a huge black centrifuge inside my head. I saw a tall figure in a floor-length evening gown approach

the centrifuge with a vase-sized glass tube of blood in her hand. As the figure turned around I saw to my horror that it was me and that there was
blood all over my dress, cape, and long white gloves. I watched as the figure
carefully put the tube of blood into one of the holes in the rack of the centrifuge, closed the lid, and pushed a button on the front of the machine. The
centrifuge began to whirl.

Then, horrifyingly, the image that previously had been inside my head
now was completely outside of it. I was paralyzed by fright. The spinning of
the centrifuge and the clanking of the glass tube against the metal became
louder and louder, and then the machine splintered into a thousand pieces.
Blood was everywhere. It spattered against the windowpanes, against the
walls and paintings, and soaked down into the carpets. I looked out toward
the ocean and saw that the blood on the window had merged into the sunset; I couldn't tell where one ended and the other began. I screamed at the
top of my lungs. I couldn't get away from the sight of the blood and the
echoes of the machine's clanking as it whirled faster and faster. Not only had
my thoughts spun wild, they had turned into an awful phantasmagoria, an
apt but terrifying vision of an entire life and mind out of control. I screamed
again and again. Slowly the hallucination receded. I telephoned a colleague
for help, poured myself a large scotch, and waited for his arrival.

I first met the man who was to become my psychiatrist when he was chief
resident at the UCLA Neuropsychiatric Institute. Tall, good-looking, and a
man of strong opinions, he had a steel-trap mind, a quick wit, and an easy
laugh that softened an otherwise formidable presence. He was tough, disciplined, knew what he was doing, and cared very much about how he did it.
He genuinely loved being a doctor, and he was a superb teacher. During my
year as a predoctoral clinical psychology intern he had been assigned to su-
pervise my clinical work on the adult inpatient service. He turned out to be
an island of rational thought, rigorous diagnosis, and compassion in a ward
situation where fragile egos and vapid speculation about intrapsychic and
sexual conflicts prevailed. Although he was adamant about the importance
of early and aggressive medical treatments for psychotic patients, he also had
a genuine and deep belief in the importance of psychotherapy in bringing

about healing and lasting change. His kindness to patients, combined with an extremely keen knowledge of medicine, psychiatry, and human nature, made a critical impression upon me. When I became violently manic just after joining the UCLA faculty, he was the only one I trusted with my mind and life. I knew intuitively that there wasn't a snowball's chance in hell that I could outtalk, outthink, or outmaneuver him. In the midst of utter confusion, it was a remarkably clear and sane decision.

I was not only very ill when I first called for an appointment, I was also terrified and deeply embarrassed. I had never been to a psychiatrist or a psychologist before. I had no choice. I had completely, but completely, lost my mind; if I didn't get professional help, I was quite likely to lose my job, my already precarious marriage, and my life as well. I drove from my office at UCLA to his office in the San Fernando Valley; it was an early southern California evening, usually a lovely time of day, but I was—for the first time in my life—shaking with fear. I shook for what he might tell me, and I shook for what he might not be able to tell me. For once, I could not begin to think or laugh my way out of the situation I was in, and I had no idea whether anything existed that would make me better.

I pushed the elevator button and walked down a long corridor to a waiting room. Two other patients were waiting for their doctors, which only added to my sense of indignity and embarrassment at finding myself with the roles reversed—character building, no doubt, but I was beginning to tire of all the opportunities to build character at the expense of peace, predictability, and a normal life. Perhaps, had I not been so vulnerable at the time, all of this would not have mattered so much. But I was confused and frightened and terribly shattered in all of my notions of myself; my self-confidence, which had permeated every aspect of my life for as long as I could remember, had taken a very long and disquieting holiday.

On the far wall of the waiting room I saw an array of lit and unlit buttons. It was clear I was supposed to push one of them; this, in turn, would let my psychiatrist-to-be know that I had arrived. I felt like a large white rat pressing paw to lever for a pellet. It was a strangely degrading, albeit practical, system. I had the sinking feeling that being on the wrong side of the desk was not going to sit very well with me.

My psychiatrist opened the door and, taking one long look at me, sat me down and said something reassuring. I have completely forgotten what it was—and I am sure it was as much the manner in which it was said as the actual words—but slowly a tiny, very tiny, bit of light drifted into my dark and frightened mind. I have next to no memory of what I said during that first session, but I know it was rambling, unstrung, and confused. He sat there, listening forever, it seemed, his long six-foot-four-inch frame spread out from chair to floor, legs tangling and untangling, long hands touching, fingertip to fingertip—and then he started asking questions.

How many hours of sleep had I been getting? Did I have any problems in concentrating? Had I been more talkative than usual? Did I talk faster than usual? Had anyone told me to slow down or that they couldn't make sense out of what I was saying? Had I felt a pressure to talk constantly? Had I been more energetic than usual? Were other people saying that they were having difficulty keeping up with me? Had I become more involved in activities than usual, or undertaken more projects? Had my thoughts been going so quickly that I had difficulty keeping track of them? Had I been more physically restless or agitated than usual? More sexually active? Had I been spending more money? Acting impulsively? Had I been more irritable or angry than usual? Had I felt as though I had special talents or powers? Had I had any visions or heard sounds or voices that other people probably hadn't seen or heard? Had I experienced any strange sensations in my body? Had I ever had any of these symptoms earlier in my life? Did anyone else in my family have similar sorts of problems?

I realized that I was on the receiving end of a very thorough psychiatric history and examination; the questions were familiar, I had asked them of others a hundred times, but I found it unnerving to have to answer them, unnerving not to know where it all was going, and unnerving to realize how confusing it was to be a patient. I answered yes to virtually all of his questions, including a long series of additional ones about depression, and found myself gaining a new respect for psychiatry and professionalism.

Gradually, his experience as a physician, and self-confidence as a person, began to take effect, much in the same way that medications gradually begin to take hold and calm the turmoil of mania. He made it unambivalently clear that he thought I had manic-depressive illness and that I was going to need to be on lithium, probably indefinitely. The thought was very frightening to me—much less was known then than is known now about the illness and its prognosis—but all the same I was relieved: relieved to hear a diagnosis that I knew in my mind of minds to be true. Still, I flailed against the sentence I felt he had handed me. He listened patiently. He listened to all of my convoluted, alternative explanations for my breakdown—the stress of a stressed marriage, the stress of joining the psychiatry faculty, the stress of overwork—and he remained firm in his diagnosis and recommendations for treatment. I was bitterly resentful, but somehow greatly relieved. And I respected him enormously for his clarity of thought, his obvious caring, and his unwillingness to equivocate in delivering bad news.

Over the next many years, except when I was living in England, I saw him at least once a week; when I was extremely depressed and suicidal I saw him more often. He kept me alive a thousand times over. He saw me through madness, despair, wonderful and terrible love affairs, disillusionments and triumphs, recurrences of illness, an almost fatal suicide attempt, the death of a man I greatly loved, and the enormous pleasures and aggravations of my professional life—in short, he saw me through the beginnings and endings of virtually every aspect of my psychological and emotional life. He was very tough, as well as very kind, and even though he understood more than anyone how much I felt I was losing—in energy, vivacity, and originality—by taking medication, he never was seduced into losing sight of the overall perspective of how costly, damaging, and life threatening my illness was. He was at ease with ambiguity, had a comfort with complexity, and was able to be decisive in the midst of chaos and uncertainty. He treated me with respect, a decisive professionalism, wit, and an unshakable belief in my ability to get well, compete, and make a difference.

Although I went to him to be treated for an illness, he taught me, by example, for my own patients, the total beholdenness of brain to mind and mind to brain. My temperament, moods, and illness clearly, and deeply, affected the relationships I had with others and the fabric of my work. But my moods were themselves powerfully shaped by the same relationships and work. The challenge was in learning to understand the complexity of this mutual beholdenness and in learning to distinguish the roles of lithium, will, and insight in getting well and leading a meaningful life. It was the task and gift of psychotherapy.

At this point in my existence, I cannot imagine leading a normal life without both taking lithium and having had the benefits of psychotherapy. Lithium prevents my seductive but disastrous highs, diminishes my depressions, clears out the wool and webbing from my disordered thinking, slows me down, gentles me out, keeps me from ruining my career and relationships, keeps me out of a hospital, alive, and makes psychotherapy possible. But, ineffably, psychotherapy *heals*. It makes some sense of the confusion, reins in the terrifying thoughts and feelings, returns some control and hope and possibility of learning from it all. Pills cannot, do not, ease one back into reality; they only bring one back headlong, careening, and faster than can be endured at times. Psychotherapy is a sanctuary; it is a battleground; it is a place I have been psychotic, neurotic, elated, confused, and despairing beyond belief. But, always, it is where I have believed—or have learned to believe—that I might someday be able to contend with all of this.

No pill can help me deal with the problem of not wanting to take pills; likewise, no amount of psychotherapy alone can prevent my manias and depressions. I need both. It is an odd thing, owing life to pills, one's own quirks and tenacities, and this unique, strange, and ultimately profound relationship called psychotherapy.

From *Thinking in Pictures, and Other Reports from My Life with Autism*

Temple Grandin

Autistic Emotions

Some people believe that people with autism do not have emotions. I definitely do have them, but they are more like the emotions of a child than of an adult. My childhood temper tantrums were not really expressions of emotion so much as circuit overloads. When I calmed down, the emotion was all over. When I get angry, it is like an afternoon thunderstorm; the anger is intense, but once I get over it, the emotion quickly dissipates. I become very angry when I see people abusing cattle, but if they change their behavior and stop abusing the animals, the emotion quickly passes.

Both as a child and as an adult, I have felt a happy glee. The happiness I feel when a client likes one of my projects is the same kind of glee I felt as a child when I jumped off the diving board. When one of my scientific papers is accepted for publication, I feel the same happiness I experienced one summer when I ran home to show my mother the message I had found in a wine bottle on the beach. I feel a deep satisfaction when I make use of my intellect to design a challenging project. It is the kind of satisfied feeling one gets after finishing a difficult crossword puzzle or playing a challenging game of chess or bridge; it's not an emotional experience so much as an intellectual satisfaction.

At puberty, fear became my main emotion. When the hormones hit, my life revolved around trying to avoid a fear-inducing panic attack. Teasing from other kids was very painful, and I responded with anger. I eventually learned to control my temper, but the teasing persisted, and I would sometimes cry. Just the threat of teasing made me fearful; I was afraid to walk across the parking lot because I was afraid somebody would call me a name. Any change in my school schedule caused intense anxiety and fear of a panic attack. I worked overtime on my door symbols because I believed that I could make the fear go away if I could figure out the secrets of my psyche.

The writings of Tom McKean and Therese Joliffe indicate that fear is also a dominant emotion in their autism. Therese stated that trying to keep everything the same helped her avoid some of the terrible fear. Tony W., another man with autism, wrote in the *Journal of Autism and Developmental Disorders* that he lived in a world of daydreaming and fear and that he was afraid of everything. In my case the terrible fear did not begin until puberty, but for some autistic people it starts in early childhood. Sean Barron reported that he felt pure terror during the first five or six years of his life. The highly structured environment of the classroom reduced some of his fear, but he was often afraid and anxious in the hallways.

The intense fear and anxiety I used to experience has been almost eliminated by the antidepressant medication I've been on for the last thirteen years. The elimination of most of my fears and panic attacks has also attenuated many of my emotions. The strongest feeling I have today is one of intense calm and serenity as I handle cattle and feel them relax under my care. The feeling of peacefulness and bliss does not dissipate quickly like my other emotions. It is like floating on clouds. I get a similar but milder feeling from the squeeze machine. I get great satisfaction out of doing clever things with my mind, but I don't know what it is like to feel rapturous joy. I know I am missing something when other people swoon over a beautiful sunset. Intellectually I know it is beautiful, but I don't feel it. The closest thing I have to joy is the excited pleasure I feel when I have solved a design problem. When I get this feeling, I just want to kick up my heels. I'm like a calf gamboling about on a spring day.

My emotions are simpler than those of most people. I don't know what complex emotion in a human relationship is. I only understand simple emotions, such as fear, anger, happiness, and sadness. I cry during sad movies, and sometimes I cry when I see something that really moves me. But complex emotional relationships are beyond my comprehension. I don't understand how a person can love someone one minute and then want to kill him in a jealous rage the next. I don't understand being happy and sad at the same time. Donna Williams succinctly summarizes autistic emotions in *Nobody Nowhere:* "I believe that autism results when some sort of mechanism that controls emotions does not function properly, leaving an otherwise relatively normal body and mind unable to express themselves with the depth that they would otherwise be capable of." As far as I can figure out, complex emotion occurs when a person feels two opposite emotions at once. Samuel Clemens, the author of *Tom Sawyer*, wrote that "the secret source of humor is not joy but sorrow," and Virginia Woolf wrote, "The beauty of the world has two edges, one of laughter, one of anguish, cutting the heart asunder." I can understand these ideas, but I don't experience emotion this way.

I am like the lady referred to as S. M. in a recent paper by Antonio Damasio in *Nature*. She has a damaged amygdala. This part of the brain is immature in autism. S. M. has difficulty judging the intentions of others, and she makes poor social judgments. She is unable to recognize subtle changes in facial expression, which is common in people with autism. In developing many varied, complex ways to operate the squeeze machine on myself, I keep discovering that slight changes in the way I manipulate the control lever affect how it feels. When I slowly increase the pressure, I make very small variations in the rate and timing of the increase. It is like a language of pressure, and I keep finding new variations with slightly different sensations. For me, this is the tactile equivalent of a complex emotion and this has helped me to understand complexity of feelings.

I have learned how to understand simple emotional relationships that occur with clients. These relationships are usually straightforward; however, emotional nuances are still incomprehensible to me, and I value concrete evidence of accomplishment and appreciation. It pleases me to look at my collection of hats that clients have given me, because they are physical evidence that the clients liked my work. I am motivated by tangible accomplishment, and I want to make a positive contribution to society.

I still have difficulty understanding and having a relationship with people whose primary motivation in life is governed by complex emotions, as my actions are guided by intellect. This has caused friction between me and some family members when I have failed to read subtle emotional cues. For instance, it was difficult for my younger sister to have a weird sister. She felt she always had to tiptoe around me. I had no idea that she felt this way until years later, when she told me about her childhood feelings toward me. Motivated by love, my mother worked with me and kept me out of institutions. Yet sometimes she feels that I don't love her.

She is a person for whom emotional relationships are more important than intellect and logic. It pains her that I kicked like a wild animal when I was a baby and that I had to use the squeeze machine to get the feeling of love and kindness. The irony is that if I had given up the machine, I would have been a cold, hard rock. Without the machine, I would have had no kind feelings toward her. I had to feel physical comfort in order to feel love. Unfortunately, it is difficult for my mother and other highly emotional people to understand that people with autism think differently. For her, it is like dealing with somebody from another planet. I relate better to scientists and engineers, who are less motivated by emotion.

At a conference a man with autism told me that he feels only three emotions, fear, sadness, and anger. He has no joy. He also has problems with the intensity of his emotions, which both fluctuate and get mixed up, similar to sensory jumbling. My emotions don't get mixed up, but they are reduced and simplified in some areas. The emotional jumbling described by this man may be like the sudden emotional changes that normally occur in two-year-old children. They can be laughing one minute and having a tantrum the next. The tendency to shift emotional states rapidly often occurs in autistic children at a later age, whereas older autistic children may have the emotional patterns of a younger child.

During the last couple of years, I have become more aware of a kind of electricity that goes on between people which is much subtler than overt anger, happiness, or fear. I have observed that when several people are together and having a good time, their speech and laughter follow a rhythm. They will all laugh together and then talk quietly until the next laughing cycle. I have always had a hard time fitting in with this rhythm, and I usually interrupt conversations without realizing my mistake. The problem is that I can't follow the rhythm. Twenty years ago, Dr. Condon, a Boston physician, observed that babies with autism and other developmental disorders failed to move in synchrony with adult speech. Normal infants will tune into adult speech and get in synch with it.

The work I do is emotionally difficult for many people, and I am often asked how I can care about animals and be involved in slaughtering them. Perhaps because I am less emotional than other people, it is easier for me to face the idea of death. I live each day as if I will die tomorrow. This motivates me to accomplish many worthwhile things, because I have learned not to fear death and have accepted my own mortality. This has enabled me to look at slaughtering objectively and perceive it the way the cattle do. However, I am not just an objective, unfeeling observer; I have a sensory empathy for the cattle. When they remain calm I feel calm, and when something goes wrong that causes pain, I also feel their pain. I tune in to what the actual sensations are like to the cattle rather than having the idea of death rile up my emotions. My goal is to reduce suffering and improve the way farm animals are treated.

People with autism are capable of forming very strong emotional bonds. Hans Asperger, the German doctor after whom the syndrome is named, states that the commonly held assumption of poverty of emotion in autism is inaccurate. However, my strong emotional bonds are tied up with places more than people. Sometimes I think my emotional life may appear more similar to those of animals than humans, because my feelings are simpler and more overt, and like cattle, I have emotional memories that are place-specific. For instance, I am not aware of a subconscious full of memories that are too painful to think about, and my emotional memory is very weak. It is highly doubtful that cattle become emotionally aroused when they think about a cowboy who whipped them, but they will have symbolic doors. I was partly afraid that the door would be locked, like the blocked burrow of a tunneling animal. It was as if an antipredator system deep in my brain was activated. Basic instincts that we share with animals may be triggered by certain stimuli. This idea has been suggested by respected scientists such as Carl Sagan in his book *The Dragons of Eden* and Melvin Konner in *The Tangled Wing*. Judith Rapoport suggests in *The Boy Who Couldn't Stop Washing* that obsessive-compulsive disorders, where people wash their hands for hours or repeatedly check whether the stove is off, may be the result of an activation of old animal instincts for safety and grooming.

The fear of blocked passages persisted in both my visual symbolic world of doors and in the real world long after I stopped using door symbols. In my early days I would find the doors that opened up to the roofs of the highest buildings on the school campus. From a high vantage point I could survey the danger that lurked in the next stage of my life. Emotionally I was like an animal surveying the plains for lions, but symbolically the high place signified striving to find the meaning of life. My intellect was trying to make sense of the world, but it was being driven by an engine of animal fears.

Nearly thirty years ago, when I was navigating my visual symbolic world of doors, I recognized that fear was my great motivator. At that time I didn't realize that other people experience other major emotions. Since fear was my major emotion, it spilled over into all events that had any emotional significance. The following diary entry shows very clearly how I attempted to deal with fear in my symbolic world.

> October 4, 1968
>
> I opened the little door and went through tonight. To lift up the door and see the wide expanse of the moonlight roof before me. I have put all my fears anxieties about other people on the door. Using the trap door is risky because if it were sealed shut I would have no emotional outlet. Intellectually the door is just a symbol but on the emotional level the physical act of opening the door brings on the fears. The act of going through is my overcoming my fears and anxiety towards other people.

The intellectual side of me always knew that making changes in my life would be a challenge, and I deliberately chose symbolic doors to help me get through after the first door almost magically appeared. Sometimes I had massive activation of my sympathetic nervous system—the system that enables an animal or person to flee from danger—when I went through a door. It was like facing a lion. My heart would race and I would sweat profusely. These reactions are now controlled with antidepressant drugs. In conjunction with vast amounts of stored information in my memory, the drugs have enabled me to leave the visual symbolic world behind and venture out into the so-called real world.

Yet, it has only been during the last two or three years that I have discovered that I do not experience the full range of emotions. My first inkling that my emotions were different came in high school, when my roommate swooned over the science teacher. Whatever it was she was feeling, I knew I didn't feel that way toward anyone. But it was years before I realized that other people are guided by their emotions during most social interactions. For me, the proper behavior during all social interactions had to be learned by intellect. I became more skilled at social interactions as I became more experienced. Throughout my life I have been helped by understanding teachers and mentors. People with autism desperately need guides to instruct and educate them so they will survive in the social jungle.

QUESTIONS

1. It's been said that madness and artistic genius often co-occur. If some future form of gene therapy could significantly reduce your children's risk of developing mental illness but at the cost of also reducing their potential artistic genius, would you do so? Why or why not?

2. Is depression qualitatively or quantitatively different from sadness? Find a copy of the *DSM* (*Diagnostic and Statistical Manual of Mental Disorders*) and study the definition for depression. Do you think the definition is more likely to be too strict (excluding some people who are genuinely depressed) or too loose (including some people who are not genuinely depressed)? Is there anything about the diagnostic criteria that you find surprising?

CHAPTER SEVENTEEN

TREATMENT

Five hundred years from now, our early-twenty-first-century techniques for treating psychological disorders may seem as crude to our descendants as nineteenth-century bloodletting and surgery with unsterilized instruments seem to us today. But therapy and drugs are not just the best we've got—they really do work. Although in some cases scientists have only a vague idea why these treatments work, both therapy and drugs have been scientifically proven to help alleviate symptoms in people suffering from disorders such as depression and anxiety.

This book is not the place to cover every method in the vast array of techniques clinicians have tried; instead, I have chosen readings that illustrate the two major approaches: therapy and medication. I include an excerpt from Peter Kramer's *Listening to Prozac* (1993) not because I think that Prozac is the best drug for treating depression (there are by now many competitors, and there is a constant search for still better drugs), nor because drugs are the only solution, but because the pharmaceutical approach is here to stay. In that light, it's worth understanding something about how psychiatric medications are developed.

Similarly, although cognitive therapy is by no means the only form of remediating psychological disorders, the selection by pioneering clinical psychologist Aaron Beck—whose work is still sound after thirty years—does an excellent job of laying out some of the fundamental tenets of therapy. Much of what he says in *Cognitive Therapy and the Emotional Disorders* (1976) may be good advice for all therapists, regardless of their specific theoretical orientation.

From *Listening to Prozac*

Peter D. Kramer

Though the reception accorded Prozac is unique, it is not unprecedented. The first modern antidepressant, iproniazid, enjoyed its own meteoric career. Iproniazid was developed as an antitubercular drug in the early 1950s and at first it appeared successful. Not only did it decrease the number of tubercule bacilli in the sputum, it also stimulated patients' appetites, gave them energy, and restored to them a general sense of well-being. Iproniazid was immortalized in an Associated Press photograph of 1953 that shows residents of the Sea View Sanatorium on Staten Island, attractive black women in ankle-length cotton print skirts and white blouses, smiling and clapping in a semicircle while two of their number do what looks like the Lindy Hop. "A few months ago," the caption read, "only the sound of TB victims coughing their lives away could be heard here."

Iproniazid did suppress the replication of bacteria, but the patients' inclination to dance did not derive entirely from the remission of their illness. Iproniazid was discovered to be a "psychic energizer," to use the phrase of Nathan Kline, the psychiatrist who investigated the drug's effects on the mind. Kline hoped an increase in a patient's vital energy would reverse depression. Using the language of psychoanalysis, then the dominant theory of mind, Kline wrote: "The plethora of id energy would make large amounts of energy easily available to the ego so that there would be more than enough energy available for all tasks. Such a situation would result in a sense of joyousness and optimism."

The drug's manufacturer was unenthusiastic. Iproniazid had been superseded by other antituberculars, and the company was ready to stop production. But in April 1957, *The New York Times* reported the contents of papers to be given at a research conference in Syracuse indicating preliminary successes in treating depression with iproniazid. Years later, Kline wrote:

"Probably no drug in history was so widely used so soon after the announcement of its application in the treatment of a specific disease."

Approximately four hundred thousand depressed patients were treated in the first year. Unfortunately, 127 of these patients developed jaundice. Given the prevalence of viral hepatitis, this was probably a small number of cases for the population involved, but the manufacturer thought (wrongly) that it had a more potent antidepressant coming to market, so, rather than fight the bad publicity, it withdrew iproniazid. Iproniazid's reputation had been fatally tainted by the report of side effects, and it was never heard from again.

The extraordinary initial reception of iproniazid had been due to two factors. First, it had already been used in the treatment of tuberculosis. As a result, doctors were comfortable with it, and when the research results were announced, it was already on the market, ready for use. Second, the pent-up demand was enormous. Depression is an extraordinarily prevalent affliction, and there was at the time no acceptable way to treat it biologically. It was well understood among physicians that, though certain medications could alleviate one or another symptom of depression, short of such extreme interventions as inducing a seizure through administering high doses of insulin or through shocking the patient's brain electrically, there were no physical treatments that gave relief from the whole spectrum of symptoms and ended the episode of depression.

While Nathan Kline was on the lookout for energizing drugs, a leading researcher in Switzerland, Ronald Kuhn, was pursuing a different line of reasoning. At the time of the discovery of iproniazid, the most effective drug treatment for depression was opium. Opium was recognized as an odd substance. It caused some of the symptoms of melancholy in healthy subjects and alleviated symptoms in the depressed. Kuhn thought opium presented the proper model for a true antidepressant.

For unknown reasons, rare depressed patients even today will respond to no medicine except opiates, and a few researchers into depression have become newly interested in these substances. Fifty years ago, most patients who felt better on opium probably valued it for its ability to ameliorate scattered symptoms, such as sleeplessness, anxiety, and a general sense of malaise. Perhaps for mistaken reasons, Kuhn took the occasional success of opium to set the standard in the search for antidepressants. The hallmark of opium was that it restored energy in the depressed without being inherently energizing. Kuhn set out "to find a drug acting in some specific manner against melancholy that is better than opium"—that is, a nonstimulating antidepressant.

Iproniazid met only part of the standard. In some patients, it ameliorated all the symptoms. But it also seemed to have the ability to stimulate a variety of people—witness the dancing tubercular women—so it was not clear at first whether its effects came from reversing a basic process of depression.

In his search for a nonstimulating antidepressant, Kuhn began by looking at antihistamines. Antihistamines are the drugs, like Benadryl, used to treat allergies. Many antihistamines are sedating—indeed, the active ingredient in Sominex, the over-the-counter sleeping pill, is the same as the active ingredient in Benadryl. Kuhn was interested in sedation because opium is sedating, and he was interested in the antihistamines because the first modern psychotherapeutic medicine, chlorpromazine, was an antihistamine.

Chlorpromazine (Thorazine), introduced in 1952, constituted a breakthrough in the treatment of schizophrenia—it is known as the drug that emptied the state mental hospitals. Chlorpromazine had some efficacy in depression, calming agitated patients. Kuhn had already tested new antihistamines to see whether they were effective as sleeping pills. He now returned to the sedating antihistamines, especially those whose structure resembled that of chlorpromazine, to see how they affected depression.

In September 1957, less than half a year after the reports regarding iproniazid's initial success, Kuhn announced that he had found a substance that sedated normal people but relieved depression. As Kuhn put it: "We have achieved a specific treatment of depressive states, not ideal, but already going far in that direction. I emphasize 'specific' because the drug largely or completely restores what illness has impaired—namely the mental functions and capacity and what is of prime importance, the power to experience."

Kuhn's new drug was called imipramine. The theoretical importance of imipramine (Tofranil), the first nonstimulating antidepressant, is underscored in a memoir by Donald Klein, the pharmacologic researcher who so eloquently opposed the spectrum theory of mental illness. Klein worked with imipramine on an experimental basis in 1959. He later wrote:

> We knew that amphetamine was ineffective in the treatment of severe depressions, but we hoped this new agent would be much more stimulating and blow the patients out of their pit.

Imagine our surprise when we found that giving imipramine to severe depressives first resulted in sedation, and shortly after that in an increase in appetite, hardly stimulant effects. Further, marked mood improvement was usually not evident for several weeks. At that point many patients' moods returned to normal but they rarely became overstimulated....

Therefore this drug was certainly not a stimulant. Further, when given to normals it did not cause stimulation or elevation of mood, but rather sedation. So, whatever the drug was doing was the result of an interaction between the medication and the pathophysiological dysregulation that produced the pathological state. In this sense the drug seemed a normalizer, not a stimulant.

In other words, imipramine was the grail—the true antidepressant, a substance of more conceptual importance even than iproniazid.

Despite the enthusiasm of isolated researchers, the announcement of the efficacy of imipramine was mostly met with skepticism. An entirely new medicine with no other indication than the treatment of depression, imipramine took some years to catch on. Though slower out of the blocks, imipramine was to enjoy a fate happier than that of iproniazid; but it turned out both drugs were antidepressants. The nearly simultaneous demonstration of the efficacy of imipramine and iproniazid signaled the opening of the modern era of research into human emotion. The two medications still set the terms for our contemporary understanding of the biology of mood.

In discussing patients' responses, and my own, to the success of psychotherapeutic medication, I have alluded to the tendency to "listen to drugs" as if they could tell us something about how human beings are constituted. (If Julia's fastidiousness diminishes in response to Prozac, then it "really" was a penumbral form of OCD; Sam's prurience, similarly, is revealed as a biological obsession. Tess has "really" been depressed all her life, and her social failures are a consequence of that depression.) Listening to drugs is not merely a popular phenomenon. For the last half-century, scientists have relied on medication response to infer the cause of disease.

"Pneumonia is not caused by a lack of penicillin" is the sort of statement used to ridicule such reasoning. But, in the absence of other easy approaches to the human brain, researchers have tended to use drugs as probes and to try to understand mental disorder in terms of the mechanism of action of effective medication. The great result, in terms of our theoretical understanding of mental functioning, has been the biogenic-amine theory of depression.

Stated simply, the theory holds that mood is determined in the brain by biogenic amines—complex chemicals a part of whose structure resembles that of ammonia. Even before the discovery of antidepressants, amines were known to be involved in the regulation of a variety of functions, from heart rate and gut motility to alertness and sleep. The discovery of iproniazid and imipramine led scientists to conclude that these amines also regulate mood.

Shortly after the drugs were introduced, it was shown that both iproniazid and imipramine influence the way nerve cells terminate messages. Nerves communicate by releasing "transmitter" substances—in this case amines—into the space, or synapse, between cells. The message is then ended by a two-stage process in which the amines are taken back up into the transmitting cell and inactivated by "janitorial" enzymes. Imipramine slows the reuptake of amines from the synapse into the transmitting cell, thus leaving the amines active in the synapse for a longer period of time. Iproniazid poisons the janitorial enzyme that digests the amines. Poisoning the enzyme makes more amine available for use in transmission. Thus, both known antidepressants (imipramine and iproniazid), by different mechanisms, made biogenic amines more available in relevant parts of the brain. This finding was taken as strong support for the hypothesis that depression is caused by a deficiency of amines.

If the amine theory held true, then (by somewhat circular reasoning) iproniazid and imipramine acted on the core biological problem in depression. They were increasing the efficacy of necessary, naturally occurring bodily substances. The amine theory was a very attractive model of mood regulation, because it made depression look like illnesses whose causes were well known. A person who has too little insulin suffers from diabetes; an excess of insulin causes low blood sugar (hypoglycemia). Thyroid hormone can be too high (hyperthyroidism, as in Graves' disease, suffered by President and Mrs. Bush); or it can be too low (causing hypothyroidism, or myxedema). Under the amine hypothesis, mood disorders now looked like those ordinary illnesses. An excess of amines was thought to cause mania (not least because an overdose of iproniazid could sometimes precipitate mania), and a deficiency, depression. For technical reasons, it was impossible to deliver biogenic amines directly to the relevant part of the brain. But the deficiency state could be ameliorated by slowing the breakdown or reuptake of the amines.

The amine hypothesis is perhaps false and at least incomplete. Like the evidence supporting the amine hypothesis of depression the evidence against it came from drug effects. For one thing, researchers identified antidepressants (not in use in this country) that have no direct effect on the amines. For another, there is a curious time lag in the onset of action of antidepressants. Imipramine can block the reuptake of neurotransmitters in a matter of minutes or hours. But it takes about four weeks for patients on imipramine to begin to feel less depressed. Why should a patient with effective levels of the relevant neurotransmitters not experience an immediate change in mood? Why do some depressed patients not respond at all? The amine hypothesis cannot answer these questions.

A particular line of evidence made it clear early on that the biogenic-amine hypothesis was imperfect. There are drugs that deplete the brain of complex amines, in effect doing the opposite of what antidepressants do. (One of these drugs, reserpine, has been used for many years to lower blood pressure.) Depleting the brain of amines should cause depression, and it does—but only in about 20 percent of patients. People who get depressed in response to amine depletion tend to be those who have already been depressed in the past or who are under stress in their lives. Depletion of amines is not enough in itself to cause depression.

From the time it was propounded, researchers understood that the amine hypothesis could not be the whole story. Indeed, the amine hypothesis is, in a sense, a self-deceptive form of listening to drugs. Most drug development takes place by homology. If one drug is effective, researchers will create physically similar substances, chemicals structured with what some cynics call the "least patentable difference" from the already successful medication. Scientists synthesized a host of substances similar in chemical structure to imipramine, and the success of these medications in treating depression strengthened the hold of the amine hypothesis. Almost all drugs on the market could be shown to affect amines—not surprising, given the modes for their development. The second popular way of developing drugs is through analogy: if one chemical that works as an antidepressant affects amines, then researchers will look for antidepressants among structurally different substances also known to affect amines. The potential for circular reasoning in this case is even more evident.

Only 5 percent of neurotransmission in the brain occurs via amines, but amines are the lighted streetlamps under which the secret of depression is most often searched for. The amine hypothesis may some day be superseded. In the meantime, its usefulness in predicting the effectiveness of compounds for the treatment of depression, and its heuristic power to explain their mechanism of action, have led it to dominate the scientific landscape. That these compounds were developed by analogy or homology with other compounds that affect amines is the irony embedded in the amine hypothesis.

Imipramine is a highly effective antidepressant. Perhaps 60 or 70 percent of classically depressed patients—those with insomnia, depressed appetite, low mood, and low energy—will improve on imipramine, as will certain patients with a variety of other disorders. But imipramine has serious limitations. One is side effects.

When Ronald Kuhn chose to look at antihistamines as a source for antidepressants, he created a complication the field did not overcome until the advent of Prozac. The antihistamines known in the 1950s, as well as most developed thereafter, tend pharmacologically to bring on the body's fight-or-flight response. They do this by interfering with a neurotransmitter called acetylcholine. When acetylcholine-related nerve transmission is diminished (as imipramine causes it to be), the body is ready for action. The heart beats rapidly, and energy is withdrawn from functions that can be postponed, like evacuation of bodily wastes. As a result, imipramine can cause a host of side effects—sweating, heart palpitations, dry mouth, constipation, and urinary retention among them.

Iproniazid and its relatives arouse the fight-or-flight response somewhat less often. This advantage alone might have made them popular. But an unexpected effect on blood pressure emerged in those drugs, a complication that pushed them to the sidelines, at least in the United States, and left the field to imipramine.

The drugs related to iproniazid are of particular interest because, although they are chemically quite distinct from Prozac, they can be seen, in terms of their effect on patients, as Prozac's predecessors. Like Prozac, they seem to reach aspects of depression that imipramine does not. In particular, it was recognized as early as the 1960s that they can be especially effective in patients who may not suffer classic depression but whose chronic vulnerability to depressed mood has a global effect on their personality.

The relatives of iproniazid are called monoamine-oxidase inhibitors, or MAOIs. Monoamine oxidase is the janitorial enzyme that oxidizes (burns, or inactivates) certain amines. By inhibiting monoamine oxidase, MAOIs prolong the effective life of those amines in the brain. In the years before Prozac was available, a doctor might have considered putting a patient like Tess on an MAOI, especially after she experienced an incomplete response to imipramine; but the doctor likely would have hesitated, because of concern over what else an MAOI might do: in the 1960s, a rash of deaths from brain hemorrhage was reported among patients taking MAOIs; other patients, though they did not die, experienced severe headache on the basis of extremely high blood pressure, an odd occurrence because the MAOIs were used to *lower* blood pressure in people with hypertension.

The means by which MAOIs make blood pressure skyrocket was elucidated in an interesting way. A British pharmacist who read a description of patients' headaches wrote a seemingly naïve letter noting that they resembled those his wife suffered when she consumed cheese, but not butter or milk. He asked whether the reaction might not be related to an interaction between MAOIs and some substance in cheese. Barry Blackwell, the doctor to whom the pharmacist had written, at first dismissed the suggestion—no drugs were known to interact with food substances in this way. But then he began to observe a series of patients on MAOIs who suffered headache and even extremely high blood pressure upon eating cheese.

Convinced that the "cheese reaction" was real, Blackwell set out to identify the offending ingredient. It turned out to be a chemical, ordinarily broken down by MAO, that causes nerve cells to release complex amines. Aged cheeses contain large amounts of this substance—so much that, when the janitorial enzyme is poisoned, a cheese eater on MAOIs will be flooded with biologically active amines, including ones that raise blood pressure.

Once the problem had been explained, it was a simple matter to advise patients to avoid foods that interact dangerously with MAOIs. But sticking to a restricted diet is constraining—the list of proscribed foods has grown over the years, and includes such disparate items as Chianti wine, fava beans, and ripe figs—and the requirement is dangerous for impulsive patients who "don't care if they live or die." MAOIs remained in widespread use in England, where they have been mainstay antidepressants for over thirty years. But in America the drugs were withdrawn from use, and even though they were later, reintroduced, American doctors remained wary of them. Imipramine and related compounds dominated the medical treatment of depression.

Imipramine, however, is a "dirty" drug—a drug that affects many systems at once. Not only are its side effects wide-ranging—the result of its action on nerves using such chemicals as histamine and acetylcholine—but imipramine's main effects are also nonspecific.

From the time antidepressants were developed, two different amines were understood to influence mood: *norepinephrine*, a substance that was familiar to pharmacologists because of its close relationship to adrenaline, and *serotonin*, another substance that is active throughout the body but about which less was known. Imipramine is "dirty" in its main effects and its side effects because it affects both norepinephrine and serotonin. Once imipramine's mechanism of action was understood, pharmacologists set out to synthesize a "clean" antidepressant—one as effective as imipramine but more specific in its action.

This goal proved unexpectedly elusive. In the three decades after imipramine's introduction, pharmacologists synthesized and tested many chemicals similar to it in form. Like imipramine, the better known among these drugs, such as the antidepressants Elavil (amitriptyline) and Norpramin (desipramine), had three carbon rings in their chemical structure, and thus the group came to be called "tricyclics." Each new tricyclic antidepressant, as it was introduced, was said to have fewer side effects than imipramine—to have less effect on the acetylcholine or histamine pathways—or to act faster on depression. Some of these claims held up marginally. But most of the purported advantages evaporated as the drugs came into general use. None of the tricyclics is more effective than imipramine, probably none has a different time course of action, and all are "dirty" in the sense of influencing pathways involving both histamine and acetylcholine.

The only increase in specificity was the development of drugs that affected norepinephrine (and histamine and acetylcholine) without affecting serotonin. Desipramine, for example, is perhaps fifteen hundred times more active on norepinephrine than on serotonin pathways, and as a result a good deal of modern research has been done using this drug. But two goals eluded researchers: finding an antidepressant without side effects related to histamine and acetylcholine, and finding an antidepressant that preferentially affects serotonin.

This last goal was especially enticing. As the years passed, it seemed a number of conditions, ranging from atypical forms of depression to OCD and eating disorders, might involve derangements of serotonin. Here the

MAOIs sometimes played a role. The MAOIs were very dirty. They affected not only norepinephrine and serotonin but a third amine, dopamine, the substance implicated in schizophrenia and Parkinson's disease. But the MAOIs were often more effective than the tricyclics for the disorders thought to be related to a lack of serotonin. Pharmacologists came to believe that the MAOIs' distinct efficacy might have to do with a strong effect on serotonin pathways, and that the tricyclics' limitations related to their lack of potency in raising serotonin levels. The new grail, pursued throughout the 1960s and 1970s and well into the 1980s, was a drug that would be like imipramine but that would selectively influence serotonin.

In its search for a clean analogue of imipramine and for an analogue that would strongly alter serotonin levels, psychopharmacology treaded water for over thirty years. This stalemate was frustrating to clinical psychiatrists. I remember as a medical student, and then again as a psychiatry resident, struggling to memorize charts regarding the characteristics of the tricyclic antidepressants. Generally, these charts would have a list of drugs running down the left-hand side and a list of neurotransmitters across the top. In each cell where the drug and a neurotransmitter intersected would be a series of plus or minus marks. Thus, a given drug would be + + + + for norepinephrine, + + for serotonin, − − for histamine, and − − − for acetylcholine. Medical students and residents for the most part do not mind this sort of chart; it makes demands on familiar skills and helps psychiatry seem like the rest of medicine. But the charts for antidepressants had no reliable relation to patients' responses.

The embarrassing truth about clinical work with antidepressants was that it was all art and no science. Various combinations of symptoms were said to be more serotonin- or norepinephrine-related, and various strategies were advanced for trying medications in logical order for particular sorts of patients. But these strategies varied from year to year, and even from one part of the country to another. It was true that a given patient might respond to one antidepressant after having failed to respond to another, but the doctor would have to manufacture a reason to explain why.

Psychiatrists were reduced to the expedient of choosing antidepressants on the basis of side effects. A patient whose depression was characterized by restlessness would be given a sedating antidepressant to be taken at night; a similar patient who complained of lack of energy would be given a stimulating antidepressant to be taken in the morning. But these choices said nothing about how the medications acted on depression: in all probability, both drugs amplified the effect of norepinephrine. It was as if, after discovering penicillin, researchers had synthesized a series of antibiotics, some of which incidentally made patients weary and some hyperalert—and then, when treating pneumonias, clinicians chose between these antibiotics not according to the susceptibilities of the infecting bacteria but according to whether the patient was agitated or prostrated by the illness.

Hopes that a more specific agent would make a difference were dampened by the advent of Desyrel (trazodone) in the early 1980s. Desyrel worked via serotonin, but its effects were difficult to distinguish from those of earlier antidepressants. Much of the problem, again, was side effects. Desyrel was so sedating that it had been marketed first in Europe as an antianxiety drug. You could do with Desyrel what you had been able to do with the tricyclics—treat a fair percentage of seriously depressed patients—but patients would tend to become tired or dizzy before you could get them on doses that radically changed the functioning of nerves that use serotonin.

This was the stage onto which Prozac walked: thirty years of stasis. The tricyclic antidepressants were wonderful drugs, but in practical terms they were all more or less the same. And it was not clear whether a drug that was pharmacologically distinctive would be any different in clinical usage from the many antidepressants that were already available.

Prozac was made to be distinctive. In the history of therapeutics, the development of Prozac belongs in a different chapter from the stories of lithium, imipramine, and iproniazid. Prozac was not so much discovered as planfully created, through the efforts of a large pharmaceutical firm, using state-of-the-art animal and cellular models and drawing on the skills of scientists from diverse disciplines. And yet, as was true in the cases of lithium and iproniazid, the development of Prozac required serendipity.

The story begins in the 1960s, with Bryan Molloy, a Scots-born organic chemist who had been synthesizing cardiac drugs for the pharmaceutical firm Eli Lilly. Molloy was interested in acetylcholine as a regulator of heart action. In the 1960s, a pharmacologist, Ray Fuller, came to Lilly to test potential new antidepressants. Fuller had worked with a method, using rats as test animals, for measuring drugs' effects on serotonin pathways; he tried to convince Molloy that the availability of this method made the time ripe for research in brain chemistry. Fuller proposed that Molloy leave his heart research to look for a substance that could affect amines in the brain without acting on nerves that use acetylcholine.

Like prior researchers, Molloy thought the right place to start in looking for an antidepressant was the antihistamines. He did not know whether he could develop an antidepressant without antihistaminic properties, but he thought he might have a tool that would allow him to minimize the acetylcholine-related side effects—dry mouth, urine retention, and rapid heartbeat—that so limited the use of the tricyclics.

In his cardiac research, Molloy had hooked up with Robert Rathbun, a member of the group at Lilly called the "mouse-behavior team." Rathbun was working with a model in which mice were given an opium variant, apomorphine, which lowers the body temperature in mice. Antihistamines block this response—except for antihistamines that also affect acetylcholine. Using Rathbun's model, Molloy hoped to be able to distinguish drugs that work purely on the histamine pathways from ones that affect acetylcholine as well.

Molloy synthesized compounds to test. He began with Benadryl, the antihistamine in common use as a remedy for stuffy noses and allergic rashes. He played with the Benadryl molecule, substituting one or another chemical group at one or another spot in its structure. Molloy developed dozens of compounds, including several that were good at blocking the effect of apomorphine on body temperature in mice. He thought he might be on the path toward eliminating acetylcholine-related side effects.

Meanwhile, a fourth researcher at Lilly, David Wong, had become dissatisfied with his area of work. Wong had been looking at mechanisms within the cell that allow antibiotics to combat infection, but to date all his research had led to medications for agricultural uses. He wanted to make drugs for humans, not animals, and in 1971 he began moonlighting in the area of neurochemistry. A particular book had caught Wong's attention, a newly published summary of what was known about the chemistry of mental disorder. Whereas by 1970 most research in America was focused on norepinephrine as the key chemical in mood regulation, this book summarized findings, better appreciated in Europe, that pointed to a role for serotonin.

The paths of Wong and Molloy crossed at a lecture by Solomon Snyder of Johns Hopkins University. Snyder is one of the great minds in modern biological psychiatry, a man whose name is often mentioned for the Nobel Prize. Most major developments in American biological psychiatry rely to some degree on an element of Snyder's work. Snyder had been invited to Lilly's laboratories in 1971 to receive an award and deliver a lecture. As his topic, Snyder chose his research into neurotransmission.

Snyder had been trying to isolate the nerve endings that handle biogenic amines. He found that, by grinding up rat brains and using various techniques to divide the ground-up products, he could produce a collection of nerve endings that still functioned chemically. This preparation he called a "synaptosome."

The synaptosome promised to be immensely useful in neurobiological research. You might, for example, pretreat a rat with imipramine, allowing the drug time to bind to nerve endings. Then you could kill the rat, grind up its brain, centrifuge and separate out the nerve endings, and produce an extract that was still active—still worked like the terminals of living nerve cells. You could then expose this extract (the imipramine-treated synaptosomes) to a neurotransmitter, such as norepinephrine or serotonin, and see how much of the neurotransmitter was taken up. This procedure almost defied belief—you could more or less blenderize a brain and then divide out a portion that worked the way live nerve endings work—but in Snyder's hands the technique succeeded. Not only did Snyder lecture on synaptosomes, he also instructed the Lilly team on the fine points of what neurochemists call "binding and grinding."

Wong immediately set about applying the bind-and-grind technology to Molloy's series of promising antidepressants. It turned out that the compounds on which Molloy was focused, those that worked in Rathbun's apomorphine-mouse model, were, like drugs already on the market, potent blockers of norepinephrine uptake in rat synaptosomes. But Wong did not stop there. His research showed that the rat synaptosome, and presumably the human brain, treated very similar drugs differently. If one chemical blocked the uptake of norepinephrine, a structurally similar chemical might block the uptake of serotonin. So Wong decided to look also at chemicals in Molloy's series that had failed in the apomorphine test.

One of those compounds, labeled 82816, blocked the uptake of serotonin and very little else. In all, Wong quickly tested over 250 compounds, but none looked as selective in its effect on serotonin as did 82816. The chemical was then tested in Fuller's rat system, the one that had initially sparked Molloy's interest in brain chemistry. There and elsewhere, 82816 selectively blocked the reuptake of seroronin into transmitting cells.

Compound 82816 was fluoxetine oxalate; it turned out to be easier to work with a related preparation, fluoxetine hydrochloride. Fluoxetine hydrochloride is Prozac.

In June 1974, David Wong's laboratory and Bryan Molloy publicly reported that fluoxetine is a selective inhibitor of serotonin uptake into synaptosomes of rat brain. Fluoxetine was two hundred times more active in inhibiting the uptake of serotonin than of norepinephrine—and it did not affect the histamine or acetylcholine systems either. Fluoxetine was a clean drug. Wong and Molloy understood they had a new powerful research tool with which to study the functioning of serotonin, as well as a potential new type of antidepressant. Later research showed that the drug was suitable for the treatment of depression in humans.

From *Cognitive Therapy and the Emotional Disorders*

Aaron T. Beck

If we wish to change the sentiments it is necessary before all to modify the idea which has produced [them], and to recognize either that it is not correct in itself or that it does not touch our interests. —*Paul Dubois*

We have seen that the common psychological disorders center around certain aberrations in thinking. The challenge to psychotherapy is to offer the patient effective techniques for overcoming his blindspots, his blurred perceptions, and his self-deceptions. A promising lead is provided by the observation that a person responds realistically and effectively to situations not related to his neurosis. His judgments and behavior in areas of experience beyond the boundaries of his specific vulnerability often reflect a high level of functioning. Furthermore, prior to the onset of illness, the neurotic frequently shows adequate development of his conceptual tools for dealing with the problems of living.

Psychological skills (integrating, labeling, and interpreting experience) can be applied to correcting the psychological aberrations. Since the central psychological *problem* and the psychological *remedy* are both concerned with the patient's thinking (or cognitions), we call this form of help cognitive therapy.

In the broadest sense, cognitive therapy consists of all the approaches that alleviate psychological distress through the medium of correcting faulty conceptions and self-signals. The emphasis on thinking, however, should not obscure the importance of the emotional reactions which are generally the immediate source of distress. It simply means that we get to the person's emotions through his cognitions. By correcting erroneous beliefs, we can damp down or alter excessive, inappropriate emotional reactions.

Many methods of helping a patient make more realistic appraisals of himself and his world are available. The "intellectual" approach consists of identifying the misconceptions, testing their validity, and substituting more appropriate concepts. Often the need for broad attitudinal change emerges with the patient's recognition that the rules he has relied on to guide his thinking and behavior have served to deceive and to defeat him.

The "experiential" approach exposes the patient to experiences that are in themselves powerful enough to change misconceptions. The interactions with other people in certain organized situations, such as encounter groups or conventional psychotherapy, may help a person to perceive others more realistically and consequently to modify his inappropriate maladaptive responses to them. In encounter groups, the interpersonal experiences may cut through maladaptive attitudes blocking the expression of intimate feelings. Similarly, a patient, in response to his psychotherapist's warmth and acceptance, often modifies his stereotyped conception of authority figures. Such a change has been labeled "corrective emotional experience" (Alexander, 1950). Sometimes the effectiveness of psychotherapy is implemented by motivating a patient to enter situations he had previously avoided because of his misconceptions.

The "behavioral" approach encourages the development of specific forms of behavior that lead to more general changes in the way the patient views himself and the real world. Practicing techniques for dealing with people who frighten him, as in "assertive training," not only enables him to regard other people more realistically but enhances his self-confidence.

If neurosis is the outcropping of the patient's maladaptive attitudes, why can't he change these attitudes through life experience or through the help of parents or friends? Why does he need a professional helper? Obviously, in many cases the troubled person works out his problems by himself or with the help of a "wise, old neighbor." Many people improvise quite independently—and successfully—the kinds of techniques that are the stock-in-trade of behavior therapists by gradually exposing themselves to frightening situations or imagining themselves in these situations ("systematic desensitization"), or through patterning their behavior after others ("modeling"). Others tap the "folk wisdom," the cumulative experience of their cultural group, through the advice or suggestions of friends or relatives.

Those who come to the professional helper, and inadvertently acquire the label of patient or client, are drawn from the residue who have failed to master their problems. Perhaps their reactions to their problems are too acute or too severe to respond to usual life experiences or self-help. The patient may have been too fragile to develop coping techniques, or his problems may have been too deeply ingrained. In some cases, the troubled person becomes a patient simply because he received and followed "bad advice" or because no assistance was available from nonprofessional sources. And, while the folk wisdom is often helpful and is probably at the core of much psychotherapy, it often is blended with myths, superstitions, and misconceptions that aggravate an unrealistic orientation. Moreover, many people are not motivated to engage in a "self-improvement" program unless it is instigated in a professional setting.

In any event, psychotherapy can have the greatest impact on problems because of the considerable authority attributed to the therapist, his ability to pinpoint the problems, and his skill in providing an appropriate systematic set of procedures.

Targets of Cognitive Therapy

Cognitive techniques are most appropriate for people who have the capacity for introspection and for reflecting about their own thoughts and fantasies. This approach is essentially an extension and a refinement of what people have done to varying degrees since the early stages of their intellectual development. The particular techniques such as labeling objects and situations, setting up hypotheses, and weeding out and testing the hypotheses are based on skills that people apply automatically without being cognizant of the operations involved.

This kind of intellectual function is analogous to the formation of speech in which rules of pronunciation and grammatical construction are applied without consciousness of the rules or of their application. When an adult has to correct a speech disorder or attempts to learn a new language, then he has to concentrate on the formation of words and sentences. Similarly, when he has a problem in interpreting certain aspects of reality, it may be useful for him to focus on the rules he applies in making judgments. In examining a problem area, he finds that the rule is incorrect or that he has been applying it incorrectly.

Since making the incorrect judgments has probably become a deeply ingrained habit, which he may not be conscious of, several steps are required to correct it. First, he has to become aware of what he is thinking. Second, he needs to recognize what thoughts are awry. Then he has to substitute accurate for inaccurate judgments. Finally, he needs feedback to inform him whether his changes are correct. The same kind of sequence is necessary for making behavioral changes, such as improving form in a sport, correcting faults in playing an instrument, or perfecting techniques of persuasion.

To illustrate the process of cognitive change, let us take as a rather gross example a person who is afraid of all strangers. When we explore his reactions, we may find that he is operating under the rule, "All strangers are unfriendly or hostile." In this case, the rule is wrong. On the other hand, he may realize that strangers vary, but he may not have learned to discriminate among friendly strangers, neutral strangers, and unfriendly strangers. In such a case, his trouble is in applying the rule, that is, in converting the available information in a given situation into an appropriate judgment.

It is obvious that not all people who think erroneously need or want to get their thinking straightened out. When a person's erroneous ideation disrupts his life or makes him feel miserable, then he becomes a candidate for some form of help.

The troubles or problems that stimulate a person to seek help may be manifested by distress of a subjective nature (such as anxiety or depression), a difficulty in his overt behavior (such as disabling inhibition or overaggressiveness), or a deficiency in his responses (for example, inability to experience or express warm feelings). The kinds of thinking that underlie these problems may be summarized as follows.

Direct, Tangible Distortions of Reality

Distortions familiar to everybody are the thoughts of a paranoid patient who indiscriminately concludes when he sees other people (even people who are obviously friendly toward him): "Those people want to harm me." Or, as one patient once told me, "I killed President Kennedy."

Less obvious distortions of reality occur in all neuroses. For example, a depressed patient may say, "I have lost my ability to type, to read, to drive a car." However, when he becomes involved in the task, he may find his performance is still adequate. A depressed businessman complains that he is on the verge of bankruptcy, yet examination of his accounts indicates that he is completely solvent and, in fact, is prospering. The label "distortion of reality" is justified because an objective appraisal of the situation contradicts his appraisal.

Other examples of distortions that are relatively simple to check are ideas such as, "I am getting fat" or "I am a burden to my family." Some judgments require greater work to authenticate; for example, "Nobody likes me." The therapeutic sessions, particularly when the patient has been trained to report his automatic thoughts, provide an excellent laboratory for exposing distortions. The therapist may readily identify certain distortions, for instance, when a patient toward whom he has warm feelings reports the thought that he believes the therapist dislikes him.

Illogical Thinking

The patient's appraisal of reality may not be distorted, but his system of making inferences or drawing conclusions from his observations is at fault: He hears distant noise and concludes someone has fired a gun at him. In such instances, the basic premises may be erroneous or the logical processes may be faulty. A depressed patient observed that a faucet was leaking in a bathroom, that the pilot light was out in the stove, and that one of the steps in the staircase was broken. He concluded, "The whole house is deteriorating." The house was in excellent condition (except for these minor problems); he had made a massive overgeneralization. In the same way, patients who have difficulties as a result of their overt behavior often start from inaccurate premises. Someone who consistently alienates potential friends because of his overaggressiveness may operate according to the rule, "If I don't push people around, they will push me around." A timid, inhibited person may be indiscriminately applying the principle, "If I open my mouth, everybody will jump on me."

The Therapeutic Collaboration

Certain factors are important in practically all forms of psychotherapy, but are crucial in cognitive therapy. An obvious primary component of effective psychotherapy is genuine collaboration between the therapist and patient. Moving blindly in separate directions, as sometimes happens, frustrates the therapist and distresses the patient. It is important to realize that the dispenser of the service (the therapist) and the recipient (the patient) may envision the therapeutic relationship quite differently. The patient, for instance, may visualize therapy as a molding of a lump of clay by an omnipo-tent and omniscient God figure. To minimize such hazards, the patient and therapist should reach a consensus regarding what problem requires help, the goal of therapy, and how they plan to reach that goal. Agreement regard-ing the nature and duration of therapy is important in determining the out-come. One study has shown, for instance, that a discrepancy between the pa-tient's expectations and the kind of therapy he actually receives militates against a successful outcome. On the other hand, preliminary coaching of the patient about the type of therapy selected appeared to enhance its effec-tiveness (Orne and Wender, 1968).

Furthermore, the therapist needs to be tuned in to the vicissitudes of the patient's problems from session to session. Patients frequently formulate an "agenda" of topics they want to discuss at a particular session; if the ther-apist disregards this, he may impose an unnecessary strain on the relation-ship. For instance, a patient who is disturbed by a recent altercation with his wife may be alienated by the therapist's rigid adherence to a predetermined format such as desensitizing him to his subway phobia.

It is useful to conceive of the patient-therapist relationship as a joint effort. It is not the therapist's function to try to reform the patient; rather, his role is working with the patient against "*it,*" the patient's problem. Placing the emphasis on solving problems, rather than his presumed de-fects or bad habits, helps the patient to examine his difficulties with more detachment and makes him less prone to experience shame, a sense of in-feriority, and defensiveness. The partnership concept helps the therapist to obtain valuable "feedback" about the efficacy of therapeutic techniques and further detailed information about the patient's thoughts and feelings. In employing systematic desensitization, for instance, I customarily ask for a detailed description of each image. The patient's report is often very informative and, on many occasions, reveals new problems that had not previously been identified. The partnership arrangement also reduces the patient's tendency to cast the therapist in the role of a superman. Investigators (Rogers, 1951; Truax, 1963) have found that if the therapist shows the fol-lowing characteristics, a successful outcome is facilitated: genuine warmth, acceptance, and accurate empathy. By working with the patient as a collab-orator, the therapist is more likely to show these characteristics than if he assumes a Godlike role.

QUESTIONS

1. Kramer describes how Prozac was designed to be a "clean" drug, but that doesn't mean its makers fully succeeded. Use the pubmed database (pubmed.gov) to search for five recent studies on Prozac's long-term costs and benefits. Is Prozac genuinely "clean"?

2. What do you think are the most important differences between Beck's cognitive theory and Freud's psychoanalytic approach? What, if anything, do you think they share?

PERMISSIONS ACKNOWLEDGMENTS

Huff: Excerpt from Ch. 8 of *How To Lie With Statistics* by Darrell Huff, illustrated by Irving Geis. Copyright © 1954, 1982 by Darrell Huff and Irving Geis. Reprinted by permission of W. W. Norton & Company, Inc.

Hughes: Excerpt from Ch. 1 of *Sensory Exotica: A World Beyond Human Experience* by Howard C. Hughes. Copyright © 1999 by the MIT Press. Reprinted by permission of the MIT Press.

Jamison: Excerpt from *An Unquiet Mind* by Kay Redfield Jamison. Copyright © 1995 by Kay Redfield Jamison. Reprinted by permission of Alfred A. Knopf, a division of Random House, Inc.

Kagan: Excerpt from Ch. 4 of *Galen's Prophecy* by Jerome Kagan. Copyright © 1994 by Basic Books, Inc. Reprinted by permission of Basic Books, a member of Perseus Books, LLC.

Kramer: Excerpt from Ch. 3 of *Listening to Prozac* by Peter D. Kramer. Copyright © 1993 by Peter D. Kramer. Reprinted by permission of Viking Penguin, a division of Penguin Group (USA) Inc.

LeDoux: Excerpt from Ch. 6 of *The Emotional Brain: The Mysterious Underpinnings of Emotional Life* by Joseph LeDoux. Copyright © 1996 by Joseph LeDoux. Reprinted with the permission of Louise Aibel at Brockman, Inc.

Marcus: Excerpt from *The Birth of the Mind: How a Tiny Number of Genes Creates the Complexities of Thought* by Gary Marcus. Copyright © 2004 by Gary Marcus. Reprinted by permission of Basic Books, a member of Perseus Books, LLC.

Nasar: Excerpt from the Prologue of *A Beautiful Mind* by Sylvia Nasar. Copyright © 1998 by Sylvia Nasar. Reprinted by permission of Simon & Schuster Adult Publishing Group. All rights reserved.

Nisbett: Excerpt from Ch. 5 of *The Geography of Thought: How Asians and Westerners Think Differently . . . and Why* by Richard E. Nisbett. Copyright © 2003 by Richard E. Nisbett. Reprinted by permission of The Free Press, a division of Simon & Schuster Adult Publishing Group. All rights reserved.

Pinker: Excerpt from Ch. 1 of *How the Mind Works* by Steven Pinker. Copyright © 1997 by Steven Pinker. Reprinted by permission of W. W. Norton & Company, Inc.

Pinker: Excerpt from Ch. 2 of *The Language Instinct* by Steven Pinker. Copyright © 1994 by Steven Pinker. Reprinted by permission of William Morrow, a division of HarperCollins Publishers, Inc.

Richerson: Excerpt from *Not By Genes Alone: How Culture Transformed Human Evolution* by Peter J. Richerson and Robert S. Boyd. Copyright © 2004 by The University of Chicago Press. Reprinted by permission of the University of Chicago Press.

Sacks: Excerpt from Ch. 3 of *The Man Who Mistook His Wife for a Hat and Other Clinical Tales* by Oliver Sacks. Copyright © 1980, 1981, 1983, 1984, 1985 by Oliver Sacks. Reprinted by permission of Simon & Schuster Adult Publishing Group. All rights reserved.

Sapolsky: Excerpt from Ch. 10 of *Why Zebras Get Ulcers* by Robert M. Sapolsky. Copyright © 1994 W. H. Freeman and Company. Reprinted by permission of Henry Holt and Company, LLC.

Schacter: Excerpt from Ch. 6 of *Searching for Memory* by Daniel L. Schacter. Copyright © 1996 by Daniel L. Schacter. Reprinted by permission of Basic Books, a member of Perseus Books, LLC.

Stanovich: Excerpt from Ch. 6 of *How To Think Straight about Psychology*, 7th edition, by Keith E. Stanovich. Copyright © 2004 by Pearson Education. Reprinted by permission of Allyn and Bacon, Boston, MA.

Taylor: Excerpt from Ch. 6 of *The Tending Instinct: How Nurturing Is Essential for Who We Are and How We Live* by Shelley E. Taylor, Copyright ©2002 by Shelley E. Taylor. Reprinted by permission of Henry Holt and Company, LLC.

Watson and Rayner: Excerpt from "Conditioned Emotional Responses" by John B. Watson and Rosalie Rayner, originally published in *Journal of Experimental Psychology*, 3(1), pp. 1–14, 1920.

Wegner: Excerpts from Ch. 1 and 2 from *The Illusion of Conscious Will* by Daniel M. Wegner. Copyright © 2003 by the MIT Press. Reprinted by permission of the MIT Press.